Also by Ann Wroe

Lives, Lies and the Iran-Contra Affair

A Fool and His Money:
Life in a Partitioned Town in Fourteenth-Century France

PONTIUS PILATE

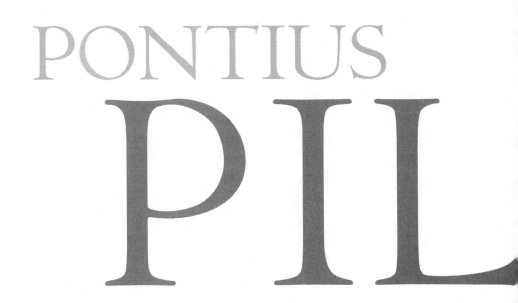

PONTIUS
PIL

ANN WROE

RANDOM HOUSE   NEW YORK

Library of Congress Cataloging-in-Publication Data
Wroe, Ann.
    Pontius Pilate / Ann Wroe.
        p.   cm.
        Rev. ed. of: Pilate. 1999.
        Includes bibliographical references and index.
        ISBN 0-375-50305-6
        1. Pilate, Pontius, 1st cent.   2. Bible. N.T.—Biography.   I. Wroe, Ann.
Pilate.   II. Title.

BS2520.P55 W76 2000
226′092—dc21   99-043000

For my husband

Contents

Introduction

"WHY PONTIUS PILATE? Couldn't you choose a different subject?" cries the demon Woland to the Master in Bulgakov's *The Master and Margarita.* And well may the Master wish he had chosen something else. His novel about the fifth governor of Judaea, the man who crucified Christ, has been rejected by his editor and savaged by the editorial board. So he has burned it in the stove, and now finds himself in Dr. Stravinsky's hospital for the insane.

The Master tells his story to Ivan Nikolayich Poniryov, also in the asylum for Pilate-related reasons. The demon has sown thoughts of Pilate in Ivan's head. Because he cannot stop talking about him, he is regularly injected with ether and subjected to reflex therapy with hammers. He is told that it is hazardous to his health to think about Pilate at all. Of course, he is not put off. He wants to struggle free and report everything to the police. The head of the asylum tells him, kindly, that if he were to turn up at the police station dressed as he is, in his underpants, saying he has met a man who has met Pontius Pilate, he would rapidly be recommitted.

"Because of my underpants?" Ivan asks.

"Chiefly because of Pontius Pilate."

When I first read Bulgakov, I laughed at this exchange. Once Pilate was under my skin, I began to worry. How had he arrived there? Could he be made to go away? Did I really want to pursue this and, if I did, how much charred ash would my manuscript produce?

There were other difficulties, beyond failure and scorn and madness. Pilate would bring me up against two redoubtable tribes, biblical scholars and classical experts. I would be plunged into the dark waters of anti-Semitism—for Pilate's reputation has often, though not always, risen and fallen with attitudes toward the Jews—and drawn into impossible controversies about the Resurrection. I would find myself arguing over obscure dates and personalities, while Pilate—that strange amalgam of human struggling and human failing—would slip away from me.

Friends were no help. "Pilate? But surely we know nothing about him!" they'd say. Their next question, invariably, was "So, was he a goodie or a baddie, then?" When I mumbled some response (I still do; how many flaws and failings, how often repeated, make up a bad man?) they would leap in with details they felt sure I would appreciate. One friend told me she had heard that Pilate was Hungarian (Hungarians, I'm sure, think he was Romanian). Another exclaimed: "Ah! Fortingall!" His story was that Pilate was born in this village, seven miles west of Aberfeldy on Tayside, the son of a Roman ambassador and a daughter of the clan MacClaren. On the site of the earthworks there, known locally as the Praetorium, the Roman dignitary and his Scottish lass had some-how come together under the northern rain to produce the dour inter-rogator of Christ.

For three years or so I did research on Pilate. There was almost noth-ing to go on. We do not even know his *praenomen,* the name his mother and wife and friends called him by. The only physical evidence we have of this man is one inscribed stone and a few small coins. All the records he kept, as he was bound to keep them, have disappeared, and so have two chapters of Tacitus, covering A.D. 30 and 31, that might have men-tioned him. The only documentary sources for Pilate are a few para-graphs in the writings of Josephus, a Romanized Jew who wrote forty years after the governor was recalled from Judaea; two or three pages from Philo of Alexandria, a defiantly non-Romanized Jew and one of Pi-late's contemporaries; one sentence in Tacitus, looking back from the time of Hadrian; and those almost too-familiar scenes from the New Tes-tament. All these have their biases. Each offers a version of Pilate's char-acter, but so wrapped in propaganda or agendas that it is difficult to detect what, if anything, may be true in them.

Plenty of people have tried to fill in the gaps, though. They have fallen over themselves to make Pilate up, because he stands at the center of the Christian story and God's plan of redemption. Without his cli-mactic judgment of Jesus, the world would not have been saved. With-out Christ's death—pronounced by Pilate—there would have been no Resurrection, no founding Christian miracle. To have a faceless bureau-crat at the heart of this drama was unacceptable: something had to be made of this man.

Early Christian apocryphal writers scrambled to embroider Pilate's conduct before, during and after the trial of Jesus—especially after, when they imagined he began to feel Christian sympathies. Medieval writers invented his origins, which they took to be German, and built up his disreputable childhood and youth. Tremendous myths were created to account for the lost last years of Pilate's life. As a result, although the real Pilate is frustratingly hard to uncover, the mythological Pilate emerges ten feet tall.

This was the next stage of my research. I ransacked the London Library for the apocrypha and hagiographies of Pilate, written by obscure clerics centuries ago and translated with nineteenth-century enthusiasm into huge quarto volumes. I read fairy tales, legends, travelogues, guidebooks, to follow where his ghost had walked around Europe. With (almost) unflagging ardor, and usually in dusty solitude, I checked every life of Christ on the fifth-floor Theology shelves to track how Pilate had been seen by commentators in Europe and America for the past two centuries. Then, as an antidote, and to try to get close to some shadow of the Roman Pilate, I read whatever literature I could find from his lifetime or from shortly before or after. I did this not just to find out the duties of governors or the monstrosities of emperors, but to try to ascertain the view of the world someone in his position might have had. This would always have to be an approximation; however vivid, this Pilate-shadow would never be the real one. But it was better than nothing.

At the end of three years, I emerged with two things: the shadow, and the myths. It did not seem like the stuff of biography. But biography is often more speculative, more selective—even more fictional—than writers admit or readers suppose. Much of it begins as a mass of reported or unsubstantiated stories, reflections, impressions, legends, which must then be filtered through the views and attitudes both of the biographer and of the age. Aspects of a life belittled in one biography are central to the next. Characters themselves ebb, flow and go on growing after death. Even the sternest of biographers let their imaginations play with their subjects. They speculate on their motives, pass judgment on their actions, fill in the gaps. Their own sense of a man's importance—their own mythology of him—flavors every sentence. And through it all the real man slips, eluding capture.

Pilate is an extreme case: successive writers, intoxicated by what he represented and unhindered by knowing much about him, invented him almost from scratch. All these Pilates contribute, in greater or smaller degree, to the Pilate we suppose we know; they are fragments of his life. This book reflects that. It proceeds as a collage of biographical scenes moving sequentially through the life of Pilate. Some are Roman, some Victorian, some medieval, some early Christian, some even modern. Centuries may shift at the turn of a page. But the constant thread, which readers should hold on to, is the life and character of Pontius Pilate from his birth to his death, and then some.

This is not a search for the "real" Pilate. Nothing here—save that stone and those coins—is "real" in the sense that an archaeologist or historian would understand the term. Even the Roman reconstructions, as plausible as I have tried to make them, rely on the accounts of writers with their own agendas, or on the experiences of other people. We long for records, letters, diaries, the memories of friends; but everything is the surmise of different centuries, including the late twentieth century looking back at the first. "What is truth?" asked John's Pilate, and we ask the question with him. We are all grasping at shadows.

Perhaps all this striving to invent Pilate should just be dismissed as fiction. But then again, it isn't fiction at all: it's an attempt, made in different ways in every age, to express what the character of Pilate means and why he is important. The Pontius Pilate we think we know is a mixture of dozens of invented men, each symbolic of something: the State facing the individual, the pagan world opposing the Christian one, skepticism versus truth, ourselves facing God. He represents either man's free will, or his hopelessness before fate, or his struggle to distinguish good from evil, or the tyranny of hard choices. He is the tyrant and oppressor, the implacable man of law, the perfect example of imperial authority; but also the grand equivocator, the modern democratic politician reading his polls and spinning his message, sliding from one expedient to the next. People ceaselessly project their own ideas and anxieties on him. They use him, and have always used him, exactly as they want to, often revealing in the process as much about themselves as they reveal about him.

Yet somewhere behind all this philosophy and fantasy lurks a flesh-and-blood Roman. And this world—this real world in which Pilate moved—is every bit as strange as the mythological one. It's tempting to feel we understand the Romans: that they were men and women much like ourselves, civilized, sophisticated, worldly, rational, only wearing different clothes. Pilate is often treated this way, as a modern man (of any age) distinguished only by his toga and his haircut. Yet there is of course another side, one of utter distance and difference. I was sometimes made startlingly aware of it: not just in the grand arcana of Roman myths and gods, or their revolting quack medicine, or their sensual appreciation of blood, but in the details.

Marcus Aurelius in his *Meditations* tries to describe at one point the beauty of small, almost unexpected effects in Nature. He wonders at "the cracks and little breaks in the surface of a loaf . . . figs, which, when they are ripe, open and gape; and olives, which when they fall by themselves and are near decaying, are particularly pretty to look at." This image of putrescence as beauty brought me up short: these were different eyes looking at the world.

This was the real reason I couldn't shake Pilate off. There was too thrilling a tension between the man and the symbols, between Pilate as he probably was and Pilate as we have imagined him. He saw the world in his way, but we all want him to see it in ours. And he was never really important in that provincial job of his; but he has become hugely important since.

This, then, is a book about all our Pilates. Some are familiar characters, but more are surprising. They have depths and contrasts that are unexpected. They do extraordinary things. Among these surprises are the hints we can occasionally get of a man actually walking on a marble floor in Caesarea, feeling his shoes pinch, clicking his fingers for a slave, while clouds of lasting infamy gather overhead.

PONTIUS PILATE

PILATE ON THE BEACH

ON THE SEVENTEENTH OF SEPTEMBER 1870, a gale of extraordinary force swept ashore in Blackpool. By eight in the evening, it was impossible to walk along the beach. Men in stovepipe hats and newsboys in caps struggled, bent horizontal, across the sandflats. The tide ran fast with unaccustomed foam; toward Ireland, the night sky towered like a bruised fist.

All night the wind blew. Behind the Manchester Hotel, the sea destroyed the embankment of the Lytham and Blackpool railway. The rail bent and sagged over gaping air. In two places the waves crashed through the promenade, sweeping away field walls and pouring in a torrent across the Lytham Road. John Knowles, a local farmer, lost four fields of oats, reduced to a mass of blackened straw floating with the scum of the sea.

In the morning, bleary walkers found the water knee-deep inside the Blackpool gasworks. Bathing vans had been blown all over town, tipped on their sides in the middle of roads, or upended in fields far from the water's edge. Their spars stuck up like the horns of giant cattle. Oddest of all was the fate of the wooden confectioner's kiosk that had stood at the corner of the Foxhall Hotel. It was found upside down in the middle of the bowling green, as if challenging customers to exchange their woods for gobstoppers, jawbreakers and fizzing sherbet balls.

Two days earlier, Her Majesty's Ship *Captain* was caught in the same gale off the coast of Finistère. The *Captain* was an ironclad battleship of a new and unusual design. She carried cannon on turrets at stem and stern; she boasted the tallest masts in the Royal Navy, and the greatest area of sail. The ship was 857 tons heavier than she should have been, and her sides rose a mere six and a half feet above the water. During previous voyages to Vigo and back, water had often washed over the decks in relatively calm seas. The former Secretary of the Navy had condemned earlier ships of this design as "wretched low-lying, ill-ventilated, wave-washed, unworthy abortions." Even the *Captain*'s captain recognized her liabilities: that at an angle of more than 21 degrees, for example, she could not right herself. His advice was trenchant: "Don't hesitate if you get into bad weather to furl all sails, use steam and get her bow to the sea."

The *Captain* had been out with the rest of the squadron that afternoon, all flying their ensigns about twenty miles west of Cape Finistère. Admiral Milne, on board the *Lord Warden,* admired the *Captain*'s speed but noticed that, even in a moderate wind, the sea was washing over the lee side of her decks. By midnight the barometer had fallen and the wind had increased. Milne saw the *Captain* "heeling over a good deal to starboard, with the wind on her port side." At about 1:30 A.M. he noticed that he could not see the *Captain*'s red bow light; but by then it was "thick with rain" and the *Lord Warden* herself was laboring in a heavy cross-sea. Milne never saw the *Captain* again.

On board the *Captain,* Robert Hirst, an able seaman, was stationed on the foredeck for the starboard watch. Like most of the officers and crew, he was a West Country man. His frightened burr still sounds in the account he gave later to the man from *The Times.*

> There was a strong wind, and the ship was then under her three top sails, double reefs in each, and the foretopmast staysail. The yards were braced sharp up, and the ship did not seem to have much way upon her. As the watch was mustered, I heard Captain Burgoyne give the order, "Let go the foretop sail halliards," followed by, "Let go fore and main topsail sheets." By the time the men got to the topsail sheets the ship was heeling over to starboard so much that the men were washed away off the deck, the ship lying down on her side as she was gradually turning over, and trembling with every blow which the short jumping seas (the sea was now white all round with the squall) struck her, and the roar of the steam from the funnels roaring horribly above everything, and continuing to do so even when under water.

Hirst and two of his companions rushed to the foredeck netting and jumped overboard. Almost at once, they found themselves washed scrambling and sliding on to the ship's bottom; and then the ship went down, taking them with her.

The next thing Hirst knew he banged against a floating spar, to which he tied himself with his black silk handkerchief. It kept him buoyant for a while, until the tie broke. Tossed here and there on the foaming seas, he managed to catch hold of the stern of one of the *Captain*'s launches, still with its canvas cover lashed around it. Clinging to the cover were half a dozen other men. One produced a knife, hacked away the canvas, and set the launch floating. Hirst and his colleagues then tried to row back to the *Captain* to rescue Captain Burgoyne, but the boat was immediately swamped by the sea, and two men were washed out of her. Back went Hirst a second time, bailing out the boat with a cap, but so many oars had been washed away that the craft was barely maneuverable in the raging seas. "Nothing could be done," he concluded; "Captain Burgoyne was away to starboard, clinging to the bottom of a boat, in all that storm of broken water."

All this time, they had not been alone. They had been able to make out the red and green bow lights of the other members of the squadron, but could not attract their attention. Their companions never knew they were in trouble. After the squall, as the weather moderated, the heavy bank of clouds rolled away to the east; the stars came out, and the moon shone down on an apparently empty sea.

At last, at around five in the morning, the drifting remnants of the *Captain*'s crew saw another light, that of the Finistère lighthouse. Day was breaking. The men struggled to the shore and collapsed. By good fortune, they had found the only place on that rockbound coast where a safe landing was possible.

Five hundred men had been on board the ship. Eighteen survived. Captain Cowper Coles, who had designed the *Captain* despite his complete lack of training in naval architecture, was drowned in his own invention. In the morning, as the disconsolate squadron regrouped, there seemed to be no trace of the missing vessel. But by sunset the *Psyche,* coming up from Vigo, reported having passed "two cutters, painted white, bottom up, with a large amount of wreck." Among the wreckage floated the body of a seaman with "Rose" marked on his flannel underwear.

There was one more survivor. Before the *Captain* sailed, the second lieutenant, John Trevithick, had cut a parchment page from an Ethiopian manuscript and given it to a friend, a sailor on HMS *Malibu.* It is doubtful whether Trevithick could read the Coptic in which the manuscript was written. He had been on attachment to Lord Napier's expedition of 1858, helping to chart a course for ships through the Hormuz

Strait at the entrance to the Persian Gulf. Boxes of such manuscripts had
come home with him as plunder. The page in question was attractive,
with well-spaced, looping Ethiopian script traced in black ink and scattered with red ornamental crosses, which formed the points of punctua-
tion. One column was almost filled with a painting of a group, one man
and five women, placing a body in a tomb. It made a decent present, and
the rest of the manuscript went with Trevithick's luggage in his cabin on
the *Captain.*

A few months later, Trevithick's friend handed the page to the Ashmolean Museum in Oxford as a curiosity. And it is curious enough. Beneath the scene of the burial stands a man in priest's vestments, his arms
outstretched. He is praying in the manner of ancient and modern Christians, palms uplifted and fingers spread. Unlike the swarthy figures at
the tomb, this man is white-faced: a European. It is Pilate at the tomb of
Jesus, making a profession of repentance.

To the Victorians who saw and translated it, this relic was unbearably
poignant. The only written remnant of the wreck of the *Captain,* beyond
poor Rose's nametapes, was Pilate's prayer for forgiveness from the man
he had sentenced to death: a prayer which, in its short Coptic cadences,
also reads like the words of a man gasping for air.

> *I believe*
> *that you have risen*
> *and have appeared to me, and*
> *you will not judge me,*
> *oh my Lord, because I acted*
> *for you,*
> *fearing this*
> *from the Jews.*
> *And it is not that I*
> *deny your resurrection, oh*
> *my*
> *Lord. I believe*
> *in your word and in the*
> *mighty*
> *works you wrought*
> *among them when you*
> *were alive, you raised*

many
dead. Therefore, oh my God,
be not angry with me
because of what

A whole fantastical story was originally wrapped around this prayer. Most of it has since become part of the silt and sand at the bottom of the Bay of Biscay, or perhaps has been cut out of fish on the kitchen slab, as rings and jewels were cut out of cod in the fables of old Europe. Trevithick's page itself turned out to be missing its bottom half, so that the columns of script broke off in the middle. Even this tiny part of the story was in inconsequential pieces.

On the page that survives, the Jews and Pilate have quarreled after the burial of Jesus. The governor has gone to the tomb; it is not "proper" or "desirable," the Jews tell him, that a high Roman official should do that. Besides, the body laid in the tomb is not even Christ's. Disquietingly, it belongs to someone else. Why should Pilate cause such horror among the Jews on account of some corpse of no importance? But Pilate is disconsolate, thinking of the evil that has been done by the "injustice" of the crucifixion of Christ. He begins to pray for the resurrection. As he stretches his hands over the tomb, a voice comes from inside, from the mouth of the dead: "Roll away the stone, my Lord Pilate, that I may come out in the power of my lord Jesus Christ."

The next section is lost, but it is clear that a miracle occurs. Pilate cries out in joy, and is next found standing at a distance in a state of rapture and enchantment. He himself has raised the dead; and besides, the cloths that remain are heavy with the sweetness of Christ. He had noticed that before, begun to tremble before, even as he had approached the tomb.

he said,
"Oh my brother, don't you see
how
it smells and is beautiful, the
fragrance
of those linen cloths, and it is not like
the smell of the dead, but like
the fine purple of kings'

wrappings?"
The Jews therefore said
to Pilate,
"You know yourself how Joseph
put spice on him,
and incense, and rubbed him with
myrrh and aloes, and this is why
they smell fragrant." And Pilate said,
"Although they put ointment on the
linen cloths,
why is the whole sepulchre
like a chamber, which has in it
musk and sweet spices, and is warm
and smells fragrant?" And they said,
"The perfume you smell, Pilate,
is the smell of the garden
which the winds blow into it."

So the wind blew. The wind of God that had upended the *Captain* and had whirled the confectioner's stall across the close-cropped green beside the promenade, scattering humbugs and toffees and sticks of colored rock, now blew out sweetness from the sepulchre of Christ. The Jews said it was no miracle, no reversal of corruption; only the wind in the garden. But as he stood beneath the lifting branches, with the breeze in his hair, the pagan governor began to believe. Or so the Ethiopians said.

It was only a fragment, after all. Like so many other scraps of Pilate's story, it survived only by chance. Yet it is still worth laying these fragments out, as on that desk in the Ashmolean (if the daylight is dim, you can adjust the lamp), to see if they approximate the outline of a life.

Chapter 1

THE FORUM
AND THE
FOREST

I.

HE WAS BORN a few years before Christ, somewhere in Italy, most probably in Rome. But this was not, in the deepest sense, his country. His ancestors were mountain men from Samnium, south of Rome. There in the brutal hills the men scratched at stony plots, the women spun wool; they worshiped oak groves and springs and woodpeckers, and their talk was of war. From time to time the Samnites would descend to the poppy-strewn fields of Campania, which they devastated. For years they fought the Romans, but in 290 B.C. Rome defeated them. The struggle had always been unequal.

After that defeat—much of their territory gone, and their power broken—the Samnites slowly and sourly picked up Roman ways. Some even became citizens. But they were still mostly peasant fighters, as intractable as their mountains, and when civil war broke out between Marius and Sulla in 86 B.C., the Samnites tried to wrestle free again. This time Sulla defeated them just outside Rome itself, right by the Colline Gate, and the reprisals were brutal. The few Samnite leaders who survived were executed; their mountain villages were burned like torches; the people were killed or scattered, and soft-skinned Roman colonists were sent to take their places.

Cicero, writing about it later, described this as the milder sort of war. The Romans were not fighting the Samnites as enemies, only as rivals for supremacy. They thought them rough and brave as Spartans; they respected them. But the difference in treatment was sometimes hard to perceive. Cicero himself described how, after the "respected" people of Marseilles had forfeited their supremacy, a wooden model of the city was carried through Rome in triumphal procession "to show the world that they had been defeated." In the case of the Samnites, though the names of their various families were scattered all over northern and central Italy, the polity was destroyed. There would never again be a mountain redoubt where people dreamed of liberty in quite the same way.

That is why we do not know where Pilate was born. His tribe, the Pontii of Samnium, was dispersed and broken. The Samnites were known in Rome as rustic buffoons, gallumphing creatures who were wild and clumsy as horses. Horace described one he met on the road with such a scar on his face from the removal of warts "that he could dance the Cyclops-shepherd dance without a mask." The older ones spoke not Latin but Oscan, primitive country words that Pilate may have heard from his grandfather: *sollo* for *totus, abzet* for *habet, pipas* for *clamas.* "Petis pipas?," addressed to a child, meant "What are you chirping for?" Even in the gladiators' ring these men were comic turns. It was traditional to deck them out in particolored plate and helmets with huge bobbing crests, in mockery of the gorgeous new armor they had once proudly worn, according to Livy, to one of their defeats by the Romans. They would go into the ring heavily but ludicrously armed, with wooden swords and quarterstaffs, and simply belabor each other for hours, until darkness fell and the audience went home.

Yet the tribe of the Pontii was of the Samnite nobility, and it was not without heroes. The Pontii were even slightly larger than life, numinous with legends and fame. If Pilate's father ever aspired to an *atrium,* an entrance hall decorated with painted wax masks of the family ancestors (in which a small boy could slide on the tiles in his slippers), it might well have contained a mask of Gavius Pontius, who had defeated the Roman army in 321 B.C. in a high mountain pass called the Caudine Forks. Under those walls of rock, loud with the sound of water, the Romans had fallen on their faces. But Gavius Pontius did not kill them. He simply took their weapons, made them strip to their tunics and drove them home under a triumphal yoke of three spears lashed together. Thirty years later, he met the Romans again; they took him prisoner, sent his own men under the yoke and killed him, showing him no shred of the mercy he had shown them. The defeated Samnites, too, were made to strip to their tunics, giving up to the Romans the marvelous leather belts, studded with bronze clasps, that were the symbols of their liberty. Only the buffoon gladiators wore such belts after that.

Next in the parade of family heroes came two brothers, both of whom had been caught up in the fighting in 82 B.C. after the Social War. Many of the Pontii were Roman citizens now, but they had been weaned on the legend of Gavius. The first brother, Pontius Telesinus, commanded the Samnite contingent for Marius against Sulla; he died beside the Colline Gate as the battle raged in the dark, cut down on the point of entering Rome. Those Samnites who survived were slaughtered by Sulla in the Campus Martius, where Pilate might later have wrestled or played handball in the dust.

The brother of Telesinus was besieged with Marius' son in Praeneste, outside the city. Heartlessly, Sulla sent them the severed heads of Telesinus and his men. At the sight of those gagging faces, with white eyes and bloodied hair, they resolved to die by each other's hands. The younger Marius drew his sword and offered it to the breast of his friend, who fell on it. He then drew it out, shining with Samnite blood, and fell on it himself. "And so perished," wrote a modern Italian historian, "the noblest and last of the sons of Italy, the soul of resistance to Rome."

These were the stories: a collection, thrilling as a Boys' Annual, of desperate battles, struggles for liberty, magnanimous gestures, heroic sacrifices. The boy Pilate could glean from them that mercy shown to your enemies was both noble and futile: had Gavius Pontius killed those Romans, he might not have died by public execution. From the scene in the cell in Praeneste, where the two friends embraced each other and the cold blade in the dripping darkness, he could deduce that suicide for the honor of one's nation was the ultimate act, and that death was all the nobler for being premeditated, sealed by mutual resolution and carried out with quiet efficiency. There were many such deaths to admire, from Socrates onward.

There were lives to admire, too: for many of the Pontii had struggled after the dispersal, and their sense of illustriousness was difficult to recover. They had lost a generation of young men in the 80s B.C., the generation of Pilate's great-grandfather, and for fifty years afterward the Samnites scarcely appeared in any public capacity in Rome. Within two generations the most thriving members could be classed as just below patrician rank, respectable but decidedly second-class. Julius Caesar recruited Samnites for their valor; they became *equites illustriores,* then special administrators, prefects and private imperial troubleshooters. Yet not all could escape their origins. Titus Pontius became one of Caesar's centurions in the civil war; when he refused to abandon his leader he became a hero of sorts, but only of sorts. "The great lights of our country," wrote Valerius Maximus, "will not be offended to see big-hearted centurions [like Titus] beside their own glorious and resplendent names. . . . Nobility should encourage, not scorn, a natural goodness that springs from the breast of obscurity." A little later on, gracious Valerius summed up Titus again: "Sine ullis imaginibus nobilem animum!"—"What a noble soul, even with no masks of the ancestors in the hall!"

It may have been during these years—if Pilate did not earn the name himself later—that the cognomen "Pilatus," "Skilled with the Javelin," became attached to his family. Javelin-throwing was thought to have come from the Samnites anyway, and the Oscan version of "Pilatus," *eh-peilatus,* has been found on an inscription from Capua. It is another clue to Pilate's origins: an indication of the violent past that beat, however faintly, behind him.

So his father, if not Pilate himself, held and balanced the javelin, which quivered in his hand like something living. This was the second skill of the Roman soldier, after he had been trained in the use of sword and shield. The *pilum* was five feet of wooden shaft and two feet of tapered iron, of which the bottom half was left soft and untempered. When the point lodged in a shield the shaft would bend and hang down, making it impossible to throw back. A trained javelin thrower could tilt his heavy weapon skyward, flex his body, hurl the javelin thirty yards, and hit the mark. His training had consisted precisely in aiming at a fixed target, aiming again, aiming again, until his arm, bruised from the effort, could smoothly direct the missile anywhere he wanted. If you were called *pilatus,* it meant you excelled at doing that: you showed decisiveness, strength, straightness of aim. But not all qualities could be transferred from the field of battle to public life.

His army service done, Pilate's father probably settled down as a member of the Roman knightly class. We assume this because prefect-governors in the early empire were knights and sons of knights; it was not yet done to open the postings to freedmen. His father, then, had his own large house, with an *atrium* and colonnaded garden and piped water; several slaves would wait on him. He had a patron to whom he would present his morning greetings, but also a few men dependent on himself. Perhaps, like so many of the knights lampooned by contemporary writers, his aspirations ran ahead of his taste in furnishings, tableware and statues; perhaps, like them, he needed to impress and feel secure. And the vital element of his security was his children, the next generation. These would be given every piece of ceremony, training and education in order eventually to recover the rank the *gens* had held before. By the time Pilate was born, the clan of the Pontii was on the point of producing

Roman consuls and Roman millionaires, and expectations had grown accordingly: an official's *toga praetexta* with its purple border, a private bath with windows overlooking a view, a litter for the streets, a villa by the sea. Wordlessly, these ambitions were laid on the shoulders of the next male child in line.

No one knows what Pilate's first name was. As a child, whether he was called Marcus or Gaius or Lucius would have mattered; but as he grew older his friends and even his lovers would have used his cognomen, Pilate with three syllables in the vocative, when they talked or wrote to him. "Mi Pilate," my Pilate, would have been a term of endearment or a nickname for the man, but his mother bending over his cradle would have whispered a name that history has rubbed away.

As a baby he would have been presented to the gods and given a *bulla,* a little golden pouch containing a lucky charm, which was hung around his neck. As a child he sat through several years of rote learning in school, scratching with a metal stylus on a wax slate over which his long curls fell, absorbing the rudiments of mathematics, reading, rhetoric and writing. To learn to write, he would put his small hand inside the strong hand of an adult; together they would trace the wobbly characters until he was ready to draw them on his own. A rich boy would have slaves to carry his book rolls. Perhaps Pilate had one, or perhaps he carried the rolls himself, "slate and satchel slung over his left arm," as the poets described it. At Saturnalia in December he was given presents: sweets, nuts and little terra-cotta figures you could fight with, at least until they broke. Richer boys got ponies and parrots.

In the last years of school he learned, like a little lawyer, to unpick the multiple sides of every question. The questions were well-worn: "Should Alexander have sailed the ocean, or not?" "Should the Spartans have fled when they were sent against Xerxes?" "Should Cicero have begged Antony's pardon?" Each had its series of set opposing answers, the different "colors" of the schoolman, and these he would have learned too, declaiming them as well as he could with the right hand movements and the right pitch of his breaking voice. This may have been most of his training in the practice of the law.

At the age of seventeen he would have been given his first ceremonial shave in front of the family shrine. The down was consigned to a tiny decorated box; then, dressed in the white toga of a new adult, the *toga virilis,* he was taken through the Forum to pray in the Temple of Jupiter.

The *bulla* was left behind at the family shrine, among the statuettes and fading flowers, and there may have been times in the years ahead when he regretted the leaving of that little piece of luck.

His days now had to be spent preparing for a career in public service. This usually meant trying for a commission in the army as a junior officer, for which he would need a recommendation to the commander. He would begin, therefore, the routine Roman round of getting himself known and noticed by the powerful. In the morning he would pay his respects, arriving at dawn at the entrance hall of the man he hoped would be his patron. He would have to wait until the *nomenclator* (only a slave, but the sort of slave who reveled in his authority) noticed him in the throng of hopefuls and passed on his name to his master. The nervous greetings were passed on too: "Quid agis? Quid commode vales?" "How are you? I hope you're well?" and in exchange might come a commission, a recommendation, or a little money. By these means he learned the essential etiquette of Roman life: all paths to advancement lay through politeness, persistence and the favor of richer and nobler men.

Horace described the ritual in painful detail. As soon as he aspired to any rank or any noble friendship, he wrote, "people start asking, 'Who is this fellow? What was his father?' " Approaching the would-be patron was agony:

> On coming into your presence, I said a few faltering words, for speechless shame stopped me from saying more. My tale was not that I was a famous father's son, nor that I rode about my estate on a Saturian steed; I told you what I was. As is your way, you answered little and I withdrew; then, nine months later, you sent for me again and bade me join your friends. I count it as a great favor that I pleased you. . . .

Part of Horace's social disadvantage, though he did not say so, was that he was a provincial, from Venusia in Apulia. Those "few faltering words" showed that he was still rough-cut, without polish, and with a country accent that could be heard; he still needed to learn the soft urbanity of Roman speech and manners, as perhaps Pilate did.

At last, somehow, the right impression was given. Having found a patron, Pilate would do whatever tasks he was assigned. He would run errands, take messages, whirl between the rich man's house and the Janus Arcade, where the bankers were. Sometimes he would ride in his patron's carriage, where (by Horace's account) he would be favored with such conversation as "What's the time?" or "Do you think Thraex is a match for Syro the Chicken?" But on his free afternoons he would enjoy himself. At the games he and his friends would sit for hours on the hard benches, discussing the muscles and stamina of fighters and the blows they had endured. There was no greater thrill than to see a man still fighting, still struggling out of the dust, when he was painted like an actor with the streams of his own blood. At that point the nameless criminal or captive, oiled and caged and conveyed to the circus in a cart, acquired a name and a reputation; he acquired the dignity of a man. And he died with that dignity on him, his own scarlet cloak.

Young men would build up their bodies in conscious imitation of their heroes. To be strong in every way, *vir fortis ac strenuus,* the steely character in the steel-hard body, was the Roman ideal. Together Pilate and his friends would attack the baths in style, leaping in off the side, splashing all and sundry with their ferocious strokes, wrestling one another like dolphins, belting out songs in the wonderful echo of the changing rooms. In the exercise yard they ran, lifted weights, did the long jump and played ball until their bodies were pink with effort; then, exhausted, they made for the wine seller and the hot-sausage man. They were oiled and rubbed on adjacent tables, hung their clothes on adjacent pegs, used the same cold sponge in the latrines, fainted for the same mistresses.

Possibly Pilate was treated to a repetition of the famous lecture on sex once given (the story ran) by the philosopher Archytas to Herennius Pontius, the father of Gavius. Cicero related this story in his treatise *On Old Age,* recording, too, that Herennius was so deeply studious and intellectual that he had debated with Plato. "No more deadly curse than sensual pleasure," Archytas told Herennius, "has been inflicted on mankind by nature. It is a fruitful source of treasons, revolutions, secret communications with the enemy. In fact, there is no crime, no evil deed, to which the appetite for sensual pleasure does not impel us. . . . Intellect is the best gift of nature or the gods. To this divine gift and endowment there is nothing so inimical as pleasure . . . since, when more than ordi-

narily violent and lasting, it darkens all the light of the soul." But perhaps your soul was not too much darkened if, during the Floral games in
April, you watched the actresses take their clothes off.

In any case, sex took second place when the call to the army came
through. It would have taken Pilate away from Rome for years. There
seems not much doubt, from the record of his actions in office, that he
was a soldier first and a diplomat second. Some have imagined he fought
as a legionary, acquiring a taste for blood he never lost. Yet his class dictated against it. If he had really been a foot soldier, the sort of blunt and
thick-headed strongman who is sometimes pictured, he would hardly
have risen to become the governor of Judaea. Legionaries spent their careers in the army, but Pilate joined in the military tribune class that
would lead, eventually, to a foreign posting as the governor of a province.

In the late Republic there was no longer an obligatory five-year stint
of service before a man could become a military tribune, or legionary
staff officer. The minimum age for the office was eighteen, when a boy
had scarcely shaved and might have been a soldier for only a year or so.
His duties could be rigorous, but the experience could also be as much a
shambles as military service in France in the 1970s. "Although our early
manhood was spent in camp," wrote Pliny, "it was at a time when merit
was under suspicion and apathy an asset, when officers lacked influence
and soldiers respect, when there was neither authority nor obedience, and
the whole system was slack, disorganised and chaotic, better forgotten
than remembered."

Pliny, bound for the civil service, would leave in a couple of years,
but Pilate seems to have taken a harder path. He probably did several
tours of military service, both as a tribune and as a prefect of cavalry or
auxiliaries. Since he was a commanding officer, even of a relatively lowly
sort and barely out of his teens, he wore lighter armor and had few en-
cumbering weapons. The mark of his office was the *parazonium,* a waist-
band that carried the sword on his left side, where ordinary soldiers wore
it on the right. When he drew his sword the action was statelier and
slower, crossing his chest like a half-salute, and he was not required to do
it so often. The hardest marching, too, was not required of him. Slaves
carried his gear; lowlier soldiers dug the ditches and put up the camp
palisades. Superior commanding officers included him in their meetings,
and sometimes offered him dinner in their tents.

Pilate was less a fighter than an administrator, keeping things straight behind the lines. For this he was paid fifty thousand sesterces a year, about as much, the elder Pliny noted, as some connoisseurs would pay for a nice chandelier. He was in charge of the pay, food and floggings for his unit; he had to keep his men motivated and see they did not desert. Modern soldiers would call it a soft billet, yet it was still active military service. He took the same oath as any foot soldier, every third of January and on the anniversary of the emperor's accession, to obey the emperor and his superior officers. Inside the camp palisade he would sleep as the others did, wrapped in his regulation red cloak under the cold stars, and in the morning he too woke to the long summoning blast of the army bugle. He ate the same porridge, drank the same sour wine—the wine that was offered to Jesus on the cross—and sang the same bawdy songs, like the mocking soldiers' tribute to Julius Caesar known as "The Triumph over Gaul":

> *Watch your wives, everyone, here we've got a man*
> *Who may be bald but fucks the girls in any way he can.*
> *Guess who's spent your money on many a Gallic whore?*
> *He's used up every penny, and he's coming to borrow more.*

He also took part in the same wars of conquest. Some suppose he fought in the German campaigns of Tiberius in A.D. 9, or of Germanicus in 14, where it was sometimes cold enough to wear trousers and ride along muffled in a cloak. These were campaigns of victory, fought by legions nicknamed "The Triumphant" and "The Indomitable" to impose the peace of Rome on bearded and foul-smelling barbarians. Whether or not he was fighting, Pilate would have ridden out most mornings, his bridle heavy with his service medals, to see the standards with their silver medallions and wreaths and eagles flashing in the sun; and most evenings, tired, hungry, aching, he would relive his part in the day's engagements. He was not constantly in the thick of things, but he was sometimes close enough to be in danger of enemy spears and to dread that his horse would be cut down under him; close enough to see the dilated eyes of the enemy and hear again the screams of the dying as he lay in the dark.

This was unlikely to have bothered him. The war he was fighting was generally considered a good one, a war for the future of civilization, protected by the gods. Military discipline, wrote Valerius Maximus at about the time Pilate left for Judaea, was "the principal glory of the Roman empire and its most secure foundation"; it was the one ancestral virtue that had been preserved intact by the soft and corrupted Romans of his day. Others among the prefects and tribunes, more languid young men doing their part-time service only because they had to, may have taken a more cynical view; like Catullus, they may have called it "playing billiards with our world." But even Pliny, not much of a soldier, could recall with emotion "life under arms, the camps, bugles and trumpets, sweat and dust and heat of the sun"; and Pilate probably took his soldiering seriously.

He could have gone to Judaea straight from his military postings and never become a civil servant in Rome. Yet he was not without position there. He was possibly a knight, an *eques,* by virtue of successive tours of military service, and it is likely that by inheritance he was also an *eques* in the civilian sense, with a minimum net worth of 400,000 sesterces. That would buy him two medium-sized houses in the city. He was entitled to wear a gold ring and to sit in the first fourteen rows at the theater, where he would not be "elbowed or besmirched by the mob," as Martial put it; although he was not so elevated that, naked at the baths, he could not be gently but firmly moved aside by the slave of an equally naked man of praetorian rank.

As a professional soldier, he did not have to stay abroad to qualify for governorship of a province. Although many a governor-to-be passed through the same junior ranks, ending up as a military prefect on some difficult frontier, what was important was to catch the attention of the powerful at the right moment. For that, it was useful to linger in the city for a while. Another of the Pontii, C. Petronius Pontius Nigrinus ("the Black-Haired"), was a consul when Tiberius died in A.D. 37, and there were other rich and influential relations. But Pilate's own reputation still rested on exploits performed far away, and he would need to burnish it somehow at home.

If he stayed for a time in Rome, he may have become a member of the Praetorian Guard, the thousand-strong personal bodyguard of the emperor himself. Tiberius, obsessed with security, had reorganized the Guard, taking them out of their scattered lodgings around the city and giving them a permanent camp in which to nourish their esprit de corps. If Pilate was among them, this would explain (since Praetorians were famous for it) his well-attested public devotion to the emperor, his cult and his welfare. And it might have produced an association that was to make, as well as almost break, him.

Many scholars suppose that Pilate was taken under the wing of Lucius Aelius Sejanus, the brutal commander of the Praetorian Guard who, from A.D. 23 to 31, held sway over the emperor's affections. Tacitus wrote that Tiberius, "always dark and mysterious with others, was carefree and outspoken only with him." Sejanus was hardy, daring and spirited, but he could affect humility when he needed to; he was a strange combination of the energetic and the watchful. In his military duties he ingratiated himself with the troops, perhaps with Pilate too, by mixing with them and learning everybody's names. Some of those names he would then put forward to advance his own designs.

Sejanus commended himself to Tiberius by his efforts, in A.D. 22, to put out the fire that almost destroyed Pompey's theater. When the theater was rebuilt, a bronze statue of Sejanus was placed in it. Others were put up around Rome and in the shrines of the legions, and his birthday was publicly celebrated with the burning of incense and candles before them. But he was deeply unpopular. Like Pilate, he was a knight, not a noble; he was something of an upstart and, worse, an ambitious one. This made him anathema to Roman historians, even apart from his misdeeds. According to them, Sejanus wished to destroy the older heirs of the imperial house in order to gain control over the younger ones, and he was not scrupulous about how he achieved his end. He was said to have murdered Tiberius' son Drusus by slow poison in 23 with the connivance of the victim's wife. It is possible that Pilate glimpsed Tiberius, already graying and withdrawn, on the day when, as Tacitus recorded, he came to the Senate to rebuke the senators for weeping for his son. He made a speech of perfect, indeed chilling, composure until the very end, when he suddenly appealed to the consuls "or anyone else" to relieve him of his power. Tacitus thought these remarks were stupid. They may have been tactical, to shore up his authority. But what might Pilate have made of this show of humanity and despair on the part of his emperor?

Sejanus then began to work toward the downfall of the rival house of Germanicus, headed by his widow, Agrippina. He sowed fears in the emperor's mind about the threat of civil war, and succeeded in getting two of the widow's close friends charged with extortion and treason. Other charges followed against other enemies; all of them fell, as the favorite wormed himself still deeper into Tiberius' affections. But in 25 Sejanus overplayed his hand by asking to marry Livia Julia, the widow of Drusus. His letter to Tiberius and the emperor's reply, included by Tacitus in the *Annals,* are possibly both forgeries. But, genuine or not, they give a vivid impression of the social handicaps of an *eques* such as both Sejanus and Pilate were.

Sejanus said he was deeply grateful for the favors he had received. He insisted that he had never sought high office, because it was an honor merely to serve such a master as Tiberius, to whose ear he brought his hopes and desires "as readily as to the gods." He could think of no honor higher than marriage to a member of the imperial house; and Augustus himself, after all, when he was looking for a husband for his daughter, had considered men of equestrian rank. So, if Livia Julia was thought to be in need of a husband, would the emperor kindly think of him?

Tiberius, in answer, said he would speak plainly. Livia Julia, already in her seventies and once the wife of Gaius Caesar, would never agree to grow old with "a mere Roman knight." Even if he, Tiberius, agreed to it, the leading men in the state never would. They already thought Sejanus had been promoted well above "the permissible levels of equestrian advancement." Yes, Augustus might have considered equestrian suitors for his daughter, but he went no further; she had married nobles. If Sejanus continued to prove his devotion and his usefulness, "there are no heights you may not reach"; but for the moment, nobility was out of the question.

Rebuffed, Sejanus went on plotting. Over the next months and years he persuaded Tiberius to leave the smoke and noise of Rome and go into exile in Capri, surrounded by Greek scholars. He poisoned his mind still further against Agrippina, engineering an imperial dinner party at which she refused to take apples, imagining them poisoned, from the emperor's hand, and he managed to save Tiberius' life by shielding him from a rockfall as he dined at a villa called the Cave. His sense of power was perhaps never greater than when, crouching on hands and knees, braced beneath the rocks, he found himself face-to-face with the terrified emperor, only inches between them, and calmly held his death away.

For four or five years now, Sejanus had been suggesting appointments. He had recommended men as centurions, as tribunes and as governors. At dawn the leading citizens would congregate in his house, bringing the private petitions they wished to communicate to Tiberius. It is likely that Pilate was a regular until A.D. 26, the year he was posted.

He must have known that hall at first light and sat on the famous couch that eventually collapsed, on New Year's Day in 31, under the weight of all the petitioners. Sejanus' recommendations to the emperor in the 20s were seldom turned down. If he had suggested Pilate for the governorship of Judaea, Tiberius would have concurred.

Yet there is no firm evidence that Pilate was Sejanus' creature. He was certainly not so close to him that after his fall he had to die, as several other governors did. Sejanus would have known and presumably approved of him; Pilate for his part, whatever his private feelings, would have been careful to remain in Sejanus' favor. And maybe that was all. Tiberius was also known to make governors on a whim, on no formal recommendation. Tacitus gives some idea what his criteria were: decent behavior, good character, but not "outstanding merit," because that might threaten him. At times, too, "decent behavior" was put aside. Pomponius Flaccus was made governor of Syria on the strength of a thirty-six-hour orgy of drinking, with the immortal imperial endorsement on his commission: "A good fellow at all hours, day or night!"

In 22, during the trial of a former governor of Asia, one senator suggested that it might be an idea if no one "of scandalous life and reputation" were allowed to be a governor in future; it might save grief. But Tiberius disagreed. Many governors, he said, had surprised people, since "important positions stimulate some natures and blunt others." His candidates were often unknown quantities, clay to be molded by fate. He preferred them that way.

Pilate's presumed Samnite origins would not have commended him. Tiberius disliked both Samnite-style gladiators and the "old Oscan farce," a long-running series of hit shows called the Comedies of Atella which featured young male actors in the grotesque roles of Bucco the Braggart, Dossenus the Hunchback, Maccus the Glutton and Pappus the Dotard. He had closed such shows down and sent the actors packing. But he seemed to trust Pilate enough (or think him insignificant enough) to send him to his province once he had appointed him, rather than detain him in Rome on trivial excuses, as was the fate of several other governors.

So, one day, Pilate received his imperial promotion. It came on a five-leaved wax tablet, the official form; the standard response was to go to the temple to offer thanks and sacrifice. And then the knight Pilate, blooded in war, approved by the favorite, but still full of social insecurities and with his Samnite chip on his shoulder, set off for Judaea.

II.

So runs the most plausible version of Pilate's early life. But a second, proposed with equal confidence, holds that he was a Spaniard. Giovanni Rosadi, an Italian magistrate, put forward this theory in 1908, though several sorts of Spanishness had been claimed for Pilate centuries before.

Some said he was born in Seville, a city whose residents had the right of Roman citizenship. There is a large house off the Plaza de Arguelles, built in a mixture of Gothic and Moorish styles, with marble doorways, Roman columns, Spanish balconies, iridescent blue tiles and a garden which, in nineteenth-century guidebooks, was running wild and scattered with sculpture like a stonemason's yard. This was known from the fifteenth century, and is still known, as Pilate's house, although it was also the palace of the dukes of Alcalá. It boasts a *praetorium,* or governor's judgment hall, and the table on which Judas is meant to have thrown down his thirty pieces of silver, as if they had been carted back as souvenirs of Pilate's time in Judaea.

Alternatively, he was born in Tarragona on the coast of Catalonia, the citadel city where the great Augustus wintered after his Cantabrian campaign. This was another favored imperial town, with golden ramparts on the seaward side. Among these ramparts, in a great square tower, "a ruin among ruins," Pilate was born. The walls were twenty feet thick in places and, as late as the 1950s, the tower was still in use as a prison. Every eastern window looked toward Rome across the crawling sea. Tarragona smelled of fish and onions; white banners of cambric fluttered from the houses, and the slow *sardana* was danced in its squares. Pilate stayed and soldiered in the region for some years, and troops from Tarragona were supposed to have formed the "Italian legion" that later scourged Christ outside the real *praetorium.*

The little Spaniard was called Lucius: Lucius Pontius Pilate. He grew up crunching garlic, sucking on oranges and revering the black bulls of Las Marismas; but he was also taught to look on Rome as the center of the world. His father, Marcus Pontius, fought in the Cantabrian campaign and helped to suppress the Asturians, although he should by rights have defended his fellow Iberians against the might of Rome. For this treachery he was honored and given the title "Pilatus." Lucius followed after him, joining the suite of Germanicus and fighting with him through the German campaigns. Then, still young, he made for Rome, intending to have fun.

Spaniards in Rome had a flashy reputation, even a dangerous one. Any brigand or robber was "a Spaniard." Spanish sea captains, Ovid said, dealt only in meretricious baubles, and their wine was good only to get drunk on. Being Spanish and knowing no one, Pilate needed to ingratiate himself. He became an *adsectator cenarum,* a supper scrounger, one of those young men found loitering in bands on street corners in the evenings, hoping to be invited to dinner; or one of those sycophantic morning greeters, all smiles and fluttering Spanish scarves. The poet Catullus described one such irritating Spaniard he knew, who would flash his bright white teeth on every occasion: in court, as the defense wound up a moving peroration, or at funerals, "where on every side heartbroken mothers weep for only sons." Perhaps, Catullus mused, this Spaniard was merely trying to prove that he washed his teeth, but all civilized people did that. The only difference he knew of was that Spaniards used their morning urine as mouthwash.

So Pilate, saturnine and ingratiating, hung around Rome, and especially around the court of the emperor. Men like him were called *umbrae,* shadows clinging to their patrons. He was at the edge of every intrigue, behind every curtain. In the interests of self-improvement, he made himself as servile as possible: there was nothing he would not do. He was prepared to cut up the courtiers' food and wait beside their litters; if the mere shadow of the emperor crossed his path, he would abase himself before it. He kept his own pride, which was considerable, locked up like a wasp in a bottle, and was prepared never to release it if that would help in his advancement.

One day, at the court of the emperor, he caught sight of a girl. Not just any girl: this was Claudia Procula, the youngest daughter of Julia, the daughter of Augustus, who had married Tiberius as her second husband. The notion that Pilate's wife came from the imperial house was popular from the earliest years of Christianity; it gave an extra edge to Christ's defiance if his judge was so close to the emperor. Julia, the story ran, had been banished by Tiberius for her passionate and adulterous behavior, and in exile she had taken up with a Roman knight, Claudia Procula's father. At the age of thirteen, Claudia Procula was sent to Rome to acquire noble manners and to find a husband. She was spirited, pretty, curious and intelligent; at least some of her blood was royal. A marriage might have been arranged for her with any of the young men at court. But the one who asked for her, who worked his way for several years toward that tremendous request, made of the emperor himself, was the strange young Spaniard with the haunted eyes and the strained, determined servility; and Tiberius agreed.

Their courtship, socially unequal as it was, did not follow the practice of other young Romans. Ovid in his *Amores* described the usual mating games: hanging around the Palatine Hill or the Temple of Diana to lure girls from the giggling, bangle-jiggling crowd; writing words in wine on the table at parties; the endless exchange of wax tablets with scribbled notes, "Come tonight," or "Don't come"; the snuggles and cuddles in the close press of the racetrack or the gladiator shows, fanning your partner with your program, adjusting her stool and her cushion, letting her bury her head in your shoulder when the action became too bloody to watch. Even if Pilate enjoyed these flirtations with other girls, the daughter of the imperial house demanded a certain distance: as when a man was obliged to watch his love from a different couch at a dinner party, unable in the dim light to see the subtle sign-language used by lovers and too far away to touch her slippered foot with his own. He would content himself with tiny, poignant acts. When she passed him the cup, he would brush with his lips the place where she had drunk; when she passed the bread, he would touch it where she had done; at night, silently, he would leave on her doorstep the chaplet of roses he had worn at the party. And after a while she would notice him.

On the day of the wedding all was as it should have been. The auspices had been consulted. The hall of Procula's house was hung with flowers and branches, and a garland of myrtle was fixed on Pilate's door. Procula, with her hair in six braids and wreathed with flowers under a veil the color of flame, was led into the hall. Pilate, also crowned with flowers, waited for her while the contract was signed and then took charge of her. He took her right hand in his, and they were married to each other.

Among the twelve witnesses to the wedding was Tiberius himself.

The imperial signet ring was impressed into the soft wax of the marriage seals, and the imperial litter, attended by eight slaves, waited outside the house. Procula left first, with her girlfriends, to start the procession to Pilate's house. She ran down the steps in her yellow slippers, while behind her the pitch-pine torches showered sparks into the dark. Scattered voices sang the bride-song, "Io! Hymen Hymenaeus!," and the flutes sang out like nightingales. Pilate made to follow her, burning to possess her on the myrtle-strewn bed in his own house, but he found himself snagged by a gray, aging hand: the hand of Tiberius. The emperor said nothing. Instead, he fumbled inside the breast fold of his toga and drew out a scroll of paper. He handed it to Pilate, climbed into his litter, and was carried unsteadily away.

The paper was Pilate's order to leave at once for Judaea. A war bireme was already in the harbor, waiting to take him to Caesarea. He was to be the governor. It seemed an important posting, but it was also an exile and a punishment for having dared to marry so far above himself.

Meanwhile, Procula and her friends were nearing the door of his house. The ill-omened torches still tossed in the darkness, far away. The happy cries were fainter; the flutes had become the whine of insects. How did Catullus describe what was meant to happen next?

> *Shed your concealment!*
> *New bride,*
> *hear our bride-speech,*
> *see, the shower of torch-flakes!*
> *shed your concealment!*
>
> *Your husband will lie*
> *only in the valley of your breasts,*
> *a hero caught in your arms*
> *as the grape pole*
> *caught in the twisting vine.*
> *See! the day fades:*
> *shed your concealment!*
>
> *Venus will shine for him*
> *in the vague night,*

blaze
at midday.
The day fades.
New bride, shed your concealment!

But Pilate stood in the street without her. The last onlookers watched him curiously, wondering what he would do. In one hand he held the order, in the other the bag of walnuts and confetti which the new bridegroom was meant to scatter to the crowd. His wreath of flowers was still on his head. But between conjugal love and the emperor's order there was no competition. Heartbroken, he turned and walked toward the harbor.

He did not see his wife again for six years. But out of the depths of his bitterness and sadness and sexual frustration, he tried to rule over Judaea.

III.

That is the second version. But a third, hugely popular in Europe from the Middle Ages onward, insists that Pilate was German. He was born at Forscheim, near Mainz, on the Rhine. This was sandy country, a region of fir woods and hop gardens; the air smelled of beer and resin. A pasture near the town, with cows and horses grazing the uneven ground, is still called Pilate's Field, and his red trousers—the favorite color for a child's first pair of trousers in this part of Germany—were still on show in 1936 in the Forscheim museum.

The story is found in the *Golden Legend,* a thirteenth-century compendium of lives of the saints, and in dozens of other chronicles and songs. Jacobus de Voragine, the friar who compiled the *Golden Legend,* admitted even then that it was apocryphal; he had "read it in a history." But it was worth retelling.

Back in the days when rulers were skilled in the seven liberal arts, there was a king whose name was Tyrus. He was born in the diocese of Maginise, in a castle called Leich, in the district of Babenberg. This king loved to hunt; but in the evenings, when he could no longer see the shadowy stags among the trees, he studied philosophy, as kings do. He understood the temperance and humors of the air; he measured the span of heaven; he observed the astrological signs and the courses of the stars. He knew everything.

From his observations with his "subtle engine," and from the vellum pages of his great books, he saw that he was going to sleep with a woman and produce a line of descendants who would rule over many lands and islands. But on the day he had this illumination he was a long way from his wife, out hunting again. Indeed, he was a long way from any woman at all. He made quickly for the nearest city of the district, sending before him the message that if anyone knew of a woman good enough to sleep with him, they should bring her at once. For Tyrus preferred to lie with anyone he could find, promptly and unfussily, rather than lose the hope of fathering a great dynasty.

His men went out, following their lord's orders, and searched the neighborhood. At last they seized on a girl called Pila, pretty enough, the daughter of a moneyer. They led her to Tyrus, and he slept with her that night just as he slept with his wife; then, pulling on his long hunting boots, he galloped away. The deed was done. Pila conceived a child who was royal, or at least half-royal, and when she had carried the baby as long as she had to, she gave birth to him. But then a problem arose. The baby had to be given his father's name, and Pila did not know the name of the king she had slept with. So she took her own name, Pila, and the name of her own father, Atus, and called him Pilatus.

She was proud of her invention. It sounded noble and respectable, more respectable than one would suppose for the child of a moneyer's house. Indeed, in its bourgeois aspirations it smacks of nothing so much as the name of Mr. Boffin's wife in *Our Mutual Friend,* a name to match the garish drawing-room furniture, the too-small flowery carpet, the wax fruit under glass shades and the eight volumes of Gibbon displayed on a table: "Henerietty Boffin,—which her father's name was Henery, and her mother's name was Hetty, and so you get it—."

The Pilate of the York mystery play required his knights to "get it" in just the same way.

> *My mother was Pila, Pila the proud,*
> *Pila the proud had Atus for dad,*
> *Pila plus Atus—how does that go?*
> *Yes, bold knights! That's Pilatus!*

Not everyone thought the child's father was Tyrus; some thought it was "Sir Caesar, that excellent emperor," waylaid during his German campaigns. In the York play Pilate's wife, Procula, purred over this "joyful genealogy," but her dreams of connection with gentry were dashed by other versions of the story. According to these, Pila was no moneyer's daughter, just a bad brothel girl, "a lazy, stinking nurse, a piece of dung, who conceived in a night of two ribalds rolling together." The grubby tryst was not in Babenberg but in Lyons or Mainz, near the River Zei. There the king, who was himself called Atus, stumbled out of the woods under a sky filled with stars, a long way from the city. He and his companions found an inn, where they feasted and drank prodigiously to while away the hours. After a time, the king noticed the stars that blurred and danced outside the dim window, and made his prophecy of greatness to come. There was no queen to hand, but there was Pila, a serf's daughter. His men said: "You shouldn't miss this chance, sir."

The king was quickly persuaded. "Matters raced on"; in no time, Pila was pregnant, and the child was born. A messenger was sent to tell the king the news. As Atus rejoiced in the birth of his wonder child, the bringer of victories, the messenger asked: "Do you have a name for him, your majesty?"

"Let's have something easy," said the king. "I'm Atus, his mother's Pila; join them together, that makes Pilatus! Call him that."

So the messenger returned. He went back either to the inn on the edge of the forest, or to a serf's hut, or, as some say, to the dwelling of Pila's father, a mill on a stream in the depths of the woods. There, bending over the crude wooden cradle, he bestowed the name of Pilatus on the tiny child.

As the child grew, these were his memories. In the moneyer's house, the fierce glow of the forge; hands adjusting a balance; shavings of silver that bit into the skin; the pleasurable shifting of coins in a purse. In the inn, violent nights; floors being slopped down in the morning; candles in extravagant icicles overhanging their conches; the iron taste of wine mingling with the sweetness of milk. In the serf's hut, smoke, oatmeal, cows' breath. In the mill, water ceaselessly roaring and foaming; white meal in the folds of a dress; the damp green powder of moss on a fence; a boat, half-submerged, with its cargo of black leaves.

However shadowy these scenes, they had a proper geography. They belonged in Lyons, in Mainz, in Babenberg, somewhere along the wooded border of Germany fringing on Gaul. Pilate came from the edge, the appalling German forest gloomy with firs and overrun with wolves. He wore barbarians' cloth trousers, his hair was flaxen, and in his cold blue eyes was the gleam of the north. A fourteenth-century poem from Vienne, in the foothills of the Alps, left no doubt of his ancestry:

Teutonicae gentis, crucifixor omnipotentis.

This was the forest where Publius Quinctilius Varus had come with his Roman legions in A.D. 9 only to see them slaughtered to a man, pinned among the crowded trees; and it was where Germanicus in 15 had come to avenge him, gathering and piling up the bones of the dead for dreadful mass funerals. Tacitus described the first sight of that woodland clearing, scattered with white bones and pieces of spears, skulls grinning where the barbarians had nailed them to the mangled firs; and in the dreams of one horrified Roman commander, Varus himself, coated with blood, rose up from the marshy ground.

Tiberius, too, had campaigned there for Augustus, eating and sleeping on the bare ground under the stars, and counting it a lucky omen if his lamp blew out in the dark. In that dark, in the depths of the forest, strange birds flashed like fire. Here the trees grew so thickly that swords and shields were caught in them, and branches snared your clothes as you tried to run away. And supposing you ran, you might blunder into one of those sacred coppices where the Germans worshiped what Tacitus called "that mysterious something" that could not be contained within walls; or into a grove where white horses that had never been ridden raised their heads from the close-cropped grass.

Medieval listeners gave this setting an even stranger coloration. This was the land where young men, sent out on difficult journeys, became confused and enchanted. They would find their path branching in the woods, with the easier way leading to misery and the harder to treasure, honors and love. In hopes of remembering where they had come from they would scatter trails of crumbs, but the birds would devour them. Here, behind towering thickets of thorn, princesses would prick their fingers and shed their blood in fulfillment of old prophecies; but then they were kissed awake, and every stone knight and sleeping hound would stir into life around them. Here trees talked, cloaks made men invisible, and bargains were struck that brought nothing but grief to the proposer; while, in the dark vaults of the forest, the merest touch of light was enough to send a benighted prince wandering the face of the earth for seven years.

Here Pilate grew up. Some say he was prudent and good-looking; indeed that, like the child Jesus, he increased every day in wisdom and beauty:

> *Crevit Pilatus et fit prudens adolescens,*
> *corporis et mentis gemina virtute nitescens.*

Others say that he was brought up badly, never punished, and "proud as a toad." Cassius Parmensis' scurrilous description of the child Augustus would have suited him: "You're a lump of your mother's meal, which a money-changer took from the nearest bake-house and kneaded into some sort of shape, with his hands all discolored from the fingering of money." When he was still a boy—as young as three, some say—he was sent to the king his father. The king was delighted to see him; but this was a child who dragged trouble in his wake.

The king and queen already had a son of their own, about the same age as Pilate. Pilate enjoyed playing with him, and as they grew older the two often wrestled, or boxed, or shot at birds with a sling. But the king's son was always a little better than Pilate: not only of nobler birth, but also more skillful, faster and stronger. This began to rankle. Their arguments multiplied, until they could be found in furious tangles on the grass or bleeding in the corridors. Pilate was so consumed with jealousy, and already so bilious with liver trouble, that one day he simply killed his rival with a huntsman's twist of the neck.

Prostrate with grief, the king and queen called a meeting of the royal council to determine Pilate's punishment. The councillors were cautious. "We weep for you and your wife," they told the king. "But if one son is dead, how will it help to kill the other? Pilate deserves punishment, for sure. Indeed, he deserves death, but it would be better to warn him never to do such a thing again. Don't kill him; send him to Rome, and make sure he never comes back."

.   .   .

So the boy Pilate, the slayer of innocence, was sent to Rome. He went as blood money, replacing the annual tribute which the king his father sent to the emperor. But no sooner had he arrived there than he fell into trouble in all kinds of ways. As he himself put it later, in one of the medieval "songs" of his life, "My heart was boiling with all the ardor of youth, even though I was only so high. When those folk from Lyons sent me to Rome, they did what they liked and I did what I liked, for good or bad." In fact, he fell in with a fine young nobleman, the son of the king of France, or possibly the son of the king of the Angles. He played and sparred with him, just as he had with his brother; and, more or less inevitably, jealousy overcame him again. In the course of a heated argument, he put his hands around his friend's white neck and throttled him.

Now it was the Romans who wondered what to do with him. He deserved death all over again, but they could not insult his royal father. Perhaps such a ruthless young man could be useful to the empire. They could send him somewhere safely far away to put down the enemies of Rome. There was, as it happened, a savage island called Pontus off the coast of Asia Minor, famous only for producing poisonous herbs and beaver oil. The most poisonous weed of all, yellow aconite, grew thickly there around the mouth of the cave that was one of the back doors to the Underworld. The people were shaggy and uncivilized, roaming among trees that ran with red resin as thick as tar. In one eye they had a double pupil, in the other the image of a horse, and they could not be drowned even with their clothes on. They had never accepted a ruler; instead, they had put all their would-be lords and kings to the sword. In that same medieval song, "Caesar"—any Caesar, any emperor with a beard and crown—sent Pilate to take charge of them, since he thought his wickedness would tame their perversity. "And if it doesn't," he remarked, "then he can get what he deserves."

Pilate, who was no fool, realized that his life hung in the balance. To everyone's surprise, once he reached Pontus he conducted himself modestly, with verbal threats and blandishments rather than killing. He even lived honestly. The people took to him, and he became popular; they obeyed his laws and behaved themselves. Pilate made such a success of the job that he was called, after the island, Sir Pilate of Pontus, or Pontius Pilate.

From afar, in Jerusalem, King Herod noticed him. He liked his methods, and invited him to be his chief justice in Judaea. There Pilate amassed enormous power and huge heaps of silver. He was dangerous, clever, brittle, beautiful and cruel, "a perilous prince" in every sense. He and Herod were friends at first, in a watchful sort of way. But when Pilate petitioned Tiberius for all the authority and privileges that Herod possessed, and tried to buy the office of justice for life—the *Golden Legend* said—"with so much money you could hardly count it," the king fell out with him. From then on, relations were strained between them. And it was Pilate alone, with his German soul, his love of the forest, his wanderlust, his huntsman's indifference to killing, who was left to rule the country where Christ had already been born.

IV.

What did he look like? However men imagine him. On early Christian sarcophagi and ivories he is a stocky judge in a shoulder-clasped cloak. In a sixth-century mosaic at Ravenna he has grown a neat dark beard and has melancholy eyes. In a thirteenth-century fresco by Giotto he is clean-shaven and vigorous, with a golden chaplet on his head. In either case his face is benign, and his robes long like a lawyer's; he has thin protesting hands. The Pilate of early medieval iconography was always simply a civilian ruler, with no hint of the military about him. He was neither good nor bad but reasonable and baffled, in line with the version of his character that had sprung up in the apocryphal versions of the New Testament. There was no suggestion that he would get his way by anything other than the rule of law.

This changed around the fourteenth century, as residual neutrality about Pilate faded and he became both a dandy and a prototype bad man. His robes began to shorten (short or girded-up robes being then, as in Roman times, the mark of a man of action) and he acquired exotic hats and weapons. Only his ghost, which haunted the shores of a little lake in the Swiss Alps, dressed plainly, in the red robes of a local magistrate. When color was applied to Pilate, he tended to alternate between gold, the color of nobility, and red, the color of blood: literally becoming, as Oscar Wilde described him, "the scarlet figure of history."

Most medieval manuscripts show him bearded, with a decorated tunic and a nobleman's hat. Stage directions for the Lucerne passion play stipulate that he should be "a German nobleman, finely dressed, with pointed hat, heathenish, civilian coat with sleeves down to his knees, sabre and boots, scepter or staff." The accounts for the Coventry Corpus Christi play show that Pilate's expenses ran to a cloak, a hat, a canvas doublet (one shilling and tenpence), gloves (fourpence), gold braid (twopence) and a skein of green silk for the mending of his gown. The medieval stage Pilate was an aggressive fashion plate, treated by everyone (including himself) as the most handsome figure in the house. In the York play, he pointed out that this was only natural:

> For I'm the loveliest lapped and laid, with favor fair in my face; my forehead is brown and broad, and my eyes glitter like gleam in the glass; my hair glistens like gold wire; my cheeks are both ruddy and red, and my colour is clear as crystal.
> I'm as blithe as blossom on briar. . . .

Nobody dared contradict him. "Loveliest lord, we bow to your beauty," was a typical greeting not only from his servants, but also from the chief priests of the Jews, who seemed to shrivel in his presence as if he sapped the life from them.

Yet apart from the mystery plays, in which the actor who played Pilate was sometimes paid more than Christ for his vigorous command of the action, his portraitists tended to make him passive and almost dreamy. Among these creations, none is stranger than the haunting Pilate of Piero della Francesca's *The Flagellation*. At first glance, it seems that Pilate should be the man who stands in a group of disinterested observers in the foreground, a close-cropped, bull-like thug with a broken nose and a gorgeous gown of blue and gold brocade. But no; he is a lean, distant figure, in a recessed room lined with marble columns where the flagellation of Christ is taking place. He sits, as Pilate probably sat in life, on a spindly curule chair (the X-shaped chair of judgment of a principal magistrate) of blue-and-gold-painted wood. His costume is extraordinary: a short pink jacket, baggy dark blue trousers, vermilion slippers and a hard-brimmed hat with a flopping pink peak. He is lightly bearded, and wears his hair long in the style of the early Renaissance. Slightly hunched, his hands loose in his lap, he is watching the flagellation with no pleasure. Indeed, it would seem that he had nothing to do with it, were it not for the fact that the hands of the beaters break into his calm rectangle of space, drawing him into the consequences of his orders.

To make Pilate authentically Roman was not important to these artists. As a symbol of earthly authority, he made his point more dramatically if he looked like a contemporary lord. That changed in the sixteenth century, when painters began to attempt fantastical historical reconstructions. In the paintings of the high Baroque period he was put in turbans and silk robes like an Arab carpet seller, and his beard grew long. In Tintoretto's *Christ Before Pilate* his gray beard curls to his chest, and he is given the high domed forehead of a philosopher. Were it not for the presence in these paintings of Pilate's universal trademark, the bowl of water, he could be mistaken for an elder of the Jews. Indeed, the mistake is made by cataloguers, too. Gerrit van Honthorst in 1617 painted a picture of Christ before a questioner who is wearing a caftan and a trimmed fez and whose finger is wagging dramatically, as if declaring the lowest price in the souk. This is a man who has been dragged out of bed, his eyes bleary, his beard tousled, and with what looks suspiciously like a nightshirt gaping under his gown. It is catalogued now as *Christ Before the High Priest,* but was happily accepted by earlier generations as *Christ Before Pilate.*

Decades passed; and when the trial scene became a favorite subject again, with the rise of the startling popular religiosity of the midnineteenth century, Pilate had recovered proper Roman dress. His plain white toga might have made an unsatisfactory contrast with the simple white robe of Christ; but painters made sure it was elaborately draped, to suggest his vanity, and slightly overlaundered, to suggest hypercivilization. Against this whiteness his face could be sallow, where Christ's face against his comparatively dirty robe could glow with divine luminescence. The governor had also put on weight; and as he confronted Christ, gesturing prissily, or slumped in his chair apparently examining his fingernails, the folds of his toga could not quite disguise the middle-aged paunch and the plumpness of his thighs. His neck was thick, too, like a gourmand's, or like the neck of a man used to barking orders on the parade ground.

This image lasted a while, until Hollywood changed it. As a figure of tragedy and perplexity, Pilate was better thin; as a representative of the gross materialism of the Roman empire, he needed dressing up. In *The*

Last Days of Pompeii (1935), Basil Rathbone, better known as Sherlock Holmes, made a more than acceptable thin Pilate, with long tapering fingers and a long tapering nose. Subsequent Pilates, younger and better-looking, relied heavily on decoration. Gold braid was sewn on the borders of their togas; more braid and jewels were glued to their sandals. In *The Robe* (1953), Pilate's wrists were heavy with bangles, and his fingers were so encrusted with rings that he could hardly squeeze the absolving water between them.

From here it was only a small step to sexual ambivalence and foppery. Indeed, to the Roman Pilate, any man with more than one ring and a clutch of bangles would have been flagrantly effeminate. This tendency reached its apotheosis in the silly, lisping Pilate of *Monty Python's Life of Brian* of 1979 ("Whom shall I welease? I shall welease Woger!"). In Martin Scorsese's *The Last Temptation of Christ* (1988) the governor was played by the gaunt and eerily hermaphrodite David Bowie. And the actor who played Pilate in the only film made exclusively from his point of view (the French-Italian *Ponzio Pilato* of 1962) was Jean Marais, for many years the lover of Jean Cocteau. Marais was astonishingly handsome, "with all the characteristics," Cocteau wrote, "of those blue-eyed hyperboreans mentioned in Greek mythology." It was Marais' profile that Cocteau drew again and again in the doodles that littered his notebooks: blond curling hair, the straight brow proceeding to the straight nose, the small imperious mouth. Oddly enough, that face corresponds almost exactly to Pilate's preening description of himself in the York play: the same "noble forehead," the hair like gold wire, the hard and glittering stare.

Yet, for all this, Pilate's face remains a blank. The Christs of history bear a startling similarity: dark brown hair centrally parted, a modest beard, brooding eyes. Of Pilate only two things can be said for certain: that he was, according to the imperial fashion of the day, short-haired and clean-shaven. That in itself suggests a good deal. He would submit himself to the barber each morning, after his cursory breakfast of water and bread, and perhaps again in the course of the day, if he was dark and his beard was strong. It was always a long ritual. Julius Caesar was famous for reading reports while he was being shaved; other men wrote memoranda. The procedure included minute inspection of the skin, extraction of unwanted hairs, combing and clipping: the barber's tools of razor, scissors, strap and different sizes of tweezers covered a whole table. So, on most mornings, the barber would comb Pilate's hair, snipping it in places, and then tie a towel around his neck. A servant brought cold water, and with two or three deft movements of his hands the *tonsor* would slather it, without lubrication, on Pilate's cheeks. He then began the long, slow razor work.

The blade dragged across the skin. The skin became sore, and the blade dragged across it again. In the interests of passivity, master and barber did not talk much. The only sounds were the blade dipped in water, the hiss of the strap, and the tiny scratch of metal against the beard, like a bird's claw. Quite often, the blade slipped. There was a quick, fierce pain; blood on the governor's fingers, when he instinctively raised his hand to the place; and a curling flower of blood in the water.

What would he have done? Slapped him? Called for a mirror? Endured in silence? We do not know. But we know what the barber would have done: opened one of his little pots of salve made of leaves or mud or tallow or cobwebs, taken a little on the tip of a finger, dabbed the cut dry with his other hand, and smoothed the ointment over Pilate's skin. Some barbers offered patches, but these were thought as effeminate as scratching the head with one finger or wearing long-sleeved gowns; Pilate would probably have refused them. Instead he took, on the smarting cut, a strange piece of stuff like tamped gray cotton wool. And it may well have been like this—chafed, cut, sore, but mollified with a little fresh pomade—that Pilate went out on that Friday morning to have his encounter with Christ.

V.

Even this is fancy, of course. And we have little more to rely on when we come to his age, or his marriage, or how bright he was. Of his age, we can only be certain that he was not younger than thirty when he went to Judaea. That was the minimum age for governors. But his behavior there— enthusiastic, sarcastic, nervous, occasionally brutal—suggests he was not much older. The two ancient Jewish sources, Philo and Josephus, whose biases we shall unravel later, recorded a remarkably similar personality. Their Pilate could behave with efficiency, but not with maturity. His trademarks were calculated affronts, crude deceptions, stubbornness to a degree. This was a character not yet made smooth by experience.

The Gospels, too, suggest he had a short fuse. Roman arrogance is the implied reason for it—combined, in the case of the trial, with some early-morning grumpiness. Medieval writers recognized this as a hangover; so, in the mystery plays, Pilate is usually a prodigious drinker, urging those around him to "sit down and wet your whistle," and sleeping the thick, drugged sleep of the sozzled man. The accounts of the Coventry play show that "wine for Pilate" was a large expense. Whoever played the governor seemed to go on drinking it offstage, keeping in character, while even Jesus confined himself to beer.

Pilate's wife usually drank with him. He was married, history has assumed, not just because of the legend of his callously interrupted wedding, but because Matthew introduced a message from his wife into the trial of Jesus, begging him to leave the prisoner alone. (The passage was probably invented, but it was harder to invent the wife.) Like Caesar's Calpurnia, or the trembling soothsaying wives in Babylonian fables, Pilate's wife is a harbinger of cosmic disruption: leaves wither, birds shriek, the pallid moon overfills the tides. It was the writers of the Apocryphal Gospels who first suggested she was Claudia Procula, of the imperial blood of Rome. The medieval playwrights preferred to call her Procla or Percula, treating the name as if it were a diminutive in the Roman style, like *libellus* (little book) or *hortulus* (little garden). The Romans had a habit of playfully diminishing even unexpected things: Cicero's letters include "dear little cohorts" and "dear little mint leaves." So Pilate's dear little woman trips through history.

Her character has grown alongside her husband's. The earliest Christians supposed she was fascinated by Judaism and curious about Jesus, to the point where her eagerness to see him upset her dreams. Origen thought she was the first Gentile to believe in Jesus' teaching, "the proselyte of the Gate." The Greeks and Copts made a saint of her because of her attempt to save Jesus, and put her among the women who went to the tomb to pray. Nineteenth-century romantics saw her as delicate and spirited, confined in the Herodian palace as if in some nunnery, but nonetheless glimpsing from the window the pale Galilean as he passed; for if she had never encountered him, how could she see him in her dreams? In the Slavonic version of Josephus she was imagined to have had a desperate illness for which both she and Pilate sought the healing of Jesus, and writers through the ages have imagined her nervous headaches, the result of hysteria and insomnia, alongside her husband's puffed and aching liver.

For centuries Procula was kept indoors, virtually confined to the bed from which she would spring after her appalling dream of the innocence of Jesus, screaming for Minerva and her maid while trying to cover her nakedness with sheets. Her only communication with the wider world was by folded notes, scribbles on tablets, whispers in a messenger's ear. She seldom, if ever, committed the indiscretion of trespassing in a man's territory. It was not until the 1930s that Procula was emancipated, attending Christian rallies in Galilee in the middle of expeditions to the carpet shops of Judaea and, on celluloid, hobnobbing in glossy lipstick with Jesus in the street.

Medieval playwrights had by far the most fun with her. Pilate and Procula were seen as classic canoodlers: lovebirds, in fact. She calls him "my friendliest"; he calls her "the fairest figure that ever food fed." There is no couple they resemble so much as Chanticleer and Pertelote, the besotted cock and hen from Chaucer's "Nun's Priest's Tale." Beautiful Chanticleer, with his golden feathers and jet beak, his scarlet comb and azure spurs, is the king of the farmyard; pretty Pertelote is his paramour. On the top perch in the henhouse they cuddle together, sing "My love is out faring," and mate constantly in a flurry of feathers. In their case, it is Chanticleer who has the bad dreams. But the chemistry between them, with Pertelote, the stronger-minded, building up her flashy but wavering husband in order to encourage him, is precisely mirrored in the medieval passion plays.

Procula, like Pertelote, knew she was sexually gorgeous. She was always dressed and played extravagantly. Women "lent their gear" for the part in the Coventry play, and on one occasion "Ryngold's man Thomas" played the part in outrageous drag. In the York cycle, just before the opening of the trial of Christ, the First Couple of Judaea are found together embracing on Pilate's couch, which doubles as his bed. Procula (one imagines the extravagant sigh, the fussing with her hair) is determined to improve on Pilate's glowing description of himself:

"The Jews have never had another judge like you, darling! You doughty duke, you doomer of damnation—so nobly born, so debonair! You tell everyone where to go."

"Certainly do."

"I bet all the other procurators take lessons from you. If someone dis-
obeys an order of yours, you kill them, don't you? If anyone drags their
feet, you have him stoned, don't you? Just reduced to a pile of rags."

"Try to."

"Lucky me! Dame Precious Procula, wife of Sir Pilate, prince without
peer! And wife without peer, too! Witty, wise . . ."

(Pause.)

"Don't you think my skin's smooth? So comely and clear? It's just
like the rest of me. And this dress . . . it's ravishing, don't you think?
Though I say it myself, wouldn't you agree—no lord could have anyone
sweeter than me?"

"I agree totally."

"Love you, darling."

"Love you, too. In fact, if I don't kiss you, I'll go crazy."

"Kiss away then, darling. No one's stopping you."

"Hey, fellows, see how lucky I am! These lovely lips are all mine! Lus-
cious, lovely lips . . . all mine . . ."

(A long pause, while he kisses her.)

"I just want to stay in bed all morning, loving you."

"Me too."

This steamy little episode was interrupted only by "jangling Jews" at the
door; but it was not only medieval playwrights who gave a high erotic
temperature to Pilate's life. Edwardian commentators in their boned col-
lars also liked to imagine him in love ("at least as a man of his nature
could love") because it softened the military and legal rigors a little, and
possibly also because it confirmed the governor's moral weakness. Like
some character in a Galsworthy play, Pilate could struggle between cruel
masculine imperatives and a clumsy desire to please his wife. The man's
world would win, as it had to, but not without a moment of sentimental
hesitation, when Jesus was on the brink of being handed over like a
pretty necklace or a new dress.

She was vivid enough, but Procula is impossible to trace. In life she
could have come from the clan of the Proculi, wealthy Roman knights of
the same social background as Pilate, who lived—at least in the mid-
80s—in a "gleaming smart" house on the Palatine Hill. Martial described the journey to this house from the Quirinal, where he lived: past
the Temple of Vesta, across the Via Sacra, through the Forum, until

"right before you on the left stands a building with a shining facade, the hall of a lofty house that bids you enter." This was possibly a route Pilate took to see her, his heart pounding as he negotiated the stalls, the carts, the building sites, the muddy drains. We can imagine that Procula wished her hair blond, wore Coan silks in pastel colors, softened her skin with bean meal and wove Pilate's clothes with her own hands; but we are deep in the realm of conjecture here.

The presence of Procula in Judaea, if she was there, has often been taken as an indicator of love. In the early years of the empire, wives did not normally accompany their husbands to the provinces. They were seen as a security risk. Augustus had enforced this law absolutely, allowing only one visit in winter, when travel was often impossible because the sea-lanes closed. In A.D. 21, not long before Pilate left, an attempt was still being made in the Senate to keep the wives at home. The proposer claimed that women were frail, extravagant, easily tired and "made a Roman army look like an Oriental progress." Sternness of this sort was hard on marriages. Aelius Rufus, Cicero's friend, described the fate of one such couple in a letter. "Paulla Valeria, the sister of Triarius, has divorced her husband without assigning any reason, on the very day that he was to arrive from his province. She is going to marry D. Brutus. She has sent back her whole wardrobe."

Some writers suppose that Procula was there because she had asked Tiberius especially for this favor, at the end of six years of anguished correspondence from Pilate on his own in Judaea. But this would not have been necessary, since by then both sentiment and the law had changed. As a spokesman for the majority put it during that same Senate debate in 21, weren't governors entitled, when they returned from their labors, to relax with their wives? Was enforced celibacy really ideal? It was true, of course, that husbands were often corrupted by bad wives, but who was the stronger party here? "If a woman misbehaves, it's her husband's fault."

This argument won the day, although in the minds of Roman males the women were still barely controllable: half-expected, like the medieval Procula, to scour the markets for dresses and baubles, or, like the flapper Procula, to hitch up their skirts and run after preachers in the wild hills of Galilee. Yet Matthew's Gospel suggests that Pilate took Procula not only to Judaea but also on his party-and-peacekeeping trips to Jerusalem, at moments when the city was manifestly unsafe. Perhaps they loved each other with the passionate dottiness suggested by the

Roman poets, whispering in the dark "Mea rosa," "mi anime," "passercu-lus" ("little sparrow"), "melliculum" ("little honey"), "mea vita" ("my life"). Tradition has them clinging together like limpets in his uncom-fortable posting, and it was in Jerusalem that Procula committed the in-discretion that invented her life and her career, as well as gaining her admittance to the canon of Greek and Coptic saints.

So Pilate, from a shadow, was given his passionate and colorful wife; and, by logical extension in the Middle Ages, he was also given children. There were usually two offspring in the Pilate household, two boys or a boy and a girl, aged somewhere between six and twelve. In the York cycle the boys are little yobs, hanging like puppies around the feet of the knights as they bring Jesus to trial. "Here, Jesus, you caitiff," cries one, "why don't you fall flat on your face for fear of my father? I reckon you don't know how wise he is. But I recommend you obey him, you brawler." In the Coventry play Pilate's son is a miniature king in gown and hat, with his own small scepter and gilded poleaxe; but he is a child of better manners, essentially waiting on his parents, like a baffled ser-vant in the wake of their gaudiness.

The most childlike children belong to a fifteenth-century French passion play, a boy and a girl whose role, like small chirping birds, is to be the conscience of their father as he deals with Jesus. They appear first with Procula, who wants to shoo them away as she talks to Pilate; but they tug at her skirt, demanding, "When are we going to see the prophet they want to torture?" The little boy adds: "We know where to find him. He's where no one has pity on him, but everyone really hates him."

The little girl then says, alarmingly, "God, who made the world, take care of my father."

"And God give *you* honor and grace, my lovely daughter," Pilate hap-pily answers her.

"Father, I'm really sad you've treated that prophet so badly. No one's complained about him except the Jews. He has such a good character, everyone says so. Let him go. Have pity on him."

"What are you saying, sweetheart? The Jews will kill me if I do that; they'll have the eyes out of my head."

At this point, the little boy comes in with a disturbing singsong verse of his own:

God who made the wind and rain
Let my father not be ashamed.

There are echoes here of Shakespeare's fools, like Feste in *Twelfth Night* ("For the rain it raineth every day"): innocent creatures who see to the heart of the action and are somehow allowed to speak plainly, without being beaten. Pilate does not hear the warning in his son's words; he simply takes it as a sweet song, hugs the child, asks what he really wants. His son has opened a window, letting into the palace great blasts of cold air and dark water, but Pilate is always the indulgent father. In the same way, the brutish little boys of York are ignored, or flattered with the title "Sir" and told to wait on their mother; the girls are called pretty and delightful, however disquieting their chatter. The medieval Pilate, a villain in most respects, is made pliant and disorganized by any show of goodness, in his children as well as in Jesus. He is a fearsome ranter, and yet he is domesticated: the managing director who, in the midst of some towering crisis—a takeover bid, a liability suit—comes home from work to kneel on the floor and mess around with model trains.

Lastly, there is Pilate's dog. Bulgakov's Pilate in *The Master and Margarita* has a wolfhound called Banga, a great gray dog with pointed ears and a gold-studded collar. Banga is the only creature Pilate loves, and the feeling is mutual. They sleep together on a couch out on the balcony of Herod's palace, under the stars, the governor's arms around the dog's neck; they walk together in his dreams up the long path of light toward the moon. Cruel and sharp with everyone else, with Banga Pilate is a child. There is almost no characterization of him that does not contain some peculiar, almost discordant element of innocence. The man may be a schemer but, in a deep way, he has barely the faintest notion of what he is doing.

VI.

Perhaps he was not very bright. His learning, or the lack of it, is once again a subject we know nothing or everything about. He was either a rough soldier, or a philosopher of acute and skeptical intelligence, or any possible gradation in between. One phrase above all has served to pigeonhole him: the question, seemingly too strange to have been invented, which he asks Jesus in the Gospel of John—"What is truth?" And our assessments of his intelligence spring, too, from what he apparently did next; turned on his heel and, in Francis Bacon's words, "would not stay for an answer."

Bacon thought he was "jesting." Perhaps he was. Even as a chance remark, with all deeper meanings stripped out of it, it has been taken in all kinds of ways. Most probably Pilate thought Jesus was out of his depth and was simply tossing the subject back to him, as confident men do. (This sense is wonderfully caught in the broad Yorkshire of the Northern Passion: "What is sothefastness? *You* tell *me.*") Possibly he had never in his life wasted his time thinking about truth; possibly he racked his brain on the subject daily. Yet that last suggestion, that he was a thinker, seems to suit the Pilate of the ancient accounts least of all. Josephus, Philo and the Gospels agree that this is a man who believes in action, even—and often—at the cost of reflection.

The author of the fourth-century *Acta Pilati* went to some lengths to make Pilate more thoughtful and intelligent. These *Acta,* which were supposedly an account of the Passion events recorded by Pilate's Jewish "friend" Nicodemus, had an interest in gilding the governor. This is a man who, largely for reasons of early Christian prejudice, is being drawn in deliberately reasonable contrast to the supposed fanaticism of the Jews. It is he who takes delivery of the priests' "memorials," written in Hebrew and providing the conclusive evidence of the Resurrection, and preserves them—with Roman efficiency—so that later Christians may make use of them. Although he knows almost nothing of Jewish culture, he is intellectually curious and sharp. He may feel occasionally at sea, but he is not about to let anything pass him by.

In the *Acta,* just before the trial of Jesus, a messenger runs in to tell Pilate and the chief priests that he has seen Jesus coming into Jerusalem and has heard the crowd cry: "Save us, you who are in the highest! Blessed is he who comes in the name of the Lord!" The priests dispute this, and point out that the messenger must have got the message wrong; after all, the shouts were in Hebrew, and he is Greek. Stung, the messenger retorts: "But I asked one of the Jews, and he explained it." Pilate then butts in, throwing out a question to the Jews in the room:

"What did they cry out in Hebrew?"

"*Hosanna membrome baruchamma adonai.*"

"And what does that mean, *Hosanna* and the rest?"

"It means, save us now, you who are in the highest."

"So, if you yourselves say your children shouted that, how has my messenger sinned?"

The chief priests cannot answer him. And this is not the last of Pilate's clever interjections. In the middle of the trial of Jesus he suddenly accuses the Jews of "always rebelling" against their benefactors, and goes on:

> According to what I've heard, your God brought you out of Egypt out of hard bondage, and led you safe through the sea as by dry land, and in the wilderness he nourished you with manna and gave you quails, and water to drink out of a rock, and gave you a law. And in all these things you provoked your God to anger, and sought out a molten calf, and angered your God and he tried to kill you; but Moses made supplication for you, and you were spared.

This breathtaking précis of Jewish history is all the more impressive because Pilate has encountered neither the Bible nor the Scriptures. His first sight of the Bible comes a day later, in the Temple itself, when the chief priests, *grammatici,* scribes and teachers of the law produce one for him. It is heavily inlaid with gold and glittering with precious stones; four ministers stagger under it. Pilate, deeply impressed, commands the chief priests to consult the book and to tell him in which year the Son of God was meant to come. The chief priests answer in arithmetic:

- from the third son of Adam to the coming of Christ, 5,500 years.
  - length of the Ark of the Covenant, ... $2\frac{1}{2}$ cubits
                              plus breadth, ... $1\frac{1}{2}$ cubits
                              plus height, ... $1\frac{1}{2}$ cubits
                              equals .... $5\frac{1}{2}$ cubits

Therefore the coming of Jesus Christ in the ark of his body was to be after 5,500 years.

Alternatively—

- from the making of heaven and earth and the first
  man to the Flood, ...2,212 years
- from the Flood to the building of the tower, ... 531 years
- from the building of the tower to Abraham, ... 606 years
- from Abraham to the coming of the children of Israel
  out of Egypt, ... 470 years
- from the leaving of Egypt to the building of the
  Temple, ... 511 years
- from the building of the Temple to its destruction, ... 464 years
- from the burning of the Temple to the coming of
  Christ, ... 636 years

equals 5,500 years [*sic*]

Pilate drinks all this in, and takes notes. We imagine him bent over the calculations, hanging on the numbers; he too, impatiently, can do the addition and subtraction. But that image remains less impressive than the one of Pilate, like the Inca Atahuallpa, facing the Book. He is half afraid of it, half contemptuous; he will not read it himself, open it or even touch it, because it glitters like a reptile. Yet he waits for it to enlighten him.

In the medieval plays, Pilate is seldom faced with the teachings of the Jews. When he is, it is plain that Jewish history and religion mean nothing at all to him; he has brought in something superior. The York Pilate boasts that he made his reputation among philosophers, while the Towneley Pilate still has a law teacher, a bedraggled fellow who complains that his careful teaching about right and wrong seems to be falling on deaf ears. Yet, even when he is a buffoon, Pilate is still more intelligent and usually more cunning than anyone else on the stage. He never has much time, and does not suffer fools gladly. In the Gréban play Caiaphas, painstakingly listing the charges against Jesus, is urged, even rudely, to get to the point. As the high priest drifts again, Pilate barks, "Keep to the matter, sir!"

But it was the nineteenth-century biographers of Jesus who drew the boldest and wildest pictures of Pilate's intellectual formation, his favorite reading and the color of his thinking. Curiously, whether they were English or not, they often gave him an English character, as if in deference to the imperial power of the day. Thus Giovanni Papini, an Italian, stated confidently that a Pilate transplanted to Victorian London would have read John Stuart Mill and Swinburne ("Thou hast conquered, O pale Galilean; The world has grown grey from Thy breath"); that he would have enjoyed the romantic vigor of Byron and the sentimental cadences of Tennyson; and that he would have read *The Times.* Ernest Renan, a Frenchman, was sure that Pilate would have been a Tory. Papini thought he would have voted Liberal (hence Mill); both were convinced of an overwhelming superiority complex on the British colonial model, allied to rather lush and disjointed reading. It therefore followed that Pilate was "one of those skeptics of the Roman decadence corrupted with Pyrrhonism, a devotee of Epicurus, an encyclopaedist of Hellenism without any belief in the gods of his country"—an odd conclusion, since by their lights Pilate was almost bound to have been a card-carrying member of the Church of England.

It was provocative and fantastic, and it made Victorian writers feel closer to Christ, to dress Pilate up as a man in a top hat and astrakhan coat who worried about the Irish Question. Yet it did not shed much light in the darkness. How intelligent might this man have been? How thoughtful, and how well equipped to deal with the spiritual challenge that was set before him? In Pilate's Rome the *equites,* often new men with new money, were assumed to be magpies in the matter of knowledge too: ostentatiously organizing readings of their own poems, buying pocket cribs of the philosophers, rejoicing in arcane self-improvement. A knight who was truly learned or wise was something to remark on. More typical was the man Tacitus sat next to at the races, who "after discoursing on several learned subjects," suddenly asked, "Are you Tacitus or Pliny?"

So to return to Pilate's own famous question, the one John says he threw out at Jesus with much the same abruptness as that racegoer threw his at Tacitus. "Ti estin aletheia?" was what he said, according to John; and, if indeed he said it, Greek was very probably the language he used. This was the lingua franca of the eastern empire. Even a rough soldier would have a smattering of it, and a governor could not work without it, unless he dared to put himself at the mercy of interpreters. Seneca, apparently voicing the general opinion, thought Greek a bit vague and sissyish beside the forcefulness of Latin. It fitted with other soppy Greek things, such as the slippers (rather than sensible Roman shoes) that Tiberius had slopped around in during his exile in Rhodes. Cicero scattered Greek through his letters to express the sort of refined, snobbish concepts for which English-speakers use French: *bons mots, double entendre, banal.* To him, too, it was a literary language first of all, although he noted in his treatise *On the Nature of the Gods* that "in matter of style we've now made such progress that even in richness of vocabulary the Greeks do not surpass us."

Perhaps Pilate thought the same. It is easy to imagine him mangling his Greek as English-speaking diplomats still mangle French, falling back into the cadence of inky blotters and tear-stained lists of verbs. The state of Pilate's Greek, possibly fluent, possibly awful, adds a peculiar poignancy to his supposed exchanges with Jesus and the Jews during the trial. Perhaps he repeated the same question over and over not out of judicial cussedness, but because his phrasebook Greek could not stretch much further; perhaps he was baffled by Jesus' answers not because he could not penetrate the philosophy, but because he could not understand the words. These "conversations," heavily theological in any case, could also be read as the dialogue of two men adrift in a half-known language: meanings missed, questions and answers not quite connecting, like two dim-sighted explorers extending their hands to make out the shape of the other.

Even some Greek would have laid Pilate open to the influence of Homer, Plato, Aristotle and the Greek theater, just as his Latin laid him open to Virgil, Ovid, Cicero, Propertius, Horace, Lucretius. Had he read any of them? Did he think of them at all? Did he carry in his head scraps of the *Aeneid,* as Pliny did, or Greek tags, as Augustus did? Could he debate the finer literary points of the *Odyssey,* as Tiberius could? Or was there a contemporary mishmash of Greek and Roman adventure stories, the clashing of oars, the wine-dark sea, Scipio falling on his sword, Odysseus tied to the mast, the heartbreaking presentation of pious Aeneas as the founder and savior of Rome? There may have been all these things, as well as the common maxims and quips that men carry around with them. The ones below came from *Cato's Collected Wisdom,* a popular little book of the time.

What you don't need is dear, even when it's cheap.
Know yourself.

Be thrifty with time.
Only a fool stubs his toe on the same rock twice.
Forgetting trouble is the way to cure it.
Fortune favors the brave.
Nothing in excess.
Expect to be treated by others as you have treated them.
Don't ask for what you'll wish you hadn't got.

Something of this blunt practicality could have colored Pilate's question, too. "What is truth?" was not a mystical remark. If Pilate meant it as anything more than a knee-jerk challenge, it would have been purely philosophical. A Roman could practice religion and pursue philosophy almost without the two colliding, for his religion, ritualistic, pragmatic and superstitious, was in a separate compartment. It was entwined not with higher thinking, but with politics; not with lofty abstractions, but with matters of practical loyalty and even of life and death.

Modern minds think of this religion—the obsessive auguries, the pompous state sacrifices, the dry decisions of the Board of Fifteen for Religious Ceremonies and the Board of Seven for Sacrificial Banquets—as essentially empty. But Augustus' reformation of Roman religion around the cult of the emperor, together with the inexorable spread of the Roman empire and the Roman peace, could make this worship in Pilate's time relevant and even affecting: the divine Augustus was the savior of the world, and what Rome was doing was a work approved by the gods.

As a young man, Pilate may have watched the defining scene of the cult: the moment in A.D. 12 when Tiberius returned from his German campaigns and, alighting from his chariot, knelt at Augustus' feet. It appears, at any rate, that the governor wore his religion on his sleeve. His god was the emperor, and he not only surrounded himself with holy imperial objects—military standards, votive shields, coins with religious insignia—but also tried to foist them, like an evangelist, on the outraged Jews. To return to the Victorian metaphor, he sometimes seems like one of those British governors of India who, partly out of nostalgia for home, partly out of desire to civilize the natives, partly out of eagerness to keep in with the establishment, built Anglican cathedrals in which to take their ostentatious Communion.

Did he really believe in Roman religion, and in the imperial cult that now colored it from top to bottom? It is difficult to say. Public devotion was often a cover for private doubt. Several modern writers have assumed that he believed in nothing at all: "neither gods nor men, nor Pontius Pilate," as Nikos Kazantzakis put it. It is tempting to make him indifferent, even nihilistic, if only for the satisfaction of a real intellectual clash with Christ. But the evidence of the ancient sources—both written and archaeological—suggests a different picture.

His philosophy, if he dabbled in any, is even harder to pin down. If he was a skeptic or a Pyrrhonist, he would scarcely have bothered with book-learning beyond what he had absorbed as a child; there was no point. Pyrrhon taught that certain knowledge of anything was unattainable. For any given proposition, the opposite could be proposed with equal reason; no assertion was more valid than another. The man of wisdom, rather than declaring "This *is* so," could only say, "This *seems* so." The Academicians followed this teaching later, but, said Cicero,

> We are not men whose minds wander in uncertainty and never know what principles to adopt. For what sort of mental habit, or rather what sort of life would that be which dispensed with all rules for reasoning or even for living? We don't do that; but, where other schools maintain that some things are certain and others uncertain, we . . . say that some things are probable, others improbable.
>
> What then is to stop me from accepting what seems to me probable, while rejecting what seems to be improbable, and from shunning the presumption of dogmatism, while keeping clear of that recklessness of assertion which is as far as possible removed from pure wisdom? And as to the fact that our school argues against everything, that is only because we could not get a clear view of what is "probable" unless we could make a comparative estimate of all the arguments on both sides.

An Academician Pilate asking "What is truth?" would be neither mocking nor world-weary. He would simply be exposing Jesus for being so recklessly certain. Like Polonius, he himself could accept whatever seemed probable, especially if his superiors suggested it to him.

> HAMLET: Do you see yonder cloud, that's almost in the shape of a camel?

POLONIUS: By the mass, and 'tis like a camel indeed.
  HAMLET: Methinks it is like a weasel.
POLONIUS: It is backed like a weasel.
  HAMLET: Or like a whale?
POLONIUS: Very like a whale.

Other teachings too might have flickered in Pilate's mind. Epicurus would have told him that he had no overriding obligations to the gods or the state, that no one had claims on him, that peace lay in withdrawal from outside influences and in the revealed truth of his own sensations; but that was hardly a line a Roman governor could take. The Stoics would have taught him the tranquil virtue of the wise man, so fixed on the divinity within him that he could become oblivious to pain, to money, or to promotion. Pilate did not seem to take that path either, or not successfully. Some civil servants never read philosophers.

Besides, even if we know what his references might have been, we still do not know what store he set by reading. Julius Caesar read at the games, which was thought bad form; Cicero read at picnics, lying on a blanket on the grass; Pliny (like many contemporaries) had books read during and after meals, and even took his notebooks out when he was hunting boar, "so that I shall have something to bring home even if I catch nothing." Among governors and proconsuls there was a presumption of literacy and cultivation. The governor Lucilius, to whom Seneca addressed his *Moral Letters,* wrote poetry and contemplated, though not without nervousness, the highest reaches of philosophical inquiry. A governor's job was not one that kept him too busy for reading or self-improvement; Cicero congratulated one friend on becoming a governor simply for the acres of leisure time he would have.

It was also a job that required much written self-expression. Letters were sent, and from the homesick they were long ones, "filling the reader's left hand" as he unrolled them; crowds greeted the flashing white topsails of the mail boats as they jostled into the harbor. In Pilate's luggage, too, as he left home must have been the paraphernalia of his thinking life: empty scrolls, bundles of papers, waxed notebooks to be kept in the breast fold of his toga, cuttlefish ink, iron pens. Possibly somewhere too, among the stacks of white togas, the cloaks and shoes, the bric-a-brac and the statuettes of the household gods, were the favorite books.

The best ones were usually kept in rectangular boxes impregnated with cedar oil. They may have been new, purchased for the journey, "new books with new ivories, inscribed on Augustan Royal, the lines lead-ruled, red tabs and red wrappers, the ends shaved with pumice," as Catullus described some he had bought himself. Or they were well-worn scrolls, cracked with constant unrolling, marked in the margins, tied with frayed string. And what was on them was whatever we want to imagine.

The journey from Rome to Caesarea, Pilate's seat of government, took at least twenty days. By tradition, a new governor set out from the temple of Mars the Avenger, the huge new temple built by Augustus from which all campaigns against "impious foes," to the east or the west, were always started. The doors and walls were hung with weird weapons taken from defeated foreigners, all hides and feathers and spikes, while above them, serenely, Romulus and Aeneas and the rest of the heroes blessed the new hero on his journey.

From Rome to the coast the governor would pass in parade with his escort, waving to any crowds that gathered. The sea voyage started from Brindisi. We do not know exactly what time of year Pilate left, but the elder Pliny recorded that the sea was opened to voyagers "when the west winds soften the wintry heavens" and the sun occupied the twenty-fifth degree of Aquarius. This meant mid-February, just before the rising of the wind that brought the swallows. If a man was important or devout, he sacrificed to the waves before embarking; a man of regular piety would go on board *adoratis sideribus,* having paid his respects to the stars. The recommended route was by way of Alexandria on ships which, according to the Emperor Gaius, were sailed as swiftly as "a charioteer handles race-horses."

Each morning, the sun rose over the sea in the direction in which he was sailing. Above the crack of the sails and the chants of the oarsmen the night sky grew ragged, and the mottled clouds were filled with light. Did Pilate see, with Homer, the goddess of the rose-tinged dawn rising from the couch of Tithonus, harnessing her two-horse chariot and ascending the heavens to announce the coming of the sun? Did he feel, as the Stoics felt, some stirring of the divinity within himself in tune with the divinity outside? Or did he merely see, as Hamlet saw, whales and weasels in the flat and unknowable sky?

One line at least he might have remembered, common to every school of thought, as the low coast of Judaea came into view. "Nunc animis opus, Aenea, nunc pectore firmo!"—"Ah now, Aeneas, be strong and stout of heart!"

Chapter 2

GOVERNING
JUDAEA

"But how," you ask, "does one attain the highest good?" You do not need to cross the Pennine or Graian hills, or traverse the Candavian waste, or face the Syrtes quicksands, or Scylla, or Charybdis, although you have traveled through all these places for the bribe of a petty governorship; the journey for which nature has equipped you is safe and pleasant. She has given you such gifts that you may, if you do not prove false to them, rise level with God. Your money, however, will not place you on a level with God; for God has no property. Your bordered robe will not do this, for God is not clad in raiment; nor your reputation, nor a display of self, nor a knowledge of your name spread throughout the world, for no one has knowledge of God. The throng of slaves which carries your litter along the city streets and in foreign places will not help you; for this God of whom I speak, though the highest and most powerful of beings, carries all things on his own shoulders. Neither can beauty or strength make you blessed, for neither of these qualities can withstand old age.

What we have to seek for, then, is that which is untouched by Time and Chance. And what is this? It is the soul—but the soul that is upright, good and great. What else could you call such a soul than a god dwelling as a guest in the human body? A soul like this may descend into a Roman knight as well as into a freedman's son or a slave. For what is a Roman knight, or a freedman's son, or a slave? They are mere titles, born of ambition or of wrong. One may leap to heaven from the very slums. Only rise,

And mold thyself to kinship with thy God.

SENECA, *Moral Letters*, XXXI

I.

BEYOND IDUMAEA AND SAMARIA, wrote the elder Pliny,
Judaea extends far and wide. The part which joins up with Syria is called
Galilee, while the part which is nearest to Arabia and Egypt is called
Perea. This last is thickly covered with rugged mountains, and is sepa-
rated from the rest of Judaea by the River Jordan.

The River Jordan rises from the spring of Panias. It is a delightful
stream and, as far as the terrain allows, it winds along its course and
lingers among the dwellers on its banks. With the greatest reluctance, as
it were, it moves on toward Asphaltites [the Dead Sea], a lake of a gloomy
and unpropitious nature, by which it is at last swallowed up; and its celebrated waters are lost sight of as they mingle with the pestilential
streams of the lake. Because it is so reluctant to get there, as soon as the
valley through which it flows affords the opportunity, the Jordan dis-
charges itself into a lake known as Genesara [Tiberias], sixteen miles long
and six miles wide. This lake is skirted by the pleasant towns of Julias and
Hippo on the east, Tarichea on the south . . . and Tiberias on the west,
where there are health-giving hot springs.

Asphaltites produces nothing whatever except bitumen, to which it
owes its name. The bodies of animals will not sink in its waters, and even
those of bulls and camels float there. In length it exceeds a hundred miles,
being at its widest point twenty-five miles, and at its narrowest six. The
country of the Arabian tent-people faces it on the east, and Macharus on
the south, which was at one time the most strongly fortified place in
Judaea, next to Jerusalem. On the same side lies Callirrhoe, a warm
spring, remarkable for its medicinal qualities.

Lying on the west of Asphaltites, and sufficiently distant to escape its
noxious exhalations, are the Esseni: a people that live apart from the
world, and marvelous beyond all others throughout the whole earth, for

they have no women among them. To sexual desire they are complete strangers; they have no money; the palm trees are their only companions. Day after day, however, their numbers are replenished by the crowds of strangers that resort to them, driven there to adopt their customs by the tempests of fortune, and wearied with the miseries of life. So it is that through thousands of years, incredible to relate, this people eternally prolongs its existence without a single birth taking place there: so fruitful a source of population is the weariness of others.

Below the home of this people [stands] the town of Engadda, second only to Jerusalem in the fertility of its soil and its groves of palm trees . . . and next to it is Masada, a fortress on a rock, not far from Lake Asphaltites.

So much for Judaea.

Strabo in his *Geography* provided a few more details. On the plain of Hiericus, near Jericho, was a wonderful grove of fruit trees and date palms one hundred stadia long, watered by streams and dotted with fine buildings, including a palace built by Herod. (Horace confirmed this: he wrote that in Herod's palm groves "a man might idle and play and smooth himself with oil," a Roman's heaven.) Near the palace stood a "balsam park," where workers tapped the spice-scented shrubs for their milky juice; "and when it is put up in small quantities, it solidifies, and is remarkably good for curing headaches and incipient cataracts and dimness of sight." But for Strabo, too, it was Asphaltites that summed up the strangeness of this country. He noted that the asphalt was blown to the surface, leavened with bubbles, until it looked like a hill, and that it tarnished every metal that touched it. When the local people knew it was rising they would venture out in reed boats to gather it in. This required the chanting of spells and the softening of the asphalt, with their own urine, before they could chop it in pieces and bring it home. The fire and fumes that underlay Judaea also rose up in other places, so that in Gadaris the lake water corroded the hooves of sheep, and near Masada the high cliffs dripped with pitch.

Pilate arrived in this land of bitumen and balsam in about A.D. 26. We assume this date because his predecessor, according to Josephus, was appointed immediately after the death of Augustus in 14, and served for eleven years; and because when Pilate was recalled, in 36, Josephus remarks that he had been in Judaea for a decade. Some think he arrived in

19, which would have made him more experienced when he encountered Christ; but Josephus' calculations seem good enough.

He was the fifth prefect—a word that is best translated, for familiarity's sake, as "governor." The word in Greek was *hegemon,* the title he would officially have been addressed by, although Greek-speakers under his orders would have called him Kratiste, "your Excellency." Before him came Coponius (A.D. 6–9), M. Ambivius (9–12), Annius Rufus (12–15) and Valerius Gratus (15–26). Short tours were normal policy under Augustus, but Judaea was not known as a place that enticed men to stay longer. Did any of his predecessors advise Pilate, give him briefings, or leave the odd warning letter in the files? Possibly. Gratus, after appointing and dismissing four high priests of Judaea in as many years, had gone back to Rome. The last part of his tour was obviously bad-tempered and corrupt: the high priesthood of Judaea was generally awarded for money. So Gratus may have given Pilate a lesson in graft, and Sejanus, if he was his patron, may have trained him in anti-Semitism, for, according to Philo, Sejanus found it impossible to trust the Jews. He accused the Jews in Rome of plotting against the emperor, and the bad feeling was mutual: "He knew," wrote Philo, "that the Jewish nation would take the principal part against his own unholy plots."

However, no writer but Philo, an ardent Jew, suggests that Sejanus was especially anti-Jewish, and Pilate could in any case have picked up this everyday Roman prejudice well before his posting. A large Jewish colony lived on the "other side"—the west side—of the Tiber, known as Ward 14, which was then as now a warren of workshops and small houses. The Jews who lived here were emancipated slaves and Roman citizens, though they were careful to preserve their Jewishness: hence the dual loyalties that Sejanus mistrusted. They ran their own synagogues, in which they received "training in ancestral philosophy," as Philo put it, every Sabbath morning. Inside their small houses an elaborate system of enclosed rooms kept their women hidden, and hayboxes warmed their food on noncooking days. They did not often leave their own quarter, though by the 70s (when their numbers were swollen by refugees after the Jewish War) Jewish hawkers could be seen in the city proper, trading sulfur matches for broken crockery.

Some formal respect was shown to them. According to a decree of Augustus, Jews could not be made to appear in court on the Sabbath, which was understood to start at three o'clock on Friday afternoons; and their sacred money from the "first fruits" was always sent to receivers in Jerusalem and never touched by Romans. The law also dictated that "anyone caught stealing their holy books, or their sacred money, whether out of the synagogues or from the men's apartments, shall be deemed a sacrilegious person." Tiberius, too, was usually solicitous for these Jews, allowing them to come a day late to claim the distributions of money or corn that were made on the Sabbath.

Pilate in Rome could often have observed Jewish rhythms of life—the robes and beards, the hush of Friday evening, the hum of Saturday prayers. But he would probably not have cared to. Romans nursed some lively prejudices against Jews, based largely on misunderstandings of what they believed. Sabbath observance persuaded them that the Jews were bone-idle. Petronius Arbiter, unless he was being extraordinarily offensive, thought they worshiped a "pig-god." Horace in his *Satires* painted Jews as proselytizers, always on the lookout for drifting Romans to draw into their prayer groups, and deeply superstitious, believing for example that frankincense would combust spontaneously if placed on a holy stone. (Horace's friends roared with laughter at that one.) In the ninth Satire, another friend refuses to rescue Horace from a man who is annoying him because "Today is the thirtieth Sabbath. Would you affront the circumcised Jews?"

"I don't care. Religion's nothing to me."

"But it is to me. I'm a weaker brother, one of the many. So, if you'll excuse me, I'll talk another day."

Despite this banter, the Jewish Sabbath was not considered inauspicious for Romans. Ovid thought it was a good day for chasing girls, though he does not say why. In the end, it was their "proselytizing," real or imagined, that rankled most. In A.D. 19 Tiberius expelled the Jews from Rome after a Roman woman of good breeding had been conned into sending her treasure to Jerusalem; but Dio Cassius, a chronicler of the early years of the empire, thought they had been banished more generally for "flocking to Rome and converting people to their ways." Some four thousand Jewish men were called up for military service and sent to Sardinia, a fever-ridden place. The rest, who refused to be soldiers for religious reasons, were arrested, and their holy objects and vestments burned. At around the same time, Tiberius also banned overpriced mullets, Corinthian glass and promiscuous kissing in the street; but these eventually crept back in, and so did the Jews.

The one thing Romans knew for sure about Jews, which fascinated them in the most prurient way, was that the men were circumcised. Anyone trying to disguise himself as a Jew reckoned this was the first distinguishing mark, beyond beards or robes. But to be circumcised, for a Roman, was to lose a bit of manliness. There was therefore that suggestion too in Pilate's outraged response in John's Gospel, "Am *I* a Jew?" The very notion insulted him. The difference was physical, obvious, and there was absolutely nothing to be gained by seeking to narrow the gulf between them.

To do his job well, in Pilate's view, was not a matter of understanding the land he ruled over. He just had to use to the profit of Rome the powers he had been given. His job was not a plum appointment. It was a junior officer's billet; more experienced men got Syria or Egypt. It was also a challenge, because Judaea was such a new and recalcitrant province. Although it had a mixed population of Jews, Greeks, Samarians, Syrians and Idumaeans, all other ethnic conflicts paled beside the overwhelming cultural clash between the Romans and the Jews.

The Jewish nation considered itself in every way superior to Rome, chosen by God and essentially untouchable. Any Roman would have been disquieted by that. All his schooling, his experience, the lines of Livy and Virgil ringing in his head, told him it was his own nation the gods had blessed and appointed: "the Romans, the lords of creation, the togaed people." Cicero put it with typical bluntness: "There is no race which has not either been so utterly destroyed that it hardly exists, or so thoroughly subdued that it remains submissive, or so pacified, that it rejoices in our victory and rule." Earlier in the same speech he dismissed the Jews explicitly as "people born to be slaves." It was a constant headache to Pilate that they were of the opposite opinion.

The Jewish diaspora made his job more difficult. As Philo pointed out, the Jews were spread out across almost the breadth of the habitable world. An insult to them in Judaea could bring "myriads" into open conflict with Rome, and "the result would be something too awesome to be resisted."

Philo, always so fierce in his defense of his people, exaggerated. The desert-sweeping Parthians on the border with Syria, darkening the sky with buzzing swarms of arrows shot backward, were probably more of a threat in Pilate's mind than the massed crowds of the Jews. He might even have felt more nervous about Gauls and Germans, the "godless" barbarians he had probably fought face-to-face. Yet Judaea was fragile enough to be under the personal aegis of the emperor, rather than the Senate, and Pilate was there as Tiberius' personal representative. In the interests of stability both he and his regional superiors, "good fellow" Flaccus and Lucius Vitellius, successive governors of Syria, were bound to obey the least decree that came down from Rome. Petronius, Vitellius' successor, stated this as plainly as possible to a crowd of complaining Jews of the sort Pilate often had to face: "The emperor has sent me, and I am under the necessity of carrying out his decrees, because disobedience to them would bring upon me inevitable destruction."

Vitellius commanded four legions: the sixth ("Iron-Clad"), the third ("Gallica"), the twelfth ("Rolling Thunder") and the tenth, "Fretensis," whose symbols were the bull and the boar. He was on call to intervene in Judaea if things got out of hand—as, by the end of Pilate's stint, they had. For the first five years of his tour, however, the legate of Syria was detained in Rome on the emperor's orders, so Pilate had no one on hand to advise or restrain him. Not that he could get up to much mischief: the governor of Judaea had, at most, four thousand men in auxiliary units of cavalry and infantry. Only the senior officers, and perhaps not all of those, were Romans. The troops were Idumaeans, Samarians and Syrians, many from Caesarea itself, where they sometimes amused themselves by insulting the local Jews and throwing stones at them.

This was a fatal flaw in Pilate's forces. They were even more anti-Jewish than the governor himself was inclined to be, and less able to control themselves. Some years before, Varus (the same Varus who would later be destroyed in the German forest, who was then governor of Syria) had been only too pleased to disband similar units, "which he had not found at all useful, for the soldiers behaved themselves in a most disorderly manner, disobeying his wishes and being intent only on the profits they could make from their misbehavior." The mercy was that their numbers in Judaea were relatively small: so small that, in an emergency, there were simply not enough of them unless Vitellius joined in.

The point of the Roman presence in Judaea was to secure tax revenues, keep the peace and establish trade with Rome; it was not to colonize or Romanize it. Most Romans knew a lost cause when they saw one. Nor was their job to act like an occupying army. Pilate's troops were more of a police force, responsible for guarding important buildings, protecting the governor, controlling sheep in the streets and, when necessary, punishing malefactors. They also carried out the duties of interrogators and secret police. In 1997 part of Pilate's palace at Caesarea was excavated, revealing a room (later than Pilate's time, but built over another of similar function) with a black-and-white mosaic floor. The mosaic carried the legend "I have come to this room in the good hope that I shall be secure." Israeli archaeologists assumed it was an inner interrogation room, in which spies were debriefed or prisoners tortured to elicit secret information.

Pilate seemed to relish the military side of his job. Josephus showed he had a fondness for unusual strategy, even though it often went wrong. He was, after all, the prefect of Judaea, the title he proudly acknowledged in the only memorial that survives of him. By the time of Claudius, around 46, the title of such officials had been changed to "procurator," and Tacitus made the mistake, in about 115, of attaching this title to Pilate. He would have been offended. A procurator in the strict sense was a financial agent, like a purchaser of grain or a supervisor of mines. By contrast, in Caesar's armies a prefect was a cavalry commander. When Augustus redefined the office, the title was automatically attached to knightly officers who extended their military careers to become governors of provinces, as Pilate seemed to do. Strabo in his *Geography* noted that prefects of the equestrian order were usually sent to wild or mountainous regions, or to places where the people were "entirely barbarians." A prefect was on the front line, in harm's way, or certainly liked to assume he was.

Some of this was simply wishful thinking. As Cicero remarked, Romans were so passionate about military glory that most of their statues were in military dress. The greatest possible virtue lay in fighting and laying down your life for Rome; civilian public service could seem second-rate. Pilate would sometimes have worn his leather soldier's tunic and metal breastplate, but his public clothing was usually the *toga praetexta,* white bordered with purple, clothing so heavy and so elaborately draped that he could move only like a bureaucrat or a statesman. If he chafed at that, Cicero had comforting words for him:

> Men who in a civil capacity direct the affairs of the nation render no less important service that those who conduct its wars. . . . Diplomacy in the

friendly settlement of controversies is more desirable than courage in set-
tling them on the battlefield. . . . It takes a brave and resolute spirit not
to be disconcerted in times of difficulty or ruffled and thrown off one's
feet, as they say, but to keep one's presence of mind and one's self-
possession and not to swerve from the path of reason.

Now all this requires great personal courage; but it also calls for great
intellectual ability by reflection to anticipate the future, to discover some
time in advance what is going to happen, whether for good or ill, and
what must be done in any possible event, and never to be reduced to having to say, "I hadn't thought of that."

. . . There are, therefore, instances of civic courage that are not inferior to the courage of the soldier. Indeed, [civic service] calls for even
greater energy and even greater devotion.

In Judaea, the prefect was not just the chief soldier; he was also the chief
magistrate and head of the judicial system, carrying Tiberius' whole *imperium* into his tiny patch. Although most civil and criminal jurisdiction
continued to be exercised by the Jews through their councils, the lesser
and greater Sanhedrin, there was a tendency to refer the hardest cases to
the governor, especially when they involved unrest or might require the
death penalty.

Pilate routinely used his troops to carry out crucifixions, the favored
punishment for thieves, bandits and all low-class troublemakers. These
were performed, in peacetime, after a cursory hearing and, in times of rebellion, immediately and en masse. After the uprising under Spartacus a
century before, the Appian Way in Rome was lined with crucified slaves
on both sides; in Judaea, after one uprising, Gratus crucified two hundred Jews at once. Under Pilate there is no record of mass crucifixions,
but we can assume the punishment was common. The governor would
have seen this as good administration, the policy that would later enable
Tacitus to sum up his tour in Judaea as *sub Tiberio quies,* "under Tiberius,
peace." Crucifixion was not done without a reason, and the reasons were
advertised on the crosses themselves. The horror of this punishment, for
non-Romans, was its savagery, and for Romans its disgrace; but not ran-
domness. Rabble-rousing Jews could anticipate the cross as a matter of
course. As Luke's good thief remarked, hanging beside Jesus where Pilate
had put him, "We were sentenced justly; we are paying for what we did."

The governor's sentences were written into the record, filed in the archive and continually referred to, as were the records of his predecessors. They were annulled only if he fell into disgrace. Almost all such governors' records have vanished with the passage of time. Historians and mythmakers alike have agonized over the disappearance of Pilate's archive, and the puzzle of whether anyone saw or consulted it while it still existed. Many suspect that, if it survived for any length of time, it was suppressed for the short, sharp reference to Jesus it presumably contained.

Pilate was also the chief fiscal officer, responsible for collecting taxes, allocating revenues and keeping the wheels of his province turning to the profit of the *princeps* in Rome. According to Philo, budget matters took up most of a governor's time. Underlings called *publicani* farmed the indirect taxes for him, and there were plenty of them: "income" taxes, food taxes, the *tributum soli* (land taxes based on harvests), *portorium* (a transport tax on goods), purchase tax, customs duties. Among these, the most lucrative was the duty charged at Gaza on the frankincense brought by camel from Arabia. This was still raw, white and sticky, wrapped in the palm mats on which it had dropped, like foaming milk, from the wounded trees—but not so raw that it could not be diverted, in sticky samples, as an offering to the governor.

These dues came on top of the *tributum capitis,* the poll tax paid directly to Rome, for which the census was taken that led the family of Jesus to Bethlehem. In Pilate's time the tribute was set at one silver denarius per head, the coin that was given to Jesus to test him on the morality of Roman taxation; it raised about four hundred talents a year. This heavy load was fiercely resented by the Jews, and not only for the obvious reasons. For many of them, the tribute implied an unacceptable submission to human masters rather than to God. As for the census itself, it was the work of the Devil, since God alone had the right to know his people in that sort of statistical detail.

Venal collectors compounded the sin. In the first years of Gaius, and possibly in the last years of Tiberius and Pilate, the chief tax collector for Judaea was one Capito, who cherished according to Philo "a spite against the population." (Philo painted his villains black, but most tax collectors can seem that way.) When Capito arrived in Judaea he was apparently a poor man, "but by his rapacity and peculation he amassed much wealth in various forms. Then, fearing that some charge might be brought against him, he devised a scheme to elude the charges by slandering those he had wronged." We do not know whether Judaea made a profit or a loss while Pilate was in charge, or how much ended up in his pocket; but peace was also construed as profit, no matter how slim the revenues were.

In other provinces, governors approved all public works, reviewed the status of slaves and freedmen, adjudicated disputed wills, saw to the welfare of abandoned babies. At least some of their time was spent picking their way through overgrown gardens and swampland to see if they could bear constructions to the greater glory of Rome. They issued, or refused, permits for clubs and societies, and gave out precious licenses to use the Imperial Post. Pilate would have done all this for the Gentiles in his province, but the social government of the Jews was left exclusively to the Sanhedrin and the local councils. This greatly narrowed his scope. While the essence of his job, as he apparently saw it, was to implant the ways of Rome, in Judaea he was under strict orders not only to tolerate the local culture—standard practice in the provinces—but to make his own virtually invisible, and to keep himself as much as possible out of Jewish life.

This had financial implications. Each of his actions as governor provided an excuse for a bribe, and the habit was so endemic that it is doubtful Pilate would have resisted. This was one of the paybacks of foreign service. You were stuck in the provinces, you were homesick, bored and reviled, but at least you could shake down your subjects in exchange for the blessings of straight roads and a postal service. Cicero described one governor of Syria as "always standing with his right hand out" to get payments for favors. In official charge sheets, the various types of extortion were all described as "theft," but in common parlance a governor's payments on the side were *unguentaria,* "ointment money." You could also extort more straightforwardly, through taxes, as one governor of a Spanish province bragged in a letter to his mistress: "Hooray, hooray, I'm coming back to you solvent! Because—guess what?—I've managed to screw four million sesterces out of the Baetici."

Governors knew that their behavior was meant to be upright, but temptation loomed on every side. Foreigners had nice things. When Verres was pro-praetor of Sicily in the 40s B.C., he sent home four hundred jars of honey, fifty sofa cushions, dozens of candelabra and dozens of bales of Maltese silk, all without paying duty. Cicero was gratified and astonished that his brother Quintus, governor of Asia, should have been three years in supreme command "and not been tempted by the offer of any statue, picture, plate, garment, or slave, or by any fascination of human beauty, or any pecuniary proposal."

Pilate's presumed ancestor, Gavius Pontius, could have lectured him severely on the subject. Self-seeking behavior in public office was unpardonable to him. He had complained bitterly that fate had engineered his birth too soon, in the years before the Romans started taking bribes. Had he been born later, he said, he would have had the most glorious excuse "for suffering their supremacy no longer." But it seems safe to say that Pilate would have taken a softer, looser line.

Besides, a certain amount of conspicuous expenditure went with the posting. Embassies had to be received, friends entertained, rituals observed with music and processions. On his birthday and at Saturnalia, in December, the governor was expected to send out presents: books or bottles for the men, alabaster perfume boxes for their wives, or figs and dates to wish them (as the Jews also wished one another) a sweet new year. He was also expected by his Gentile subjects to organize games and to decide how the prizes ought to be awarded. Under Herod, Pilate's base city of Caesarea had been the site of a four-yearly festival in honor of Augustus, with athletic and musical competitions as well as wild-beast shows. Perhaps the new governor was expected to keep these up. Good shows, as much as brilliant campaigns, made a man's political reputation; some men imagined God himself as an *aedile,* a master of ceremonies, stringing the sky with lights and marshaling the shooting stars. Pilate would need to get wild panthers, keeping them in cages to judge their sinuous stretching and the thrilling flash of their fangs. He would need to recruit gladiators and worry about their morale, for it was not unknown for slave fighters to throw themselves, slippery with oil, from the carts that took them to the arena, or even to kill themselves with the cleansing sticks from the latrines. Chariots would have to be built, horses trained, and elaborate naval battles staged in a few feet of frothing water. If Pilate was a true Roman, the hours spent in the circus at Caesarea—entering to the crowd's applause, throwing out coins among the spectators, hollering on his favorite racing color as he cheered the Blues or the Greens at home— might well have been the happiest aspect of his job.

There were certainly disappointments. Since Judaea was a small and

second-rate posting, he had a shoestring staff. Governors in the larger
provinces commanded a staff of three secretaries (one of whom kept the
accounts), three judicial officers, a military commander, ten messengers,
and the usual host of guards, interpreters, clerks, military intelligence officers, torturers, spies and grooms. Flaccus, the governor of Egypt, had a
"crowd" of secretaries, and routinely took "only" ten or fifteen household
slaves with him when dining around town. Pilate's entourage was probably a shadow of this. The Gospels imply that he had no lictors, the two
men who usually walked before a magistrate carrying the *fasces,* bundles
of elm rods bound with an ax, as symbols of his penal authority. His initial inquiries about Jesus suggest that he did not even have a *quaestor,* the
man who would usually have done the background questioning for him.
Pilate seems to have done things for himself, perhaps even struggling
through in Greek without an interpreter, and his "court officers" were
mostly ordinary soldiers, who might also be in short supply. Pliny reported that Gavius Bassus, the prefect of the Pontic Shore, was highly
annoyed to find that he could claim only ten hand-picked soldiers, or *ben-
eficiarii,* to be exempted from their normal duties and assigned to his
staff. He went moaning to Pliny for more, but Pliny could not oblige
him.

Being abroad was difficult. Like most men in foreign postings, governors got homesick. They worried about the houses they had left, the estates that needed planting, unreliable tenants, and—as Cicero put
it—"being robbed in every direction by domestics in their absence." As
now, builders and architects had to be chased up at long distance. ("I
urged Longilius, the contractor, to hurry up. He convinced me he was
anxious to give every satisfaction. . . . Diphilus is outdoing himself in
dilatoriness. . . . The columns he had placed were neither perpendicular
nor opposite each other. Of course, he'll have to pull them down. Some
day or other he'll learn the use of plumb-line and tape.")

Favorite foods were elusive, too. It was hard to get oysters, chipped
ice or good Falernian aged in the bottle, although, like generations of ex-
patriates before and after, it may have been smaller things that Pilate
missed: nut-and-honey pastries bought on the run, hot sausage, Tuscan
olives. The *Daily Gazette* was unavailable and, though friends might send
it whole or in bits, the gossip was cold by the time it arrived. Foreign-
service officers missed the life of Rome, "the City," even in its tedious aspects: the endless round of dinners and recitals, the faked excitement and

assiduous applause, the ritual morning greetings and emotionless embraces. "All foreign service," wrote Cicero to Aelius Rufus,

> (and this has been my conviction from the days of my youth), is obscurity and squalor for those whose active services at Rome can shine forth in splendor. . . . All the profits of a province are not to be compared, I swear it, with one single little stroll, and one single talk, with you. . . . "Any hope of a triumph?" you say. I should have quite a glorious triumph if only in the shortening of the period of my yearning for all that is dearest to me.
>
> Rome, my dear Rufus, Rome—stay there in that full light and *live*.

From Rome, in reply, friends tried to cheer them up. Thus Seneca to his friend Lucilius, who was feeling down about his job as procurator of Sicily:

> There's no reason why you should measure yourself according to this part of the world; concentrate on where you're living. Any point which rises above adjacent points is great at the spot where it rises . . . a ship which looms large in the river seems tiny when it's on the ocean. . . .
>
> You're really important in your province, though you scorn yourself. Men are asking what you do, what you eat for dinner, how you sleep—and they find out, too.

Most governors could comfort themselves with the thought that they were gossiped about and noticed, as they could hardly fail to be: the only man in gleaming white in a crowd, the only officer to sit in judgment in the gilded chair, the man before whose carriage the army cleared the streets. Yet all this show meant nothing to the Jews. They were trained from the cradle, Philo wrote, "by the far higher authority of the sacred laws and the unwritten customs, to acknowledge one God who is the Father and maker of the world." In this frame of mind, they accepted death "as willingly as if it were immortality, to save them from submitting to the destruction of any of their ancient traditions." The culture that Pilate carried with him and, indeed, loved, made him despised even before he reached Judaea. He could no more simulate affection for the Jews than they could for him; and as soon as he landed, mistrust enfolded him like noxious fumes from the sea.

II.

It was an old story, told most vividly by Josephus, with his Jewish heart and his Roman head. Each side knew the chief events, as plainly as pictures in a child's book. The first scene was Pompey in Jerusalem in 63 B.C., standing in his sweat-stained battle clothes in the very heart of the Temple, the Holy of Holies. For months the walls had been pummeled with battering rams. Faustus, Furius and Fabius, the three centurions, had finally scaled the walls and set the city on fire on the Sabbath, when the Jews were resting; twelve thousand Jews had been killed, "but of the Romans very few." That done, Pompey and his men thrust into the Temple and made for the innermost sanctum, where they knew the treasure was. They saw things it was not lawful for any man to see except the priests: the golden table laid with loaves of white flour topped with frankincense, the holy menorah, the pouring vessels, bowls heaped with spices. Bulls' blood was daubed on the walls. In the innermost chamber, to their surprise, they found nothing at all. But in the outer rooms, musty, dark and rancid with ancient sacrifice, they uncovered two thousand talents of sacred money. Pompey would not touch it. He did not need to: Jerusalem was made a tribute city, and the Romans soon extracted ten thousand talents from it. "And so," sighs Josephus, "we lost our liberty, and became subject to the Romans." The Psalms of Solomon put it even more bitterly: "Foreign nations went up to Thy altar and trampled it proudly without removing their shoes."

Quarreling high priests had been the excuse for Roman intervention. Pompey confirmed one, Hyrcanus, in power, and sent his rival Aristobulus to Rome with his arms bound behind him. But Aristobulus escaped, as did his sons Antigonus and Alexander, and immediately began to whip up unrest in Galilee, Samaria and Judaea. Alexander slaughtered many Romans and besieged others who took refuge on Mount Gerizim in Samaria—a mountain that Pilate, too, would have reason to remember. Eventually the rebels were suppressed and the land was half-quiet again.

Until the next outrage. Crassus, governor of Syria, on his way to fight the Parthians in 55 B.C., broke into the Temple again and robbed it of its gold. He found between himself and the treasure nothing more than a high curtain, embroidered with gold and purple, hanging from a great rafter. The high priest Hyrcanus begged him to take the rafter. It was hollow, and held inside it a solid beam of beaten gold that weighed seven hundred pounds. If Crassus took this, the priest reasoned, he would not want the rest of the gold that lay inside the Temple. But Crassus took it all. His appetite for gold was so intense that when, the next year, the Parthians killed him and sent his head to their king, the king amused himself by pouring melted gold into the dead, sagging mouth.

Hyrcanus continued to preside as high priest; but at his back, increasingly, was the ambitious Antipater, the father of Herod the Great. He came from Idumaea, farther south toward Egypt. Under Antipater, the Jews helped Caesar against the Egyptians and provisioned his army with corn. Antipater was even wounded in the cause of Rome; he was made a Roman citizen and procurator of Judaea. His headstrong son Herod, who had charge of Galilee, carried on his father's tradition of ingratiating himself with Rome. He sent money and presents to Mark Antony, who was on campaign in the region between his trysts with Cleopatra. In return, Rome gave the Jews privileges. Governors (including Pilate when his turn came) were banned from raising auxiliaries within the borders of Judaea, or from extracting money from Jews for winter quarters "or on any other pretext"; they could not take away their property or expect tribute in sabbatical years, when the Jews did not plow their land or pick the fruit from their trees. In 47 B.C., at the instigation of Hyrcanus, the whole Jewish nation was confirmed by treaty as a client state of Rome.

In 40 B.C. came the apotheosis of this era of good feeling. With struggles for local control still going on in Judaea, Herod decided to claim the throne in person and to seek help in Rome. Antony and Octavian (later Augustus) took him into the Senate, where he was introduced to the senators by the master of the horse. The senators heard how fond of Rome Herod's father had been and how fond he was himself, a bulwark against the Parthians; and when Antony suggested that Herod should be king of Judaea, the Senate unanimously agreed. Then Antony and Octavian walked out of the Senate house with Herod between them. He was darker than they were, with his Idumaean skin, long-haired and bearded; even in the toga of an honorary Roman citizen, he looked like a merchant. But he walked between the two Romans as if this were his natural place. They went up the hill to the Capitol, followed by a crowd of consuls and magistrates, to spill the blood of lambs and goats on Jupiter's altar. It was a Roman sacrifice, but Herod was already half-Roman: made nervous by birds and auguries, in love with architects' designs for porticoes and white marble, thrilled to sit among the senators for the wild-beast shows. He was easy to deal with because he was only half a Jew.

His people resented that. They did not believe his wriggling apology that he put up fantastic buildings only to be polite to the Romans. Factions resisted him, and he fought them to the point where, in 37 B.C., twenty-seven years to the day since Pompey's incursion, he had to take Jerusalem by force. The Romans under Sosius helped him. Once more they battered the walls, scaled them, set fire to the porticoes of the Temple and cut down Jews in the city's maze of alleyways; and once more, smelling gold, the Romans rushed toward the Holy of Holies. This time, the outcome was different. Herod held them back and begged them not to loot the city. "Do you want to make me king of a desert?" he kept asking. "Do you want to make me king of a desert?" To encourage them to leave, he pressed money into their hands and gave Sosius a golden crown. This was an embarrassing present for a Roman, a sign of Herod's cultural obtuseness; so Sosius dedicated the crown to the gods and marched away from Jerusalem.

Herod was soon without rivals. In 31 B.C. he was confirmed as a client king, a dependent and ever-dependable ally, by Octavian/Augustus. Feeling himself secure, he became more Roman than the Romans. Great palaces and public buildings in the Roman style went up at Caesarea, Sebaste and Jerusalem, featuring vast dining rooms and floors of polished stone. The king developed a Roman fixation for fittings and statues of Corinthian bronze, which was allegedly fused with gold and silver to give it a color and patina that connoisseurs adored. His sons were sent to Rome to study. And, most offensive of all to the Jews, he instituted games outside Jerusalem in honor of Augustus. At the great amphitheater in the plain, glittering with gold and silver trophies from Herod's campaigns and inscriptions in honor of the emperor, appeared wrestlers, professional musicians, horse races, races for two-horse and four-horse chariots and wild-beast fights. Foreigners like Pilate loved these, but the Jews, said Josephus, lamented "the palpable destruction of the customs they venerated." It was no better than barefaced impiety "to throw men to wild beasts, to afford delight to spectators," almost within sight and earshot of the holiest place in the world.

In short, Herod was a hedonist and a tyrant. Even his squabbling sons turned against him. When Augustus came to Syria in 20 B.C., a people called the Gadarenes accused Herod of violence, plunder and overthrowing of temples; but Herod was so sure of the emperor's favor that he stood in the judgment hall unconcerned. His confidence was justified, Josephus said. Augustus took him by the right hand, "and remitted nothing of his kindness to him, despite the uproar of the crowd." Eight years later he reconciled Herod's sons with him, when they came to Rome to accuse their father in person. Augustus beckoned to the three of them to embrace one another; and as they did so, in floods of relieved tears, a few tears glistened also on the taut imperial cheek. This did not stop Augustus remarking, on another occasion, that he would rather be Herod's pig than his son.

The reconciliation did not last long. The family soon quarreled again, and Judaea broke up with them. Josephus, undoubtedly letting his hatred for Herod get the better of him, related how the man brought bad luck on himself by going one night into the musty vault of King David's tomb and taking out, from beneath the damp slabs, the golden ornaments that were buried there. Then he ventured farther, toward the coffins of David and Solomon, but a great flame burst out, killing two of his bodyguards and frightening Herod out of his wits. He began to suspect that all his intimates were plotting against him, and most of them were. Eventually, worn out by his sons' misbehavior, he fell ill. Age and bitterness ate up his body. His intestines were ulcerated, his feet gouty, his breathing labored. Even his penis turned to stone and generated worms, and his breath stank. In desperation he tried the warm baths at Callirrhoe, where his doctors immersed him in vats of tepid oil; but it did no good.

In 4 B.C. he died and his kingdom was divided among his surviving sons. Archelaus took the half containing Judaea, Idumaea and Samaria; Herod Antipas became tetrarch of Galilee; Philip became tetrarch of Batanaea, Trachonitis and Auranitis. Augustus confirmed the division of Herod's kingdom in the presence of fifty Jewish ambassadors in the Temple of Apollo in Rome, and this was how it was still divided when Pilate arrived there thirty years later. Archelaus had been banished after ten years of misrule, at the end of which he was haunted by a dream of ears of corn being devoured by oxen. After his banishment, in A.D. 6,

Rome had taken over his half of the kingdom; his brothers still sat in their sections. It was not a comfortable arrangement for either side. Judaea both needed Rome and hated it. It sulked and seethed.

III.

Pilate's ship docked at Caesarea, one of the most impressive cities of the eastern empire. The whole waterfront was newly built by Herod, largely of white marble. From far out at sea the buildings shone in the brilliant light: blue sky, blue sea, white stone. On the left as the ship entered harbor was a round turret, capable of withstanding the strongest sweep of the sea. On the right were two monoliths, each larger than the turret, joined together to make a sort of monumental sculpture at the entryway to Judaea.

Because this coast was difficult to anchor in, buffeted by south winds and drifting sand, Herod had built a pier of huge stones 200 feet out into the sea. Each stone was at least fifty feet long, eighteen feet wide and nine feet high, and with enormous difficulty and skill they had been lowered down through twenty fathoms of water. The leeward half of the pier supported a wall and several towers, the largest named Drusus after the stepson of Augustus who had died young. Around the harbor ran a promenade lined with arches and, behind these, with fine buildings. At the central point, facing north where the sky was clearest, a small manmade hillock was crowned with a temple of Augustus. The city was so new that even the cellars and sewers were lined with beautiful fresh-cut stone; from Pilate's latrine, the Roman filth of Caesarea's newest resident could be swiftly and neatly conveyed to the sea. The northeast side of the town held an amphitheater and the south side a theater, from which the audience for the nautical war games could look out over the shining stage of waves and salt water almost as far as the Bosphorus.

The palace in Caesarea, newly built too, was Pilate's headquarters. Little dragged him away from this vision of white marble. He spent almost all his time in a city that was trying to be Rome; he could almost forget that he was in Judaea. There were far fewer Jews in town than Syrians, Greeks, Romans and far-flung sailors, whose drunken night songs floated from the harbor arches into the thickening air. Pilate could walk out by the water in the evenings, along the curving promenade ("a most agreeable walk for those who like exercise," Josephus said), unless like Tiberius he preferred to be carried in his litter, around and around, for the sheer imperious fun of it. There, if he cared to, he could sniff the salt tang of the sea and feel the wind ruffle his hair. In the winter he could wrap his cloak twice around him and shroud his head from the spray; in the summer he could watch intrepid boys plunging in the blue-green water where, deep down, the great stones sent back a shimmering lat-ticework of sunlight. When he offered public sacrifice it was Caesar's temple he walked to, attended by his retinue; and the statues to which he raised his eyes were of Augustus and motherly Roma, comforting and es-sential images of home, though touched with foreign light in a foreign place.

On the rare occasions when he left Caesarea he could still contrive to remain in this world. The way to Jerusalem, where he went to reinforce security on the Jewish festivals of Passover, Pentecost and Tabernacles, was sixty miles south-southeast along a Roman road marked reassuringly with Roman mileposts. He did not go there willingly; few Romans did. Augustus had actually commended his grandson Gaius, when he went on tour through Judaea, for not stopping in Jerusalem to pay his re-spects. But Pilate had to make the best of it.

His lodgings there made life easier. When he reached the city he stayed in Herod's old palace on the western hill, another wonder of white marble, where glistening terraces overlooked the city in one direction and, in the other, gardens shaded with trees. The palace afforded (as Jose-phus said) "a most delightful prospect to those who wished to overlook the city," and its luxury "baffled description." Possibly he was exaggerat-ing, wishing to condemn the conspicuous consumption of both Herodi-ans and Romans; but possibly what he described was exactly what Pilate saw.

It was extraordinary. Among columns of colored marble and glitter-ing fountains flew sudden scattered clouds of white doves. Their feathers fell on pavements of mosaic, on floors of agate and lapis lazuli; their wings beat among improbably high ceilings where every beam was painted with gold and vermilion. The chairs and tables were of gold or silver inlaid with jewels, uncomfortable designer objects in which no man could relax, and Herod's gifts from his emperor friends were on dis-play in every room. In the two great marble wings, one named after Au-gustus and the other after Agrippa, dining rooms with one hundred reclining couches and table settings could accommodate three hundred diners. To a visitor with a relatively small staff it was no doubt a bemusing place, easy to get lost in: the journey to bed complicated, the bedroom vast, little things like wine and snacks and writing tablets not readily at hand. And it was into this cold but fantastic hotel that Pilate brought Christ.

He did not necessarily see much of the Jews, even in Jerusalem. There they were a largely undifferentiated, potentially dangerous crowd. He stayed above them. From his terrace he could gaze down at the low gray houses, the shanties and allotments of the Holy City, studded with mangy palms and occasional cypresses like those of home. In Caesarea he felt safe, with plenty of troops around him and the blue sea offering escape. Here, although he had soldiers billeted in both the palace and the Antonia (Herod's fort, named after his friend Antony, now the headquarters of the Roman garrison), he was surrounded by enemies. Like all provincials, to a Roman nose they had a smell about them, a sharp, foreign smell untempered by perfume sprays. When Verres was pro-praetor of Sicily he would bury his face, on unavoidable outings, in a string bag stuffed with roses. Modern writers, from Kazantzakis to Bulgakov, have imagined Pilate too seeking refuge in gardens and handkerchiefs, an aesthete suffering in an unbearable place.

Yet there was much to admire outside the palace in Jerusalem, the Temple most of all. The building was a fabulous treasure-house, replenished every year with gold and silver from every corner of the world. Herod had begun to rebuild it with the services of ten thousand workers and a thousand priests, and the work was just finished—after forty-six years—by the time Pilate first came up from Caesarea. From afar it could be seen on its hill, a giant mausoleum framed by great walls and porticoes lined with Corinthian pillars. It was impossible not to be curious.

Besides, the Romans were not without interests there. They stationed soldiers in the western porticoes during the festivals, in case of trouble; and, more strangely, they themselves sent gifts and offered sacrifice. Augustus, Livia and Tiberius sent golden vials and libation bowls to decorate the sanctuary, and the Roman administration (that is, Pilate's officers) provided the bullock and two lambs that were sacrificed there daily on Tiberius' orders for the safety of the emperor. Whether the smell of blood and incense reached the nostrils of many gods or one God was, in this case, immaterial; the emperor's subjects commended him for safety's sake to "the Supreme God," the singular God of Israel.

So, undoubtedly, Pilate got closer. He was allowed to see the front wall of the Temple, decorated with lintels on pillars and constructed of slabs of white marble polished to such a high gloss that he might almost have seen his own gazing image reflected back. The lavish gold-plating flashed in the sun. In Mark's Gospel, Jesus' disciples, too, were amazed at that colossal outer wall: "Master, just look! What huge stones! What huge buildings!" It was disconcerting proof of Jesus' radicalism that he seemed to take pleasure in imagining it wrecked, even if rebuilt afterward.

If Pilate went through the entrance in that first gleaming wall, his servants clearing a path through the beggars who crouched there in hope of alms, he would arrive in the courtyard below the porticoes where pilgrims could change money, and where hawkers sold pigeons and lambs to those who wished to offer sacrifice. He could walk across this courtyard to a small flight of steps, surmounted by a wall with a door. On the wall, however, were large signs in Latin and Greek, erected by a previous Roman administration, warning him that entry beyond this point was restricted to Jews. Trespassers, it was made clear, could expect to die. Dusty couples from the countryside went through that door, dutifully carrying their pigeons in wicker cages, as Mary and Joseph had done years before to give thanks for the infant Jesus. But Pilate could do no more than watch them.

Marcus Agrippa, Tiberius' father-in-law and Augustus' second-in-command, probably saw as much of Temple business as a Roman could observe. He came in the autumn of 15 B.C. as a guest of Herod, and was so impressed by the Temple that he could not keep away. He had seen, wrote Philo proudly, "something to be profoundly reverenced, something greater than words could describe." Every day of his stay he went back to the Temple precinct, marveling at the ritual and decorations, "the majestic aspect of the high priest wearing the sacred vestments and conducting the holy rites." These, presumably, were the ceremonies of the Feast of Tabernacles and the daily sacrifices made on behalf of the emperor. More than this he was not allowed to witness. Rumor had it, though, that when you proceeded through the third door, where even the ritually pure were required to take a bath and change into white clothes, the splendors were almost incredible: enormous doors hung with embroidered veils and flowers of purple, behind a great golden grille fantastically crafted to resemble a spreading vine burdened with bunches of grapes the size of a man, symbols of the fruitfulness of Israel.

Rumor had it, too, that the tiny innermost chamber called the Holy of Holies was empty, for Pompey had been disappointed. Tacitus wrote that he had found only "a naked dome, the sanctuary unadorned and simple," though Tacitus himself was half persuaded that it really contained the head of an ass, since a herd of wild asses had led the Jews to water during the exodus. On Yom Kippur, the holiest day of the year, the high priest, in a tunic of linen and a robe of silk brocade encrusted with jewels and hemmed with gold, entered the Holy of Holies alone to burn incense and pray for the peace of the world. It was the most secret, sacred act, and so fearful that the priest would later celebrate the fact that he had emerged alive. Yet the Romans played a tiny part in that, too. For the rest of the year the high priest's gorgeous robes, including a purple chiton with golden bells and tassels, were kept in Roman custody, though never touched. They lay in the Antonia, kept like some magic treasure trove in a sealed stone room in a guarded tower. Every day, in one of the more peculiar courtesies of the Roman regime, the commandant lit a lamp outside the chamber. Seven days before the festivals on which they were needed, he would deliver the robes to the priests; and the priests, exhaustively, with water and incense and incantations, would rub the smell of the Romans away.

If anyone told Pilate of these secret places and rituals of the people he governed, it was probably Joseph Caiaphas, the high priest. Caiaphas was there when he arrived, the last of Gratus' string of appointments, and he was there when he left. Indeed, because he was seen as Pilate's man, he did not long outlast him. His longevity in office was unusual. Was this because he was a towering figure, impressively competent? It seems unlikely. Although he was the son-in-law of Annas, an ex–high priest and the real power behind the Sanhedrin, he seems to have been more of a trimmer and appeaser. It was Caiaphas who was said to have made the crassly pragmatic suggestion, as the priests were discussing how to handle the problem of Jesus, that it was "expedient that one man should die for the people," to preserve them from Roman rage.

Did he stay, then, because Pilate forswore the chance to enrich himself by selling Judaea's premier appointment? Again, it seems unlikely, although Pilate is not presented as a man who was particularly interested in money. More probably the two men got on, after a fashion. The getting-on was greased by an annual bribe pitched by Caiaphas at a rate higher than his rivals', and Pilate felt it was safer not to rock the boat by replacing him. He relied on him too much. All through his rocky career in Judaea, the priests and local rulers almost always stayed on Pilate's side. It was the crowd, usually without leaders, that opposed him.

For his part, Caiaphas accepted—as did all the Roman-appointed high priests, and most of the Sadducees and Pharisees—that the Romans were the best protectors of the Temple against insurgents from the more violent Jewish sects. In 5 B.C., a gang of young men had climbed on the Temple roof, let themselves down with ropes and vandalized a great golden eagle set by Herod above a doorway, taking it both for a sacrilegious icon and for an emblem of Rome. Samaritans had attacked the Temple too a little later, getting into the forbidden courtyards "and throwing dead men's bones around," as the horrified Josephus reported. But the Romans defended it, and Pilate played his part: in the twenty-three years of Tiberius' rule, according to Philo, no part of the Temple was disturbed.

Through Caiaphas, over the years, Pilate might have absorbed a little knowledge of Jewish faith and practice. If he had read his Strabo on the geography of Judaea, he would also have picked up the notion that the Jews were originally Egyptians, led to Jerusalem by the pious Egyptian priest Moses "because he thought the Egyptians were wrong to reproduce the image of the Divine Being by the images of beasts and cattle." Moses believed, Strabo wrote, that God was "this one thing alone that encompasses us all and encompasses land and sea—the thing which we call heaven, or universe, or the nature of all that exists." Strabo evidently struggled with this concept, and he was not alone. Tacitus thought the God of the Jews was "the great governing mind," whom they imagined in their heads; Juvenal thought the Jews worshiped "the clouds and brightness of the heavens."

Roman writers were less tentative, and much less kind, when it came to the religious practices of the Jews. Tacitus called their religion "the reverse of everything known to any other age or country. . . . Whatever is held sacred by the Romans, with the Jews is held profane, and what in other nations is unlawful and impure, with them is fully established." Their festival days were "a gloomy ceremony, full of absurd enthusiasm, rueful, mean and sordid." They were unsociable, and seemed to hate the rest of mankind. "Obstinate" and "stubborn" were the words Tacitus used most often of them; and it was their "superstitions" and "unholy practices," he said, that had made Tiberius send them away.

Even tiny things rankled. The long finger-dates of Judaea were cherished by the Romans as acceptable offerings to the gods; Pilate might have laid them among the private deities in his bedroom as he laid down quinces or apples at home. The Jews, however, called these "common dates"; and this fact alone, the elder Pliny wrote, summed up "their contempt for things divine."

His attitude was common enough. At best (as in the case of Petronius, who was sent by the emperor Gaius to sort out Judaea shortly after Pilate left), the Romans in Judaea found the faith of the Jews impressive but baffling. At worst, they mocked it, like the detachment of soldiers described by Josephus who were sent to search a village for malefactors and, finding a copy of the Laws of Moses in one of the houses, apparently tore it up with guffaws of laughter. Between these two attitudes was insulting ignorance, of the sort displayed by Gaius in 38 when he received a delegation of Jews protesting about the proposed erection of his golden image in the Temple. This delegation included Philo, who described the scene with customary, but justified, bitterness; though he was no harder than Roman writers were on the playful, brutal man who came to meet them, waving casually from his garden gate.

"Ah, so you're the god-haters!" Gaius shouted.

When they had recovered from this, he went on, between wandering upstairs and downstairs and out into the gardens of his villa, "Why don't you eat pork?"

His hangers-on burst out laughing. The Jewish delegates, embarrassed, answered, "Different people have different customs."

"Yes," said someone, "just as many don't eat lamb, though it's easy enough to get."

"Quite right, too, because it's not nice!" cried Gaius. The company burst out laughing again; and the emperor, ignoring what the Jews were trying to say to him, wandered off into other rooms to order new windows and new paintings. "Under such befooling and reviling we were helpless," wrote Philo sadly.

By the end of his tour, Pilate could probably have distinguished his Pharisees from his Sadducees. Josephus in the *Antiquities* made the differences clear enough, and so did Jesus in his parables. The Pharisees were the ones with their tassels and broad phylacteries, as Jesus described them, who prayed and swayed in the streets; or who, as the Pharisee Josephus said, lived simply, followed the guidance of reason and directed the religious observances of the people. They were not of the highest social rank and, as far as religion went, were open to and interested in change. A Roman would suppose they were not to be trusted because, during the time of Augustus, they had refused to make a pledge of goodwill to him. Then came the Sadducees, like Caiaphas and the rest of the priests: sturdy traditionalists, keepers of the Temple ritual, rejecters of novel theories such as the immortality of the soul and, though "a disputatious elite" to Jews like Josephus, ready and willing to accommodate with Rome. Last came the Essenes, "addicted to virtue," Josephus said, who dressed all in white, shared everything, refused to keep slaves and lived without sex in the desert. Pilate may never have seen an Essene; yet even these may sometimes have intruded on his dreams.

When all was said, his interest in Judaism was simple. He had to know whether it was dangerous or not. Judaea in his time seemed quiet, but in the vacuum left after Herod's death and before the Roman prefecture it had filled up with mavericks, prophets and impostors. A man called Judas, the son of a robber chief, had gathered a gang together, stormed the palace at Sepphoris in Galilee and made off with a stash of weapons in the hope that the raid would make him king. Another called Simon, one of Herod's servants ("tall, robust and handsome," said Josephus), put a crown on his head and had himself proclaimed king; he then went on a rampage, burning down all the royal palaces he came across, until the legions stopped him. Next came a band of shepherd brothers with individual gangs of their own, who engaged in constant guerrilla warfare and, in the end, revolt against the Romans. Varus put this down by crucifying two thousand of the rebels.

Still this was not the end of it. Another hothead called Judas sprang out of Galilee when Coponius was governor, exhorting the Jews to resist Roman taxes; even if they failed they would be glorious, because God was on their side. And in Pilate's time, just as he arrived in Judaea, a man called John appeared in the desert, shouting about the Kingdom of God and the mountains tumbling. Was this dangerous? What was it supposed to mean? The "pretext of public welfare," as Josephus called it, was intensely worrying; more so was the flammable mixture of politics and religion. All risings in Judaea had this cast. The hand of God, not merely of His people, was raised against the Romans; His sword would smite them; His anointing floated about the rebel leaders, balsam and frankincense, the odor of holiness. Those prophets who seemed the maddest of all might be precisely those who could not be ignored.

Nor did these discontents ever disappear. They lay under the hide of the land. It might be true, as Josephus remarked, that Judaea was a nice place in parts, with "a light and fertile soil for agriculture, thick woods, abundant fruit, singularly sweet water and a higher milk yield than other districts"; it was true that Herod had scattered it with magnificent fortresses done up, like the palace in Jerusalem, with mosaics and swimming pools and painted marble. But to the north and east of Jerusalem the wilderness unfolded, apparently empty. The bare limestone hills were scattered only with stones, or with sheep that resembled stones. The dry fissures held no water, only washes of gravel. Brown thistles and thornbushes were the only crops, and the hilltop villages were coated, like the hills themselves, with baked gray dust. Tacitus wrote later that the whole landscape seemed to bear the marks of "celestial vengeance," though he himself thought it was only the exhalations from the great dead lake that withered the flowers into black dust and, near the coast, petrified the alluvial sands into rivulets of glass.

In the great Judaean survey made by Quirinus in A.D. 6, just after Rome had assumed direct control, all these places had been inspected, their people counted and their taxes assessed. Although the governor of Judaea was evidently thought too junior to carry out a census himself, it was part of Pilate's job to know these numbers: to see why this collection of mud and stones could not pay tribute, to see why that goat-infested hollow needed a road or a water supply. In practice he preferred, as any Roman would have done, to keep to the Jordan valley, the lakeshores or the haven of Caesarea, where he could sit in the shade of palms with a plate of fresh dates and a flask of decent wine. But his domain was largely mountains, wilderness and trouble.

From time to time he would not have been able to avoid this part of it. Perhaps he was carried, but his litter was more suited to the streets of Caesarea, and out in the desert there was no one to impress. Few sights would have been odder, in the howling waste, than the governor's litter with its gilded wood and shimmering silk curtains, tipping this way and that among the rocks. It was safer to ride, though not alone; the imperial governor of Nearer Spain had been killed by a peasant not long before while traveling unguarded in just such country, steep, pathless, strewn with stones. Pilate therefore went surrounded by military outriders under heavy arms. Even then, the emptiness of the scene was terrifying. In the imagination of the Romans the desert was riddled with caves and the caves stuffed with *lestai* and *sicarii,* bandits with small curved swords. As you passed a hillside, armed men the color of dust might rise up from the ground, as men had sprung from the stones thrown by Deucalion to repopulate the earth. And the far beckoning blue of the sea was no sea at all, only poisonous Asphaltites where, as over Avernus, the birds dropped dead as they flew.

It was a job; and it was a continuous bad dream.

"EVERY NATIVE, I verily believe, is corrupt," wrote one governor. Another, kinder, confided to a friend: "As you know, the vast majority of the people are ignorant and illiterate and easily swayed by sentiment and emotion. And yet, it always seems to me wonderful that in spite of trouble and disturbances, British rule in India has lasted and continues notwithstanding."

To Christ's biographers of the late nineteenth and early twentieth centuries, in Europe as well as in Britain, the plume-hatted representatives of the King-Emperor seemed to be much like Pilate. Their problems were seen as comparable, different mostly in scale. A sunbaked, hard terrain in which you were forced to seek breezes, fans and shade. A surface veneer of roads, government buildings, imported legal structures and a pompous shared vernacular; but beneath that sulking clerks, untrustworthy officials, even outright bandits. Every so often—for their own good, naturally—the people's rights under law were suspended. They could be arrested without warrant and detained without trial, and officers acting in good faith against unruly elements were not obliged to justify their actions. As one writer put it in 1931, drawing an explicit comparison with Pilate and his circumstances, "There is almost no severity of provincial repression which will not be enthusiastically supported by a cultivated upper class at home."

Imperial power was not absolute. Local princelings ruled in their own states, controlled the local factions, were more gorgeously arrayed and had better table manners. One complained that the wife of the governor general ate her cheese with her knife. They were schooled in England, had beautifully pointed diction, drank tea at the right time, and brimmed with courteous contempt. Yet these were the easiest Indians to get on with. In the north the Sikhs were heavily armed with knives and swords, fiercely defensive of their Golden Temple; as late as 1919, four hundred Sikh protesters, this time without arms, were killed by General Reginald Dyer's troops at Amritsar. General Dyer had been sent to restore calm after rioting in the town, and was angry to find that his orders banning public meetings were ignored. After the massacre, he said he would have used the machine guns on his armored cars if he had been able to get the vehicles into the square. Those Sikhs who continued to cause trouble were forced to crawl on hands and knees, or were publicly flogged. It was natural, our writer of 1931 continued, that contemporary scholars should seek to defend Pilate, since to condemn him "might lead to unpleasant contemporary applications."

Governors trained for India by cultivating social graces. A nominee for governor in the 1920s had daily riding lessons in Rotten Row, studied marksmanship so as to be able to pick off tigers from the swaying perch of a howdah, and took up ballroom dancing. He learned no Indian language, and he studied cultural peculiarities only to avoid giving social offense. His day, after all, was largely diplomatic and ceremonial. A ride in the cool dawn, breakfast, council meetings, or the handling of reports; lunch with guests, more meetings, interviews, more reports; official dinners, balls and receptions. When he was traveling, the state Rolls-Royces would wait in the drive with their motors running, followed by lorries for the luggage and the servants, and liveried men would stand with torches at twenty-yard intervals along the railway line.

Why were they there? To claim and hold and preserve the empire, its language and laws. To keep revenues flowing from the landowners to the coffers of the imperial government, according to Cornwallis's Permanent

Settlement, which had assessed what taxes the land could sustain. To relieve famine, build aqueducts, lay roads, educate children, and set up a
model of civilization. If necessary, governors could be kingmakers; but in
general they preferred to keep power out of Indian hands. Racial superiority decreed it, just as it decreed a lower level of proof in trials and
harder seats in railway carriages. If you gave Indians some partnership in
governing, one governor wrote, this would instill in them "an increased
feeling of existing subordination and a realisation of everything by which
this subordination was expressed."

In 1925, Lord Reading, then governor general, concluded that "in
ultimate analysis, the strength of the British position is that we are in
India for the good of India." A year later, on his way home, he carried the
thought further:

> As I wend my way home, I return with a deeper realisation of the benefi-
> cent outlook of the British Empire, with a wider understanding of its du-
> ties and responsibilities, with a larger conception of the influence and
> power of that great commonwealth of nations. I glory in the high purpose
> it is our duty as citizens of the Empire to seek to achieve; in the moral
> standpoint of public service we try to inculcate; in the endeavour to im-
> prove the conditions of the poorer and less fortunate people, in the earnest
> wish that this country may be the better for our efforts, that we may have
> contributed to the cause of humanity, and that we may have assisted in
> promoting the welfare and happiness of India.

So wrote one of the better governors on one of his better days. Yet even
he was not above mass arrests, racial snobbery and unbalanced trials. One
of these was the trial of an inoffensive-looking, clerkish man in a dhoti,
with spindly bare legs, who had come to visit him at the viceregal palace
some months before. Reading admitted that Gandhi's moral thinking
was "on a high altitude"; he was bothered by, but could not work out, his
politics. What most impressed him was that when he ordered tea,
Gandhi ordered hot water, and would not touch his cup until the governor general had touched his. "I have to admit I liked him," he wrote afterward. Yet he also felt he had to crush him as a fomenter of dangerous
ideas, and did so as soon as he could act with impunity, immediately after
an expensive and successful visit by the Prince of Wales. His standing

with the King-Emperor was secure; his management of India was applauded; a nationalist uprising seemed unlikely. The chink of teacups could be replaced by the iron fist.

Gandhi was tried and convicted on a charge of sedition. It was the same charge on which Pilate tried and convicted Christ.

IV.

H E LEFT ALMOST NO TRACES behind him. No roads, no milestones, no public buildings. Some miles from Jerusalem runs an aqueduct that may be his, solidly built of brick and lined with lead. Beyond that, all that remains is a block of calcareous stone and a handful of coins.

The stone was found at Caesarea in the summer of 1961. By then, nothing remained of the fabulous city but traces of the rampart, a few scattered ruins of the Temple of Augustus, and two colossal right feet from the statues of Augustus and Roma: feet that Pilate had probably grasped to give him safety, or to bring him luck. Herod's granite blocks still shone at the edge of the pier, beside the tumbled walls of his theater.

Among those blocks was Pilate's stone. In the manner of the ancient stones built into the walls of medieval Italian buildings, this one had been hacked from its original position and put to another use. It formed a landing between flights of steps at one of the entrances to Herod's theater when, in later years, the theater was rebuilt to stage water sports. The endless passage of sports fans' feet had worn away the inscription and chipped away the sides until almost nothing remained but this:

S TIBERIEVM
TIVS PILATVS
ECTVS IVDA--E

Most photographs of the stone show it against a neutral background, as in a museum. One, startlingly different, shows it as it was found at the edge of the sea. The chiseled letters on the small, smooth slab grow out of a massive rock encrusted with limpets and barnacles. Beyond it are other ruins, low spars of stone lying in shallow water. The sun, setting, bathes the scene in a light the color of old bronze. This might be a battlefield strewn with bodies and rusted blades, except that all have been caught and half-covered by the bright evening wash of the sea.

For weeks the Italian team of archaeologists pored over the stone, cleaned it with water, brushed away the sand. They willed the letters to reveal themselves among the dancing molecules of limestone. In the end, their best guess was this:

CAESARIENSIBUS TIBERIEVM
PONTIVS PILATVS
PRAEFECTVS IVDAEAE
DEDIT

"Pontius Pilate, Prefect of Judaea, has given this Tiberieum to the citizens of Caesarea."

The second-best guess presumed that Pilate would have preferred to offer something to the gods of the imperial house rather than to the Caesareans; and perhaps that was true.

DIS AVGVSTIS TIBERIEVM
PONTIVS PILATVS
PRAEFECTUS IVDAEAE
FECIT, DEDICAVIT

"Pontius Pilate, Prefect of Judaea, has made this Tiberieum and dedicated it to the Augustan gods."

The block was of limestone quarried at Kabbara, a few miles north of the town; it was thirty-three inches high, twenty-seven inches broad and eight and a half inches thick, with lettering two and a half inches high. This suggests it was at eye level, where people could read it, in a building of modest size. It is strange, even revealing, that the inscription is in Latin, since Greek was the common language of all public notices at that time in the east. Even here, perhaps, Pilate's love of Rome insisted on showing itself; or his devotion to Tiberius, who, though fluent in Greek, once apologized to the Senate for using the word "monopoly." It is revealing, too, that at a time when abbreviation (especially of titles) was the rule and fashion in inscriptions, Pilate proudly spelled out in full the words "Praefectus Judaeae."

That said, it was not an impressive piece of work. The lettering is deeply incised, but cramped and irregular. "Tiberieum" is elegantly done, but for the name of the governor the inscriber has let himself go: he follows the contemporary fashion of making some letters, especially the "T" and the "I" of "Pilatus," taller than others, but the effect is slightly untidy. Perhaps it was hard to find good stonecutters in Judaea. But Pilate was presumably satisfied with it, and possibly even wanted his name to be inscribed that way. It would not have graced the building without his approval and a ceremony of dedication, with flowers and fat-laden smoke, on the breezy site beside the water.

The word "Tiberieum" may have been Pilate's own invention; it occurs nowhere else. Perhaps because it was new, he made sure the final "e" carried a flamboyant accent to lengthen the vowel, and took this convention through to the fourth line (where an accent is all that remains), accenting the "e" of "dedit" or "dedicavit" in a way that was unusual and even unnecessary. Yet the construction of the word was common enough. It meant that this was a building in honor of Tiberius, just as a Caesareum was a building in honor of Augustus. The usual centerpiece of such buildings was a shrine, but around the shrine—as in the famous Caesareum in Alexandria—might be courtyards, libraries, picture galleries, even "sacred groves." The budget at Caesarea would not stretch as far as that, and Pilate's Tiberieum was possibly closer to a basilica or a meeting hall. But it could well have been a temple, in which the emperor's image was worshiped every month with offerings of wine and incense, and prayers offered for his health and the prosperity of Rome.

Either way, Tiberius would have found the building embarrassing. According to Suetonius, religion meant almost nothing to him; he cared only for divination and the more obscure sides of literature. He rebuked people who called him "Lord," was highly annoyed to be addressed as a god, and once asked a man who had called his work "sacred" to change the word to "laborious." He had, of course, deified Augustus, but Pliny was of the opinion that Tiberius had given the emperor "his place among the stars" merely to reflect upon himself the glory of the man who had adopted him, and to terrorize the people. He continued to resist suggestions of temples or cults of himself, at least in the west, maintaining that the emperor could be worshiped only after his death and that, meanwhile, "my temples are in your hearts."

On the other hand, people knew he did not usually mean what he said. Even in Rome his effigy was used as a sacred amulet by criminals, who knew that by clasping this image of a god they could escape prosecution; and in the eastern empire, in Asia, Tiberius had at last allowed a temple to be built to him. In Rome in 27 the Senate suggested that one of the city's hills should be given extra veneration because, when fire had ravaged it, the only object spared had been a statue of Tiberius in a house there. Far away in Caesarea, hearing these stories, Pilate might have imagined he would bolster both himself and Rome with his intemperate devotions.

His coins tell a similar story. Prefects' coins were tiny; the largest ones issued under Pilate were only three quarters of an inch across, weighing about two grams. They were worth a demi-quadrans, or the eighth part of an as; two of them could get you into the public baths in Rome. All the coins that survive are of bronze. They were simple small change for the man in the street, but not without use as propaganda.

When Pilate arrived in Judaea, the coins of Gratus were in circulation. These carried uncontroversial devices, with a wreath or a cut branch of vine on the obverse and, on the reverse, various symbols of fruitfulness: double cornucopias, lilies, branches of leaves. The emperor's name was abbreviated and given in Greek. Other, weightier coins in circulation included silver denarii with the head of the emperor, but these were not minted in Judaea because they were offensive to the Jews.

Gratus had found a way around Jewish sensibilities with his branches and flowers, but Pilate wanted to honor Tiberius properly. Since a portrait was unacceptable to his subjects, a graven image that violated the second commandment, Pilate devised the next best, next most offensive thing: images of objects used in Roman religious rites. These were not his own design. They were in circulation in other parts of the empire, but were not recommended for Judaea, and were never seen there until he introduced them. Some scholars doubt whether this was his idea; they note that he issued no more coins after A.D. 31, when Sejanus fell. But Sejanus, unlike Pilate, had no motive for flaunting Roman superiority in Judaea.

Some of Pilate's coins showed the *simpulum,* a small vessel used to pour out oil or wine upon the altar. Others showed the *lituus,* or augur's wand, as carried in the right hand when reading the future from the slippery entrails of beasts. On the reverse of his coins he kept his symbols innocuous: three bending ears of barley, a wreath with berries. This side at least would not annoy the Jews, although it made no difference in one way: his coins would still be unacceptable in the Temple. The reason why the outer court was full of changing tables—tables soon to be upended by Jesus—was because no coin with a pagan symbol could be used, or even dropped in a box, in that holy place.

The *simpulum* was the holiest of these images: "How pleasing to the gods are the *simpula* of the priests!" Cicero had written. These were made of clay as a mark of respect to the earth, the mother of all things. The *lituus,* too, was deeply sacramental: it was the wand by which Augustus had saved the world by establishing universal peace, the instrument through which the will of the gods was made manifest in him. It was also, for those who knew, a particular sop to Tiberius and his love of divination. His mother had divined his own birth by warming an egg in her hands until a cockerel hatched from it; an eagle had perched on his house in Rhodes before he was made emperor; he was warned of a popular revolt when he found his pet snake eaten by ants. As emperor, although he banned the use of astrology by others, he spent so much time in the company of his astrologer, Thrasyllus, and studied the subject so avidly, Suetonius said, that he could even tell when his dreams were deceiving him. At the end of his life, he decided to depend on divination to fix the succession to the empire; it fell to Gaius because one morning he came in to Tiberius first, while his rival Drusus waited for breakfast. All the emperor's frightening fascination was caught up in that magic wand, curled like a seahorse, that Pilate impressed upon his coins. And around the image lay his title, "Tiberius Kaisaros," spelled out by Pilate in full, just as he had spelled out "Prefect of Judaea."

Beyond the coins and dedicated buildings lay more routine expressions of respect. Governors made annual vows, with prayers and celebrations, on the anniversary of the emperor's accession, and at the beginning of the year they offered public prayers for his safety and that of the state. They were also bound to remember his birthday. (In his early years Tiberius would not allow any special celebration, but this changed as he got older.) As in the British Raj, imperial birthdays meant special services, ceremonies and reviews of the troops. Condemned men were usually not punished on that day, and the crucified were taken down and allowed to be buried; "for it was thought fitting," says Philo, "that the dead should also have the advantage of some kind treatment on the emperor's birthday, and also that the sanctity of the festival should be maintained." Tiberius' birthday was on the sixteenth of November, the sixteenth before the Kalends of December, and Pilate's dutiful note to Rome would doubtless have resembled Pliny's of a little later: "It is my prayer, sir, that this birthday and many others will bring you the greatest happiness, and that in health and strength you may add to the immortal fame and glory of your reputation by ever-new achievements." Doubtless, too, the form reply came back from the emperor's secretary: "Thank you. I hope the gods ensure you're right."

Between the emperor and his servant-governor there was an almost continuous stream of communication. Governors were expected to keep a minute record of everything that happened, every day. They were issued *tabellae,* thin leaves of wood coated with wax on which to jot notes and write memoranda, and from these they drafted reports. These formed the basis of the *commentarii,* the governor's official diary. Copies of the *commentarii* were filed in the provincial archives, and edited extracts were sent to Rome. Governors—especially imperial deputies like Pilate—did not do this for their own amusement. They did it for the emperor, as his eyes and ears on the spot.

Surviving records show that the writing was done in cursive script, on parchment or papyrus, by a secretary. The governor then read them through and wrote, in his own hand, "lecta," "read." These reports were sometimes posted up in public, like news sheets, but eventually they were pasted on a long roll to be stored in the archives. Similar reports went out in letter form to the emperor or to colleagues, sometimes written by the governor himself in moments of emergency but generally, again, dictated to the secretary. These, too, would be scanned for errors. That done, the governor sealed the report or letter with his signet ring. This gesture was as personal as a signature and, according to Cicero, was to be used with as much circumspection: as he advised his governor brother Quintus, "Let your signet ring be your very self."

Day by day, this was Pilate's routine: dictation, scanning, signing, sealing. Rummaging in his memory as he fiddled with pens at his desk, or paced the room with his hands behind his back; the squeak and scratch of a reed pen; the search for phrases that might justify, conceal, cast in a flattering light; the ring pulled from the fourth finger of his left hand and pressed into the yielding wax. The worries did not end when the letter was sent. Ships were slow, and couriers could be delayed; letters often crossed, or arrived two at a time. The most important letters were sent out in duplicate with duplicate messengers, but even this did not guarantee safe delivery. Worst of all, the governor's report was sometimes not the only version of events the emperor saw. More than once, Pilate's "subjects" wrote their own letters to Rome complaining about him. On the last occasion, they succeeded in removing him.

Messages arrived in such quantity that the emperors were reduced to reading them as they were being shaved and while they watched the games; they seldom climbed into their litters but a sackful of letters went with them, to be read between the jolts of the journey. When Caesar was murdered, his arms were full of papers. A wise governor would have seen some virtue in not burdening the emperor with unnecessary words from the provinces. Yet alongside the temptation to leave "the sovereign of earth and sea" alone, there was a stronger urge to get his attention and to flatter him.

None of Pilate's letters survive, nor do any of his reports. Yet he presumably wrote from time to time, as Pliny wrote from his postings in Pontus and Bithynia, hoping for imperial guidance on matters large and small. An emperor, it seemed, could be bothered with most problems: the promotion of school friends to the Senate, the correct form of punishment for slaves discovered in the army, permission for a wife to use the Imperial Post to visit her aunt, the site of a new bathhouse. ("I've looked around Prusa and chosen one which is occupied at present by the unsightly ruins of what I am told was once a fine house. We could remove this eyesore and embellish the city without pulling down any existing structure.") He could be asked about suitable prizes for winning the games, and petitioned for extra troops to control traffic. Other governors sent nature notes: the governor of Gaul reported Nereids, bristling mermaids, washed up on the beaches of his province and singing sadly as they died, while the governor of Africa reported an encounter with a giant squid ("its head the size of a ninety-gallon barrel, its tentacles thirty feet long and covered with suckers the size of plates") on which he had set his hunting dogs. The governor of the Alps reported a sighting of an ibis, never previously seen outside Egypt, and the governor of Lycia in Asia Minor sent an account of his night inside a giant plane tree, "where the sound of the rain falling on the leaves was more delightful than any gleaming marble or gilded paneling."

What could have intrigued Tiberius about Pilate's little patch? The skeleton of the sea monster to which Andromeda had been exposed had turned up in Jaffa, forty feet long, and with ribs bigger than an elephant's; but it had been taken away long ago. A chunk of bitumen from Asphaltites, intriguing as it was, would land in the imperial palace like an insult. In any case, an emperor's interest in a small province like Judaea was not expected to be great. Nonetheless, anything that touched remotely on the dignity of the emperor or the enforcement of the *pax Romana* demanded imperial notification and imperial instructions.

So Pilate doubtless wrote, although the only letters that "survive" are medieval inventions. His letters probably began with the laborious official formula to someone of higher rank, S.V.B.E.V., *Si vales bene ego valeo,* "If you are in good health, I am well too." They proceeded with utmost care—Augustus had once dismissed a governor for misspelling *ipsi* as *ixi* in a letter—and doubtless they ended on much the same note as Pliny's, if less elegantly expressed: "I trust you will think that my obedience was correct, for I am anxious for every word and deed of mine to receive the sanction of your own supreme standards." With emperors as suspicious as Tiberius and his successors, the sycophancy had to be laid on thick, not least because governors were too far away to gauge the political temperature at home. (A man who was out of favor or had lost his influence would be dismissed with the single word *friget,* "he's cold.") When Flaccus, governor of Egypt, was trying to make things right between himself and the emperor Gaius, his written dispatches "overflowed with flattery," according to his enemy Philo, while his public speeches were "strings of fawning words and long screeds of insincere encomium." And for all that, in his case as in Pilate's, it is never clear whether the emperor gave him much of a reply.

By the time Pilate was appointed, in 26, Tiberius had already been persuaded by Sejanus to retire from Rome and from much of the business of government. He was, after all, sixty-eight years old, and although his health was good he was worn out by fears, suspicions and debaucheries. The rugged cliffs of Capri and the deep blue sea entranced him, not least because access was so difficult. When a fisherman scrambled up the rocks behind him to present him with a fresh-caught mullet, Tiberius was so terrified at this breach of security that he ordered the man's face to be scrubbed raw with the fish. (When the man cried out, "Thank goodness I didn't give him the crab," Tiberius ordered him to be scrubbed with the crab as well.) In Capri, however, he gave plenty of receptions and entertainments, and it may have been here that Pilate was entrusted with his province. The commission was not necessarily bestowed in person, but it was a personal appointment; so it is likely that, on this occasion at least, the two men met formally.

Pilate had almost certainly seen the emperor before. If he was a Praetorian he might even have walked beside him, providing part of the constant bodyguard that kept Tiberius safe from the knives he imagined under every arm. If not, he would still have seen him at a distance: perhaps at the funeral of Augustus in A.D. 14, when Tiberius had appeared, in dark robes, to offer incense before the body and to deliver the oration; or across the arena at the games Tiberius so disliked, where Pilate would have found himself watching every gesture, every movement, every change of color and expression on the imperial face.

Tiberius was tall, robust and reasonably handsome, according to Suetonius, but his face was often pimply or patched with plasters. He wore his thinning hair untidily long at the nape of the neck, a style Pilate may have copied, and cut it only when the moon was in conjunction with the sun. He was shortsighted, which made him peer at people with his large unblinking eyes; though, as Dio Cassius noted, he could see well enough in the dark. When he gave receptions he liked to take leave of his guests by standing in the center of the room with a lictor beside him and addressing each person by name, sometimes clasping their hands. This may have been the treatment Pilate received and the touch he remembered, as the fan remembers the touch of the star. We know, too, that Tiberius talked with deliberate slowness, a sort of affected drawl, and made slow movements with his fingers; but those fingers (which touched Pilate's?) were also strong enough, Suetonius said, to bore a hole in an apple, or to draw blood when they flicked the head of a child.

Reading this man was exceptionally difficult: indeed, it was forbidden, as some men believed it was also forbidden to explore the nature of God. Every ancient writer remarked how dour and cryptic he was. Dio spoke for all of them:

He never let what he desired appear in his conversation, and what he said he wanted he usually did not desire at all. . . . He would show anger over matters that were very far from upsetting him, and make a show of affability where he was most irritated. He would pretend to pity those whom he severely punished, and would retain a grudge against those whom he pardoned . . . in short, he thought it bad policy for a sovereign to reveal his thoughts. . . . He became angry if anyone gave evidence of understanding him, and he put many to death for no other offense than that of having grasped what he meant.

His friends, confidants and helpers were very few. Suetonius estimated that he needed twenty people at close hand to help administer the empire, but that he had killed all but two or three of them. He trusted no one, and had a gloominess about him that repelled intimacy. In his early years, suspicion had made him modest and even diffident. He was shrewd and wise then, despite Augustus' reservations about his "sourness"; he literally fell over himself to get away from flatterers. But in his killing mood, which lasted for most of the time Pilate was governor of Judaea, he executed his enemies on the least word of any informer; and informers were everywhere. "All offenses were capital," wrote Suetonius, "even speaking a few words without any bad intention." Tacitus said that if Tiberius' soul had been exposed it would have shown, like the scourged back of a slave, the lash marks of his cruelty.

Those who offended him were dragged through the streets with hooks, sent sprawling down the Gemonian Steps and thrown into the Tiber, if they did not kill themselves first. Nobody could trust his favor, even if they thought they enjoyed it. There is a sharp chill in the words of Seneca when he describes how Montanus, a mediocre poet known as "the sunrise and sunset man," was famous for being touched by *amicitia Tiberii . . . et frigore,* both Tiberius's friendship and his coldness. Whatever may be true or untrue in the Gospel accounts of the trial of Jesus, one moment, from John, is highly plausible: Pilate's total loss of composure when the Jews suggest that, if he spares Jesus, "You are not Caesar's friend."

Was he ever his friend? The Jews at the trial used the official title, *philos tou kaisaros,* attached to members of the emperor's innermost circle, but there is no evidence that Pilate was ever so close. The Jews appear only to have meant that he was loyal to Tiberius and sensitive to his interests. The later story of an imperial connection through marriage to Procula was almost certainly invented. Yet a friendship of some sort was not socially impossible. There was always the example of the "mere Roman knight" Sejanus: the one who had made the emperor laugh when, for others, even a tempered smile was unsafe. If Pilate had been recommended by Sejanus, he could have been Tiberius' golden boy for a time. Yet to be close to the emperor, any emperor, was no particular advantage. Juvenal said you could spot these men at a glance, by their drawn white faces. Imperial favor not only laid a man open to the emperor's jealousies, but tarred him by association with his excesses and his horrors.

These Tiberius displayed in plenty. He was nicknamed Biberius Caldius Mero ("Tippler of Hot Wine with No Water Added") because he drank too much, and the Old Goat for his lecheries on Capri, frolics so disgusting that the Victorian translators of Suetonius could mark them only with rows of blushing asterisks. Grottoes were made in the woods where his buggery could take place unobserved, and off the rocky beaches of Capri he indulged in naked swimming-and-sex sessions with minors of both sexes. These things were the talk of Rome. Tiberius was mocked on the stage, where the goat jokes brought the house down; and in more serious vein, around 27, an anonymous poem appeared.

> *Fastidit vinum, quia iam sitit iste cruorem;*
> *Tam bibit hunc avide, quam bibit ante merum.*

> All he wants now
> Is undiluted gore,
> Just as he guzzled
> Undiluted wine before.

At some slow remove, this talk must have reached Caesarea too. By all accounts, the public so loathed Tiberius that when his death was announced they could scarcely contain themselves for joy, although they were terrified of showing it until the death was confirmed. This fear and loathing also suffused the city, and the empire, when he was alive. It is not hard to imagine dinner parties in Caesarea at which Pilate's guests, visiting from Rome, would regale him with blood-soaked stories and sexual details that would make the women cover their ears; while Pilate would listen in the awful, sinking knowledge that this was the man to whom he owed his career, from whom he drew his authority, and whose safety he prayed for. Doubtless in some sense he could disconnect the man from the office, as people under any regime can close their eyes to the personal sins of their rulers. But there may have been times when he could not; when, amid the genteel litter of wine beakers, chicken bones, roses and clowns, the prefect of Judaea would find himself suddenly sickened by the obscenity of his protector, as by the flopping fall of an augur's bird.

V.

Pilate stayed in Judaea ten years. This was much longer than some of his predecessors, but it did not necessarily mean that he was doing a good job. Tiberius did not believe in changing his lieutenants abroad. Suetonius supposed this was because he did not care about government in general, and because he especially wanted to avoid provoking unrest overseas. Tacitus remarked of one aged record holder—twenty-four years in various governorships—that he was kept on "not for any outstanding talent, but because he was competent and no more."

Josephus had a more interesting theory. Tiberius was a man who made an art of procrastination, and could justify any form of it. He kept prisoners waiting for trials and the condemned rotting in prison, to draw out the agony of punishment. Ambassadors, too, were always made to hang about, in case new ones were about to be appointed who would have to be treated with all over again. The same excruciating slowness and shrewdness, Josephus supposed, colored his attitude to the running of the empire.

Tiberius thought that all governors were grasping, out to wring as much from their provinces as they could. If they were given short tours, it meant that they would fleece their subjects unbearably in the effort to fill their pockets before they were recalled. If, on the other hand, they were left in place, they would be sated with their spoil and become less keen on pillaging. The emperor's unlovely analogy—typical of a man his schoolteacher described as "mud mixed with blood"—was of flies swarm-

ing on a wound. If you drove the flies away, new ones would settle that
were famished for food. If you left the old flies alone, they would become
so gorged with blood that their bite no longer hurt.

So Pilate, trusted or ignored, remained for a decade. His job carried
with it certain expectations. Clearly Tiberius assumed, and Pilate assumed, that he would enrich himself personally; his salary, of around
100,000 sesterces a year, was understood as a basis only. But he was not
supposed to be brutal about it. This was both dangerous and counter-
productive. Of one governor of Egypt, who suddenly sent the emperor
more money than his province was down for, Tiberius remarked: "I told
him to shear the sheep, not flay it." Senatorial governors, at his insis-
tence, were regularly condemned for extortion. Contrary to his style in
domestic affairs, Tiberius' advice to his men abroad was almost benevolent. Suetonius records him saying—and possibly Pilate heard him saying—words that now carry an unavoidable ring of irony and poignancy.
A governor, he said, ought to be "a good shepherd."

Was Pilate ever that? There is no Roman assessment of his career.
The chapters of Tacitus' *Annals* for 30 and 31, which might have mentioned him, have vanished. Instead the most famous summary of his career comes from Philo, that highly educated Jewish contemporary who so
hated (with some reason) the treatment of his people by the Romans. His
description of Pilate was tucked into an impassioned letter supposedly
sent to the Emperor Gaius by Agrippa, Prince of the Jews, in the course
of his ill-fated diplomatic mission to protest against an imperial statue in
the Temple. Agrippa cited Pilate as a governor who, though bad and un-
reasonably devoted to Roman symbols, would not have been allowed to
go that far. He was "inflexible, stubborn and cruel." He was induced to
behave decently only because he was so afraid that Tiberius would hear
bad things of him, and there was plenty bad to report: "venality, violence, robbery, assault, abusive behavior, frequent executions without
trial and endless savage ferocity."

Philo's words have weight because he was a contemporary of Pilate's,
and some of his charges are backed up elsewhere. But Agrippa's letter
had a purpose that depended on painting Pilate black. It was meant to
show Tiberius in the best light, the mild and wise ruler contrasted with
his rapacious deputy; and it was also intended to advance Agrippa's own
claims to be the ruler of Judaea, the soothing Jewish presence that the
province needed. Philo's habit, in any case, is to present characters in

fierce black and white, either good or bad. In *Flaccus,* his book-length attack on the governor who failed to prevent the pogrom of 36 in Alexandria, Roman governors are summed up as a breed in much the same words he applied to Pilate specifically. Philo may have had good reason to hate Pilate, but he was not disposed to treat anyone impartially.

Josephus, writing forty years later and with Roman sympathies, provides a milder view. Although he does not favor Pilate, he does not object to him particularly. He relates the governor's most brutal actions in detail, but never accuses him generally of anything worse than "tumult." When the governor of Syria eventually sent Pilate home, Josephus reports that he rescinded the tax on grain sales; he does not say that it was burdensome, but he implies that it was part of a regime that was hated. As a Romanophile, perhaps he was too kind to Pilate; or perhaps he thought the governor's reckless and clumsy actions spoke for themselves. Yet Josephus could be sharp enough in his accusations against other governors who were violent and corrupt: witness his descriptions of the "mad insolence" of Sabinus, or his verdict on Gessius Florus, governor of Judaea under Nero:

> It was as though he had been dispatched to Judaea on purpose to display his crimes, ostentatiously showing his lawlessness to our nation, never omitting any rapine or unjust punishment; for he was not to be moved by pity, and was never satisfied with any amount of gain . . . but went fair shares with the robbers.

On Pilate, however, Josephus passed no judgment, and sometimes gave him the benefit of the doubt. Over ten years, he cites three incidents in which the governor provoked his subjects, once severely enough to induce them to appeal to Rome against him. Out of this, and out of the Gospel accounts, there emerges a character consistent in many ways with Philo's picture: obstinate, proud, patriotic, cunning, flippant, heavy-handed. But the obstinacy wavers, in Josephus too, even becoming repentance; the heavy-handedness is sometimes unintended, the result of incompetence and insecurity; and between the provocations, whether malicious or thoughtless, Judaea is at peace. The "endless savage ferocity" is not substantiated. What we seem to have is someone immature and hotheaded, entranced by schemes that don't work, who seems less on the edge of destroying the Jews than of destroying himself.

A temperament like this was not unknown in governors. Cicero rebuked his brother, a man of high intelligence, for similar "violent outbursts of temper" and "abusive or insulting language" in his post in Asia. These were worse in his first year, because, Cicero supposed, "the general insolence you came across took you by surprise, and struck you as intolerable"; but his second year was kinder, "because you improved in tolerance and mildness as the result of getting used to things and reasoning things out, and also, I believe, because you read my letters."

If any such progress occurred in Pilate's case, it was not recorded. He may simply have lacked good advice, or not listened to it. But he was not a Jew-hater as we, in our supposedly more civilized times, would understand the term. He did not like them; he felt superior. But in some ways, he believed he was there to make their lives better. And most of all he wanted to leave Judaea in the good graces of the man-god who had sent him there. Cicero's words in *The Laws* may not have been far-fetched as a motto for Pilate's enthusiasm: "For Rome it is our duty to die, to her to give ourselves entirely, to place on her altar and, as it were, to offer to her service all that we possess." The most sentimental hymns of the British Empire said exactly that.

VI.

So the devotion played itself out. It centered around the issue of the emperor's graven image. The Jews would not accept it anywhere, in any form. Pilate's predecessors, as far as we know, had respected Jewish sensibilities. The new governor, more arrogant or more desperate to please, was not inclined to.

The emperor's image belonged on all buildings, monuments, coins and insignia, and in most cities of the empire it was standard practice to put it there. Philo describes how the city of Alexandria was full of tributes to the emperor, "shields and gilded crowns and slabs and inscriptions." Most especially, his image belonged on the sacred standards of the army, which, along with the silver eagles, were carried with every unit and brought good luck in battle. After victories, incense was burned before them as if before gods; on holidays they were anointed with perfumed oil, despite their sharp points and cutting edges; and the very precinct of the camp where they were stored was considered holy. When

Germanicus went back to Germany after the defeat of Varus to restore the honor of Rome, his piety consisted not merely in burying the dead, but in recovering the standards.

The image attached to the standards was a gold medallion about six inches across, enclosed in a border engraved like a triumphal wreath bound up with ribbons. The whole thing, about the size of a carving plate, was attached to the standard a foot from the top, where the insignia met the shaft, and could be taken off if necessary. Not only the image of Tiberius but also that of the favorite, Sejanus, glittered on the standard poles when Pilate took over in Judaea. Only the legions in Syria had refused to display it.

Pilate's sense of security in Caesarea depended not merely on the armor and number of his men, but also on the gleaming spiritual barrier provided by the standards. He needed their protection even more on his rare visits to Jerusalem. Yet his predecessors had conceded that the fully decorated standards would never be taken there, into the city sacred to the Jews. Instead, they were dismantled and the images were left in the guardroom at Caesarea, among the extra blankets and the broken swords. Jerusalem was thus the only city in the empire where people did not bow in the public squares to the image of the emperor. Indeed, it was the only city where they had no glimpse of imperial paraphernalia at all.

The moment Pilate arrived in Judaea, according to Josephus, he decided on a different policy. The next time the troops were ordered to Jerusalem for garrison duty, they would not dismantle the standards but would take them, fully accoutred, under cover of darkness. Still in the dark, they would fix them to the walls of the Antonia fortress. If Pilate was thinking tactically at this point—rather than vengefully or emotionally—he might have reasoned that the fortress was not a holy part of the city; it already had Romans in it. He was simply planting Rome's standards in a Roman-occupied place, as any conquering general would do. Then, when the Jews woke up, the beauty and power of the emperor's authority would hit them in the face. The first rays of the morning sun would gild his profile all along the battlements: Tiberius, Tiberius, Tiberius, Tiberius.

In the *Antiquities,* Josephus suggests that this was part of a larger, more outrageous plan: to move the army to winter quarters in Jerusalem and "to abolish the laws of the Jews." But it would have been odd to move the troops in winter to a colder, snowier place, and in his earlier work, *The Jewish War,* he does not mention any such motive. Instead, the aim of the standards policy seems to have been much simpler: to show the Jews who was in charge at the start of Pilate's term. He did not, after all, parade the standards flagrantly through the streets by day; he had just enough sensibility to do it in the dark. Abolishing the laws of the Jews was nowhere in the brief of even a foolishly headstrong governor of Judaea.

The new standards policy had only one airing. Some days after the garrison had gone to Jerusalem, Pilate awoke to find a huge crowd of Jews outside his palace. They were right below the walls, under the windows. Most had plainly walked the sixty miles from Jerusalem. Some had their feet bound with rags; many, since it was almost winter, were bundled in cloaks and overcoats. The crowd seethed with noise or perhaps, more unnervingly, with silence. And it stretched as far as he could see.

According to Josephus, the Jews petitioned him for days to take the standards down. For most of the time they did so with ritual swaying and incantations, praying that his soul would be softened and that he would see sense. Josephus suggests that they also negotiated directly; but perhaps they did not get too close. Pilate would have suffered them to approach and salute him with the usual deep bow of subject people; but in their eyes the Roman governor, though freshly bathed daily and scraped with the strigil and full of the magnetism of his authority, was impurity itself, from which they wished to keep their distance.

They therefore could not really negotiate. These were, in effect, two religions colliding: two notions of the sacred that could not be reconciled. Again and again the Jews pleaded with him: "Please, sir, remove the standards. They offend us, and they offend the laws of our ancestors. Please remove them."

"No."

"Your predecessors did not offend against our laws. They respected them. Please remove the standards, sir."

"No."

"Will you tell us why you will not remove them, sir?"

"Because it would be an insult to the emperor," Pilate answered. "And I will not insult him."

The Jews stayed for five days. On each day, for hours, they petitioned him. He refused to budge, and so did they. Pilate seemed too surprised to ask his troops to clear them. He went about his duties. Then, on the sixth day, he forced a confrontation in the Great Stadium. He let himself get to the point of killing them because they would not leave; his soldiers had their swords at the Jews' throats. Then, when they showed themselves quite indifferent to death, he was so shocked that he backed down. Their invisible God was stronger than his, whose image surrounded him. The order was given for the standards to be taken out of Jerusalem, and Pilate retreated to his palace.

It was his first defeat, and perhaps the hardest to take. Not only the emperor's honor had been at stake, but his own ability to keep order and impress Roman ways on his province. His humiliation so delighted the Jews that they appointed a new feast day, the third of Kislev, to commemorate the day "when the standards were taken away from the pavement of the Temple." The fact that Pilate removed them without apparent clearance from Rome suggests that the whole affair was his idea from the beginning, and that he had only himself to blame for the debacle that resulted. The honor of Tiberius in this small, symbolic case was not worth a massacre of the Jews, and Tiberius himself would have been the first to point that out to him.

So he returned, smarting, to his chambers by the sea.

After a while he had a second idea. It was less contentious; indeed, it was benevolent and kind. It was futile to imagine that the Jews would ever like him, but perhaps a little murmur of appreciation would fall from their stubborn lips.

He would build an aqueduct. There was nothing better to mark the advent of Roman civilization: massive masonry at the service of safe and convenient drinking water. This was a resource Judaea was almost without. In the high desert, the overwhelming impression was of unwatered stone. From Beersheba to Bethel there were perhaps six tiny streams; no lake, no river, no waterfall. Shepherds led their flocks to pools that were almost illusory, trembling among improbable trees. Even in Jerusalem, where rain could fall copiously in winter, the precious water sank immediately into deep limestone, where every resource of ingenuity was needed to catch it. The city was riddled with man-made pools and cisterns, including, it was said, a fantastic complex of reservoirs sixty feet beneath the Temple: a "fountain of perennial water," as Tacitus called it, hewn in the solid rock. Pilate may have only heard rumors of this reservoir, but there were countless others, such as the two pools beside the Antonia fortress and the two pools of Siloam, beside which lay the abandoned crutches of the men Jesus had cured.

The Jews yearned for water with a religious longing: the hart panting after the water brooks, the torrent gushing from the rock under God's power and "running in all the dry places." They feared more than anything the divine anger that could turn rivers into wilderness and springs into thirsting ground. With immense labor they built conduits, tunnels and aqueducts to bring spring water to the pools of Jerusalem. Pilate evidently thought that Roman labor could help the enterprise. His enthusiasm may well have matched Pliny's, who adored the combination of beauty, utility and *Romanitas* that an aqueduct represented. Of a similar project, the linking of a lake with the sea, Pliny wrote to the Emperor Trajan:

> In consideration of your noble ambition which matches your supreme position, I think I should bring to your notice any projects which are worthy of your name and glory and are likely to combine utility with magnificence. . . . The king [who started it] despaired of finishing the work. This, however, only fires me with enthusiasm to see you accomplish what kings could only attempt. You will forgive my ambition for your greater glory.

The aqueduct Pilate built was, by all accounts, impressive. It ran for twenty to forty miles (Josephus ranges between two hundred and four hundred furlongs); it was lined with lead and lime mortar, and the water in it gleamed blue as metal. It is thought to have been the aqueduct that linked the springs in the Wadi el Arab to Solomon's pools near Bethlehem, from which two great "high- and low-level" aqueducts, probably built by Herod, conveyed the water northward to Jerusalem. To a Roman, the completed project would have looked wonderful. But the Jews were not grateful. According to Josephus, "they were not pleased with what was done about the water."

There could have been many reasons for this. Perhaps there were casualties in the building works, or perhaps the Jews were simply indulging the age-old and reasonable dislike of monstrous modern stoneworks marching across the landscape. It appears, too, that part of the aqueduct may have run through a cemetery, rendering the water ritually impure. But the main problem was that Pilate allegedly financed the project with *corban* money, the sacred treasure stored in the Temple. The account in Josephus' *Jewish War* suggests that he exhausted the treasure completely.

Corban was the adjective applied to all money that was either vowed to one holy purpose or was deliberately removed from the use of others. It applied to other objects, too: a beast bound for sacrifice was *corban* once it had been chosen for the altar. The sacred money flowed in from Jews all over the empire, as well as from the poor widow whom Jesus saw depositing her two mites, "which make a farthing," in the box in the Temple courtyard. Every male Jew over the age of twenty paid a half-shekel tax every year toward this treasure, and people also gave their clothes, jewels and ornaments. The money could be used for public works of benefit to Jerusalem as well as for ritual observances; indeed, Jesus himself criticized the way that the notion of *corban* tended to turn spontaneous generosity and social duty into narrowly ritualistic "gift-giving." Cheekily, he told the collector to pluck his own Temple-tax out of the jaws of a fish. Among his followers, he suggested, the *corban* idea should be treated skeptically or even dismissed in favor of unrestricted love: but not by Romans.

The most famous misuse of the *corban* treasure was not by Pilate, but by the Sanhedrin itself. It was *corban* money, thirty pieces of silver, that was said to have been given to Judas by the chief priests as payment for betraying Jesus. Whether or not such a use was legitimate in their eyes, the priests in Matthew's Gospel refused to take it back from Judas when he changed his mind and tried to return it. It had become impure, and was unwanted. It would have been equally impure, of course, if Pilate had tried to give it back.

How he got hold of the treasure is unclear, but he did not seize it by force. A Roman would have known as keenly as a Jew that it was sacrilege to steal anything entrusted to a holy place; his own temples were stacked, like banks, with boxes of money. Even Philo noted that in the time of Tiberius the Temple was never disturbed. Josephus says simply that Pilate "used" the treasure, without saying that he committed any sacrilege in getting it. Probably some secret deal was made with Caiaphas, and the money was simply transferred. But however it was done, the Jews violently objected.

When Pilate next visited Jerusalem a great crowd assembled, just as they had done to protest about the standards. Yet this time there was no pretense of submission; "God's gift," the holy money, was at stake. Enraged, they formed a ring around Pilate's tribunal and screamed abuse at him. This would have shocked Pilate; Josephus, always sensitive to etiquette, was apologetic, almost embarrassed ("crowds will do that sort of thing"). But Pilate was not proposing to apologize; he considered himself the injured party and, in his view, there was nothing to be sorry for. Instead, knowing in advance that he was going to face trouble, he had already concocted one of his plans. He had made his soldiers put on Jewish dress (long robes, head cloths, perhaps the odd false beard; since most of them were Samaritan and Idumaean auxiliaries, there was no need to touch up the skin with ink or green-walnut juice). In the *Antiquities,* Josephus says they had daggers under their costumes, but were ordered not to use them if they could help it. In the *Jewish War* he says they had swords, but that Pilate ordered them only to use their cudgels to beat "the noisy ones." With this sort of muddled thinking, the stage was clearly set for a calamity.

Pilate continued to face the crowd from the tribunal. He was alone, as he had been at the Great Stadium in Caesarea; yet not as alone as all that, because, as before, he had his troops hidden and ready. He loved to challenge the Jews in this way, to appear courageous, to take a risk that was, in fact, no risk at all, because he had brute force hidden up his sleeve. Yet experience would have taught him not to feel entirely secure: the Jews had quite as much cunning as he had.

He sat in his curule chair and told the Jews to go away. The reverse happened; the crowd surged forward. They came right up to him: close enough, Josephus implied, actually to hurt him. When they waved their fists, he flinched; when they spat, he felt the spittle in his face. Most of what they shouted he could not understand, but it needed no translation. He had touched the holy money; he had defiled the Temple. While the water in his aqueduct might be pure, the aqueduct itself was filthy, hateful and degraded, and so was he. The Jews came so close that they almost trampled the hem of his toga: so white, so immaculately fullered with bean meal and potash, so uselessly clean.

He bore this for a while. He knew that when he had had enough, he could give the signal. And something broke his forbearance in the end, as it was bound to. Possibly he was frightened, or felt he was getting too close to humiliation. Possibly someone touched him, that unbearable contact of flesh against flesh that suggested equality, common humanity and the threat of capitulation. He gave the signal. At once, his legionaries in disguise fell upon the fringes of the crowd.

The local auxiliaries who made up his raggle-taggle army always relished such a chance. Their animosity toward the Jews was something Pilate could never control entirely; here, he could not control it at all. Instead of sticking to their cudgels, the soldiers used everything they had, and Pilate did not intervene to call them off. Of course, he should have done. As Valerius Maximus could have told him, "The force of the empire is in the soldier; once out of the straight line, that force soon becomes oppressive unless it is swiftly controlled again." Instead, perhaps deliberately, he froze. His men slashed and cut as if the Jews were armed, when they had no weapons at all. Many who escaped the blows were killed as they ran away, trampled by their own people as they tried to squeeze through the narrow streets to safety. The bloodshed may have extended to the courtyard of the Temple, where the pigeon-sellers and money-changers were; this may have been what Luke meant when he recorded Jesus being asked about "the Galileans whose blood Pilate had mingled with their sacrifices." Perhaps within the holy place, certainly outside it, Jewish blood was on the flagstones and smeared along the walls. How much water from the new aqueduct would it take to wash them clean?

Pilate had not left the scene. The brutalities took place on the edges of the crowd; it is uncertain how much he saw, except that, as Josephus noted, it was much more than he had commanded. When it was over the rest of the crowd remained, terrified and silent, staring at him. We do not know with what feeling or with what expression Pilate looked at them.

That was his second mistake. He probably analyzed the failing, if he saw it as a failing at all, as a loss of control over his men, but the Jews saw it as a violent lack of regard for the things they thought holy. This was a lesson Pilate seemed incapable of learning.

Philo records that some time later he had some shields made, coated with gold and dedicated to Tiberius, and had them put up in Herod's palace in Jerusalem. Why he did this is unclear. If it happened around 32, and Pilate was indeed a protégé of Sejanus, it may have followed on the news that the favorite's star had fallen. Sejanus had reached such heights that he seemed to share the emperor's power: receiving his own ambassadors, becoming the object of prayers and sacrifices. At the shows, he even had his own gold chair beside the emperor's. In distant Judaea, Pilate too would have sacrificed to him, set up his bronze statue among his household gods and entered his name in the records alongside the name of Tiberius. It was standard practice. But then Tiberius, afraid of the favorite's ambition, sent a letter to the Senate ordering his arrest. Sejanus, after a moment of stunned disbelief ("Me? You are calling me?"), was accused of treason and garrotted, and his relatives and friends were rounded up and killed. If Pilate had been a friend of any sort, he desperately needed to make a show of loyalty to the emperor. What he may not have known was that Tiberius, as part of his policy of destabilizing Sejanus, had actually forbidden the proposal of honors either to the favorite or to himself. To make such a gesture now was almost as dangerous as making none at all.

Yet there the shields were. The Greek word Philo used for Pilate's action was *anatithesin,* "consecrated"; the word for shield, *aspideion,* meant one that was dedicated in thanks for services rendered. Shields like this were not normally hung up in private houses, however grand. They were hung up in public buildings or in the temple of the god who had been prayed to and had answered the prayer, as engraved tin tokens are still put up around statues of the Virgin in Catholic Europe. Horace recorded the hanging of a votive tablet, together with his dripping clothes, in the temple of the god of the sea of love in which he had just escaped drowning; Ovid promised to erect one, engraved in his own hand, in the temple of the goddess of childbirth, if only his girlfriend Corinna might be saved from dying from a self-induced abortion. They were very simply worded: "Horace to Neptune" was all that was required to make the prayer of thanks. So Pilate thanked his emperor.

Philo thought differently. He assumed that Pilate had put the shields up simply to annoy the Jews. This is plausible enough, but even Philo had to admit there was nothing on the shields that was obviously offensive: "no image work nor anything forbidden by the law, apart from the barest inscription stating two facts, the name of the person who made the dedication and of him in whose honor it was made." They were not on public display, but seem to have been set up inside the palace in Pilate's private apartments, which he could presumably decorate as he liked. Yet some reference to divinity was likely from the mere fact of their consecration, and would have been deeply offensive. Besides, part of the penalty of being so unpopular was that anything Pilate did could be turned against him. So people began to talk about the shields and, in the end, to complain with vigor.

Such sensitivity was not new. Something similar had happened when Herod, who liked to give prizes at the games, devised some out of blocks of wood to look like miniature armed men. The Jews took enormous offense at these prizes, claiming they violated the Law. Even when Herod invited them to inspect the little "images of men," and to tap the blocks of wood beneath the gilded decoration, several of them still accused him of profanity. A little later, the incident was cited as one of the reasons for a "holy and pious" revolt against him. This happened all too often in Judaea: out of simple decoration, martyrdom.

Philo claims that the four Herodian princes came in embassy to Pilate to ask him to take the shields down. (This must have happened at a festival; there were few other occasions when all the local rulers were in Jerusalem together.) They begged him not to violate their traditions and disturb their customs, "which have been safeguarded through all preceding ages by kings and emperors." But Pilate dug in his heels. Inflexibly, stubbornly, "with his usual mixture of self-will and relentlessness," as Philo described it, he refused to do what they wanted.

The Herodian delegation is difficult to identify, but it clearly included Herod Antipas of Galilee and Philip the Tetrarch as chief spokesmen. These men were all virtual kings in their own right: bearded, richly dressed, exotic, attended by trains of servants. They were not cowed by Pilate. It was their father, not his, who had once hung on the arm of Augustus and had been on gift-exchanging terms with Mark Antony. If they cared to, they could put on Roman airs and adopt Roman practice, and they knew which strings to pull at the court of Tiberius. They pulled them now.

"Don't arouse sedition," they pleaded with him. "Don't make war, don't destroy the peace. You don't honor the emperor by dishonoring ancient laws. Don't take Tiberius as your pretext for outraging our nation;

he doesn't want any of our customs to be overthrown. If you say he does, produce an order or a letter or something of the kind, so that we can stop pestering you and can go and petition him."

Pilate listened to all this in a cold, sulking fury. To him, the shields were holy; they had been dedicated, and now he could not possibly take them down. Besides, how much fuss could the Jews make over inscriptions? How could the mere geometry of letters offend them? It was impossible to live with such exquisite sensitivity, in which the gleaming angles of an "A" became a weapon, and the curves of an "S" an obscenity. Besides, as the princes knew, there was no order from Tiberius. There was no letter, either. It was ridiculous to think that the emperor would send one, or the governor could produce one, ordering the customs of the Jews to be overthrown. Pilate's compulsion and enthusiasm were his only authority; it was all in his own head.

But it was the last point—the possibility of Jewish tale-telling— that most exasperated him. More than anything, he didn't want the Jews to write to Tiberius. He would have no control over what they said, and there were, according to Philo, many aspects of his rule that were better hidden. He was cautious in what he revealed to the emperor through his regular reports; he could even instruct the messenger to loiter, not to rush in, to make sure the emperor was smiling and unirritated before handing the letter to the Praetorian guard to be delivered. He could not bear to think that anyone else should represent him. But if he did not want the Jewish princes to write, he would have to remove the shields and dishonor the emperor by removing them. He was stuck.

A silence followed, in which Pilate's conscience and his pride struggled like desperate wrestlers. "With all his vindictiveness and furious temper," wrote Philo, "he was in a difficult position. He had not the courage to take down what had been dedicated; nor did he wish to do anything that would please his subjects. At the same time, he knew full well the constant policy of Tiberius in these matters."

The Herodian princes watched Pilate closely: four fierce, imperious heads. He would not concede. He would not back down. The protocol for listening to requests from subject people was to keep your head bowed and your gaze fixed on the floor, so that your expression gave nothing away. But no matter how still he sat in his curule chair, draped in the resplendent white folds of his office, his mind squirmed. Something of his torment must have shown in his face, in a twitch of the lips or a glimmer of compunction in his furious eyes. Perhaps, like many Romans, he showed his unutterable frustration by biting his nails. For somehow the princes divined, according to Philo, that for all his stony refusals he had, in fact, repented. He was sorry, but he was damned if he would ever admit it to four petty local rulers.

They left him then and wrote, as they had threatened, their letters of complaint to Tiberius. This was not an entirely hostile act. They could see that Pilate was trapped in his own pride and, to some degree, in his terror of offending the emperor, and this was a quandary from which only Tiberius could release him. Yet the moment of release, when it came, was appalling.

Tiberius would have received the letters on Capri, on his terrace dappled with the light of the sea. Philo, relishing the scene, says he read them through quickly (not in this case procrastinating, or waiting until his romp-of-the-day was done) and immediately erupted with anger. This was not unusual. According to Suetonius, the emperor wavered between being a timid and quasi-scholarly old man who would make a nuisance of asking abstruse questions ("What was the song the Sirens sang?" "Who was Hecuba's mother?") and a terrifying brute who scourged almost to death a centurion who failed to clear a road of bushes to let his litter pass. Had Pilate been there in front of him he might have dreamed up some exquisitely appropriate punishment, such as nailing him up spread-eagled to the walls like a votive shield himself. But since he was far away, Tiberius merely cursed him to the skies and tore him limb from limb with words. "What language he used about Pilate!" crowed Philo in delight. He then dictated that language to his secretary, not caring to wait until the white heat of the moment had passed.

A letter "full of reproaches and rebukes for his audacious violation of precedent" was sent off to Pilate. The wording can only be guessed at now, and what Philo suggests it was should probably be taken with the same grain of salt as his assessment of Pilate himself. All we know is that Pilate was told to take the shields down and transfer them to the Temple of Augustus in Caesarea. But very little imperial displeasure was needed to have a petrifying effect at the other end of the line. Plainly, this was one of those communications that coats a man in a cold rush of fear from the scalp downward: the fear of a job, or a life, in pieces.

Amicitia Tiberii et frigore.

Pilate took the shields down. A man went up a ladder, prized them off the walls, packed them in boxes or wrapped them in cloth, and sent them back to Caesarea. Each time after that when Pilate stood in the Temple of Caesar Augustus on the little hill above the harbor, gazing at the image of the emperor's adoptive father through the sweet rising smoke, he would see the gleaming shields along the walls. Stupid, sang the shields, stupid and rash, stupid and rash; count yourself lucky not to be fired. Or words to that effect.

Presumably he kept the letter. It was awful, but it was from Him, and so could not be part of the selective culling and cleansing of correspondence that went on from time to time. His shadow would have fallen across it as he dictated it, in his marble villa by the deep blue waters in the center of the world. His ring had impressed his image on the heavy purple seals. Besides, the letter was not wholly critical. Tiberius had shown him mercy, which was the prerogative of great men. And if he had hurt him, that too was his prerogative. As Ovid said, when Augustus exiled him for a crime that remains obscure, "et iubet et merui"; "he orders it and I have deserved it."

To feel the wrath of Caesar was, the poet said, to be crushed by God. He was the *princeps,* the life of the world, the most merciful, "he who sees all things." It was never necessary to name him: he was *ipse,* Him, and he had the power to give or take a man's life. Although he was mortal, his soul was becoming divine. The stars beckoned, and he was already "immeasurably removed" from the thin petitions of his subjects. Poets, of course, exaggerated. But if Pilate's feelings were anything like this, it could be that the idea for the Tiberieum grew out of the humiliation of the dismantled golden shields. In Jerusalem, he could not put a prayer of loyalty on an inside wall; but in Caesarea he could build in stone and put up altars.

In any case, Pilate now needed to begin the long process of working himself back into his boss's affections. It was difficult. He could try to send him something, some natural curiosity, as governors often did; the deputy governor of Africa once sent Augustus a parcel, heavy with damp sand, of nearly four hundred shoots obtained from a single grain of wheat. Tiberius had his likings, strange as they were: for Setinum wine and wild German parsnips and cucumbers grown all year under glass.

Perhaps these could be grown in Judaea, to save the imperial gardeners the trouble of making cucumber beds in little carts that could be wheeled around to catch the sun. They might be grown in strange shapes that would tantalize him. Or he could be sent dates again, the famous Nicholas dates that a philosopher from Damascus had once presented to Augustus: four inches long, flesh-white when you crushed them, oozing with a juice like honey, and grander by far than those that Pilate offered to the gods beyond the clouds.

Yet he had gone wrong once, and there was always the numbing possibility of going wrong again. From distant Judaea, it was impossible to tell. Tiberius, in his palace, sucked the sweet flesh from a fig and wished his name to be respected; and Pilate, far away, harried, keen for approval, put up the gleaming shields. On whose orders? the princes had asked him. But he could not answer. He could not bear to admit that there was no order, nothing in writing, only a prompting of the heart and a deep urge to ingratiate himself: as with the whispered bon mot, the watchful eye at the great man's back, the steer by the elbow to a place of safety, if only he were close.

Chapter 3

GOD'S SECRET
AGENT

Don't bother.
It's all worked out beforehand
The match is rigged
And when he appears in the ring
surrounded by magnesium lights
they'll thunder the Te Deum *fit to deafen you*
and even before you've got out of your chair
they'll ring the bells at full tilt
they'll throw the sacred sponge in your face
and you won't have time to fly towards his feathers
they'll throw themselves on you
and you'll crumple
your arms out stupidly, like a cross
in the sawdust
and you'll never make love again

JACQUES PRÉVERT,
"The Fight with the Angel" (1949)

I.

H
E MAY HAVE WONDERED, from time to time, why he had
been sent to Judaea. Any number of later theologians and
scholars could have told him. He was sent because the stars
were in alignment and the other players in place. This was what God had
planned from the beginning of the world. His son would be put to death,
a symbolic death on a tree, to save sinners. But it would appear to be a
routine execution by a governor who did such things all the time.

The place was set. To cite the words of Peter and John in the fourth
chapter of the Acts of the Apostles, "In [Jerusalem], in fact, both Herod
and Pontius Pilate, with the Gentiles and the people of Israel, gathered
together against your holy servant Jesus, whom you anointed, to do
whatever your hand and your plan had predestined to take place." Both
God and, below him, the astral spirits, were involved in this design.
When St. Paul wrote of "the rulers of our age" crucifying Christ, the
Greek phrase he used—"archontes tou aionos toutou"—meant not only
the present authorities but also the demonic powers, seated in the plan-
ets, who governed the order of the world and the lives of men. It was the
archontes who brought about the crucifixion. The authorities, Caiaphas,
Annas or Pilate, were merely their agents.

The Catholic Catechism adds: "For the sake of accomplishing his
plan of salvation, God permitted the acts that flowed from their blindness." But this is a refinement, in which God allows free will and incor-
porates it into his design. The unrolling of Scripture suggests a different,
inexorable motion: the "free" acts of Pilate and the others were already
part of the plan. Although the Roman governor had never heard the
voices of the prophets, he fulfilled them in every detail by trying Jesus
and condemning him.

Even the time was prefigured. As St. Thomas More confidently expressed it, "Adam was created and fell into sin in the month of March, on
Friday the sixth day of the week and at the sixth hour of the day, and

Christ chose to suffer on the day in March on which his coming was announced and on which he was put to death—the sixth day, Friday, at the
sixth hour." *Christ chose to suffer.* Yet he suffered at a time apparently determined by Pilate's schedule. At a certain hour, Pilate went out on the
Great Pavement outside Herod's palace to hold the tribunal that would
sentence Christ to death. From the hour of that hearing, the crucifixion
was set. As far as Pilate knew, the precise timing of the tribunal was determined by how quickly he came downstairs once the Jews had summoned him; how well he had slept, whether he had made love, whether
he had paused to dip bread in wine for breakfast, whether urgent letters
had arrived from Rome. Yet perhaps these things, too, were factored into
the divine chronometer: each crumb, each kiss, each delay, each stroke of
the razor, until at the appointed time Pilate took his seat, prepared to
send Christ to the predetermined cross. The exact time of his sentence
(which More did not "record," but John did) was noon, the very moment
that the lambs intended for Passover began to be killed in the precincts
of the Temple.

Pilate would have believed in Fate, though to what degree we cannot
possibly tell. As a schoolboy he would probably have repeated, as the
elder Seneca said he had done, the famous epigrams of Furnus: "The moment we are born, the day that will end our life is fixed; we are hurried
off to a destiny that is not announced to us beforehand." Since Pilate was
a magistrate with *imperium* and the highest official in Judaea, it would
have been his duty from time to time to take the auspices himself: to observe the warm entrails, the flight of birds and the "carefully designated
parts of the sky," in case the gods had somehow revealed in them their
plans for his province. He would know what to look for: the bad luck of
a missing heart, or one spongy and distended by disease; the good luck of
a liver folded at the bottom like a pocket. He was obliged on such occasions to show belief in the augur's rites and to speak the ritual words with
all possible solemnity, though Cicero remarked that most men seemed to
put on "an outward show, with no belief in the reality."

Nonetheless, lists were kept, and all oddities recorded, in case their
significance could be detected. Julius Obsequens kept records of portents
by consulships, so that men could read how under Gaius Valerius and
Marcus Herennius a bronze statue sweated, a kite was caught in the Temple of Apollo, and at Volsinii flame flashed through the sky at dawn.
Some of these incidents evidently predicted the fate of Rome. During the

victorious campaigns in Spain in 75 B.C., blood appeared on the outside of the soldiers' shields; this meant triumph. Before the conspiracy of Catiline in 63 B.C., bronze tablets containing laws were struck by lightning. Marcus Crassus in 54 B.C. disregarded a black fog and the sinking of a standard in the Euphrates; and so he perished, with his whole army, in the war against the Parthians. A foaling mule meant civil war, and a swarm of bees on the standards would bring ruin. Just after Pilate left for Judaea the collapse of a jerry-built stadium at Fidenae, which crushed hundreds of spectators, was taken as an omen of Rome's abandonment by Tiberius.

Most Romans tended to believe there was a message of some sort in these things, something involving higher powers, even if they did not quite know how. Only an Epicurean would have no time for it, calling it old women's tales; he would claim that natural forces made the world work, while the gods basked in indifference and idleness. A Stoic would tend to believe in an unbroken chain of causation proceeding from the soul of the universe, which was Fate, or Providence, or Jupiter, or Nature, or "every name of power." The very beauty and organization of the world, said Cicero, was enough to demonstrate that some intelligence was in charge of it, just as the beauty of a sundial or a water clock displayed the skill of the craftsman. The very greatness of Rome was a proof that the gods had poured out their favor on her. How could this order be fortuitous? "It would be as if by making countless copies of the twenty-one letters of the alphabet, of gold or whatever you will, and throwing them together in some receptacle and shaking them out on the ground, you could produce the *Annals* of Ennius, all ready for the reader."

Between these views came what ordinary men believed. It was a mishmash: the whimsical tinkerings of heavenly beings, Jupiter's nods, Mercury's tricks, Venus's breathy interruptions, and the implacable decisions of the goddess-of-what-must-be, balancing in the scales the illustrious and the lowly:

> *aequa lege Necessitas*
> *sortitur insignes et imos.*

Fortune herself was a goddess, as was Misfortune; both had temples in Rome, and both needed propitiation. The stars themselves, scattered over the bowl of heaven, were attached to each man and displayed his fate: the brightest belonged to the rich, the dimmest to the worn-out and poor. Some flared up, flashed and vanished, like a lamp fed with too much oil. A man could be boldly rationalistic, no longer believing literally in the three old stooping Fates with their spindles and shears who paid out the thread of his life, yet certain that what happened to him was not random, and that he did not drift in time undirected. Even Trimalcho's great burlesque in the *Satyricon* of Petronius Arbiter was not without some vestige of belief:

> Under the Bull are born ox-herds and men who have to find their own food. Under the Twins tandems are born, and oxen, and debauchees. . . . Under Virgo are born women, and runaway slaves, and chain gangs. Under Libra, butchers and perfumers, and people who put things to rights; under Scorpio, poisoners and assassins; under Sagittarius cross-eyed men, who take the bacon while they look at the vegetables; under Capricorn, the poor folk whose troubles make horns sprout on them; under Aquarius innkeepers and men with water on the brain; under Pisces chefs and rhetoricians. So the world turns like a mill, and always brings some evil to pass. . . .

The most stalwart believer in the power of the stars was Tiberius himself. According to Dio, he would not appoint a man to high office without first ascertaining, from the day and hour of his birth, whether he might present some danger to him in the future. He had almost certainly read Pilate's horoscope, and divined enough from it to know the limits of his ambition and potential; he could already tell, from the lines of his fate, whether he might need to kill him. And Pilate, equally, would understand what the nature of his official clearance was. It lay in the stars.

In his own mind, then, Pilate was not free from otherworldly interference. And he may not have been mistaken. We imagine we are free agents, but possibly do not realize how steadily Fate moves us along the road we think we have chosen. A woman wakes in the morning and gives her hair a hundred strokes of the brush; if she had given it seventy-five, she might not have crossed the road in front of the car that killed her. A man spills a teaspoon of sugar between the packet and the cup, and stops to sweep it off the table; if he had not bothered, he would not have been at the crossroads when the woman stepped from the pavement. A boy stoops to tie his shoelace, and avoids the bullet that passes a foot away; a businessman decides not to take the airplane that plunges into the sea. A young Roman makes the right contact at the right dinner party, picks an opportune moment, passes the wine bowl with acceptable obsequiousness, and finds he has ended up with a foreign posting he might as well accept: even Judaea.

His life had been moving in parallel with Christ's almost from the beginning. Christ was sent to earth at just the moment when Judaea was passing under Roman control. He was born as his parents submitted to the Roman tax assessors: in Luke's words, "the decree of Caesar Augustus that all the world should be taxed, which was first made while Quirinius was governor of Syria." His birth thus paralleled the triumph of Augustus, one divine bringer of peace beside another. When Jesus, at the age of twelve, began his precocious teaching in the Temple, Pilate in the army was impressing Roman teaching on barbarians. As Jesus hammered nails in his father's workshop, Pilate was directing men to hammer up the palisades of camps; as Jesus observed the netting of fish and their battering to death on stones beside the Sea of Galilee, Pilate saw much the same fate meted out in the circus to prisoners taken in the German campaigns. One medieval legend imagined the child Jesus at the carpenter's bench, blond curls over blond curling wood, already fashioning small models of the cross on which Pilate would hang him.

Those legends also emphasized that Pilate's father had been an astrologer. He had foreseen his child's power in the stars and had passed on to him, together with an arrogant smile and a love of hunting dogs, certain presentiments and forebodings. These trouble Bulgakov's Pilate, too. He finds himself haunted by images of death and physical dissolution, vials of poison and fearfully dissolving trees; but also strangely drawn to his philosopher-prisoner Jesus, who also has the gift of foreseeing things. "You and I will always be together," Jesus tells him. "Whenever people think of me, they will think of you." In Pilate's dreams, the two walk in comforting lockstep up the long beams of light toward the moon, that twister of fate and arranger of the tides, as if they are grafted to each other.

And perhaps they were. Man's salvation was assured because at the appointed moment Pilate was ready, and in his place. As an early Russian catechism expresses it, with utmost confidence: "God and man undertook to compass our redemption, by interceding for us with his father, by suffering for us under Pontius Pilate, and by satisfying, by his death, burial and resurrection, the demands of divine justice." When God had proceeded from God and the Light from the Light, when Christ had come down from heaven and was made flesh, there was Pilate, waiting: a crop-haired prefect with a grumbling liver, a pretty wife, a sarcastic streak and an obsession with clean water. Or so he was imagined. Here was a man who, like us, found his eyes bleary in the mornings, picked dirt from his fingernails, savored a good wine, thought he made his decisions for himself; and had no notion of the part he might be playing in any higher scheme of things. Well done, thou good and faithful servant! *Ad majorem Dei gloriam.*

II.

It began in a garden. In the center of that garden, planted by God in Eden, grew the tree of knowledge of good and evil. Fruit hung from its branches. The Book of Genesis does not say what sort of fruits these were; the Arabs think they were figs, some say they were pomegranates or green plantains; but at least since the time of the apocryphal Gospels, men have imagined they were apples.

The apple, *malum,* also meant "the bad thing." It could not be evil in itself; it was the concentration of God's sweetness. But men could not cope with it. It symbolized not only dangerous knowledge, but contention and power. Men longed for it almost without knowing why. Hercules traveled the world for the golden apples of the Hesperides, which also grew in a tree guarded by a coiling serpent; he tricked Atlas into fetching them, but Atlas refused to hand them over. Eris, also called Discordia, tossed a golden apple among the gods to spoil their celebrations. Apples were irresistible, but carried risks. Men or women who longed for apples were about to get into trouble.

Adam and Eve in the garden desired the apple, ate, and fell. What is less well known is that Pilate followed them. The *Golden Legend* relates how one day he stood at the window of his palace, gazing at a nearby orchard. The trees were heavy with red apples, and Pilate was seized with such a fierce desire for the fruit that he almost fainted. He called his servant to him and said, "I want that fruit so much that if I don't get some, I shall die."

The scene was supposedly set in Judaea, but it sounds like northern Europe. It is a version of the story of Rapunzel, in which the pregnant wife longs for the wild garlic that grows in the witch's garden. Her husband, believing her when she insists that she will die without it, scales the wall. But the witch exacts a penalty for the stolen plant: she demands the child that is to be born. A bargain of the same sort was about to be made with Pilate, that loss and death would come of his desire.

He did not exactly order the apples to be stolen, but they were stolen anyway. That is the way with apples. They invite the stealing, then the excuses. ("The woman gave it to me, and I ate." "The serpent beguiled me, and I ate.") Typically, the guardian of the apples—the owner, the higher authority, the conscience—is absent or asleep. The apples ask to be stolen, inveigle themselves into outstretched hands. Thoreau, the most moral of men, wrote in his diary of sampling apples in the woods of Massachusetts; they belonged to someone, but their very splendor made it more of a sin to leave them than to take them. "I pluck them," he wrote,

> fruit of old trees that have been dying ever since I was a boy and are not yet dead . . . Frequented only by the woodpecker, deserted now by the farmer, who has not faith enough to look under the boughs. Food for walkers. Sometimes apples red inside, perfused with a beautiful blush, too beautiful to eat,—apple of the evening sky, of the Hesperides . . . Let the frost come to freeze them first solid as stones, and then the sun . . . thaw them, and they will seem to have borrowed a flavor from heaven through the medium of the air in which they hang.

Stolen apples, as the proverb says, are always sweetest. They impart knowledge, love, authority, charisma, to those who are not ready to have them yet. The immature king (or the immature governor) holds the orb, the "golden apple" of power; the teenager fondles the orbs of his girl's breasts. If apples are so bewitching, perhaps God has put them there deliberately to provoke the crime: to unleash the longing that will lead to the fall.

So Pilate, in his palace, longed for the apples beyond the wall. His servant went over to fetch them, scrambling, jumping, filling his pockets. On the way he encountered the owner of the orchard, a man he did not recognize, and killed him with a stone. Then he delivered the apples to Pilate, shining, blood-red, and watched as he cut the white flesh to the core. As Pilate ate, the servant told him what the price of the apples had been.

Adam, too, had eaten the apple boldly for a while. But it turned to ashes. He realized that he was naked; and then, *sciens bonum et malum*, knowing good and the apple, he was driven from the garden. The cost of that apple, too, was blood. According to Augustine, "Eve borrowed sin from the devil and wrote a bill and provided a surety, and the interest on the debt was heaped upon posterity. . . . She wrote the bill when she reached out her hand to the forbidden apple." And in the end, adds the *Golden Legend*, "Christ took this bill and nailed it to the cross."

That cross itself, some said, sprang from the forbidden apple tree. Centuries before, Japheth, the son of Noah, had taken into the Ark a cutting from the tree of knowledge in the garden of Eden, and planted it in the garden where Christ was arrested. By the time Pilate needed it, it was high enough to hang a man.

The Song of Songs offered a different speculation. There Christ was both the apple and the tree: the outstretched arms and the drops of blood.

> *As the apple tree among the trees of the wood,*
> *So is my beloved among the sons.*
> *I sat down under his shadow with great delight,*
> *And his fruit was sweet to my taste.*

It was sweet to Pilate also. The governor desired the apple tree and its sweet hanging burden, without knowing why, because of the job he was destined to do. Christ was the tree, Christ the apple; Christ was the temptation and the satisfaction. And if Pilate did not pluck him, peel him, pierce him, crush him till the juice flowed, he would never unleash for fallen men the possibility of salvation.

So Pilate stood at the window, longing so deeply that he thought he would faint away; and his servant stood at his shoulder. But this was no ordinary servant. He was Pilate's deputy, his soul mate, and a man who understood at a snap of the fingers the deepest inclinations of his master's heart. His name was Judas Iscariot.

Medieval mythmakers believed the two men must have been thrown together some years before the betrayal of Christ. Their careers were bound to cross. Like evil twins, they needed to plot together and strengthen their complicity in each other's company. No one else would willingly be their associate; but in the gloomy halls and mountain passes where such lost souls met, they could comfort each other. Thus, in one modern Italian novel about Pilate, Judas tells him: "We are the indispensable artisans of the redemption. We are the instruments of the supreme outrage required to shake the moral conscience of the world. . . . You will be execrated, but console yourself. He knows that he could never have redeemed mankind without my pretended betrayal and your pretended cowardice."

Thomas de Quincey, in his opium haze, also understood this. Judas, he wrote, should never have been flung into the Potter's Field after his suicide on the elder tree. He had served Christ's purposes; he had been the force that pushed him into action. Pilate had then pushed Christ further, toward the result that God intended.

The *Golden Legend* recounted how Judas' life, like Pilate's, had begun with portents, though they were more in the nature of bad dreams. One night, after Ruben, his father, and Cyborea, his mother, had made love, she fell into a half-sleep, only to wake up screaming. She had dreamed, she said, that she was going to have a son "so wicked that he would bring ruin to all our people." Ruben scoffed at this; he thought "some divining spirit" must have infected her. But she insisted through her sobs that it was not; the son she was bound to have would be "a revelation of the truth."

The nine months passed, and Cyborea bore a son. His parents did not know what to do with him. His little body was perfect, but he was red-haired, a sign of criminality and bewitchment. At last, feeling that they must dispose of him, they put him in a basket woven of green rushes and set him afloat on the sea.

After a while, the basket drifted ashore on an island called Iscariot. The queen of the island, who was childless, was walking along the beach. She saw the basket bobbing on the surf, and asked her maids to bring it to her. The child's face within the basket shone with fraudulent beauty;

and the queen sighed. "If I had a child like that," she said, "the royal line would be secure." So she had the child rescued and secretly put to a nurse, while she herself pretended to be pregnant. Later, amid national rejoicing, she produced Judas as her own son.

In this way, though his origins were obscure, he was brought up royally: as, at some distance, Pilate was. And in Judas' case, too, there was competition that his proud nature found unbearable. Not long after the queen's false pregnancy, she gave birth to a true son conceived with the king. So Judas, like Pilate, had a brother who was by blood and breeding superior. As they grew up and played together, Judas often mistreated the royal child and made him cry. Sometimes the Devil himself got into Judas, making him bite anyone who came near him; if there was no one near, he would bite his own arms and the backs of his freckled hands.

In despair, his mother took him at last to a child in Nazareth, Jesus, who was said to work miracles. The child touched Judas, and at once the Devil slunk out of him in the shape of a black dog; but not before Judas had bitten Jesus on the hand and the right side, which made him cry. The scar of the bite in his side later provided a marker for a half-blind centurion to pierce him on Pilate's orders.

After the visit to Jesus, Judas was better for a time; but it did not last. He somehow found out that he was not the queen's son but a foundling, a piece of jetsam washed up on the beach. This filled him with such shame that he secretly killed the queen's true son and fled to Jerusalem, hiding himself in a company of young men who were being sent there as tribute. Daring to emerge, he took service in the household of Pilate, who was governor. Pilate was deeply charmed by him: a strange-starred child like himself, a half-prince, a brother-killer, a tribute-boy. On every level they understood each other, "screw to screw and false to false," as a medieval writer described it. In no time, Judas became Pilate's favorite. They walked together, drank together, laughed at each other's jokes. Pilate gave Judas the post of chief steward, and Judas did for Pilate anything he requested.

Pilate made a strange employer. He was capricious, filled with sudden longings and peculiar impulses, and each of these Judas was bound to satisfy. When he went to fetch the apples from the orchard, the man he encountered was Ruben, his own father. Unwittingly, since neither man recognized the other, Judas slew him with a stone to the nape of the neck. The governor, the bright fruit at last in his hands, barely registered the cost of the errand.

When he did, after the body was discovered at dusk under the blue trees, he awarded all Ruben's goods to Judas: including Cyborea, Judas' mother. The governor, morally impervious or possibly still dreaming, seemed unaware of the enormity of what he had done. So Judas, like Oedipus, killed his father and, at Pilate's urging, married his mother, until the day when she suddenly burst into tears among the tangled sheets. Learning the truth, Judas at first had no idea what to do; but Cyborea saved him. She urged him to repent of his awful sin by joining Jesus and his band of disciples. Judas agreed, for, as it happened, that too fitted perfectly with the schemes which he and Pilate were hatching together.

For Pilate had longed for apples, the symbols of Christ, but this was nothing compared to his desire for Christ himself. He had heard reports of his disturbances but also snippets of his teachings, including the idea that this man, too, had a royal parentage that was distant and confused. It was impossible to make a public show of his curiosity; but repentant Iscariot could become Christ's follower, and infiltrate the group of disciples on Pilate's behalf.

He succeeded admirably. He became a favorite among the disciples, and was trusted with the group's store of cash, not that there was much of it. Meanwhile, Jesus' doings were faithfully reported back to Pilate. When those doings became too dangerous, too strange, smacking of alternative authority, it was Judas who was sent to turn Christ in: to jump over the wall, seize the fruit that so tortured Pilate, brush his lips against it and bring it before him. He would not know—as Pilate himself did not know—whether Pilate was motivated by rage, curiosity, jealousy, cruelty, or something like love. His own role was not to ask questions. It was to jump, fetch, deliver, feign and fawn, like any good little red-headed spy.

Perhaps the relationship was like that. The medieval playwrights thought it was more distant, at least in the beginning. Their Judas did not cross Pilate's path until the Passion story was already fast unfolding, with Jesus waiting outside Jerusalem and receiving the tender ministrations of Mary Magdalene. This Judas was a stranger and a pest; he had his uses, but he would not leave Pilate alone. In the York play he makes his appearance just as the Jews, mainly in the persons of Annas and Caiaphas, are trying to persuade Pilate that Jesus is dangerous. From off-stage then comes that piping, whining voice: "I hate him, Jesus, that Jew."

Judas' fate is already clear. He wears his cloak like a shroud, and a noose is around his neck; his hair blazes red as if it is on fire. He pours out his hatred for thirty lines to the porter at the gate of the palace. While they were all at supper, a woman came and poured ointment over Jesus' feet. As treasurer, Judas objected: the ointment could have been sold for "three hundred silver pennies to give to the poor," and he could have taken his secret cut, his ten percent. In order to recoup it somehow, he now wants to sell his master to "Prince Pilate and the priests."

But the porter refuses to admit him. There is something about this "glowering gadling," this "beetle-browed briber," that bothers him. It is not just the beard, as Judas rather plaintively supposes, but the whole personality. So the two argue on the doorstep. Pilate meanwhile sits behind them, in his golden robes, on "a bench with banners bright," but he can hear nothing. The man Judas has to persuade is a statue caught in amber, sitting beside the gesticulating Jews, and pouring himself the occasional drink.

"You look like an utter loser to me. If you don't clear off, I'll beat you to a pulp!"

"Look, just this time . . . It's all true, I swear it is."

"Tell me another."

"Look, just get me a word with him. In proper council, if you like. I don't see why everybody shouldn't hear it."

"Wait here."

The porter goes in to Pilate, composed on his golden bench. Annas and Caiaphas are at his elbow. Two doctors in wide-brimmed Jewish hats perch on the steps, and a soldier stands guard behind them. The porter says, "I suppose I'd better keep nothing from you, my lord."

"Tell me," says Pilate.

The scene is stately and sycophantic. The Jews are telling Pilate how beautiful he is, a theme as constant as sunlight in the York play; he, in turn, is being gracious. The news that there is a man at the door "hilt-full of ire" merely intrigues him. He says, "What has he come for?"

"I don't know him. He's wrapped in a cloak. All I know is, you wouldn't want to kiss him."

"Go and get him, so we know what his trouble is. We'll give him an open hearing."

The porter fetches Judas. He sidles in, cloak around his head, noose around his neck, and bows to them. "Come on, look sharp!" the porter bellows. "Say what you want to say, and don't make trouble! Step up lively, and take care not to upset us!"

"Flower of fortune and fame, may we all find favor with you."

"Thank you," says Pilate. "Welcome. I like that."

Caiaphas comes bustling up, in his bishop's miter, and hooks a long finger in Judas' sleeve. "Can't you hear, knave?" he cries. "You should be on your knees! On your knees!"

"Don't worry about them," says Pilate to Judas. "Caiaphas, stop mocking him; you should be ashamed, sir. And you, fair sir—come in properly. Don't stand in the doorway and be bashful."

They connect at once. Even in traditions like York that make the two men strangers, they understand each other. The priests irritate Pilate, and he ignores them; Judas he wants to deal with man to man. And the deal begins when they have scarcely met. Judas makes his offer: "If you want to bargain or buy, I'll sell you Jesus." Some of the bystanders whoop, but Pilate simply asks: "What's your name?"

"Judas Iscariot."

"You're a just man. So Jesus will be justified by our judgment, Judas."

These two conclusions are plucked from thin air. The York Pilate has seen Judas for two minutes, knows nothing about him, but is immediately prepared to do business with him. More than that, he is prepared to alter the course of history with him by "justifying Jesus," or, in other words, letting him do his work of salvation. The partners in crime fall smoothly into each other's arms. "Now, what shall we pay?" asks Pilate. "Is that price all right with everyone?" "Do you agree, Judas?" "That's great." He even repeats Judas's pregnant phrase, "a knot for to knit," redolent of both the plot and the noose. Their fates are tangled together in an instant.

Only one sticky moment occurs, when it emerges that Judas is a disciple of Jesus. Pilate doesn't like that: "Say, man, to sell your master—what has he done wrong?" Judas answers: "Done me out of as much money as I'll get from you, if everything goes right." Pilate wavers for a while, but as Judas describes his plan to the Jews, his motions to catch Jesus, the governor softens again. He smiles at this awful creature, this "lurdan," this "harlot": "Abide in my blessing and bring what is best, Judas. It would be good to clear this little difficulty up. As soon as you can."

"I haven't had any money yet."

"You'll be paid soon, really soon. Then you'll have reason to love us. So, Judas, no more moaning—"

As if on sudden impulse, he takes out the bag and thrusts it at him. Judas yelps with delight; the priests rear back their mitered heads.

"Take your silver. Take it all."

"That's fine. I feel great now. I'll bring you that traitor before you know it. I'm so happy now."

"Keep your word, do your work well, and you'll have our love and support; that's a promise."

The crowd presses to the door, priests, doctors, soldiers, all eager to catch Jesus. But Pilate's last words are for his agent, his new accomplice, promising precisely what he cannot give him: "Solace to your soul."

L ET ME INTRODUCE YOU to this Judas. He is the direct descendant of the servant-spy of the *Golden Legend* and the mystery plays, but his name is not in the newspapers. He is Judas only in his own head, in the heads of those who suspect him (but they can never be sure) and in the head of the man, like Pilate, who runs him on the Leader's behalf in the name of internal security. It is a little drama of loyalty, cruelty and betrayal that is played out daily in the hearts of all oppressive regimes. The Cold War saw such Judases everywhere, but now you will most easily find them in a city like Havana, where there is still a sense of people trapped like insects in historical forces larger than themselves.

You may not spot him at first. He could be the taxi driver outside the Hotel Nacional, or the young blood who offers ham sandwiches in the street. The man lying on the seawall, his cap over his eyes, or the one selling greenish oranges from a tilting market stall. A boy on a bicycle, chewing sugarcane like a stick of rock; or a lanky mulatto who mops, with languorous insouciance, the floor of the meeting hall of the local political committee. All these, like him, are watchers. They note who visits, who knocks, who leaves, who parks for a while in a car with foreign plates. But Judas is the one who reports to the man in the government office who reports to the Leader himself. He can command his attention, bother him at odd hours, and can also be sure that if trouble comes he can be disowned and brushed aside, as easily as Pilate can be brushed aside by the Leader in the villa in Miramar.

Carefully, Judas maps out his days. In the morning a shave with a cutthroat razor and a cup of domestic coffee, made mostly of pulverized dried peas. Down the damp peeling stairs into the street, where the heat is already rising among the tattered palm trees. A better cup of coffee at the Esplendido, where the tourists stay. A table inside, in the cavernous tiled dining room, or his customary seat on the leather sofa just inside the door. From there he can banter with the doorman, another watcher, and with the taxi drivers, who will work only for hard currency and the promise of conversations worth recording.

He himself records other things. The room numbers of foreigners; the addresses on the cards they innocently post in the black box in the foyer, to which he has the key; descriptions of nationals consorting with tourists and the objects—a pen, a roll of tape, candied peanuts wrapped in brown paper—they exchange. He writes on anything he can find, including cigarette packets and the margins of his newspaper. He imagines he is safe; no one could read writing so oblique and small.

As he leaves the hotel, the sun is vertical above the streets. His lunch is a hot corn fritter from a stall in the market, washed down with weak beer. He makes it last as long as the siesta, an hour or so. After this, he strolls the streets, making for the flat where he will spend his afternoons. It is this flat that holds the information Judas' boss needs, where Pilate longs to go himself with the security of a pistol under his jacket; but instead he must sit, and smoke, and wait for the moment when Judas will report to him.

The flat is on a side street, up two flights of concrete stairs. It belongs to an eminent national philosopher, now out of favor. He holds court there in a room bare except for his desk, two metal garden chairs, the bed where his mother sleeps, and the television set on which she watches

Brazilian soap operas. His followers cram on the bed and the floor; some stand in the kitchen, a room about the size of a small cupboard, with a sink that drains into a bucket. They talk, argue, drink glasses of sweet coffee. Everyone knows the group is infiltrated; it is their guarantee of survival, for if they were not controlled they would need to be eliminated. But no one is sure which among them is Pilate's man.

At around seven in the evening, Judas makes for Pilate's house. It is a disused embassy off Avenida Quinta; the steps to the front door are broken, the garden overgrown, the elegant balcony lined with empty drums of cooking oil. Because this man is important he merits a sentry, who sits in a glass-sided kiosk with his rifle cocked. The bushes down the avenue's central divide are rustling with girls in Lycra and lipstick; but they do not look at Judas, because he has no money.

All he has is information, as good as treasure to the man he has come to see. Pilate wants not only the philosopher's movements but also his ideas. To him, these ideas are as dangerous and as exotic as bright fruit on a tree, the tree he himself—as a good party member—has been ordered never to touch. But once he tastes them, he will not fear them; he will be able to debate them, counter them and, if necessary, crush them. Knowledge will give him the advantage over these subversive people.

So night after night they talk together; screw to screw, false to false, across a desk with only an ashtray and a packet of cigarettes. The room in which they sit was once beautiful, with the remains of cornices now crumbling in the humidity; but the black plastic sofa is party issue, and the walls are stained with nicotine. Pilate keeps the Leader's picture on the wall behind his desk.

Steadily, Judas stokes his curiosity. He retails the philosopher's stories and, by doing so, spreads the word himself: agent and double agent. He cannot gauge the effect he is having. Sometimes Pilate laughs, snorting smoke at the ceiling; sometimes he seems perplexed, almost afraid; more often he launches into an impassioned diatribe on some scarcely related subject. If it gets too late, a taciturn woman—perhaps his mistress, perhaps his wife—will appear and put down before him a plate with rice, fried plantain, pork, fish. Judas barely waits for the moment of invitation before he is eating, fast and furtively, like a small and lucky dog.

Around them the regime moves toward its inevitable dissolution. The people are resentful, the revolutionary murals fading; the soldiers are preparing to put their guns away. In the great scheme of things, Pilate and Judas are battling against ideas that will inevitably prevail. Indeed they themselves, by alternately bullying the dissenters and relaxing their grip, are agents in their state's collapse, just as a trickle of water freezing and expanding may topple the monuments of concrete and cement. They themselves are advancing the events that must come. They are part of the plan.

Were it not that the air inside is thick with tobacco and the air outside still steams, like damp laundry, you might say that you were in Judaea.

III.

In the beginning was the Word, and the Word was with God, and the word was God.

He was in the beginning with God.

All things were made by him; and nothing came into being except through him.

In him was life; and the life was the light of men.

And the light shines in darkness, and the darkness did not understand it.

There was a man sent from God, whose name was John. In 26, as Pilate's ship approached Judaea, this man had just begun to preach in the Judaean wilderness. He roamed in that frightening expanse east of Jerusalem, running down toward Asphaltites. People surged out to find him from the whole province, and now that delightful river, the Jordan, was full of people up to their knees in the dappling water.

The two strangers appeared together: the new governor in his rippling toga, snacking nervously on the recommended Judaean dates, and the Baptist in his camel-hair loincloth, crunching locusts with wild honey. The crowds that followed both of them were not merely interested in their new, foreign faces: they wanted to hear promises, receive instructions, form some notion of what the future might be like. Auxiliary soldiers came to John, as doubtless they came to Pilate, to ask what they ought to do. He answered: "Don't hurt anyone or accuse anyone falsely, and be content with your wages." The *publicani,* or collectors of Roman taxes, came too, and John told them: "Exact no more than you're supposed to." In the wilds of Judaea, they may well have obeyed him with more alacrity than they did the man who was still exploring, and mentally redecorating, the rooms of the palace in Caesarea.

Herod Antipas kept an eye on John. He was fascinated by him, and wary of his capacity to provoke disorder. If Pilate and Herod shared intelligence in those early days of cautious diplomacy, or if Pilate sent his own spies out, he would have heard that "all Judaea" was streaming out to John to hear his teaching. Much of it did not make a great deal of sense: he spoke of fire, winnowing flails, sandals. But he mentioned also "the wrath to come," a code phrase for the Roman aggressors, and spoke of someone more disturbing who was to come after him. Beyond that there was, to Roman ears, a strange perversion in his most persistent teachings. He called for straight paths and baptism by water, whose purity would make all men new. Pilate, too, could offer straight roads and clean water; indeed, it was almost all he could bring that would remotely interest the Jews.

Although John was on Pilate's territory, it was Herod Antipas who took action against him, showing the new governor both how such mad creatures could get under a ruler's skin, and how hard they were to eradicate. Josephus, as well as the Gospels, reported his anxiety. He feared, said Josephus, "that the great influence John had over the people might lead to some rebellion"; he therefore thought it best to prevent mischief by putting him to death, "and not bring himself into difficulties by sparing a man who might make him repent of his leniency when it would be too late." On the other hand, according to Mark, Herod liked John and even thought him holy, or at least possessed of spiritual powers. The fox of Galilee in his sumptuous court liked to watch and listen to this disheveled, half-naked man; he imprisoned him as one might cage a curious animal at the zoo. John was dangerous, but he was compelling and probably in command of magic; so Herod wavered. It was not until his new wife, Herodias, inveigled him, through her daughter Salome, to kill John that he found the courage to do so, and had him beheaded.

Even then, the tetrarch never got over him. He did not shed his guilt or forget his fascination. When Jesus appeared, according to Mark, there was no doubt in Herod's mind who he was. This was John risen from the dead, "and that's why mighty works show themselves in him."

"No, no," said others around him. "It's Elias."

"It's one of the prophets."

But Herod insisted. "It's John, the one I beheaded. He's risen from the dead."

From then on his court swarmed with rumors. And perhaps it was not only the Jews who were so credulous, believing in maverick preachers who did not die but assumed different shapes. Perhaps Gratus, Coponius and Pilate were haunted also, in their elaborate beds. Not only the Jews had prophecies. Virgil in his fourth *Eclogue* had foretold the coming of a golden child "filled with the life of the gods" who would bring in a kingdom of love, in which hounds and deer would steal to the stream to drink together. The sins of men would fade away then, and they would no longer need to struggle to make the earth fruitful: grapes would hang on brambles, the oak trees would run with honey, and soft waves of wheat would spread across the fields like sunlight. Augustus had inaugurated the Age of Gold, the *pax deorum;* Fortune had crowned him, and from his cornucopia the earth was springing already with fruit, and flowers, and peace.

Back in Rome, lines like this would be politely applauded in lecture rooms for the elegance of their meter and for their sentiment: the golden child could safely be identified as the son of one of the consuls. There was no need to be mystical about it. Yet in Judaea prophecies were shouted in the market, howled in the desert; their broken rhythms were of no importance. They were urgent and true. Ideas that would never have disquieted a governor in the mocking air of Rome gained a disturbing life from the fervor with which men believed them in Judaea. At night, with the oil lamp almost out and the bedtime reading (Livy? Propertius?) laid aside, the imposed order of the working day gave way to creeping moonlight, Hebrew songs, the cries of distant birds and, most unnerving to an urban Roman, silence. Rationalization was no good in the dark.

Every governor ran spies and informers, but there were other means of getting information. Pilate's soldiers, on duty all through Judaea and Samaria, could send reports. An odd incident in the mountains; people moving on the road like refugees but without their goods, as if called out to see something; their litter, broken bread and fish, spread over a hillside. The story would be picked up in bits and pieces from the hysterical healed woman, the surprised tax collector, the small boy with crumbs in his pockets. These were unreliable witnesses, of course, their tales the sort of rubbish heard in drinking houses. Would you believe water turned into wine, or a herd of pigs falling rump-over-snout into the sea?

Nonetheless, the stars were in alignment, and the land of Judaea swarmed with intimations of Christ. In Isaiah, the Lord had promised that the desert would fracture into streams that were full of him, that the hills would sing with the thought of him, and that the stony beds of dragons would become soft paths of holiness on which Christ would tread. Everyone expected him, and the secret could not be kept. Reeds at the edge of Lake Tiberias took in the message and whispered it, as their cousins had once whispered the secret of the folly of Midas. The turpentine trees that grew among the rocks overheard, and impressed the message on their many-fingered leaves. The leaves shivered and, before the wind, exposed the name of Christ on their pale undersides. Some fluttered down, turning in the air like the Sybil's distracted prophecies, to carry Christ into gullies where sheep huddled, or into dry stream beds to be kicked aside by boys.

A citron tree in a garden overheard; and when its fruit was picked the name of Christ was in the pith, bitter and white. A row of bean plants overheard and, when they blossomed, the name of Christ was inscribed on their flowers.

Shells held to the ear on the beach whispered "Christ," and the sea itself sighed and roared him.

Last, word came to the swallows that darted around the eaves of the houses in Caesarea. All day they swooped and dashed across the terraces and into the cool tiled halls, squeaking the name of Christ. In his palace, Pilate watched as the birds flew to and fro to their nests among the joists of the ceiling. And in his ears, on his plate, in his kitchens, in his garden, in the breast of the blue sea, past the shining piers, one name resounded: Christ, Christ, Christ.

A spy in the crowd that followed John would have seen him baptize a man whom he called the Lamb of God. He dribbled the water over his head at the place where the River Jordan flowed into dead Asphaltites. John said he had seen the spirit of God descending on this man like a dove. The man began to gather disciples of his own, who also began to baptize. To a Roman governor, the names of some of these disciples were disturbing: two brothers who were called Sons of Thunder, and a man called Simon the Zealot. Perhaps these titles had no political connotation to the disciples or to Jesus, but they carried echoes of rebellion, which Pilate would not have missed.

For a while, Jesus put no particular strain on him. He did not want the earthly authorities to be provoked. For most of his ministry he stayed in Galilee, out of Pilate's way. He told his disciples expressly, as he sent them out, that they were not to go "into the way of the Gentiles," though he knew they could not help encountering them; even if they were "prudent as serpents," as he advised them to be, they would still end up "brought before governors and kings for my sake."

Yet Jesus avoided Judaea less for fear of the Romans than for fear of the Jews; and the Gospels suggest that, but for the suspicions of the Pharisees, he would have been left alone. He is not bothered by the Romans, though he calls them "enemies," "wolves" and "dogs," and they are not yet bothered by him. Their presence in the Gospels is virtually invisible. They are scarcely seen, heard or even talked about, an extraordinarily muted performance for an armed occupation force. As Luke's Jesus implied in the parable of the Good Samaritan, they had not even made the main road between Jerusalem and Jericho safe for people to travel on. Only occasionally, as when Jesus invokes the carrying of crosses or, in the course of teaching, breaks the night into the four Roman watches of evening, midnight, cockcrow and morning, is there some sense that these occupiers have left a mark on Jewish life.

Until the Passion, there is no account of the Romans exercising their police powers except by implication. In Luke, the "enemies" who must be loved slap people on the face, take their cloaks and steal their property; they are "sinners" who, like any Roman—like Pilate—love those who love them and scratch the backs of those who scratch theirs. In the course of the Sermon on the Mount, Jesus advises his listeners that if someone asks them to go a mile, they should go two; the reference was to compulsory services demanded by Roman troops, who might, for example, get locals to carry their packs to the next village. John the Baptist told such soldiers not to intimidate or to extort money; presumably, therefore, they often did so.

In Mark, the devil driven out of a madman is asked his name; he answers, "Legion, because we are so many." A legion could only mean Romans, bristling, swarming, appropriately changed at last into a snorting herd of swine. On the other hand, the parables of Jesus show a Judaea in which people are going about their business peacefully enough. They plant vineyards, sow seed, invest money, hire reapers for the harvest, with every expectation of profit and no suggestion of political disruption. The only sour note is provided by the local tax collectors, the hated *publicani,* who collect Pilate's money for him. Yet even these Jesus has time for. It is a measure of his strangeness and his kindness that he talks to these people and eats with them: people he does not hesitate to call "sick" and "sinners" and who are usually mentioned in the Gospels in the same breath as prostitutes, because they could find no better way of living than whoring for the Romans.

Jesus made a point of the gravity of their offenses. The virtue of the publicans in his eyes was that, having fallen so far in collaboration with the Gentiles, they could only begin to repent and rise. Even these hardest cases could be saved. A publican who bowed in humility and dejection in the Temple, beating his breast in repentance for the money he had handled, was more surely justified before God than the Pharisee who fasted, tithed, prayed extravagantly, and was not "an extortioner and unjust, or even like this publican." In the grand scheme of salvation Pilate's fiscal agents had their own small role, as exemplars of the extraordinary breadth of the love of God.

The first to be saved by name was Zaccheus. He was the first indirect point of contact between Pilate and Jesus: a man who talked to, indeed took orders from, both of them. Zaccheus was a chief of the publicans, bustling, rich, and so small that he had to scramble up a sycamore tree to catch a glimpse of Jesus as he came through Jericho. Jesus spotted him in the shadow play of the leaves, which fell on his body like coins. The hiding man was called down and persuaded (though he needed no persuasion) to host a meal for Jesus. This had an extraordinary effect on him. At once, he found himself promising that "If I've taken anything from any man by false accusation, I'll give him back four times as much." Then he offered to give half his goods to the poor. If he kept those promises, the effect on Pilate's receipts would not have gone unnoticed. The governor would have wanted to know what the hell Zaccheus was doing; there can be few things more unsettling than a tax collector finding God.

On one famous occasion, Jesus was asked directly about payment of Roman taxes. The question came from "spies," according to Luke, or from "disciples of the Pharisees, with the Herodians," according to Matthew. Those "spies" have usually been assumed to be Jewish, but not necessarily so; their information would have been of the deepest interest to Pilate. These men, whatever their affiliation, approached Jesus as he was teaching in the Temple. "Master," they asked, in their wheedling way, "we know you only teach the way of God in truth, and care nothing for men or the pretensions of men. So, tell us: Is it lawful to pay tribute to Caesar, or not?"

Jesus saw at once that this was a trick question: a ruse, as Matthew put it, "to take hold of his words, and to deliver him into the power and authority of the governor." But he did not want that encounter with Pilate yet; it was not yet the hour for him to court sedition and to draw his death sentence from Tiberius' devoted representative. Instead, he demanded: "Show me a penny."

One was brought to him. This was the coin Jews used to pay the poll tax that went to the emperor's privy purse; it was not an acceptable currency in the Temple, but there would be a few of them on the money changers' tables. Unlike Pilate's small change, this was solid and silver. It was probably a coin of Tiberius with, around the edge, the words TI[BERIVS] CAESAR DIVI AVG[VSTI] F[ILIVS], "Tiberius, son of the divine Augustus," another son of a god; and it would have carried that same blunt-nosed profile, with the untidily cropped hair, that Pilate had paraded through Jerusalem on the standards of his army.

Here, then, was another close call. Jesus held in his palm, looked at, touched, the image of Tiberius: an image that counted as sacred to the man who was to kill him.

"Whose image and superscription is this?" he asked.

"Caesar's," they answered.

"So give to Caesar the things that are Caesar's, and to God the things that are God's."

This clever answer meant many things. Most obviously, it meant that Caesar could have his relatively unimportant offerings, as long as God was assured of his. But there was a strong political charge in the statement, too. The whole of Judaea, after all, was God's, and the Jews his people. Jesus might have meant that the hand of the Romans on Jewish money or Jewish property was an abomination. Indeed, he may have gone further, since he acted like a man who had scarcely handled money and had no coins about him; money itself was an abomination, and a world obsessed with money was a peculiarly Roman creation. The words "give to Caesar" may in fact have meant "pour Caesar's money down his throat," as the Parthians had poured molten gold into the mouth of Crassus. Pay contemptuously, but keep them quiet. Play games with the money, throw it in the air, hide it in a sleeve, produce it from the sea, crack their precious denarii between their well-brushed Roman teeth, mock at their desperation to collect it; but in the end, kindly, let them have it.

This would have been the Essene or Zealot interpretation of the words. They fitted in precisely with the political philosophy of Judas of Galilee, who, since the time of Coponius, had urged the Jews not to pay Roman taxes. Yet a Roman would have missed this bitter subtext; to him, the sentiments expressed would have been innocuous, even laudable. Rome too, Jesus seemed to be saying, had legitimate claims on these people. Pilate could demand his taxes, and the people ought to pay them. No one picked Jesus up then and there on this ambiguity; but when he came to trial and the Jews told Pilate that he had "forbidden them to pay tribute to Caesar," Pilate ignored the charge, implying that he did not believe them.

That said, there was no love lost between Jesus and the Romans. These were two different worlds coming into collision. Gentile values— Pilate's values—were the antithesis of what Jesus taught. Romans cared for worldly goods, fine clothes, power, and the hierarchies of their "so-called rulers." They were constantly asking "What shall we eat?" "What shall we drink?" "What shall we wear?" In the parable of the wedding feast, Jesus gave the Gentiles a walk-on role as street loafers and supper scroungers, just as some suppose the young Pilate was; but the followers of Jesus were to be simple and self-effacing, like wildflowers. When a Roman prayed, it was a series of "vain repetitions": Jesus' followers were to address God as "Father," and to mention down-to-earth subjects such as debts and bread. If a brother among the disciples did something wrong, he was to be won back with love and community discipline; but if he refused to repent, he was to be treated "like a pagan or a tax collector," a man outside the bounds of normal contact and reasonable discourse.

. . .

Mutual antipathy was essential to God's plan. Jesus had to provoke Pilate, and Pilate had to kill him. Yet this was not (as it could have been) a police murder in an alleyway; it was a set piece, including a meeting and a conversation, and the path was prepared in advance. Before Pilate met him, there was one other close encounter: the meeting with the centurion who petitioned Jesus to heal his servant. This man was probably not a Roman, despite his title. He was more likely to have been a noncommissioned officer of Herod Antipas, since the meeting took place in Capernaum, in Galilee, under Herod's jurisdiction: a native perhaps of Syria or Sebaste, speaking Aramaic. According to Luke, his sympathies with the Jews ran deep: his Jewish friends explained that "he loves our nation and has built us a synagogue." Yet he was a Gentile. He was a career soldier, as Jews never were, since they had a religious exemption; he was probably tricked out by Herod Antipas, a slavish Romanophile, in imitation Roman gear; and he knew, as a Roman would have done, that he would have to conduct his negotiations with Jews at a distance. In all these respects, he may as well have been one of Pilate's men.

In Luke, he never meets Jesus. Instead he sends the elders of the Jews, with whom he is on good terms, to petition on his behalf, and Jesus sets off for his house. When he is not far from it, the centurion sends out friends to stop him. "Lord, please don't trouble yourself" is the message. "I am not worthy that you should enter under my roof." Jesus stops, and heals the servant from several hundred yards away.

Matthew tells the story differently. Here the two men meet, but elements of distance remain. The centurion makes his request; Jesus responds by remarking about the centurion's faith to his disciples. The centurion looks at Jesus; Jesus does not necessarily look at him. It is not, in any sense, a conversation.

This was how Jesus would have acted with a Roman, too. The same invisible cordon sanitaire would have restrained him: through which he would nonetheless have sensed the centurion's sincerity, and through which the servant, stiff with pain on his damp bed, could have felt that sudden inflow of life. A Roman, of course, would not have called him "Lord"; the word *domine* was used only for evident superiors. Yet the centurion's thinking was quintessentially Roman: practical, efficient, down-to-earth. He was under orders, he told Jesus.

I am under authority myself, and I have soldiers under me; and I say to this man, Go, and he goes, and to another, Come here, and he comes, and to my slave, Do this, and he does it.

This was the authentic Gentile voice. It was obsessed with power, hierarchy, position, authority. *I am under someone, but I have people under me. This is how the world works; it depends on who is giving the orders and how strong they are. This is what counts.* Jesus did not answer these remarks directly, but he seems to have taken note of the thinking; it became the basis of the little lecture on power that he delivered later, according to John, to the Gentile who was to execute him.

Although a miracle came out of it, this was not a spiritual encounter. The centurion had heard that Jesus could do things, and he wanted him to do something for him. Although Jesus commended him for his faith, there was nothing higher in it, no glimpse of realms of light. If you can do it, do it. Just say the word. That wonderful neatness of the imperative, as soldiers knew it and as Pilate knew it: *fac, age, i, sta,* "do," "act," "go," "stay." And rise up: *surge.*

This was only the beginning of the encounter God had planned. There was not yet a proper dialogue between Christ and the Gentiles, nor even proper contact between them. Yet Jesus nevertheless heard, for the first time, the insistent Gentile mantra: do something, say something, prove yourself, define your chain of command. He was to hear it again.

IV.

For four or possibly seven years, Pilate and Jesus shared the same territory. Although Pilate was most of the time in Caesarea and Jesus in Galilee, their paths inevitably crossed from time to time. The two antagonists were sometimes tantalizingly close. Like characters in a formulaic thriller or a farce, they seemed to miss each other by seconds: one behind a door as the other enters, one looking the wrong way as the other saunters down the street.

Jesus was noted on Pilate's turf. He was reported teaching "on the coasts of Judaea beyond Jordan" and in Jericho; he was seen "in all the cities and villages" of the province, leaving behind him people marveling and fainting. But in John's Gospel he also visited Jerusalem, and at precisely the moments when Pilate, too, was there to keep order. Every year, his parents and his family went up to Jerusalem for Passover. They also went for Tabernacles (the feast of Sukkot, in the autumn), and with such regularity that when Jesus decided not to go for the Sukkot before his death it was thought peculiar, and he went up later secretly after the rest of his family had gone.

He took some precautions in Jerusalem, though the Gospels insist that this was for fear of the Jews rather than the Romans. At dusk he would leave the city to spend the night with his friends in Bethany or on the Mount of Olives. Only in the morning would he reappear. Each time he emerged, however, he caused a commotion. He healed people, performed miracles, drew noisy and rapturous crowds. According to Matthew, "the whole city was in turmoil, saying 'Who is this?' And the crowd replied, 'This is Jesus, the prophet.' " As one voice.

At the pool of Bethesda, by the sheep market, he cured the sick who had gathered there in expectation that an angel would come and stir the waters. The sick shouted as they were healed. Day after day he would walk in front of the Temple and in the Temple courtyards, teaching, as he termed it, but also haranguing the Pharisees, screaming at them. On these occasions, Luke said, "all the people hung upon him, listening." Several times the Temple guards were scrambled to get him, but held back "because his hour had not yet come." Once, at the Feast of Dedication in the winter, he was walking in Solomon's Porch in the Temple when the Jews chased him, demanded to know whether he was the Christ or not, and got ready to stone him. He fled then "beyond Jordan," but left behind a city half-crazed with him. By the time of that last fatal Passover, all the talk was of whether Jesus would come for the feast or not. The crowd knew that he had raised Lazarus from the dead, a mere two miles outside Jerusalem; they expected more wonders. Even Greeks in Jerusalem were asking, haltingly, to see him, the most famous tourist attraction after the Temple itself. Many of the chief rulers of the Jews were said to be secret believers in this man. In short, as the Pharisees lamented, "the world is gone after him."

Pilate remained in Herod's palace. In that great white mausoleum, where the marble floors absorbed his footsteps and the marble walls kept out all sound, he moved as if wrapped in insulation. Yet if he was to go to the window, or venture out to inspect the troops on duty in the western porticoes of the Temple, he might have glimpsed Jesus in the motions of the crowd, which swarmed about him like ants disturbed from the ground. He could have heard (though he would not have understood) the shout of Jesus to the crowd: "Why do you want to kill me?," and the crowd's raucous answer: "You're mad! Who wants to kill you?" Called out to the entrance of the Temple after Jesus had argued there, he might have seen him leaving: an abrupt turn of the shoulder, a whip of the long robe, face and hands still flushed with violence. To touch him, even approach him, was impossible; it was in violation of the plan. Yet Pilate could tread in his footsteps across the Temple porch, and the same beggars who had tugged Jesus' robe might be brushed aside by Pilate, too.

There were other opportunities. In the street near the Pool of Bethesda, the governor's litter might have paused. Runners were meant to clear the roads, but in a seething, distracted crowd they made no headway. Pilate waited. If he parted the curtain, he might have seen by the gloomy cisterns a man whose brown hair, as some apocryphal writings described it, fell in waves about his pale face like the leaves around a filbert: a man beneath whose touch the water trembled as if the angel of the pool had indeed descended. But it was unnecessary to notice him. The only meeting that counted was the one that was scheduled: on that day in March, on the sixth day of the week, at the first hour.

The litter jolted on.

Slowly, inevitably, by rumor and report, Pilate's antagonist was introduced to him. There was a man wandering in the district before whom a Gentile soldier had more or less knelt and prayed. And back at home that soldier's servant had swung his legs out of bed, stretched his arms, and gone back to his fetching and carrying. In general, the Jews kept their magic-working and mischief-making to themselves. This man Jesus was extending his strange ministry, in a gesture that seemed designed to catch the Romans' attention. It was as if he were embracing the cords of his own death.

Possibly the centurion delivered his own observations, to Herod Antipas or to Pilate himself: nervous, almost stammering, his helmet under his arm as he had held it, presumably, in the presence of Christ. It would not have been the usual soldier's story, but a catalogue of mystifying things. A healing at a distance, even without the touch of a hand. A magic word of some sort. And faith, that particular madness, that admission of weakness, which in the end seemed to make men strong. It could make a Jew impervious to the sword; so too it might make a centurion heedless of lying on the ground, arms out, to be whipped, as Tiberius had whipped one such jackass for stealing a peacock from his orchard. Who can feel pain when his eyes and his arms have been full of the blue of heaven?

The writers of the Apocryphal Gospels supposed that other men conveyed their thoughts to Pilate. One was Nicodemus, and some sort of contact between this man and the governor may not have been so strange. The Nicodemus of the Gospels and the rabbinical traditions is hard to pin down, but he was probably one of that group of ruling Jews who bothered, sometimes, to talk to Pilate, because he was their guarantor of order. The Jewish *Ta'an* contains the story of a man called Nicodemus (in Hebrew, Naqdimon ben Gurion), which illustrates his dealings with a "Roman lord" in Jerusalem. The heathen lord, who is in authority there, is almost certainly the governor; from the presumed date of the episode, some years before the fall of Jerusalem, he may well have been Pilate.

The scene was set at one of the Jewish festivals, when thousands of pilgrims were converging on the city and there was no water for drinking. (Another clue: there was apparently no aqueduct yet, and the incident that followed may even have encouraged Pilate in his plans to build one.) Nicodemus therefore approached the governor. He asked to be lent twelve wells of water for the pilgrims, promising to repay him by sunset on a certain date either with water—presuming it would rain in time—or, if he couldn't manage that, with twelve talents of silver. The governor agreed. When the deadline came, messages kept arriving from the governor at regular intervals, morning, midday and afternoon, demanding "Return me either the water or the money you owe me." The last message was delivered in person by the governor, who was on his way to the baths. Nicodemus replied to each, in relaxed fashion, "I still have time today."

"Oh?" replied the governor. "Seeing that no rain has fallen all year, do you suppose it will rain now?" (That sounded like Pilate, light, sarcastic, ever happy to have trumped the Jews.) And, certain that he had won the argument, he went off blithely to the baths.

Nicodemus was depressed. He went to the Temple, wrapped his cloak around his head and began to pray. Immediately the sky grew dark with clouds and the rain fell, until there was enough to fill the twelve wells with a good deal left over.

As Nicodemus left the Temple and the governor emerged from the baths, the two men met. Nicodemus said, "Give me the money for the extra water you've had!" The governor replied, "I know that the Holy One only disturbed the world for your sake, but my claim against you for the money still holds good; the sun had already set when the rain fell, so it belongs to me!"

Back to the Temple went Nicodemus, his cloak around his head, and prayed again: "Master of the universal, make it known that you have favorites in the world." Immediately the sun broke through. The governor was forced to admit that his claim had vanished; the rain had fallen in time. "But I'd still have had my claim if it hadn't," he could not resist remarking.

If there was already fraternization of this edgy, calculated sort between rabbis and their heathen governor, rumors of an astonishing or dangerous new preacher might bring them closer. Certainly the story had spread by the fourth century, when the *Acta Pilati* were produced as the "evidence" of Nicodemus, that Nicodemus and Pilate were associates and friends. The Gospels do not substantiate this, but there is one intriguing detail. According to John, Nicodemus was a secret disciple, not wanting his allegiance known. There could hardly have been better cover than friendship with the Roman governor, who in turn could hardly have found a more useful source of information.

In John's Gospel, Nicodemus visited Jesus at night, and there heard the strangest things. Perhaps circumstances dictated that he visited Pilate at night, too, or entertained him in his own house, to pass on what he had learned. He was enormously rich, with great estates near Jerusalem: estates so extensive, people said, that the stocks of wheat and wine from his fields could feed the whole city for a week. Out there, in the drowsy dusk on the white terraces, he and Pilate could talk without the governor sullying a Jewish living room; as a strict Pharisee, Nicodemus had to be careful to observe the proprieties. The governor's guards and attendants, among the clipped trees, could station themselves at a distance; delicacies could be ferried out on trays to fuel the secret conversations. If Pilate shared the fashionable taste for gold tableware, ex-

quisitely transparent glass, wine cooled in snow and meat already cut
from the bone, he was likely to find them here. Nicodemus' fabulous
wealth was known all over Jerusalem. His sister had been given a million
gold dinars as a dowry, and a niece had received four hundred dinars a
month to replenish her perfume basket. But he was also wise, and curious, and discreet.

John's Jesus had told him, as they sat in the whispering dark: "Unless a man is born again, he cannot see the kingdom of God."

Pass that on to Pilate. What would the governor make of it? Probably nothing. A man clambering back inside his mother's womb: that was
almost a ribald joke, soldiers' tent-flap stuff. Or becoming, suddenly, a
baby again, the laughable bald head soft and shining and new. How
could a man be born again? It was an impossibility.

Nicodemus had asked the same thing. Back came the answer: "Unless a man is born again of water and the spirit, he cannot enter the kingdom of God."

Pass that on. Leave aside for the moment the most troubling element, the kingdom talk. *Born of water and of the spirit.* The Jesus-
followers who did what they called baptizing were said to sprinkle water
on people's heads as they stood up to their knees in rivers; it washed off
Gentile impurity. How could such desultory, untraumatic actions add up
to a birth? Venus was born of water; when Chronos had destroyed Uranus
and the fragments of his body fell into the sea, the red-flecked foam gave
birth to the goddess of love. She rose from the sea like a shell, like a frail
skiff, her hair slicked on her white thighs. You could be born that way;
or by lustration, total immersion, ritual purification, in which you rose
up new, in a sense, to present yourself to the gods. That was a type of
birth. The water tended to be cold, the bathing place dark and cramped,
an uncomfortable womb; and when you emerged your skin was purplish
and puckered like that of a newborn child.

Was that right?

Jesus went on: *"What is born of the flesh is flesh, and what is born of the spirit
is spirit. Don't be surprised when I tell you that you must be born again. The
wind blows where it pleases, and you hear the sound of it, but you can't tell where
it comes from or where it is going. So it is with everyone who is born of the spirit."*

Pass that on. Yes, the wind blew where it wanted, but you could tell where it came from by the feel of it. Icy, shaggy Boreas fanned the face of the earth with his tawny wings, as Ovid described it, and ruffled the wide sea. Auster was drizzling and warm, the rain-bearing wind; Zephyrus brought flowers from the soft west and the land of the evening star. Eurus blew from beyond the Euphrates toward Arabia Felix and the borders of Judaea. This was the Parthian wind, the enemy wind; but it was not the worst. Boreas and Aquilo between them could sink ships, howling like war trumpets and hurling hailstones from the northeast.

God—whichever god it was who had created them—had put these brothers on earth to stir and refresh creation, but had then restrained them, when he saw how strong they were, to their own particular quarters of the sky. Their mayhem was limited. At least, this was how the poets explained it. They also spread the story that Aeolus, king of Thessaly, was in charge of the winds, catching and releasing them at any time he chose. Most of the time he kept them locked in a mountain, but when Juno hinted he threw them at Aeneas, and when Odysseus visited he gave him the bad winds wriggling and puffing in a bag. If you didn't parcel them up like that they would certainly do as they liked: tatter your sails, whip the rain in your face, blow you off course. That was why men still sacrificed to the winds, and why from November to March the wide Mediterranean was left for Aquilo to play in, separating Pilate definitively from home.

But it was strictly a poet's fancy to put the winds in cloaks and tunics and make them men. The philosophers knew it was the damp or dry exhalations of the earth that made the wind, as they squeezed into the crowded sky and struggled to get past each other. And the wind, too, was part of the plan. The four major winds and the eight subsidiary winds had been devised by Providence so that every section of the sky would be active and scoured clean. As one fell, the next rose, moving from east to west. The north winds, being regulated by odd numbers, could not blow on odd days, and the navigator Eudoxus reckoned that the exact pattern of the winds, with their exact consequences of fruit torn from the trees or boats blown back into harbor, was repeated every four years.

So wind was the air set in motion. The air moved and blew in heaven; the air moved and blew on earth, and even under the earth. Miners reported that the rivers and lakes beneath the earth also had their exhalations; "dead winds in the darkness," as Seneca was to call them. In the middle of the Underworld, not far from the banks of the Styx, stood a great dark elm tree in which dreams roosted like birds, hanging and trembling under every leaf. It must be the wind that touched them, just as a wind seemed to wrack the shivering army of spirits that stood pleading on the riverbank, as if they were leaves stripped from the autumn trees by Boreas himself, or gulls blown inland in the winter.

Was that what the man meant, that men born of spirit were like the wind? Could you see them at all? If you couldn't, how was it that this man Jesus could be seen, who was supposed to be born of the spirit himself? Did his so-called magical powers extend to spiriting himself away?

Jesus went on, as reported: *"Do you call yourself a master of Israel, and you don't know these things? If I tell you of earthly things, and you don't believe, how will you believe me when I tell you about heavenly things?*

"No one has gone up to heaven except the one who came down from heaven, the Son of Man. For God so loved the world that he gave his only son, that whoever believes in him shall not perish, but have everlasting life."

He seemed to mean immortality. That was not a foreign concept. There were plenty of immortals; they were set among the stars, engraved on the vault of the sky. Cassiopeia was there, the mother of Andromeda, whose boasting had caused her daughter to be chained to a rock to be eaten by that sea monster that later turned up in Jaffa. Perseus, who had rescued her, was there too, with his helmet and breastplate; Castor and Pollux were there, the heavenly twins, the guardians of sailors. Hercules could be seen sprawling, littering the sky with the evidence of his labors in the shape of lions and dragons; and beyond them, in sparkling drifts, was the milk that had spilled from the breasts of Venus when Cupid had been snatched away.

According to the poets (if you believed the poets) all these characters were now immortal. They were divine in very different measures: Tiberius, in his eulogy of Augustus, had even belittled Hercules as "only dealing with a stag or two and, oh, yes, a lion"; but when they had met their deaths they had all been taken up to heaven to preside and shine. It was nonsense to say, as this man Jesus did, that no one had gone up to heaven; the place was overcrowded. The real gods and the comedy stuntmen jostled one another right up to the limits of the sky.

Somewhere in the dark was the Caesar star. Farmers already knew it as the herald of good weather, coloring the grapes and the corn. Augustus was there, too, if you knew where to look for him. After his death, his soul had been taken up to heaven by an eagle which had flown out of the funeral pyre under everyone's eyes. That soul had become a comet that had blazed for seven days, and then Tiberius had placed it among the constellations. Augustus would go on forever; he would never die. Like the stars.

It could happen, in theory, to any man. The Stoics believed that each man was already a god, "if a god is that which lives, feels, remembers, foresees, and which rules, governs and moves the body over which it is set, just as the Supreme God above us rules this universe." But practical and public divinity was far away. It seemed essential to be of the right social class, the right *gens,* the right family, all somewhat higher than the ones to which Pilate belonged. Strength of character, achievements in the field, magisterial authority, favor in high places, could move a man steadily up the steep incline connecting mortals and immortals. Such a man could be an agent of heaven, doing the gods' work for them. As Tiberius had said of Augustus, "His actions and his fortunes were not such as he himself desired, but as heaven decreed."

The gods helped, giving a man violent times or raging wars in which to prove himself. There were certain qualities, too, as Cicero said, that enabled a man to ascend toward heaven: Intellect, Virtue, Piety, Fidelity. Perhaps even a governor of an obscure province could inch toward that extraordinary state. If Pilate did well in Judaea, if he ruled wisely, firmly yet benevolently, if he averted some disaster to the empire, he, too, would begin the long ascent. People would begin to applaud him. He would be given triumphs, feel the wreaths on his forehead. The people would make him consul, then repeat the honor. He would be called *pater patriae,* father of his country. Divinity would still be far off; but his brow would gleam, his eyes would shine, and his very shadow would inspire awe as it fell on the ground before him. *Et deus factus est.*

Idle dreams. Wrong family, wrong class, no likely opportunity.

Yet his soul might be immortal. It might journey on when his body died. Most people believed that; only the Epicureans dismissed it as nonsense. Even the Stoics, who thought a man simply went out like a lamp, believed that his soul then darted back to heaven, a flying spark freed from the shackles of the body. Something in a man did not die and kept on traveling, even if he did not deserve the stars. The soul went on—if you believed all this—through the caves and corridors of the Underworld, a sad-eyed moth. It was not just children, though cynics said it was mostly children, who believed in seven-headed Cerberus barking at the gate of hell, or Charon the ferryman taking the souls across. Men's spirits had sometimes wandered there as they lay on the funeral pyre, and they had revived to report it afterward. Aeneas, too, had traveled through the Underworld alive, his heart broken by the sobbing spirits of the unburied dead.

There was some comfort in believing that the spirits remained. You did not quite lose the people you loved, even if you remembered them personally only at the Parentalia in February, strewing their graves with wreaths and bread and the first few violets of the spring. That was eternal life too, wasn't it? Immortality was a name and a life remembered by your children.

But that was not the trickiest part of what Jesus had said. The trickiest part was *God loved.* Could the gods love like that, sweetly and paternally? They fell in love; they lusted and rutted like beasts. Great Jupiter came down on Ganymede, on Danae, on Io and on countless women, begetting divine sons to fornicate after him. And they loved in the sense that they picked people out to be showered with honors and elevated in the state. But this was benevolence, care for a man's interests, not that clamorous pain in the heart and that aching rush to embrace someone. It was the selective, discriminating kindness of superior to inferior. A prayer to the gods was a petition to be loved in just that way. Notice *me.* Favor *me.* And, at the end, as you lowered your arms: "Propitius sit," "God be gracious to me."

How could such prayers find purchase, if God loved everyone? How could there be beggars, slaves, victims of murder, patients with rotting sores, if God loved everyone? And why should His favor be meted out to anyone who did not love Him first? Love was not unconditional; it did not work like that. Tiberius would love him because he had loved him first. Favor was returned for favor. The client served the patron; the patron smiled on the client. This was the thrust of his letters home, the hardest part of his distance from Rome: *Mutuo me diligas,* love me as I love you, put in a word for me, press for this favor; if you are well, it is well, I am well. This was the whole reciprocal web of the world.

Most worryingly, this God loved him. He had not asked him to, but nevertheless He seemed to have found him. It was as unnerving as the thought that Jupiter selected you for thunderbolts, or that your fate was sealed when a snake slid out of the altar as you were sacrificing. You were trapped in someone else's arrangement, caught like a leaf in His burning, undiscriminating love.

Yet, having talked of love, Jesus went on: *"God did not send his son into the world to condemn the world, but so that through him the world might be saved.*

"No one who believes in him is condemned; but whoever does not believe is condemned already, because he does not believe in the Name of the only Son of God."

So he was loved, and he was condemned too—was that right? He was condemned *already;* no chance of struggle. To Nicodemus, the rabbi, the secret believer, the words presented no difficulty. He was in the light, as the man had put it; but Pilate was in the dark, in the uncomprehending Gentiles' place. Sentence had been passed. He had failed the test.

Of course, he didn't care. He didn't believe these preposterous things. But Jesus insisted on involving him in his schemes, like a trader trying to make a bargain, or a column lounger in the Forum trying to draw him into his pressure group. Luke's Jesus had once been asked directly what he thought of Pilate, after Pilate had cut down a crowd of Galilean pilgrims in the outer courtyard of the Temple, "mingling their blood with their sacrifices." Jesus said: "I tell you, unless you repent, you shall all perish in the same way."

Unless you repent. It was as if Pilate himself was doing God's work of punishment: as if he himself, despite his presence in the list under "darkness," was the winnowing flail that John the Baptist had spoken of in the desert. He was showing Judaea what the wrath of God was like; he was the implacable and violent opposite of Jesus' gentleness and healing. This made them co-conspirators. Pilate did not need to creep, like Nicodemus, to visit Jesus in the dark. He was already instructed to behave as he was meant to. He was in the plan, enlisted already, condemned already.

End of report. Will you have more wine, Governor? Olives? A cloak for the cold?

V.

According to the *Acta Pilati,* the leaders of the Jews came more than once to Pilate to tell him their complaints against Jesus. The list was long. A clerk could fill a whole stack of wax tablets with them: picking ears of wheat on the Sabbath, claiming to forgive sins, prophesying the destruction of the Temple. Several tablets could be filled with Jesus' remarks about the Pharisees alone, and these were much more vicious than anything he had to say about the Romans: the Pharisees were whitewashed sepulchres, camel swallowers, blind fools, filth, goats, trumpeters, dirty plates, mumblers on street corners. But, from the Jewish point of view, there was worse.

"We know this man," said the priests in the *Acta Pilati.* "His father's Joseph the carpenter, his mother's Mary, and he's going around this city calling himself a king and the son of God; and even though he's a Jew, he's overthrowing the scriptures and polluting the Sabbath, and says he will destroy the law of our fathers!"

"What exactly does he do that would destroy your law?" asked Pilate.

The council of the priests broke into shouts of outrage. "We have a law that we should not heal any man on the Sabbath! This man by his evil deeds heals the lame, the crooked, the withered, the blind, the dumb, the paralytic. . . . People possessed! And on the Sabbath day—"

Pilate said, "By what evil deeds?"

"He's a sorcerer. He casts out devils by Beelzebub, the prince of devils. And they're all subject to him!"

"This is not casting out devils by an unclean spirit, but by the god Aesculapius," countered Pilate.

The *Acta Pilati* left that observation hanging, as doubtless the Jews would have done if Pilate had ever uttered it. Their silence said, *"What?"* Roman and Jewish notions of sorcery and healing were simply incompatible. But the notion of Jesus as a miracle worker comes not only from the Gospels but also, with a slightly pagan flavor, from Josephus, in the section known as the "Testimonium Flavianum" in the *Antiquities.* "Now about this time," runs the passage,

there appeared a wise man called Jesus—if indeed one can speak of him as
a man, for he was a doer of astonishing deeds, a healer of people who receive gladly what they want to believe. He won over many of the Jews
and many of the Greeks.

For years, this section about Jesus (sandwiched between the reportage
about Pilate) was dismissed as a Christian forgery, but modern scholars
increasingly think that bits of it may be true: in particular, the parts describing Jesus as "a wise man," a "wonder-worker" and a healer of the
simple and credulous. Josephus does not mention what effect, if any, this
man had on Romans. But later writers built on the thought to suggest
that Pilate was intrigued by Christ's credentials as a healer, because he
himself needed help. Procula had terrible headaches and, of course, bad
dreams; according to a Slavonic version of Josephus, Pilate actually summoned Jesus, like a doctor, because his wife was dying. According to the
Golden Legend, it was his own aching liver that tortured him. In both the
Apocryphal Gospels and in Templar lore there are suggestions that Jesus
was a follower of the magi of the East, bringing with him the occult
practices that captivated more susceptible minds in Rome: minds that
demanded healing both physical and psychological.

Among modern writings, Bulgakov's Pilate is clearly in this tradition. He suffers from blinding migraines, hemicrania, brought on by the
dry dazzling sun of Jerusalem and the smell of attar of roses. When they
afflict him he can only sit perfectly still, dreaming of darkened rooms
and the touch of cold water. Jesus' response to his question, "What is
truth?" is to tell him: "The truth is chiefly that your head aches, and
aches so hard that you are having cowardly thoughts about death." Pilate
immediately feels the pain subsiding. From that point on, his line of
questioning wavers; the only thing he really wants to know is "Are you a
great physician?" When Jesus says he is not, he is bitterly disappointed.

St. Paul himself hinted that Pilate, a man caught up in forces he did
not control, may have been the prey of the demon *archontes* who ruled
both his world and his body. This did not necessarily suggest that he
would have dabbled in philters or charms, but most Romans did. He
may well have worn around his neck, or carried in a breast pocket, an
amulet of dried anemones to ward off tertian fever, or of black bryony
against scrofula. (There were so many anemones in Judaea; the Garden of

Gethsemane was thick with them.) He may have drunk the local bitumen, powdered and tangy like coal tar, in drafts of wine to treat diarrhea. It made sense to take care abroad, since this was where strange new diseases came from, like the virulent facial pox that spread to Rome when a quaestor's secretary picked it up in Asia Minor. On this disease, which had to be treated with cauterization, the legate of Aquitaine had spent two hundred thousand sesterces. The ill would seek a cure in anything, even other people's deaths. Some doctors would not hesitate to hang around the necks of sufferers from quartan fever little bags containing the hair of the crucified and nails from the cross.

This was getting close to the edge of accepted medical practice, but not too close. When the sensible advice of doctors had been taken to heart—rest, exercise, no wine, cold baths—most Romans fell back on folk medicine and, in effect, faith healing. At its worst, this was a realm of hags, witches, charlatans, fake potions concocted from lizards, leaves and entrails, anointings with grease. Practitioners of the art loitered in damp caves or, more often, in basement rooms behind screens of dirty sheets. Nothing they did was miraculous, however. Everything had some rational explanation, to be attributed to some property in the ingredients of the ghastly mixtures they made. If something could not be explained, it was better to suppress the worker of miracles, rather than let his power spread. A man once visited Tiberius, broke a crystal goblet and put it together again by passing his hands over it; Tiberius, horrified that he could not control this, had the man killed.

Healing by the agency of Aesculapius came as close as a Roman dared to the art of the miraculous. The god of medicine and healing had been spirited out of the fire by Mercury himself. He was the healer of all men and the raiser of the dead, reviving them with holy herbs. Jupiter killed him at last with a bolt of lightning, because as long as Aesculapius continued his work, men lived forever and would not die. In that sense (as perhaps in others), Jupiter and Tiberius responded to the threat of usurpation in exactly the same way.

The devotee of Aesculapius would hope to be healed by sleeping overnight in the temple of the god. He would approach quietly, in the dusk. It was not necessary to have the agency or presence of priests; he would stay there alone. Commonly he bathed or swam first, to present himself thoroughly cleansed at the altar. His hands would still be damp, the hair damp on the nape of his neck; if he had swum in the dusk, he might carry the memory of the glittering phosphorescence that had followed the motion of his arms. To cleave the water had given him the necessary shock of sacred purification. As he bowed before the altar, his body shivered and glowed.

"Heal me, O God of eternal life."

In a hessian bag he had a small snake, sacred to the god. It had been doped with an infusion of poppy seeds and flopped in his hand, opening its pale sleepy jaws. He laid it on the altar, where it coiled in on itself. When Aesculapius was born, the poets said, he had hatched from the egg of a crow; then, as his powers grew, he had conjured snakes to twine around a stick. His remedy for snakebite was inscribed on a stone at his temple in Cos: two denarii of wild thyme, two of all-heal, one of trefoil, aniseed, fennel and parsley, pounded with wine into pastilles to be swallowed one at a time. The yawning snake also prefigured the instruments of a human doctor: the puncturing, the pain, the mingling of blood.

Honey cakes were laid on the altar, too. After that, the patient wrapped his toga around his head and sat against the wall. He hoped to sleep. Supplicants who slept in the temples of Aesculapius were visited with dreams describing the means of their cure. Some saw ghostly priests who came to them with poultices and decoctions, or surgeons sharpening their knives. Some were cured merely by dreaming. Others saw only the endless repetition of a peacock spreading its blue-green tail or milestones on the coast road, solidly marching into darkness. To calm himself, to make sure that he was lucid and not beginning to die, the patient would repeat the same words over and over: Heal me. Milestones, road, darkness, spinning circles of green and purple, the bright curve of a claw, sickness in the throat: Heal me. Heal me. Heal me.

Alone, he sweated with fear. But he did not try to leave, in case the sweat itself was curative. He had brought wine, but it was dedicated and he could not drink it; besides, he wanted icy water, and the hands of a woman soothing his neck and face. His limbs were stiffening. As the night wore on he slid down the wall and rolled himself in his cloak on the unforgiving floor. Thus he would doze for a while, waiting for the touch of the god.

When dawn appeared, a slave would come to rouse him. Diffidently, as he had been trained to, he shook the patient by the shoulder and spoke into his ear. Then he wiped his face with a cloth that had been dipped in water, making him shiver and spit. Any cure would be more efficacious if a man first spat three times on the ground. Light was coming up over the city; there were slight tinkling morning sounds, the songs of birds. The patient would stand by the wall, aware of his unshavenness, composing himself.

The slave had brought a cockerel in a bag. He threw it down on the altar, wings and head trussed, beak tied with a leather thong. The creature continued to struggle feebly, its comb lying sideways and its eyelids flickering. The patient took the knife. He cut the thong first, to let the bird scream; but sometimes it was traumatized and made no sound. This was unnerving. By its hard yellow feet he swung it away from him, slashed down with the blade, and severed the cord on the bird's back. Instantly the cock was alive, striking out, flailing, screaming in a whirlwind of black wings. He managed to hold it, and cut off the head. For a minute the wings continued to whirl. His arms were full of pulsating feathers and rivulets of warm blood that ran down his chest and splashed on the marble floor.

He laid his sacrifice on the altar. There was a prayer to be said and he whispered it, holding out his crimsoned sleeves. Somewhere in the town, among the still trees, other cocks crowed. And the sun came up slowly over the red-rimmed bowl of the sea.

If not Aesculapius, then Jesus; if one could not heal, perhaps the other could. The Roman Pilate, like the Pilate of the *Acta,* would have understood the parallels of healing and blood sacrifice, both gateways to eternal life. In his curiosity, he might have risked a meeting with Jesus in the hope of getting well. He might have wanted to test his power, as much as to kill him in the cause of public order. In the world of relentlessly interlocking fates, one pretext was as good as another.

VI.

All through the Gospels the net closed on Pilate. The prophets said what he would do, and he did it. Confidently, tauntingly, Jesus predicted his decisions; for he knew "from the beginning," according to Matthew, "who did not believe, and who was going to betray him." The representative of the world's most overweening power was reduced to a stagehand who would, at a given moment—*the* given moment—draw back the curtain, turn the revolve, drop the scenery from the flies.

Even the smallest detail was prearranged. The props were laid out on the table. The blank board on which Pilate was to write "Jesus of Nazareth" was there already, with the pen beside it, for the prophets had foretold that "he shall be called a Nazarene." The nails were laid out, for, according to Isaiah, "he was pierced through for our faults." Here were the thirty pieces of silver bulging in a bag, ready to accomplish Jeremiah: "And they took the thirty pieces of silver, the price of him that was valued." And there the knucklebone dice that the soldiers would roll at the foot of the cross, drunkenly fulfilling the words of the prophet: "On my vesture they cast lots."

It was not only the coming of Jesus that was advertised as the fulfillment of prophecy but, some thought, Pilate's too. Jesus preached that when the Jews saw "the abomination of desolation" standing "where it ought not," this would be the sign of afflictions to come. At the sight of it, residents of the cities of Judaea would flee to the hills, not turning back even for their coats. This was not a vague general warning, but a specific prediction that Jerusalem would be trodden down by the Gentiles; and the beginning of that oppression, at least for some of the Jews, was Pilate's "mistake" about the standards. Eusebius, citing Josephus and Philo, said that when Pilate brought the images of Caesar into Jerusalem by night, this marked "the beginning of factions."

The Romans after Pilate were to do much worse things in Jerusalem. In A.D. 70, during the Jewish war, they smashed the Temple down. But at the time of Jesus' teaching, Pilate's blunders in Jerusalem—the shock of the standards glittering on the walls of the Antonia—would have been the first abomination that sprang to mind. It was the worst incident the Jews had seen since Crassus, the closest approach of armed force to the Temple. So Pilate signaled the beginning of those times that Jesus had come to preach about, the "desolation" of which John the Baptist warned so repeatedly. His tactless incursion coincided almost exactly with the start of Jesus' ministry. Whatever impulse had prompted him to send those standards with their images into Jerusalem, the impulse itself was preordained, God's finger nudging his back. The infamous medallions of Tiberius were on the prop table too.

Jesus got closer, more taunting still. He knew that he must die for these calamitous and glorious events to unfold, and he knew when it would happen. Openly, frequently, he talked about it. The timing was precise. When he refused to go up to Jerusalem for Sukkot, it was because his time had "not yet come." He told the Pharisees, on one of the many occasions when they came to arrest him but lost their nerve, that he would be with them "only a little while, and then I go to him who sent me." Before the Last Supper he told the people who hung on his parables that "yet a little while is the light with you; walk while you have the light." Some days before his death he began to announce that the hour had come when he would be "glorified." In Matthew he said openly that it would come at the feast of the Passover, the day of the sacrifice of the holy and unblemished lamb.

He was often equally precise about the manner of his glorification. According to Luke, he told his disciples that "this scripture must be fulfilled in me: 'And he was reckoned with transgressors.'" According to Matthew, he explained what would happen to him three times, each time in a slightly different way: "We are going up to Jerusalem, and the Son of Man shall be betrayed to the chief priests and the scribes, and they shall condemn him to death; and they shall deliver him to the Gentiles to mock, and to scourge, and to crucify him; and the third day he shall rise again."

The manner of his trial had been foretold by the prophets down to the last detail. At the prophet Jeremiah's trial in Jerusalem, despite his warning that the priests would bring "innocent blood" on themselves, they went ahead and accused him, saying he should die for "prophesying against this city." The "princes," Pilates-to-be, demurred, saying "This man is not worthy of death." Nonetheless, Jeremiah was bound and sent to an "Idumaean," just as Jesus, according to Luke, was sent by Pilate to Herod Antipas. The prophet Hosea also foresaw this scene, predicting that Jesus would be sent "bound as a present to the king." Once he was sent back, the prophecy was carried on by Isaiah: Jesus would appear before his judge "like a lamb that is dumb before the shearers, never open-

ing his mouth." For his meekness and man's sins he would then be "punished, struck by God, brought low, pierced": exact premonitions
of the orders Pilate was to give for the binding, the scourging, the laying
on the cross, the nails. God struck Jesus and the governor struck him,
one in the person of the other.

Jesus brooded on his Roman denouement. The cross seemed to haunt
him. Although he most often told his disciples merely that he would be
"killed," he never implied that he would be stoned, which would have
been his fate at the hands of the Jews, or that he would be stabbed in the
street. His death was to be in the Roman fashion, administered by the
Roman who happened to be in charge. Jesus told both his disciples and
would-be disciples to "take up their cross" and follow him; he was going
first, another of those familiar trudgers along the roads of Judaea, with
Pilate's sentence around his neck. Then, having carried the cross and allowed himself to be nailed to it, he would be lifted up, "as Moses lifted
up the serpent in the wilderness."

The serpent Moses lifted up was a brazen snake that looped from a
pole in horizontal coils; all those who were bitten turned to the serpent
and were healed. That ritual shape of upright and cross-beam had been
prefigured all through the Old Testament. Sacrificial brands had been
stacked in the form of a cross on the back of Isaac, the son of Abraham.
Lamb's blood in the form of a cross had marked the doors of the Israelites
on the eve of the first Passover, and the lamb itself, spiked with rosemary,
was roasted spread-eagled on two spits set at right angles. Moses had
stretched out his arms, crosslike, before the battle with Amalek; and Eli-
jah had met an old woman who, because she held up two pieces of wood
in the form of a cross, was rewarded by God with extra meal and oil in
her cupboards. St. Jerome contended that the form was even older than
that, elemental, suggesting birds flying in the air, a plow breaking the
soil, a man swimming.

Yet the oddest prefiguring of all was that Pilate's standards, complete
with their images of Tiberius, were also in the form of the cross. Justin
Martyr, a converted pagan and one of the earliest apologists for Christianity, described this precisely when, in his *First Apology* of around 150,
he addressed the emperor Diocletian. "And your symbols," he wrote, "in
what are called banners, and the trophies with which your processions are
universally made, display the power of this form; and by these you show
the signs of your rule and authority, even if you do it without knowing

what you do. And you consecrate the images of your emperors, on their demise, by this form, and by inscriptions you term them gods." On this reading, Pilate was the first man to carry to Jerusalem the triumphant sign of the cross.

So the form was vital: and so was the sheer spectacle, the showiness, of crucifixion. Jesus meant to be on display, so that his death could have its cosmic effect. "When you have lifted up the Son of Man, then you will know that I am he," he said once. Another remark was possibly even more specific: "If I am lifted up from the earth, I will draw all men unto me." Only one man could bring about this lifting and this irresistible attraction: the man who, as Jesus spoke, was perhaps lifting nothing heavier than the day's routine report, or a Corinthian wineglass through which, dreamily, he could see the sun.

Judas was fingered, too. Jesus knew what his role was among the disciples even before Judas was sure of it himself. He announced his betrayal as frequently as he announced his crucifixion. When the cosmic moment came at the Last Supper in the upper room, Jesus knew Judas' movements to the last detail. He would take a piece of bread and dip his hand toward the dish of vinegar that stood on the table as a condiment, prefiguring the dipping of a sponge in sour wine during the crucifixion. Their fingers would brush together. In John, he would give the sop to Judas directly, already understanding his disposition: "I know," he said, "whom I have chosen." Judas would ask, "Is it I, Lord?"—the slightly tremulous question, more a statement, of the man who cannot escape. Then he would leave, skittering down the stone stairs. He went, in the apocryphal versions of the Passion, to perform the various jobs allotted to him: to notify the priests, collect the tree of the cross, and warn Pilate that his turn was coming.

When Judas asked Jesus "Is it I, Lord?," Jesus answered: "You said it." Pilate was later to ask Jesus questions to which he would get the same irritating answer, as if to say: "Of course. Those are the words I expected, the lines written in the script for you since time began. You said them. Well done." In John, as soon as Judas had stumbled out into the dark, Jesus exclaimed: "Now is the Son of Man glorified, and God is glorified with him."

Each of these predictions, if he ever heard them, would have been like a dare to Pilate. He was being challenged to kill a man who was determined to die anyway; who, when his disciples cried that they would try to protect him, accused them of being the Devil in disguise. If Pilate killed him, it would be with his permission and encouragement: he was dying only to prove that he could rise. Augustine, in an extraordinary passage, had Jesus say: "I carried you on my shoulders, gave you back to my father, labored, sweated, pressed thorns upon my head, exposed my hands to the nails, opened my side with a spear. . . ." He was totally in control of the situation. "I lay down my life," John's Jesus said imperiously, "that I may take it again. No man takes it from me; I lay it down myself and I have power to take it again."

No man takes it from me. Would Pilate stand for that? How was he meant to react to these confident predictions of how he would behave? Some were encoded, but others were blatant: Jesus was approaching, expecting, wanting crucifixion. He needed Pilate. But what if Pilate refused to play? The sulky, resentful governor of Philo would instinctively react by refusing to indulge him; the clumsy tactician of Josephus would try to get out of the trap. Perhaps Jesus would lose his authority if he didn't do it, if he refused to rise to the dare; the prophet would miss his chance of martyrdom, and his prophecies would turn out wrong. Perhaps Pilate could simply ignore him, let him get old, allow his followers to drift away. But the uncomfortable implication of Jesus was that his arrest and death were in the stars, and that Fate had already fingered Pilate as his executioner.

Someone then—perhaps his secretary, or his military aide, or Caiaphas, or his own conscience—would ask, "So, are you going to kill him then?"

And he would burst out, furious: "Is it up to me?"

VII.

Go through the props again. Reed pen, dice, money, chair of judgment; and, in the corner, the most vital prop of all: the cross. "The tree," wrote Augustine, "which had brought about the fall and the loss of Paradise, shall be the instrument of redemption."

The type of wood did not matter. By legend and prediction, whatever timber Pilate ordered was already incorporated into God's design.

The date palm, with its unwithering fronds and clustering fruit, was the model of the Tree of Life on which, according to the Archangel Michael in the Book of Enoch, the glory of the Eternal King would rest when he visited the earth. The yew was the tree of immortality. Under the oak tree, God had made his covenant with Abraham; and according to Isaiah he had promised that "the glory of Lebanon" would come to the pine and the fir trees. The aspen tree shook with the premonition that it would carry Christ, and the apple tree was spoken for.

Five thousand two hundred and twenty years before the year of the Passion—according to the *Golden Legend* and dozens of medieval variants—the tree that formed the cross was seen in a vision by Seth, the son of Adam. Seth had been asked by his father, who was then 932 years old, to find the oil of mercy that God had promised to send them. This oil would heal the sin wounds, "sixty and ten" of them, that still covered his body and the body of Eve as punishment for eating the apple in the garden of Eden. Adam told Seth to go to the gate of Eden and beg the oil from the angel who stood there.

Seth set out from the head of the valley of Hebron and found the soft green path that led to the gate of Paradise. The track turned eastward, and soon became bare earth; this was the route that Adam and Eve had taken out of the garden. Since then, no grass had grown on it. At the end of this track, in a light like a burning fire, stood the gate of Eden.

At the gate Seth began to pray. St. Michael appeared to him. "It's useless to pray for the oil of mercy," he told him. "It won't be sent for five thousand two hundred and twenty years, until Christ dies for the sins of men. But put your head through the gate, and note what you see."

Seth did so. Inside he saw jewel-green meadows sparkling with flowers, perfumed trees, branches hung heavily with bright fruit, and the flash and cry of extraordinary birds. He wanted to live there forever. Only one thing spoiled the garden: a great bare tree, embraced by the withered remains of a snake like a dried and twisted creeper. This was the tree from which his parents had eaten the apple of fate.

Then he looked again, and saw that the tree had grown bark and leaves. It was immense now, filling the blue-gold sky, and at the top of the tree was a tiny baby in swaddling clothes. This, he was told, was the Son of God, who would bring the oil of mercy in the fullness of time.

When Seth left, the angel gave him three pips from an apple and instructed him to put them under Adam's tongue as soon as he was dead.

Seth did so, and, as Adam lay dead in the valley of Hebron, the pips began to grow into three small trees as delicate as wands, which stood in Adam's mouth in the deep earth until the time of Moses. One was a cedar, "the tree of height," denoting the Father; one was the sweet-smelling cypress, denoting the Son; and the third, the pine or the olive, was a fruit-bearing tree, denoting the gifts of the Holy Ghost. These grew until they were an ell high, and then paused to await the passage of history.

In time the Israelites crossed the Red Sea and came to the valley of Hebron. One evening Moses, walking in the valley, came upon the tiny trees. Recognizing them at once as a symbol of the Trinity, he pulled them out of the ground, and the sweetest smell came up with them. With these wands Moses healed the sick and performed miracles. When he knew he was about to die, he planted them in a stream under Mount Tabor in Arabia.

For a thousand years the wands stood in the stream, never growing. Then King David found them, on God's instructions, and took them to Jerusalem. On the way he met three "blackamoors" who, when touched with the rods, became white. It was evening when he carried the wands into the city, so he set them in a ditch and put a company of men to guard them. In the morning, he found that the wands had grown into one tree with three branches springing from the top. He did not try to move it, but built a strong wall around it and encircled it with a silver girdle to mark its growth each year. David wrote the whole of the Psalter under it, sitting in its deep shade. After thirty years the tree stopped growing.

Meanwhile, the Temple was being built in Jerusalem. David began the work, and Solomon completed it. When the work was almost finished, the carpenters found that they needed one more beam; and the only wood they could find to fit was the tree that David had planted. Solomon therefore ordered it cut down and taken into the Temple. But the carpenters found that they could never cut it to the right size; it was either one cubit too long or one cubit too short. So Solomon ordered them to make a bridge with it across the Kedron ditch. The Queen of Sheba, visiting Solomon one day, saw the beam bridge and advised him to bury it, for a man would die on it who would destroy the Mosaic law.

Solomon buried it deep. But a well sprang out of it which had miraculous powers, and the sick came to bathe in the waters. Every morning, while it was still dark, God sent his angels to stir the water so that the tree beneath would be remembered. When Jesus came to earth and began to perform miracles at the pool, the beam rose from the deep and floated. This was the tree, seasoned by water, cut down by Solomon, encircled with silver by David, uprooted by Moses, germinated under the tongue of Adam, which Pilate ordered loaded on to the back of Christ.

Others say the journey was less complicated. In the medieval *Book of the Bee,* Adam, as he was driven out of Paradise, hacked a branch from the tree, whittled off the twigs and used it as a staff for the rest of his life. The staff was passed to Abel and then to Abraham, who wielded it to smash the idols of Terah. Jacob used it, along with rods of hazel and chestnut and green poplar, to cast a fertility spell on the watering troughs where the flocks of Laban drank. For a while after that, the staff was hidden by an angel in a cave of treasures in the mountains of Moab; but it was found by Jethro as he grazed his sheep, and he passed it on to Moses. Moses used it to display the brazen serpent, and the staff then passed to Phineas, who buried it in the desert. It remained buried there until Christ was born, at which moment its whereabouts were revealed to Joseph. He dug it up, used it all his life and passed it to James the brother of Jesus; James gave it to Judas. Judas gave it to Pilate, and it was used as one of the planks on the cross that Jesus carried to Golgotha.

Golgotha itself was also preordained. Some men, like John Donne, thought it was the site of the fateful tree itself:

> *We think that Paradise and Calvarie,*
> *Christ's cross and Adam's tree stood in one place.*

But more often it was said to be the place where Adam was buried, the bald, brownish hill that held the skull of the head of the human race. Cain and Abel had brought their offerings to this place; Noah had sacrificed there when he came out of the Ark; and it was there that Abraham was saved from sacrificing Isaac by finding—caught in the brambles—a ram, which prefigured the lamblike offering of Christ. So, although crucifixions could be carried out in any prominent site and along any public road, Pilate naturally sent Jesus to Golgotha. There was no other place.

Nor was there any other time. At a certain hour on a certain day of a certain year the sun would be eclipsed. As Amos put it, "I will cause the sun to go down at noon, and I will darken the earth in one clear day . . . and I will make it as the mourning of an only son." Or as Joel said, "The earth shall quake . . . the heavens shall tremble . . . the sun and moon shall be dark, and the stars shall withdraw their shining."

The date of this eclipse was to be the twenty-fifth of March: in the Roman calendar, the sixth before the Kalends of April; in the Jewish calendar, the fourteenth of Nisan, of the year 33. Or it could have been the year 30; for it was the day that mattered, rather than the year. Since the reform of the calendar by Caesar, the twenty-fifth of March was the spring equinox: the day when the sun passed the great celestial cross, the X of Plato's *Timaeus,* formed by the equator and the ecliptic. Justin Martyr actually pointed out that the X was God's son, set crosswise in the heavens. In the great scheme of things it was bound to be on Friday the twenty-fifth of March that Christ was put to death, in order that after the necessary spell of darkness he could rise on a Sunday, the day of the *sol invictus* or unconquered sun.

The twenty-fourth of March was also known in the cult of Attis, among the Phrygians, as the "day of blood" on which the god died. The beautiful Attis was driven so mad by the jealous Cybele, goddess of nature, that he mutilated himself beneath a pine tree. His spirit passed into the tree, a resinous flash, and at the foot of the pine sprang anemones and violets from the warm rain of his blood. On the twenty-fourth an effigy would be presented of the young man tied to a sacred pine, with wreaths of violets on its branches; for two days he would be mourned as lost; and on the third his followers would celebrate his resurrection, which was also the coming of the spring.

In the case of Christ, now, the dead wood of the cross put out flowers. The scheme of salvation was also the scheme of the seasons. It was symbolically necessary that Christ should die at the coming of the spring, not at any other time; that he should die on a tree, not in any other way; and that he should not merely hang there, as on a gibbet, but extend his arms like branches with the sap of his blood flowing from his hands.

Only Pilate could effect that. Only he could provide the tau-shape of the cross, the Egyptian sign of life, on which life could be proclaimed through the act of death. His role was to be the winter to Christ's spring.

He could struggle, of course. He was free to do that. But the result of his struggling was already known: however he wriggled, he would end up as God's agent. To resist his role was unhelpful, as if Boreas were suddenly to sulk and abandon his job as scourer of the northern quarter. To be merciful and soft, in his case, would do nothing to advance the transformation of the world.

Chapter 4

BLOOD ON HIS BOOTS

. . . And we are onlookers at the crime,
Callous contemporaries of the slow
Torture of God. Here is the hill
Made ghastly by His spattered blood

Whereon He hangs and suffers still;
See, the centurions wear riding-boots,
Black shirts and badges and peaked caps;
Greet one another with raised-arm salutes;
They have cold eyes, unsmiling lips;
Yet these His brothers know not what they do.

And on His either side hang dead
A labourer and a factory-hand,
Or one is maybe a lynched Jew
And one a Negro or a Red,
Coolie or Ethiopian, Irishman,
Spaniard or German democrat . . .

DAVID GASCOYNE,
"Ecce Homo," from *Miserere* (1937)

I.

WE ARE IN VICTORIA STREET, in London, on any week-
day morning. (It is any street of any capital in the northern
hemisphere: glass towers above, sandwich shops below.) It is
raining. On both sides of the street, workers stream on their way from
the station to the desk, the computer screen, the hasty mug of coffee.
Their heads and shoulders are bent forward, under jostling umbrellas,
with the thought of the work that awaits them in the government department or the magistrates' court: the memos they will write, the rules
they will revise, the tiny drops of lubricant they will apply to the giant
wheels of the machinery of state. Try to walk against the flow of these
workers, and you are buffeted as if in a current full of fish. They swim on
inexorably down the long, rain-slicked street.

On their right stands Westminster Cathedral, across a plaza laid
with pink and gray paving. This is the Catholic Church admitted at last
as part of the British establishment, a stone's throw from Parliament and
right beside the Army and Navy Stores. On the corner stands a giant
McDonald's with seating for two hundred and a corporate presence that
spans the globe from Anchorage to China. The commuters, intent, ignore both of them.

They ignore even more the young black man who stands in the
cathedral porch, silently holding out a McDonald's paper cup. His be-
longings are stacked in a corner, under a cardboard refrigerator box
which he uses to sleep on the pavement. His rancid smell mingles with
others: incense, candles, cold stone. He lingers in a place where every
kind of power—religious, corporate, political—is oppressively represented. And by his very presence he unsettles them all.

Sixty yards from him is another confrontation. It is in stone, a bas-
relief on a pillar, the first Station of the Cross; but it is just as unsettling.
Jesus, a disheveled creature, no doubt malodorous too, stands before Pilate. Pilate sits on a high-backed marble throne engraved with the words

"Senatus Populusque Romanus"; he presides in the full and solid power of the Roman empire. Before him, a boy servant with the bowl of water kneels respectfully. Behind the governor, on the wall, in Roman capitals, march the scarlet letters recording his two irreversible decisions, the release of Barabbas and the condemnation of Christ. Memo: action taken. His throne has raised him on a level with his victim, and he stares at him with a look that is arrogant, longing, confused and cold, all at once. It is the absolute bafflement of power meeting power, but not understanding how.

Eric Gill, who sculpted the relief, labored over this expression. He worked on the piece for seventeen years in his barn at Ditchling, under the South Downs. In his working smock, with his thick-lensed glasses protecting him from chips of stone, he chiseled Pilate's features in Hoptonwood limestone. Under the soft Sussex light, the face seemed to say everything he wanted. But once it was placed in the cathedral, with "the reflected light from the floor [and] the conflicting shadows thrown by the electric lights," it looked "entirely different." Gill told a friend that the expressions on both faces had been completely changed, and that the result distressed him.

He had meant to suggest galvanizing, outrageous things. Pilate was supposed to be a symbol of the world Gill hated and from which he had retreated: the symbol of power, industry, capital, plutocracy, the exploitation of labor. In this first Station, Christ, the lover, gazed on "the essential dirtiness, dirtiness in its very being and nature, of the industrial capitalist world." It was fitting that the Station was hung in the autumn of 1914, when that world had just plunged into a convulsion largely of its own making: a bloodbath made possible by pampered armaments industries and the unstoppable efficiency of the railways.

This was not the first time that Pilate had been made to symbolize power far beyond himself. The reason why he is in the Creed, a bureaucrat set down incongruously among elemental streams of light and celestial thrones, is not merely to set Christ's death in time. Pilate represented not simply his age, but the full power structure of his age and the worst that it could do. He sat on the judgment seat of Caesar transplanted to Judaea; as Tacitus put it, leaning his full weight on the Latin *imperitante,* "Christ had, by the imperial authority of Tiberius exercised through the procurator Pontius Pilate, incurred the penalty of death." The trial of Jesus before the imperial judge was the moment when he challenged overweening power and appeared to lose; but, as the faithful knew, he burst out of the tomb and threw that power over. It was essential not merely to express faith in Christ but in "Christ crucified under Pontius Pilate," brutally killed but not—ha!—killed at all.

Among the early Christians the phrase *sub Pontio Pilato* was used almost as an incantation, an invocation, a magic spell. In one Apocryphal Gospel, St. Peter commanded a camel "in the name of Jesus Christ crucified under Pontius Pilate" through the eye of the famous needle; the tiny needle, glinting in the sand, opened "like a gate," and the camel lurched through. Demoniacs were exorcised "by the name of Christ crucified under Pontius Pilate," and converts were plunged three times in the baptismal water while Pilate's name, as well as Christ's, washed over them. The purged demoniacs immediately began to cure the sick, where other charm wavers had been unable to cure them. The names made devils tremble; and Justin Martyr makes it clear that they did not fall down merely at the mention of Christ, but at the name of "Pontius Pilate the governor of Judaea," who had administered his death "by dispensation" and had then been trumped, utterly.

The victory was all the more impressive if the odds were stacked against Christ by a bigger dose of evil and portentousness in his prosecutor. Writers through the ages therefore colored Pilate's character darker and crueler, without feeling they were exaggerating much. Tyrant Pilate is a constant. He can be traced right back to Philo's description, based after all to some extent on life, of his "venality, violence . . . abusive behavior . . . and endless savage ferocity." The Dead Sea Scrolls record him with bitterness, too: there, where Roman governors are generically known as "the Wrath," Pilate appears as "the Young Lion of Wrath," claws sharpened. Among the Jews, tyrants and lions were coterminous; both tore their subjects to pieces.

Yet this character would have grown even without Philo and even without the Scrolls. The arrogance of Pilate is there in the Gospels, even starker in Greek than in English: "Am *I* a Jew?" "Take him and crucify him yourselves." "Are you refusing to speak to me? *To me?*" His pride and stubbornness were there for the inflating, and the medieval dramatists were not slow to get to work on them. To begin with, the ancient accounts of Pilate's insults and brutalities were embroidered. Eusebius in the fourth century claimed that he consecrated the standards in Jerusalem, secretly, at night; Vincent de Beauvais in the thirteenth century added that he put up images on standards in the Temple itself; and Jean Michel's *Mystery of the Passion* (1486) insisted that he ordered the Jews to worship these images and killed anyone who refused. According to the *Scholastic History,* cited in the *Golden Legend,* it was Pilate who organized the Massacre of the Innocents; and the famous aqueduct was built to bring fresh water only to Pilate's own bath.

From there the governor could develop into a cartoon bad man, culpably weak as well as culpably strong. The drama of the Passion demanded a man who could be shamed and shown up by Christ, as well as a ruler whose power could be overwhelming. To the medieval mind, Pilate was dull when he doubted. It was when he was bad that he became magnificent, the first great modern villain of the European theater. The villain-figure of Satan, with red beard and sparking black fur, had none of the contemporary edge of Pilate, who was every bad prince that everyone knew.

Pilate was Everyruler. He was a prince, a king, a duke, a knight, and the son of the emperor of Rome. What he wore on his head was not exactly a crown; it was sometimes a helmet, sometimes a chaplet, sometimes a hat. Most suggestively, in the Coventry play, he wore a headdress of glittering gold foil; for this was a man accustomed to seeing menials lower their eyes in his presence, as Suetonius wrote that men lowered them when encountering the emperor or the sun.

Not only Pilate's headgear symbolized worldly power. That was summed up, too, in the weapons he carried. He had a sword which he swung terrifyingly, threatening to cut people to ribbons. Occasionally he was kitted out with a gilded poleax, representing a scepter with a sharp point, and with a set of leather "balls" which he seems to have hurled at his audience. Most spectacularly, he wielded a huge club of green leather stuffed with wool, covered all over with floppy leather "spikes" and ornamented with brass nails. The accounts of the Coventry play show that this was used with abandon, for almost every year it was mended at fourpence a time, or made again from scratch. In 1578 two were mended, suggesting that Pilate flourished one in each hand. Such a club, spilling out its white wool as it thwacked against pillars and heads, was a villain's trademark. The Devil was issued one, too, though at Coventry this was covered with canvas and painted. Country folk in the north of England believed that Satan usually went armed this way. When blackberries were overripe and had lost their flavor, the Devil was said to have cast his club over them.

The Devil and Pilate shared other similarities. Satan too had a set of leather balls (at Coventry, sixteen of them) to hurl around the stage. His gatekeeper at the jaws of Hell was usually the same fellow, half-sozzled on beer, who played Pilate's porter. (When Raoul de Houdaing in his fifteenth-century *Dream of Hell* found himself at the brimstone entrance, there were Pilate and Beelzebub together, crying "Raoul, welcome!") Annas and Caiaphas, gulping out their praises of Pilate in the York play, call him "most lovely of lure," exactly the compliment paid a little later by Beelzebub to Lucifer. And Satan, like Pilate, would pace the stage roaring and swearing, promising to beat to a pulp anyone who got in his way. These two great villains never colluded; they left the stage to each other. But nobody watching them could doubt that they were spawned from the same darkness. In the Towneley play Pilate actually described himself as *mali actoris,* the author of evil. His terror, both at Christ's miracles and at the thought that this man may be God's son, is, like Satan's, a fear that his power will be suddenly extinguished.

In the Coventry play, Pilate's temper was encouraged by the wine he was allowed to drink "between the stages": in 1479, a whole quart of it. He was meant to be a bibber and a gourmand not just because tradition said so, but because this was how rulers lived. Then, having drunk deep, he ranted. His voice was usually pitched like a blaring trumpet, brassily loud and high. In the prologue to "The Miller's Tale" Chaucer describes how the miller, "all pale with drink / Began to shout in Pilate's voice / and swore by arms and blood and bones . . ."

Pilate declaimed in several languages. One of them was sheer coarse English. Those who in any way offended him were "losels," "curs," "dotards," "vile factors" and "harlots," whom the Devil could "hang high to dry." On the stage even his better instincts were stained by vulgarity, as when he considered moderating Christ's flogging in the York play: "Spoil not his shape, for if the sot be sinless, it behoves us to save him."

But his ranting had another dimension. In the Chester plays he spoke French, then still the language of the English ruling classes; in the Towneley play he spoke Latin, not because he was a Roman (he was, first and foremost, a heathen, swearing by Mahound, Lucifer, Baal and "Mohammed's blood so dear"), but because Latin was the language of oppression, bureaucracy and legalese. Tyrant Pilate is never in better form than in the Towneley play in the scene called "The Talents":

> Leave me be! Men give place, *quia sum dominus dominorum!*
> He that dares to me outface, *rapietur lux oculorum!*
> Then you'd better give me space, *ne tendam vim bracchiorum!*
> Or else no man will get his grace, *contestor Iura polorum!*
> I rule in Jewry!
> *Maxime pure!*
> Town *quoque rure,*
> Me *paveatis!*

> *Stemate regali,* King Atus begat me of Pila!
> *Tramite legali,* I'm ordained to reign in Judah!
> *Nomine vulgari,* Pontius Pilate who holds you all in awe!
> *Qui bene vult fari* should call me the head of all law!
> *Judeorum*
> *Iura guberno!*
> Please me and say so,
> *Omnia firmo,*
> *Sorte deorum!*

It is unlikely that much, or any, of this was understood; it was swallowed up in the boos of the crowd and the manic thumpings of Pilate's club against the stage. But the very sound of legal Latin carried with it, to fourteenth-century ears, the ring of unfair property claims, exorbitant taxes and crooked lawyers: a whole world in which the ordinary man was ground up and spat out again. The Spanish saying "¡Que apela a Poncio Pilato!" means just this; it is still used, as the dictionary says, "for decisions from which there is no appeal or for circumstances for which there's no help, because it's too late or there's nothing left or what's happened is irrevocable . . . [it means] to cry vainly and uselessly over something that cannot be avoided or cannot be corrected."

Pilate was not imagined to do his oppressive work alone. He had accomplices and hangers-on. There were his knights, loutish and stupid, and his torturers in their black buckram jackets, who doubled (at least in the Towneley play) as the gamblers for Christ's seamless garment underneath the cross. In Towneley Pilate lists other allies too, his "dear dar-lings":

> *All false indicters*
> *Questmongers and jurors*
> *And all these false outriders*
> *Are welcome to my sight.*

Questmongers gave information against other people for the price of a dinner or a share in the fines. Jurors were bribed to give false evidence. They were welcome because Pilate was crooked himself, "full of subtlety, falsehood, guile and treachery." In fact, this Pilate is not really a king anymore; he is a local officer of the shire, but no less a tyrant for that, full of the bureaucratic and authoritarian obsessions of a big man in a little patch. He knows the law and is boastfully at home in it, using it both as a shield and as a tool for his duplicity. To medieval listeners, this made him much more a tyrant than a king was. The whole drama of the Passion was that this man, whose instruments of oppression were his law books as much as his clubs, had caught up Jesus too in his ghastly legalistic machinery. He was a technician and a specialist, one of the knowledge elite; Jesus was a peasant, even if he was God. In earthly terms, there was no contest.

Jesus was poor. Pilate, whose principles followed the warm trail of cash, had no interest in giving him a hearing. As he explained it in the Towneley play, he liked to play both sides of a case, "just as the hammer makes iron smooth: I'll support the right if it will give me advantage, but the wrong if it will avail me more." He then makes a jaunty contemporary point:

> *If I say so myself, as men of court now learn,*
> *Support a man today, tomorrow against him turn.*

This is his tactic for the trial, and a clever one from the playwright's point of view: it allows Pilate to pose as Jesus' friend, wash his hands, even proclaim him innocent, while all the time fully intending to kill him. He proposes to "tack him up," but only when he has shown him a benign contenance and flattering words. This comes easily to him be-

cause he is, after all, "a court man," skilled in every sort of social unctu-
ousness and capable of turning every vice to his advantage.

Pride, gluttony, anger, lust. Cupidity, too: in York it is Pilate, rather
than the high priests, who drives the bargain with Judas and who later
swindles the landowner out of the Potter's Field. In both Towneley and
York he purloins Christ's coat by cheating at dice, a trick everyone can
see coming: "If Sir Pilate meddles in this," says the third soldier in the
York play, "you can be sure you won't get much." The fifteenth-century
moralists could find not only the seven deadly sins in Pilate, but the
three most corrupting appetites of crooked judges: money, self-love and
fear.

All this sin was tiring. The hallmark of the medieval tyrant was a
propensity to sleep: like a small child worn out with tantrums, he had to
be put to bed to recoup his energy for the outbursts to come. In the
Towneley play, having roared at the audience not to "rake the ash of his
anger," Pilate is sleepy and petulant within a few lines, asking to be
"wrapped up well against the cold." In the York play he is found in his
hall, where he has just said a lingering good night to his wife. A couch
with rich draperies is at the side of the stage; Pilate is still on his throne,
his leather club propped against it, a beaker of wine in his hand. "Now
my wife's gone," he says mournfully. Then, in a snap of the fingers, his
mood changes. "Put me to bed, beadle. It's time for you to take care of
me."

"Yes, sir."

"Put rich robes on me, and make sure everything's as cozy as can be."

"Of course, sir. Your servant, sir. There's nothing that can possibly
annoy you, sir, once you're beautifully tucked in."

"Come here, beadle."

"Sir."

"I want to go to bed. Carry me there. Just put your arms round me
and carry me over. But be really careful how you handle me! Don't hurt
me. Pick me up really gently."

"You weigh a bit, sir."

"That's because I'm wet with wine, of course! Now, put me down.
Make sure the sheets are pulled over me neatly. I'm going to sleep for a
while. See to it that nobody disturbs me: no servants, and nobody from
outside either. I don't want the slightest noise to come near me. Understood?"

"Sir, if any warlock wakes you, it would be better for him if he'd never been born."

"If he escapes without a scratch—'scapes without a scratch . . . I'll meet him tomorrow and kill him. I'll kill him."

"Of course you will, sir."

"Teach him to feel sorry for himself."

"You just sleep, sir."

This man was a tyrant, but he was also a buffoon. His terror was full of comic gestures, and his comedy could wound. One way and another, the audience could not take their eyes off him. He controlled the stage. The crowd undoubtedly heckled him at every appearance, every exit and entrance, which gave him his cues to roar for silence: a cross-play with the mob that echoed accurately enough at least some of the encounters in Josephus and the Gospels. He was the man they loved to hate, a cumulation of all unjust authority. Their loathing was cathartic. Thomas Nashe summed up the feeling on his visit to Rome in 1594: "I was at Pontius Pilate's house and *piss'd* against it."

Pilate's dominance was reflected in his wages. At Coventry he was paid three shillings and threepence for his performance: a little less than Herod, who had to ride a horse, but almost twice as much as Jesus. This made sense, for Jesus in these plays was virtually speechless. His role was to stand there in white—sometimes in a long sheepskin, symbolizing simplicity and poverty—and to be belabored by others. Only streaks of gold paint in his hair and beard suggested his divinity. He was everything his tormentors were not: solemn where they were stupid, modest where they were vain, silent when they ranted. And so the scene was set and the metaphor displayed: pure force against pure force.

II.

There was nothing physically impressive about Jesus. He was, as Isaiah had prophesied, "without beauty, without majesty, with no looks to attract our eyes; a thing despised and rejected by men." People "took no account of him." As he himself explained to Pilate, he had no servants or officers; his kingdom had none of the accoutrements of power that Pilate would have thought essential. Yet Pilate's authority, like his medieval beauty, was skin deep. It was all violence, noise and show.

Nineteenth-century popularizers reveled in the scene of their confrontation. When they described it in words, they stressed the elements
of equivocation and uncertainty; but when they painted it, as they did
endlessly, filling Pilate's palace with grieving women with the faces of
Rossetti angels, what was paramount was the clash of authority. In these
paintings Jesus is imbued with a faint and almost imagined nimbus of
power, though his hands are bound and his feet are bare. Pilate, on the
other hand, surrounded by marble, soldiers and brass eagles, can't seem
to connect; he makes the sweeping or contemptuous gestures of a man of
power, but the observer knows they will not work. The governor is in the
presence of a man of childlike subversiveness who, as Oscar Wilde noted,
is the first figure in history to have told his followers to live "flower-like"
lives; and he has no notion how to deal with that delicacy, that lack of
substance.

The most famous of the nineteenth-century pictures appeared in 1890 in
Russia, where Tolstoy was its champion. He first saw it in the form of a
sketch which Nikolay Gay senior brought to his country estate at Yas-
naya Polyana in January that year. The weather was bitter and Tolstoy
was sleeping badly; he was distressed by the unfavorable reviews of *The
Kreutzer Sonata.* Each morning he trudged down through the snow to the
school his daughter Masha had founded in a gardener's cottage on the estate, in order to chop logs and light the stove. He then drank coffee,
wrote and revised his comedy *The Fruits of Enlightenment,* and went sledg-
ing with the children on old benches. Through this white implacable
landscape, marked with the straggling skeletons of orchards and birch
trees, Gay carried his sketch of Jesus and Pilate in a briefcase. "Very
good," Tolstoy noted in his diary, and returned to his struggles with the
stove.

In spring, the finished picture arrived. The leaves were bright green
on the birch trees, and at the base of the gleaming white trunks the earth
lay in ruts and pools where the carriages had passed. Overhead, the sky
was washed blue; beyond, the wind sighed in the forest trees. Seated in
his carriage, with his painting wrapped up on the seat beside him, Gay
bumped down the muddy drive toward Tolstoy's house. The great writer
had written to him, telling him that he longed to know how the picture

had been received. Although he had not yet seen it in a finished state, he could not stop thinking about it.

In fact, the painting had caused a scandal. It had been hung at the Wanderers' Exhibition in St. Petersburg that year, but had occasioned such an uproar that it was taken down on the tsar's orders and banned from further showings in Russia. It was subversive because it showed Jesus, unkempt and fiery, flattening himself against the wall like a rat about to spring; and because it showed Pilate as a sleek, contemptible, impervious figure, every tsar facing every rebel who had only his beliefs to sustain him.

The picture was called *What Is Truth?* It represented the moment when Pilate, invited to consider "a kingdom not of this world," flung out his infamous retort. It was, wrote Tolstoy, "the most simple motif: Christ and his teaching in conflict with the teaching of the world." This was a theme that had obsessed Tolstoy ever since, in 1881, he had written to the new tsar, Alexander III, expressing the hope that "out of Christian love and forgiveness" he would pardon the young revolutionaries who had murdered his father. Alexander had found it too hard. Now, in Gay's painting, Tolstoy saw another ruler who could not understand that love and truth might be applied to government. Passive resistance baffled Pilate; brute force was all he recognized. "With a laugh and a contemptuous gesture, he throws the words carelessly at him . . . and, evidently considering his remark decisive, goes out to the crowd."

Tolstoy then turned to the governor's body language: the plump back and the gesturing arm that took up most of the foreground of the painting. He saw there, alongside "all the dignity of that Roman figure . . . a slavish anxiety about himself: the mean trepidation of a petty soul." For all his height and majesty, Pilate was the little man, while Jesus towered. Jesus was brave, while Pilate was afraid.

This delighted Tolstoy. He embraced Gay, kissed him effusively, and decided then and there to become a champion of the painting, which he believed all the cultured classes of the western powers should see. Eventually he persuaded P. M. Tretyakov, a famous collector, to buy the picture for his gallery in Moscow and, since it could no longer be publicly exhibited in Russia, to send it on tour to Europe and America. Tolstoy wrote to George Kennan, an American journalist who worked in Siberia for Western Union, to explain the picture's vital importance:

> Pilate is a Roman governor, similar to our Siberian governors of whom
> you know; he lives only for the interests of his mother-country and, of
> course, reacts with contempt and a certain disgust to those distur-
> bances—religious disturbances to boot—among the coarse, superstitious
> people he governs.
>
> At this point a conversation occurs in which the good-natured gover-
> nor has to lower himself *en bon prince* to the barbarous interests of his sub-
> jects and, as is natural to important people, he has formed an idea of what
> he is going to ask and he himself speaks first, without any interest in the
> answers; with a smile of condescension, I imagine, he keeps saying: "So
> you are a king?"

This was not just ancient Jerusalem for Tolstoy. It was also the anteroom
of a palace in his Russia, where peasants in tunics and grandmothers in
scarves, anxious perhaps about eviction or the price of bread, waited on
hard benches. Or a room where an army commander and his casually
smoking sidekicks dealt with a conscientious objector, one who objected
perhaps to firing on demonstrators.

> Jesus is exhausted and one look at this well-groomed, self-satisfied figure,
> dulled by his luxurious life, is sufficient to understand the gulf which di-
> vides them, and how impossible or enormously difficult it is for Pilate to
> understand his teaching. But Jesus remembers that even Pilate is a man
> and a brother, a lost one, but still a brother, and that he doesn't have the
> right not to reveal to him the truth which he reveals to people, and he be-
> gins to speak. But Pilate stops him at the word *truth.* What can a ragged
> beggar, a mere youth, tell him, the friend and companion of Roman poets
> and philosophers—about truth?

One look at these marble floors, these ceiling panels, the tailcoats of the
flunkeys who open the doors, will convince these people that the problems which eat up their days are not worth pursuing; just as a little
staged contempt, with the well-polished riding boots kicked up on the
desk and a laughing flick of the newspaper, will show the political dissenters what their arguments are worth.

> He's not interested in listening to all the rubbish which this little Jew
> might tell him, and it is even rather disagreeable that this vagrant can

imagine that he can instruct a Roman dignitary; so he stops him immediately, and points out to him that people more intelligent, more learned,
more refined than himself and his Jews have thought about the word and
have decided long ago that it's impossible to know what truth is, and that
truth is an empty word. Having said "What is truth?" and turned on his
heel, the good-natured and self-satisfied governor leaves the room. And
Jesus feels sorry for the man and is terrified because of the gulf of lies
which separates him and people like him from the truth.

The picture was not a success in Germany or in America. Tolstoy blamed
the failure on lack of proper advertising, but there was a culture gap at
work too. Pilate, Tolstoy told Kennan, "is what a governor should be
now in . . . Massachusetts." But he was wrong. Nowhere in America, outside the deep South where a rebellious black might have faced a white
governor, was there the same yawning gulf between rulers and ruled as
persisted in Russia; and perhaps nowhere else in the industrialized world
was government so easily reinforced by violence. Tolstoy felt he knew
many Pilates; the character was still as fresh and menacing as Gay had
painted him. But to the bourgeoisie of Philadelphia, where Gay's painting was shown, he was inert and historical.

Gay went on refining his thoughts about the Passion, and about Pilate, for years. He began to think that power might be better depicted
without a human body at all. In 1893 he produced a painting called *Golgotha,* in which the governor, pronouncing sentence, is reduced to a
pointing hand that comes in from the left of the frame. The hand and the
arm, though naked, represent pure power and brute force; before them,
Jesus shrivels up, and the two thieves shrink back in despair. Yet the oppression is almost disembodied.

Sixty years earlier, J.M.W. Turner had had the same idea. In *Pilate
Washing His Hands,* painted in 1830, the governor has disappeared completely and only power is left: the square back of a golden chair, an explosion of light like ectoplasm, and the desperately pleading faces of the
crowd. There is no more banter, no more condescension. Instead there is
something elemental, like a storm or like the sea, which not only does
not listen but, caught up in its own noise, is incapable of doing so.

III.

The political analogies could be taken further. Tolstoy had never quite equated Jesus with political revolutionaries, but others did. In the twentieth century Jesus was increasingly a separatist, a socialist, even a Marxist, and as he changed so did Pilate, becoming every cynic or thug who faced him. No other age has been so convinced of the sheer brutishness of Pilate: a brutishness unmixed with majesty, physical charm or even much intelligence. If Jesus was the Spanish Republican martyred by the sniper's bullet, Pilate was the local Falangist strongman; if Jesus was the worker-priest, promoting liberation theology's "option for the poor," Pilate was the pinstriped *caudillo* with his mistress on his arm. The Pilate of the 1959 version of *Ben-Hur*, presiding languidly and sneeringly over the famous chariot race, seemed closely modeled on the Hitler footage from the 1936 Olympics. And if Jesus was the Jew gassed in Auschwitz or shot in Treblinka, Pilate was his Amon Goetz: the insomniac commandant, the reckless drinker, the man who "went to the work of murder as calmly as a clerk goes to his office," and who thought that his exaltation after killing came because he had performed "an act of political, racial and moral justice." For even Goetz, in Thomas Keneally's words, had his moment of toying with restraint. The most heinous thug could be, in every sense, like Pilate.

It seemed . . . that he was attracted by the thought of moderation—a temptation worthy of an emperor. Amon could imagine a sick slave on the trolleys, or returning prisoner from Kabelwerke, staggering—with that put-upon way one found so hard to tolerate—under a load of clothing or timber picked up at the prison gate. And the fantasy ran with a strange warmth in Amon's belly that he would forgive that laggard, that pathetic actor. As Caligula might have been tempted to see himself as Caligula the Good, so the image of Amon the Good exercised the commandant's imagination for a time. He would, in fact, always have a weakness for it. Tonight, his blood running golden with cognac and nearly all the camp asleep beyond his steps, Amon was more definitely seduced by mercy than by the fear of reprisal.

Restraint allows the tyrant to avoid making martyrs. Martyrs know the truth and, by dying for it, proclaim how strong it is. But if the tyrant toys with the truth, queries it, worries it, refuses to grant its importance and spares men the theatrical satisfaction of dying to uphold it, he remains the strongman and they become the fools. Most modern dramatizations of Pilate show him taking this line. He is even the originator of this approach in history, the man of apparently assured and absolute power attempting, with a bit of a joke, to jog Jesus out of his obsessive progress toward the cross. He does not always ask "What is truth?" In Dennis Potter's play *Son of Man,* he asks, "Aren't you afraid of the nails?" Yet the burden of the question is the same: "Why do you want to do this ridiculous thing? Is it really worth it?"

The martyr will always answer yes. Only mercy can thwart his determination. Yet the practice of mercy can be painfully hard for the man whose first instinct is to crush the nuisance. Pilate learned that lesson right at the start of his tour in Judaea, with the confrontation over the military standards. He had scarcely arrived when he found himself able to make martyrs; and at the same moment he felt humiliated and disarmed, because martyrdom was precisely what the Jews demanded of him.

The protesting Jews had been camped outside his palace in Caesarea for five days. In the *Antiquities,* Josephus says they lay prostrate for all that time; but it is more likely that they camped, like sit-down strikers. They sat in the gardens and on the lower terraces, only a little tidier than the drunken sailors down by the harbor, with a constant murmur and wail of prayers that a Roman could not understand.

On the sixth day, Pilate sent a messenger to order the Jews to assemble in the Great Stadium. His patience was exhausted, and they could be dealt with more easily there. At dawn he put the soldiers in, hiding them under the stadium platform. Then he took his seat in the great chair of the tribunal. On normal occasions he would have been greeted with a standing ovation, but now the stadium was unmoved. He sat there, alone except for his attendants, facing the crowd of Jews on the vast ground where the chariots raced each other. There was a saying drawn from chariot racing, if you felt in control of events and things were going well, that you were "rolling with a true axle." Conversely, if you got into trouble, you "crashed the column" that marked the turning point at each end of the track. Roll or crash.

The Jews stood there, every eye on him. Pilate let them petition him again. "This time," he said, "I will give you an answer."

They fell for it. "Please, *hegemon,* remove the standards," cried their spokesman. "They offend us, and offend the laws of our ancestors."

Pilate said, "Here's my answer."

He raised his hand, as if summoning the wine boy; or perhaps, as Caesar once did when preparing for a massacre, he shook his bright white toga from his shoulder. The troops poured from beneath the platform. In an instant they had the Jews surrounded, three deep. The Jews were terrified. They had never seen anything like this.

Now Pilate began to shout at them. "If you continue to refuse to admit the images of Caesar," he cried, "I'll have you cut down! I want you to stop disturbing me, *now*! I want you to go home!"

The Jews did not move. Pilate raised his hand again.

"Soldiers, draw your swords!"

Hundred of blades flashed in the early sun. Each was pointed at the throat of a Jew.

"Are you not prepared to answer me?"

The crowd before him seemed to waver. It was like a mirage seen from a distance in the desert; or perhaps it was only his eyes, and the strain. But no, they were wavering. They were swaying, as they swayed when they prayed in the street. Then an awful thing happened. In unison, as if by agreement, the Jews fell prostrate. It looked like a wood collapsing, with an odd, crumpling, soft sound. Surely a body should make more noise when it fell. But there was almost none. They lay there, arms outstretched, faces to the ground, among the staring troops. Every man had bared the back of his neck: a white stalk, strangely vulnerable, untouched by the sun. Pilate understood, with a dreadful surprise, that they were offering themselves to the swords of his men.

"Rather than violate our law, we will die, sir," one of them cried.

Others joined him in a confused murmur. "Yes, we would rather die, sir."

Some years later, when another crowd of Jews fell prostrate before another Roman governor, Philo expanded on their arguments. "We gladly put our throats at your disposal," they told the governor. "Let [your cavalry and infantry] slaughter, butcher, carve our flesh without a blow struck or blood drawn by us. Let them do all the deeds that conquerors commit. But why do you need an army? We'll do the sacrifice ourselves, priests of a noble order; and then, when we've bathed ourselves in the blood of our kinsfolk, the right sort of bathing for those who want to go to Hades clean, we'll mingle our blood with theirs by the crowning slaughter of ourselves. . . . We take our departure in contempt of the life that is no life."

There was not an ounce of submission in this, not an ounce of fear. The suffering was embraced and defiantly enjoyed. Centuries before Gandhi wrote down his doctrine of nonviolence, it was exactly what he recommended. "Non-violence in its dynamic condition means conscious suffering," he wrote in 1920, the massacre at Amritsar still in his mind. "It does not mean meek submission to the will of the evil-doer, but it means putting of one's whole soul against the will of the tyrant. Working under this law of our being, it is possible for a single individual to defy the whole might of an unjust empire to save his honor, his religion, his soul, and lay the foundation for that empire's fall or its regeneration."

These Jews believed, again in Gandhi's words, that "this Government represents the activity of Satan." That, too, was a concept they could be confident the new governor would not understand.

The commander was at Pilate's shoulder. "All right, sir?" he was asking.

Pilate could not speak.

"Cut them now, sir?"

He was too astonished to answer. And in his astonishment all he could say was "No."

The commander's eyebrows would have flickered, at the least, with skepticism and surprise.

"Tell them to put their swords away."

At once, the swords crashed back into the scabbards. Still the Jews stayed where they were. Standing Romans, prostrate subjects: the scene should have looked satisfactory to Pilate. Instead, it was almost intolerable: the Romans had lost, and the Jews had won. Pilate still wore his "badge of the violent," as Gandhi would have called it, armed troops everywhere; but the Jews wore their shield of the nonviolent, God himself.

It was possible to salvage some scrap of comfort from this. Pilate would have understood, through the raging in his head, that he had done something magnanimous: that he had spared people. "We are a strong nation," Propertius wrote, "as much through humanity as through the sword": "nam quantum ferro tantum pietate potentes/stamus." He had loosened his grip before snapping the bone; he had allowed the insect to go on its way uncrushed. This was what ancestor Gavius, *pius* Gavius, had done in the mountain pass, when the white necks before him had been Roman. They had bent down, expecting death swiftly, as Virgil in the *Aeneid* had described the death of Euryalus: the head flopping feebly onto one shoulder, as when a shining flower was cut by the plowshare, or when fragile poppies found that the weight of a shower was too much for them.

> *purpureus veluti cum flos succisus aratro*
> *languescit moriens, lassove papavera collo*
> *demisere caput, pluvia cum forte gravantur.*

He could have mowed down the protestors, just like that; he could have turned the sand of the stadium scarlet. Instead, he had stopped himself. He was, says Josephus, "astonished at their determination to keep their laws inviolate." The Slavonic version has him "astonished at their God-fearing purity." These men were not lying on the ground out of fear of him, a Roman governor; they were lying there out of fear of their God, whose anger was worse than cold steel severing the cords of the spine. He, Pilate, could do nothing to hurt them. Their zeal protected them.

The sun would have climbed higher now, perhaps clearing the rim of the stadium. The smell of sweat and unwashed clothes was all the stronger. That might bring the flies out; the soldiers would beat them away from him, if necessary, with their leather wristbands. Yes, he too would do as much as that. He would carefully keep the flies from disturbing his emperor as he sat in judgment. He would also prostrate himself before him, assuming Tiberius would ever ask him to. He would do all this, as to a god, if he wanted. But he did not think he should put these Jews to death to spare the emperor's honor or defend his holy standards. Yes, he feared Tiberius and he loved him. But this fear, and this love, were more impressive.

"Your order, sir?" asked the commander.

"Go to Jerusalem, take the standards down, remove them immediately, bring them back here."

"Sir."

The commander barked out the order. On hearing it, the soldiers stepped out awkwardly from behind and among the Jews. They crowded toward the tribunal, the sun now glaring from their helmets, and fell into some sort of column. They would escort Pilate away first, and then go off to Jerusalem.

He must have given some explanation, dressed up as clemency or magnanimity, but Josephus does not say what it was. Slowly, the Jews responded. After some moments, they began to register that the threat had passed. They stirred, then scrambled up, smoothing and dusting down their clothes. Pilate knew that they stared at him, but to meet their eyes would have been awful. Instead he could gaze at his soldiers regrouping, or at the neutral undemanding stones under his feet.

Perhaps the Jews thanked him. If so, it would have given him no pleasure. He would have flinched from it as from a blow. He would have left the platform with a taste in his mouth like dust, like dried blood, as if it had been he rather than they who had pushed his face into the unyielding earth.

T HERE IS NO BEATING THESE PEOPLE, though they seem beatable. The women have soft arms; they wear summer dresses, as if for a picnic or a day by the sea. The men wear ties and have polished their shoes. They wheel small children in strollers, or lead the older ones neatly decked out in Christian T-shirts. Nobody stands directly outside the abortion clinic; that would constitute illegal intimidation. Instead they stand across the road by the chain-link fence, on a piece of broken pavement that might be in Wichita, or Buffalo, or Pensacola, or Houston, in the summer of 1992.

A line of city police has taken up position down the middle of the street. They have painted a white line near the curb (not tidy, edged with little dribbles and blurs) to mark the legal limit of the demonstration. This keeps the protesters away from the clinic door, so they cannot press leaflets into the limp hands of girls escorted in for abortions, nor shout in their faces. But they have decided to drop those tactics anyway. Instead, they will simply pray and lie down in the street, daring the authorities to take violent action against them. The parallel with the Jews is not exact; these protesters face nothing worse than handcuffs and rough pushing. Yet in one respect the scenes are identical: the protesters feel themselves so empowered by God's approval that nothing can hurt or deter them.

The police are well aware of this. They know that nothing will induce these people to leave the street and go home. Even force, were they to use it—and they have been told not to—will flounder against the certainty of the just and holy cause. Violence would be easy, they have been trained to counter that. But against the passive and believing, what action can they take? Facing two dozen women, a clutch of children, six preachers in suits, the police department knows it is of no more consequence than a wire-mesh barrier or a decorative fence.

So the officers wait. The day is hot; sweat runs down their faces from under their peaked caps, and damp patches spread on their blue shirts. Police cars have sealed off the street, and the officers carry massive padded armaments at their waists. They cannot use them. Nervously, they keep the protesters confined to a corner and a few dozen yards along the edge of a tired city park of patchy grass and magnolia trees. They treat them with as much fear, and as much distance, as if their faith were a live grenade primed to explode the moment it is thrown in their direction.

The protesters have rigged up a soapbox from which, for five minutes each, the preachers speak. Each man has his own Bible, a prop as familiar as a barman's napkin, which flops open to the page confirming their enemies' damnation. They shout toward the clinic's open doors. At intervals the women sing "Our God Is an Awesome God" in voices too soft to carry far. Some, too tired to sing, lean against the fence with rosaries in their hands. They have entrusted to their children the gruesome placards of the trade: color posters of the head of a fetus in tweezers over a petri dish.

They have spent a night and a day on this. Last night they drove their campers and church vans into the woods to the north of the city. It was raining; their wheels chewed up the lush grass under the trees. In a cheerless barn they took a communal supper of sausages, orangeade and pound cake. Then, with their children on their laps, the mothers watched a slide show of saline-solution abortions and listened to testimonies and songs. At the end of the evening they made posters, while the men tried to find beer and the children ran about outside in the dripping darkness. It was all leading up to this.

Now the six preachers move forward across the demarcation line. Just beyond it they sit down, tucking their legs beneath them. They link arms. "We come in the Lord's name; he who comes in the Lord's name shall not be confounded," announces one. The blow-dried heads bend together. "Amen, brother. Let us not be moved."

The police do not react at first. They let the preachers huddle at their feet, their heads at the level of the billy clubs and guns. It is the contact of flesh against flesh they are waiting for: the assault that will allow them to call in reinforcements. But in fact, the reinforcements are already here. They poured earlier out of cars parked just around the corner by the Rees Hardware Store, and they have spent the morning working the back rows of the protesters, the women with the strollers by the chain-link fence. Aimlessly, still praying, the women stray into the side street and block the traffic. The police take their arms and lead them back to the fence, while the women go on singing in their soft thin voices.

But the preachers are determined to be arrested. They move forward a little, shuffling on their bottoms, and link arms again. A huge policeman mutters into his crackling radio, and the blue line begins to buckle. One by one the preachers are picked up and gently hauled into station wagons. Their ties are askew, but their hair is scarcely disordered; their Bibles remain in their hands. Praying, the crowd parts to let them through.

Yet this is only the beginning. The protesters have called in their reinforcements, too, and at the police station and the courthouse they are all in place. A vast assembly of bodies lies in the road, singing and praying. These are students, a tangle of jeans and sneakers and bright hair; they call themselves "Lambs of God." All summer they have been traveling from clinic to clinic, sleeping in city parks or prevailing on the kindness of strangers. When the police pluck them from the roadway they go limp, like weeds pulled from a lake; their long hair brushes the asphalt. If they are left in an open van they escape to lie down again, languidly, wreathed in smiles, in whatever space is left among their sisters and brothers.

The police cannot cope with this. They pick the protesters up; the protesters lie down again. To club them or beat them is uncalled for, for they offer no resistance. Dogs are available, but there is nothing to incite them. Gas would only bring water from those beatific eyes.

From an upper floor of the police station, the chief of operations watches from behind the blinds. No, you will say, he is not like Pilate: no taste for blood, no disposition to shed it, a position of studied neutrality between the right to abortion and the right to free speech. But he too is bound by the imperative to keep order, whatever the cost in terms of his own pride or his own convictions. And he too is astonished, angry, frustrated, as dozens of protesters sway and fall in the street beneath his window.

The noise from outside scarcely penetrates his sanctuary, which is lined with walnut paneling and framed certificates of service. His men have orders not to disturb him unless the situation gets out of hand. Outside is a jumble of bodies, vans and backed-up cars, confined in a crisscross knitting of blue and white tape. Inside, all is order. At one side of his desk stands the Police Federation flag, at the other the Stars and Stripes, both hung with yellow tassels. On the desk, among the neat papers, he has placed a foil pack of dyspepsia tablets and a cooling cup of coffee. He sits in quiet dread of the press, his superiors, his chances of promotion, the damage to his city's reputation, his own aching bowels. From the bookcase his wife and children beam their encouraging smiles.

It will happen again tomorrow, and the next day. The mild and defenseless will become possessed of an idea that makes them invulnerable. The preacher is lugged by ankles and elbows toward a waiting van. The mother, bottle-feeding a wailing child, is hustled across the sunbaked street. Their posters are torn, their hymns laughed at. But outside the Rees Hardware Store they lie down in His love, and the glow of the victor is in their faces.

IV.

Nineteenth-century writers, and later ones too, imagined that Christ would always be judged harshly by the world. There was never any doubt as to how the civil authorities would act. As Thoreau wrote in his essay *On the Duty of Civil Disobedience* in the revolution year of 1848, referring to government in general, "Why does it always crucify Christ, and excommunicate Copernicus and Luther, and pronounce Washington and Franklin rebels?"

Thoreau knew the answer perfectly well. Government could never learn to cherish its rebels, because it could not accept that the pointing out of faults or absurdities in the system might be wisdom rather than sedition. Christ's teachings made no sense in the world of power, whether Jewish or Roman. They had to be suppressed. As Pilate asks Jesus in George Bernard Shaw's preface to his play *On the Rocks* of 1933, "Am I to spare and encourage every heretic, every rebel, every lawbreaker, every rapscallion lest he should turn out to be wiser than all the generations who made the Roman law and built up the Roman Empire on it?" When Jesus warns him against "killing a thought that is new to you," because it may lead to the kingdom of God, Pilate's retort is immediate: "It may also be the ruin of all kingdoms, all law, and all human society. It may be the thought of the beast of prey striving to return."

There was a second objection, deeper and more reasonable. As a proposed framework for government, Christ's teachings did not work. Shaw, in the same preface, made the point with telling brevity. "History has borne out the case against him; for no State has ever constituted itself on his principles or made it possible to live according to his commandments." Supposing you could insist by government decree that evil should be countered by good and neighbors loved unconditionally, you could neither govern by that teaching nor uphold any system of punitive law. "Politically," as Shaw said, "it has received no more quarter than Pilate gave it." Christ's doctrine might be the absolute truth, but it was neither pragmatic nor practical. It couldn't give men what they wanted most urgently, security and bread.

This question was raised by Dostoevsky's Ivan Karamazov in what he called "this absurd thing," his essay on an imaginary meeting, around 1500, between a Christ who has returned to earth and the cardinal in charge of the Spanish Inquisition. Huddled together in a prison cell in Seville, the two men talk through the night: or rather the cardinal talks, while Christ lovingly observes him. The cardinal explains why he cannot allow Christ to come back and exercise his ministry unimpeded. He runs through Christ's refusals, during his temptation by Satan in the wilderness, to assume earthly power and, in particular, to turn stones into bread. As a result, he says, Christ has left men leaderless and hungry; he has promised them bread from heaven, when what they crave is order and solid sustenance. His work has therefore been taken over and "corrected" by the authorities, who resent that he has now returned to bother them. They have replaced damaging freedom with predictable structures of obedience, and have thereby created a world in which, as before, Christ does not fit in.

Ivan called this a "conversation." It took place on a night "heavy with laurel and lemon," and the old churchman, in his simple monk's habit, came to Christ's cell alone with a lamp in his hand. But its form and substance carried strong echoes of the confrontation with Pilate. The cardinal had arrested Jesus to get him off the streets, where his miracles were a nuisance and the adulation he inspired unnerving; and his remarks to him were couched in the form of one long, puzzled, occasionally angry accusation. Again, too, Christ would not defend himself. As it was pointed out to him that his system could not work, because it did not seem to take account of the way the world turned and what men wanted, he merely gazed at the cardinal and, at last, kissed him on the lips.

Christ's teachings implied the overthrow of institutions and the social order. Those who followed Christ's teachings, as Tolstoy never tired of pointing out, could not logically subscribe to any state that preserved itself by force of arms. They should therefore not only refuse to do military service and protest against all armies, fortifications, monuments, trophies and celebrations, but they should also refuse to pay the taxes that kept the soldiers prepared. Eventually, by logical extension, they should exclude themselves from any legislative or judicial body, since to vote in elections was to participate in the inherent violence of the government. Both Gandhi and Tolstoy recommended "non-cooperation with the whole system." For Gandhi, it was a sin even to eat the wheat that the presence of the army guaranteed for him. "I said to myself," he explained, in words that would have struck Pilate as forcefully as they struck the British authorities,

> there is no state either run by Nero or by Mussolini which has not good points about it, but we have to reject the whole, once we decide to non-cooperate with the system. "There are in our country grand public roads

and palatial educational institutions," said I to myself, "but they are part of a system which crushes the nation. I should not have anything to do with them. They are like the fabled snake with a brilliant jewel in its head, but which has fangs full of poison."

Jesus before Pilate, the conscientious objector before the general, Galileo before the Pope, all represented in some degree the world turned on its head. There was no way the powers that be could allow this. A man had to keep such convictions to himself. If he could not, it would be best to silence him in the name of law and order.

Jesus was therefore not so harmless, and he might well have seemed dangerous to Pilate. The Jews were already exceptionally resistant to the Roman state. They balked at paying taxes, had been let off military service, showed no appreciation for public works. Then came Jesus, who threatened the established order in two ways: he proclaimed indifference to it, seeming to recognize laws of his own; and he was connected by his followers with "kingship" of a peculiar and ungraspable sort.

The Romans had a dim view of kings, which they incongruously preserved long after the Republic had collapsed and the emperors had seized power. In principle, monarchy should have been the best form of government, one wise head governing the body as Jupiter ruled the universe; but the depraved reign of Tarquinius Superbus had reminded the Romans that where government depended on one man, the vices of that man could turn it to destruction. "When we think of kingship, we immediately think of an unjust king," wrote Cicero. "All those who have power of life and death over a subject people, though they prefer to be called kings, are tyrants." Few boys in Pilate's day would have escaped the set exercise of delivering a speech against "The Tyrant," a figure of fantastically stylized violence who could not be confused, even for a moment, with any ruler a Roman boy might know of.

In the end, kingship was incompatible with smoothly functioning government. Caesar himself had understood that. In 44 B.C., at the February Lupercalia when the priests of Pan ran naked through Rome, he was offered the crown of a king. It was Mark Antony, naked and drunk and shining with oil like a wrestler, who thrust it toward him. He turned it down. Antony offered it again, a laurel wreath threaded through with white ribbon, and again Caesar refused it. Then he rejected it a third time. Yet he did not object when a citizen placed a crown on his statue, nor to the golden throne set up for him on the rostrum.

Caesar got perilously close to a crown; but Augustus was more careful. He never allowed himself to be called *domine*, "lord," because it was a title of kings. Although both Caesar and Augustus would ascend to divinity, both in their earthly lives had affected proper Republican forms. Their decrees had been debated in the Senate; they had refused applause at the games; they had sometimes walked to work from their unpretentious houses, which, in the case of Augustus, had been decorated by the citizens themselves with garlands of laurel and oak leaves. (That was the house Pilate would have passed: ordinary enough, no Herodian palace, but already glossy and resinous with evergreens, like a sacred grove.) Tiberius too considered *domine* an insult, monarchy "a monstrous beast"; he described himself, at least at first, as the servant of the Senate. In contrast, contemporary kings were thought showy, tyrannical, barbarian. They could sometimes put on a gloss of civilization, as Herod could, but it seemed superficial. They always kept something of the manners of the slaves who were allowed to be kings of every Roman household at the Saturnalia in December: sprawling at the table, coupling in the hall, throwing up at last over their bunched and gorgeous clothes.

A year or so after Pilate's tour in Judaea, Flaccus, then governor of Egypt, allowed the Alexandrians to express what civilized people thought of kings—and Jewish kings at that. Agrippa, appointed by Rome as the true King of the Jews, was breaking his voyage in Alexandria in 38, on his way back to assume power in the territories once ruled by Philip and Herod Antipas. The townsmen found a local idiot called Carabas, a gentle fellow who lived on the streets in all weathers, and set him up on a throne in the gymnasium in mockery of Agrippa. A sheet of papyrus was placed on his head as a crown, he was draped stiffly in a carpet, and a papyrus reed was put in his hand. Young men carrying rods made up a bodyguard for him; others pretended to consult him on judicial decisions and matters of state. Carabas nodded and smiled, as kings did when listening to supplicants, while the crowd yelled out "Maranatha!" "Come, Lord!" to the small burbling figure in his big floppy crown.

Soldiers played "king" games too. At Saturnalia, a man was chosen by lot from the company to be King of the Feast. He would be crowned, dressed in rich robes and allowed to indulge his every whim for thirty days. At the end of this time, puffy, liverish, pale with sexual excess, he had to crawl back to his regiment. A darker version of this rite is said to have happened at the Kronia, another celebration of Saturn: the chosen soldier, after two days' royal license, would cut his own throat on Saturn's altar. This was known to have happened on the Danube in 303; it was a sacrifice all the more primitive and sinister for taking place in a makeshift temple in the king-haunted woods. Romans who overheard the blood-commemoration of Jesus among early Christians thought it was essentially the same thing, the mysteries of Saturn in the offering of blood.

In Judaea, as elsewhere in the empire, the king game seemed to survive as a barrack-room diversion. In the Antonia garrison, at the foot of the soldiers' stairways, rough symbols for a game called *basilinda,* "king," have been found carved on the flagstone pavement. The pavement dates from the second century, but the symbols belonged to a game that was older, one which Pilate, too, might have watched his men play: a crown of thorns, a saber and a "B" for *basileus,* king in Greek. *Basilinda* was apparently played with knucklebones. At the end of the game the winner would sometimes choose a victim from among the prisoners awaiting execution, crown him, robe him and call the whole company in to salute him before he was crucified.

The climax of the king game was not complicated. It was played with whatever came to hand. The cloak was an old red army blanket, the sort Pilate would have wrapped himself in on campaigns; the crown was made of any flexible plant that could be plucked and woven quickly. Scholars have insisted on identifying the thorns of the crown that was woven for Jesus; they suppose it was made of *Zizyphus spinaChristi, nubk* in Arabic, a common weed around Jerusalem, with flexible twigs and a host of small sharp thorns. Medieval Europeans supposed the material was common furze, with spines like needles; and Mandeville speculated on a series of crowns for Jesus, of whitethorn, eglantine, honeysuckle and (in Pilate's *praetorium*) "reeds of the sea, which are white, and prick as sharp as thorns." He saw half of Christ's crown at Constantinople, where it was kept in a glass jar and brought out "to show to great men and lords"—presumably shaming them to feel, uneasily, the crowns on their own heads.

Such crowns were also woven in mocking imitation of the crowns of leaves the emperors wore, or of the wreaths of laurel awarded to athletes at the games. For all his professed hatred of imperial titles and honors, Tiberius wore such a wreath almost all the time; he believed it kept lightning away. He was also depicted in diadems from which the rays of the sun shone out like thorns. So, by comparison, the most pathetic offenders against his power could be made even sillier and smaller. Cut the thorns, twine them, hold the coronation, and laugh.

V.

Who could understand the exact sort of kingship that seemed to hover around Jesus? It was "near" and "at hand," as the Jews always said, the Messianic kingdom that was to fulfill God's purpose in Israel. The persecuted would possess it, rather than the powerful, and Pilate's tax collectors would proceed ahead of the priests through the open gates. This was a kingdom of the poor, the afflicted and the thirsty; the lowest were set highest and the highest lowest, every rational ruler's nightmare. As Jesus pointed out, Romans were not meant to understand this sort of power:

> You know that among the Gentiles those they call their rulers lord it over them, and their great men make their authority felt. But this is not to happen with you. No; anyone who wants to become great among you must be your servant.

A king was presumably in charge of this vaporous domain, but Jesus seemed always to be seeking confirmation and encouragement rather than claiming the kingship for himself. He was the heir of the royal line of David if the people thought he was; he was the equivalent of Moses and Elias, worthy of a tabernacle to shield his divinity, if his followers insisted on it; but the mention of the word "Messiah" made him flinch and bolt, much as Caesar had bolted from the wreath with the ribbons. After the feeding of the five thousand, according to John, Jesus escaped into the hills rather than be taken and made a king by acclamation. Only at the end, when he wanted to force the issue with Pilate, did he begin to act the king and accept the applause.

His kingdom did not seem to be in Judaea, in any case. He disdained the world. The land to which he drew his followers was often the desert, almost the only part of the world still untouched by Rome, where he could shimmer like a mirage before their hunger. Among the wilder stories available to Pilate's spies was one of Jesus spurning the chance to float down through the air, borne up by angels. This single act would have won him the allegiance of the Jews; but he rejected it, just as he rejected the Devil's offer of "all the kingdoms of the world" spread out in blue and misty ridges under his feet. Like Scipio Africanus, who in a famous dream retailed by Cicero was given an outside view of the universe, he seemed already to know how small the world was and how little space, on that drop of a globe, the Roman empire covered. Earthly realms were inconsequential. His kingdom, he told the Pharisees, was not like this. "It doesn't come with observation," he said. "No one can say, 'Oh, look, here it is!' or 'There it is!' For the kingdom of God is within you."

Within you. The thought was perhaps less difficult for a Roman than for a Jew. The Stoics taught that there was indeed a god within you, providing all a man could approximate of virtue and goodness. The poets felt him: "It is when he stirs us that our breast grows warm," Ovid wrote. But there was no political connotation in that, no sense of competing lines of authority. You might disdain death, but you did not disdain the state because you were in possession of this secret fire. It made you placid, so that you ceased to care who was promoted over you or who went to which province; but you put up no resistance to doing what the emperor required. This Jewish kingdom of God had a different ring. Interior or not, it suggested danger, as if these people carried around with them, like snakes, a tiny sac of poison in their heads.

Any more indications, any more notes on the subject? These, perhaps, now preserved on a scrap of third-century parchment as "The Oxyrhynchus Sayings of Jesus":

Judas (not Iscariot) then said: "Who is it that will draw us to heaven, if that kingdom is in heaven? And when shall it come?"

Jesus said: "The birds of the air and the beasts of the earth and the fishes of the sea shall draw you to heaven, and also any creatures that are underneath the earth. And the kingdom of heaven is within you, and whoever knows God shall find it; for if you know him, you shall know yourselves. And you shall realize that you are the sons of the Father who is perfect; and you shall know yourselves to be citizens of heaven. For you are the city of God."

He also said:

> *"Wherever there are two, they are not without God; and where there is one alone,*
> *I say, I am with him. Lift up the stone and there you shall find me; cleave the wood*
> *and I am there."*

This was typical of him. The man had been fed questions on what this
kingdom he so continually talked of was like: what indications there
were that the kingdom was close and what a seeker might look for, like
signposts on a road. And he had blathered on about birds and fish! Perhaps he meant that, as before an earthquake, birds would fly in strange
erratic circles and animals would dig into the hillsides with frantic claws;
or perhaps he meant nothing at all, and was drunk or deliberately misleading. The kingdoms of revolutionaries were always the same. They
contained no army, no police, no institutions, no bodies of law, no currency; just idlers, love, wine, curved knives. Yet they were not always
easy to crush, for all that. Dreams could be slippery.

Lift up the stone and there you shall find me; cleave the wood and I am there.

Cleave the wood. In the balsam gardens of Judaea the harvesters took their
knives and opened the wood of the tiny crooked trees. A knife of steel
would kill them; the men used only knives of bone or stone, or a splinter
of glass. Their hands were poised steady, not daring to tremble in case
they cut too deep. Just under the bark lay perfection. It dribbled out,
drop by tiny drop, bright white and viscous as olive oil, spreading on the
air the perfume of heaven. Was that God? Why not? Only men and gods
wept, and those white drops were called tears too, tears as precious as
pearls. So you could catch God as the harvesters did, on tufts of wool, and
squeeze him in a conch shell. You could adulterate him with gum, al-
mond oil, rose oil, resin, wax, turpentine and honey that drew flies in
swarms. You could sell him, inflate his price. And when he had hardened
into red-white opaqueness, you broke him and ground him.

Or think about this. *Lift up the stone and there you shall find me.* God in
a stone. That in itself was hard enough to picture. A creature lived and
grew; a stone slept, rolled on the riverbed. It lay inert. Only with the
greatest effort could man put God into a stone. But consider how a spark
was struck out of it by flint, or by the metal tip of a boot. Was that di-

vinity? By night the spark flared gold, by day ice-blue; in that tiny burst of energy, it was not impossible to believe that a god secreted himself. Epicurus said that the whole world and the gods themselves were made of atoms like these, and that somehow life flowed among them. You could not know for certain whether and when they lived or died, but in their thousands and millions, rising and subsiding, they formed the shape of everything there was. Was that God? Why not?

But wait; God *under* the stone. God in the dark damp earth, or slithering like a millipede. God like a toad, squatting immobile before moving off, hand over plump spread-fingered hand. God in the dry leaves, in the wood ash, in the papery carapaces of wood lice that stirred and blew away. His kingdom was there even in the rubbish of creation. Every morsel of detritus smoldered with its own transferrable fire.

So God was acted on, eroded, rolled on a riverbed, flung out to sea, tossed in the air. You, too, could kick God, and flick him flatly over the waves so that he jumped like a fish. But his kingdom was coming, and at any moment you might start to feel it shift and burn under your feet.

What else did he say it was?

> *A sower sowing seed. Some good, some scorched.*
> *Bundles of tares burning. But the wheat is safe in the barn.*
> *Birds nesting in the branches of a mustard tree.*
> *Yeast in a loaf.*
> *Treasure in a field.*
> *A pearl of great price.*
> *A net cast into the sea. Fish.*
> *Laborers hired, different hours, same wage.*
> *A king forgiving a debtor. (Does this happen?)*
> *A wedding party, but nobody comes.*
> *Oil for lamps.*

You couldn't proceed against such a kingdom. It was in men's heads. To crush it with troops would make as much sense as sending the infantry in among those mustard trees, flailing with their swords until they sent up a storm of yellow petals; or into the rush-topped houses to impale the loaves of bread. It was true that you could detect a sort of revolutionary swarming in the metaphors of yeast rising and seeds sprouting; but some of the plants were choked before they grew, and the leavening stopped at three measures of meal. This kingdom's expansive potential did not go on indefinitely. It petered out, and you were left with peculiarly placid images: an old woman baking, a merchant holding a perfect pearl. Few things were more harmless than a solitary man gloating.

Yet the stories had their violence, all the same. The tares burned, and the bad fish writhed stiff-backed on the beach. There was weeping and gnashing of teeth. Jesus said his teaching would burst old bottles like fermenting wine. He was a stone on which people would break their shins, or which would smash them to powder when it fell on them. Peace, he once said, was not his purpose. He had come to bring a sword, and his followers were sometimes urged to buy them; he had come to "cast fire on the earth." So much for being harmless as doves, without shoes, without even a satchel in which to carry stones; so much for turning the other cheek and disarming your enemies with love. In his sermons Jesus had preached a doctrine of passive resistance to authority. It was the meek, not the brutal, who would inherit the earth. Yet he also implied that the meek would wreak havoc before, with gentle smiles, they proclaimed themselves the winners.

VI.

What could a governor do? He could go on ignoring the trouble, let it fester. But then again, he needed to know how dangerous this man was. He needed to know how hard he should hit him. You could put a man in prison; that cooled his heels, especially if, like Tiberius, you then affected to forget him. You could cudgel the noisier elements: this was relatively restrained but, as experience had taught him, hard to control. After that you could lash with a whip or a rope, stringing up the culprits to dangle by their feet, though this was no worse than the punishment given to slaves for dropping a glass or stanching a shaving cut with the wrong color wool; it was called "reviewing the accounts." Men survived this easily, and women were even said to pity their scars. Like slaves who had just been emancipated, they were said still to carry the marks of their master's slaps.

When all this had failed, you could start to draw blood. Scourge with the flat blades, then with the shards of bone. Flat blades were for the better class of criminal—Alexandrians insisted on them—but bone shards

opened the skin like razors; the flow of blood was exciting and astonishing. It was what you went to the games for, the bright sudden gash of
crimson spattering on the sand. "Occide! Verbera!" "Kill him! Flog
him!" You changed your seat if you couldn't see it; you cursed the orga-
nizer if the action was not right in the center of the ring. And then you
yelled, as one of the fighters began to collapse, "Adhibe!" "Lay it on!"

It was hard to recover from that sort of arousal except to go again, or
to do it again. The blood that spilled was beautiful. At certain seasons it
could seem that the whole land was drenched with it to propitiate the
gods. On the seashore it soaked into the sand, a sacrifice to Neptune,
tinting with pink the floating froth of the waves. Under the pine trees it
painted with dark purple the turf sacred to Diana; it ran red in the
streams, bubbled thickly in the fountains. The word *sanguinis* itself was
beautiful, with that aching lean on the first syllable; "Sanguine donem,"
wrote Horace, "Let me give by blood." Each pastoral had its perfect ending in sacrifice. The victim that grazed on snowy Algidus among the
oaks and ilexes, or grew fat on the Alban grass, would dye with its neck's
blood the axes of the priests:

> *victima pontificum securis*
> *cervice tinguet.*

There was nothing violent in this. The blood tinged the blades, barely
disturbing the peace of the scene. The blood-soaked earth, like black
peat, showed up the fragility of the flowers that were strewn on it. As for
the victim, it was commended to the altar by its beauty and innocence:
the pure white kid, the lamb with new horns, the boar "just practicing
its first sidelong thrusts." The sight of red against white was particularly
favored: blood against new wool, or, as Propertius wrote, scarlet petals
floating on milk. The most longed-for Tyrian purple to border white
robes was the color of congealed blood, "blackish at first glance but
gleaming in the light." It was possible, of course, bloodlessly to propitiate the gods by touching the altar with pure hands, burning incense and
spreading over the stone meal mixed with rock salt. But altars were described as yearning, like the worshipers, to see blood spilled on them at
the behest of the priests.

In Judaea, Pilate possessed every kind of blood-spilling power. He
offered sacrifice; it was his business to sever the throat vein and watch the

blood flow, scarlet on white, staining his own clothes in expiation or pro-pitiation. He held gladiatorial combats and, as magistrate or military commander, he could kill people. This was called *ius gladii,* the right of the sword, although the sword was used only for Roman citizens or, con-versely, rebels en masse. The others got the cross. This was the ultimate punishment, the most painful, the most protracted, the most public. For the Jews in particular, it was the last curse recorded in the law of God: men crucified, by whatever authority, were supposed to have incurred God's particular emnity.

The Roman attitude was more confused. This *arbor malus* or *lignum infelix*—"bad tree," "unhappy wood"—was not the most violent or bloody of deaths. For brutality, it could hardly compare with being torn to pieces by wild beasts, or with the punishment for parricides, which was to place the culprit in a sack with a dog, a cock, a snake and an ape and to throw the sack into the sea. (Even the morally acute Cicero could call this, without a qualm, "bagging people.") Against such fantastic horrors, the cross could seem almost mundane. "I ad malam crucem!" "Go and hang yourself!" was a common insult, to which the common re-tort was "I'd *rather* be hanged" (than eat with you, or listen to your sto-ries, or sit beside your wife). And although Cicero thought the language brutal, a hapless man was commonly said to be "really setting up a cross for himself." Pilate's reported retort at the trial, "Take him and crucify him yourselves," had something of this spirit: Do what the hell you like with him.

The chief horror of the cross lay in the time it took a man to die, by asphyxiation or dehydration; and in its shame. It was a punishment for slaves, bandits, hoodlums, foreign miscreants. A man could not get lower. He was *corvorum cibia,* crow food. As Justin Martyr put it, "Why on earth should we believe that a crucified man is the son of God?" You might as well believe that a worm was. Once a man was on the cross his relatives would keep trying to take him down to bury him, to get him out of the public eye; and this made crucifixion, awful as it was, also something of a black comedy. In dinner-party stories, soldiers set to keep watch would fall asleep, go off to supper, get distracted by girls, and come back to find the body gone; they would then have to run around and find another, on pain of ending up on the cross themselves. In the 30s, and possibly earlier, there was a hit play called *The Crucified Bandit* in which the star was "crucified" on stage, tried to escape, and had to vomit blood while the audience guffawed. Yet the laughter did not completely hide the terror; as Maecenas wrote, this was the worst thing a Roman could imagine happening to a man.

> *Fashion me with a palsied hand,*
> *Weak of foot, and a cripple;*
> *Build upon me a crook-backed hump;*
> *Shake my teeth till they rattle;*
> *All is well, if my life remains.*
> *Save, oh, save it, I pray you,*
> *Though I sit on the piercing cross!*

Seneca capped this in one sentence: "I think he would find many excuses for dying even before mounting the cross."

A governor could make good propaganda from this punishment. It offered maximum deterrence with minimum involvement. He could supervise a flogging, urge it on, number the strokes, but the only exercise of his power at a crucifixion was to pronounce the sentence and then dictate it for the charge sheet. It could be done as imperiously as the emperor did it at the games: a signal, the downturned thumb, the casting down of two sticks to make the shape of the cross. "Staurotheto" was all that needed to be said. The accused dragged his own load to some benighted spot outside town. Florus, one of Pilate's successors, got more involved; he had some Romanized Jews crucified right in front of him, below the terrace where Pilate scourged Christ. Flaccus in Egypt, apparently not wanting to miss the details of such deaths, turned some crucifixions of Jews into a show at the circus. They were hauled to the cross through the orchestra pit; the second act featured flautists and dancers.

The governor's heavy hand was meant to be moderated by information, investigation, inquiry, even full-blown trials. Philo claimed that Pilate did not bother much with these. He may have been right. If you wanted a shortcut, there were useful catch-all charges available, of which the most useful was *maiestas*. Tacitus called this the most momentous of all offenses: "the crime of damaging or threatening the majesty of the Roman people" or doing anything that might be thought prejudicial to their interests. The majesty of the Roman people was naturally summed up in the person of the emperor, and the emperor was high magistrate, high priest and god apparent; therefore, as Ulpian wrote later, the crime of *maiestas* was next to that of sacrilege. Every Roman official in the provinces was alert to the least whiff of *maiestas,* and it is notable that wherever in the *Acta Pilati* Pilate wants to underline an order by an oath, he swears "by the safety of Caesar," as if invoking a spell against treason.

Under Tiberius, the concept of *maiestas* had been enormously expanded: "pushed to the bitter end," as Dio Cassius said. The death penalty was now applied for criticizing anything the emperor had ever said or done, for wearing robes like his, and for allowing honors to be voted to you on the same day they had been voted to him. In the most notorious occurrence, a man was executed for *maiestas* because, in Tiberius' own words, "with my coin in your bosom you turned aside into a foul and loathsome latrine and emptied your bowels." Roman officials like Pilate, who were happy in most cases to leave their subject people in charge of their own courts, were expected to intervene with the utmost brutality over a coin, a set of clothes, or a half-joking claim to a piece of the emperor's power. Any dreaming tinkerer, like Daedalus, could potter along at low altitudes, but the flier who approached the sun would plummet downward as Icarus plummeted, blinded by filaments and quills.

Jesus refused at first to be the leader of a Jewish national movement. But when, in the end, he accepted the title of Messiah, he was setting himself up as an alternative center of power. Caesar's authority and God's were simply and directly opposed to each other: Jesus was offering a kingdom unstained by money, a spiritual ideal rather than an earthly place. If his title was purely spiritual, it could be tolerated by Rome; but, as Justin Martyr pointed out, when Romans heard that someone was seeking a kingdom, they could only assume it was a worldly one. No other sort made sense. Besides, it was gradually becoming clear that the Jews were flocking to Jesus in the expectation, misguided or not, that he would overthrow the Romans.

Mark's Gospel confirms that there was an "insurrection" that Passover, as a result of which Barabbas was arrested for murder and other "rebels," among them Jesus, were arrested for miscellaneous troublemaking. Offenders like this were generally called *lestai,* a word which could translate as "robber," "brigand" or "mischief maker"; the Good Samaritan soothed with his ointment a victim of *lestai,* and these were also the "thieves" whom Jesus expelled from the Temple. They were not necessarily, or even usually, political, but they were dangerous. And Jesus too was dangerous to some degree. Just before the disruption, outside Jerusalem, Luke's Jesus ended his parable of the king and his servants with the words: "Bring my enemies here, the ones who do not wish me to reign over them, and kill them in front of me." The Slavonic version of Josephus makes the trouble even more explicit: Jesus and his followers came to Jerusalem at that festival deliberately to mount a coup against Pilate and, if necessary, to kill him.

The governor was probably already in Jerusalem. The cold unused beds were being turned over, and blazing fires lit in the rooms. We know, from Peter's attempts to warm himself by a charcoal brazier in the tavern as he denied Jesus, that the weather was bitter. Some biographers have fancied that Pilate was in the city for some serious partying, but it is hard to imagine that he played any role in the Jewish holidays. He probably kept to the company of his entourage or of any Romans who happened to be in town, entertaining on a small scale and nervously sniffing the air for the trouble that was predicted.

The city was filling up fast, and not only with worshipers. *Sicarii,* bandits from the wilderness, came into the city at every festival, hoping to use the crowd as a cover for the various killings they had planned. Mingling unobtrusively, they would find their man and silence him. They also had a habit of kidnapping officials' slaves on the eve of festivals, forcing them to be exchanged for *sicarii* held in prison. Governors after Pilate gave in to them simply in the hope of keeping the city quiet. That, after all, was the reason they were there.

Two days before that Passover in 33—or perhaps it was 30, for the year has never been determined exactly—thousands of Galilean pilgrims streamed toward Jerusalem. This was not unusual. What was unusual was that Jesus was in the midst of them, riding on an ass. The ass was stolen. As he rode along, the dusty peasant pilgrims threw their coats in the road. The gesture was heavy with political symbolism, as the whole scene was. Jesus had taken the ass in accordance with the words of Zachariah: "Rejoice greatly, O daughter of Zion;/behold/your king comes to you . . ./He is just, and having salvation . . ./lowly, and riding upon an ass/and his dominion shall be from sea to sea,/and from the river even to the ends of the earth." The strewing of coats was based on the description in the Second Book of Kings of how the king should come, "when every man took his garment and put it under him." The crowd then broke off palm fronds and waved them, just as they had been waved for Judas Maccabeus on his triumphal entry into Jerusalem. Judas had retaken the Temple, cleared out the filth of the Gentiles and restored the menorah with its magical oil. The cleansing Jesus proposed was of the Temple, too, which for the moment the Romans were leaving alone. But there was no indication to the nervous authorities that he would stop there. He came as a king, and only Pilate in Jerusalem approximated that sort of power.

Some commentators have imagined that the procession was patently dangerous. The crowd was shouting subversive things. Over the years, "Hosanna" has been changed into a chant of angels; but on that day, some say, it was a revolutionary slogan hurled against Rome. "Hosanna, save us now, son of David!" The Galileans yelled it as they surged into the city, and the people coming out of the city took it up, too; later, youths went rampaging through the Temple shouting "Save us! Save us!"

Some of the noise must have carried to the western hill, where Pilate among the inlaid furniture was reading or eating or dictating reports. Whether it carried or not, the tumult would soon have been reported there. The *Acta Pilati* are probably right to suggest that Pilate had no idea what the chants meant, though once they had been translated he might have realized the significance of "Son of David" by himself. About "Messiah King" there was no doubt. Caiaphas could have given him the scriptural references, and they were not encouraging. Pilate may well have imagined he faced a full-scale revolt.

It contained, from the Christian viewpoint down the centuries, disarming elements of gentleness. Jesus on the humble donkey, moving slowly. Peasants with mud-stained clothes, large hands and patient eyes, the normally unprotesting lower classes mobilized into bewildered enthusiasm. Children shouting, with their innocent piping voices. A sea of palm fronds, green and pale yellow, taken from the tree that symbolized peace. So docile was this demonstration that the authorities did nothing right away, as if transfixed by the virtue of the show. But Caesar himself had declared that palm fronds meant victory, as well as peace. They were carried in triumphs in Rome, and many of them, in a stroke of irony, came from Herod's own great groves of trees in Judaea. Real violence was likely, and as soon as the crowd was inside the city gates there came the shocking scene of Jesus in the outer court of the Temple, throwing over the money changers' tables and freeing the beasts and birds: the creatures that would lead men to the kingdom of heaven.

Only John's Gospel puts events in this order, but the sequence makes sense, especially to those who see Jesus as a revolutionary and a freedom fighter. This was the necessary confrontation, the provocation that tyrant Pilate would be unable to resist. Again, everything was symbolic: the trashing of the tables with their piles of dirty denarii, Tiberius' money and Pilate's money, and the liberation of the innocents trussed for sacrifice. Jesus laid about him as he did this with a scourage of short cords, and when the business was done he retired with his disciples. Yet neither the Jewish nor the Roman authorities intervened to arrest him; the powers that be were either unimpressed with this display, or they were content to wait.

Jesus, however, was already on his guard. In response to the presumed awakening of the Roman authorities, he had become slippery and secret. He led his disciples to a house with deliberately tortuous directions. ("When you enter the city, you will see a man with a pitcher of water. Follow him into the house he enters. . . .") In the upper room, where he held the Last Supper and established the Eucharist, his disciples prepared the weapons. Even allowing for later suppression of the part Jesus played in the riot in Jerusalem, it is clear that there were swords about and that, few as they were, they were going to be used. Jesus may have loved his enemies and willingly arranged his death at their hands, but these dispositions were never transferred to his disciples. They hated the Romans and, if the Romans at last were provoked into lunging at Jesus, they intended to fight back.

This was a serious situation. Pilate may have been tempted to take preemptive steps to keep order: one of his successors, Felix, massacred four hundred people after the mere appearance of an Egyptian sorcerer on the Mount of Olives. On the other hand, the priests were saying (and Pilate probably heard) that if Jesus was so much as arrested at the feast, it would cause uproar. Some scholars think Pilate must have consulted with the priests before Jesus was arrested; he needed to know what they thought of his claims, and the priests needed to be sure that the governor would get up early enough the next day to hold the trial and finish the business before the Sabbath began. It may have been Pilate, the man who had chosen the cover of darkness to sneak the standards into Jerusalem, who suggested that controversy might be avoided if Jesus were arrested at night. Christ's more romantic biographers imagined that Pilate's palace was full of news of this man, deadening the dinner conversation; this was why Procula dreamed of him. And as she took the wine cup from her husband, softly placing her lips over the mark of his own as wives and lovers did, Jesus in the garden was resisting and then accepting the cup of death that God offered him.

John's Gospel put Pilate even closer, involving him in the arrest itself. When Caiaphas sent out the Temple guard by night to Gethsemane, carrying their lanterns, John suggests that "a captain and a troop of soldiers" (the *speira,* or cohort of six hundred men, responsible for festival duty in the western porticoes of the Temple) went along, too, as Pilate's contribution. This seems a ludicrously large number, and it is odd that they did not bring the prisoner back to him; but John was perhaps writing mystically here, of the gathering of Satan's forces in whatever guise the soldiers might have been. Certainly the Gospels record Jesus' surprise that he should be subject to a full military arrest. For their part, John's soldiers, Roman-auxiliary and Jewish alike, reacted as evil forces were bound to in the presence of God. When Jesus confirmed that he was the man they were seeking ("I am he"), they staggered backward and fell to the ground.

The disciples resisted with violence. Peter, with his sword, cut off the ear of the high priest's servant. But Jesus healed him, restoring the message of loving nonresistance. He said, "Do you think I can't pray to my father and that he can't instantly send me twelve legions of angels? But how then shall the scripture be fulfilled?" He could have hurt them if he wanted to, as he told Pilate later, but there was nothing to be gained by hitting back. He wanted them to hit him; he was still the man in charge.

As both a man of violence and a man of love, Jesus was interrogated and mocked by Caiaphas and the priests. He stood before them saying virtually nothing. In such a situation, he had told his disciples, when they were brought before "governors and powers," the Holy Spirit would tell them what to say. In the presence of the priests, the spirit apparently told him to say nothing. And these men, deciding that he deserved death—in fact, as Caiaphas said, that he was the "one man" whose death might placate Pilate and forestall reprisals against the whole nation—led him bound to the governor's palace.

They could not arrange his death themselves. Blasphemy, the crime of which they accused Jesus, was a religious charge. Pilate could no more touch this than he could touch the Temple. But the penalty, stoning sometimes followed by hanging, was one the Jews had relinquished, at least in its official and judicial form. All that remained was nonjudicial lynching, as when they had wanted to stone the woman taken in adultery, and when they had taken up stones to do the same to Jesus not so long before. If they had tried to kill Jesus that way, Pilate would not have intervened to stop them. But Jesus had to fulfill prophecy by dying on a cross; and, even without that mystical compulsion, there were other urgent reasons why the governor should have come on the scene.

The Jews seemed to want Pilate to assuage his presumed hunger for blood with this man. So far, he had sent no armies to pursue Jesus and made no attempt to kill him in battle. Other prefects faced with would-be kings had felt no hesitation; but the claims of Jesus were perhaps too nebulous, and his followers too few. The machine that would crush Jesus would not be military. But there remained the might of the criminal law, which also fed on blood.

VII.

In the York play, Judas had by now repented. The heavy bag of money burned him, so that he limped like a beggar. Under the tall eaves, in the dark, he skittered past. The beadle snoozed at the base of Pilate's platform, among the brocade and gilt chairs; in the chairs lounged Pilate, Annas and Caiaphas, drinking.

"Hey, Judas, what tidings?" called Pilate cheerfully.

"Painful tidings, Sir Pilate, I tell you," he stammered.

"Oh, surely not."

Judas, whimpering with terror, explained that he had changed his mind. He no longer wanted to sell Jesus; he wanted Pilate to let him go, take the money back. The two priests, like two fussing wimpled women, began exclaiming at once: "No, no, no, can't have that!" But Pilate took over the conversation: he was suddenly, fiercely awake.

"Who needs what you think?" he yelled at Judas. "You unhanged harlot, listen to me. Spare your speeches, there's no point; or get out of here and go to the devil!"

"Why, does that mean—you won't let him go? You won't take the money back?"

"No, traitor, I won't."

Judas began to cry. "Then I'm lost," he whispered. "Lost in bone, lost in blood. Why did I ever agree to get him killed?" His voice rose in pain, and in a sudden convulsion he threw down the money on the floor. It rolled everywhere. "Please, sirs, spare him!" he screamed. "Take back your money, all of it! Spare him, I beg you! I can't bear it!"

Pilate stood up, swaying slightly on his feet. His heavy dazzling robe seemed to hold him up, like a statue draped for a pageant. "Now look, Judas, listen to me," he said. "Just take that money back again. We don't want it. What the devil's up with you? When you first came to see us, you wanted this money badly. What's changed now to make you repent?"

Judas was on his knees, scrabbling for the coins. He gathered a handful, two handfuls, jumped up, and, still sobbing, thrust the money into Pilate's hands. Those hands were limp; the coins clattered once more to the floor. "Again, I'm giving it to you again," wept Judas. "It's to save him from ruin. That's what I mean."

"You ruined him yourself," said Pilate sharply. "You stupid fool."

He replenished his cup. Offstage, a drum began to beat. But Judas suddenly knelt among the coins and clung to Pilate's robe. "I know my guilt," he whispered. "I wish I could save him. I would do anything. Sir, if you save him, I'll bind myself to your service. I'll be your bondman forever. Sir Pilate, you can trust me! You'll find me utterly faithful—you know that—"

The red head buried itself in the folds of the robe; but Pilate brusquely detached himself.

"Find you faithful?" he snapped. "By Mahound's blood, I think you'd sell us all."

"Have mercy, lord, have mercy, have mercy!" moaned Judas. "I'm wicked, I'm wretched, I've done wrong, but please have mercy on my master!"

"Go to hell!" cried Pilate. "I don't want to hear any more."

"No more, he says, no more!" twittered Annas. "Mumbling mommet, false felon! We've expressly found you guilty!"

"You can keep the money," gabbled Judas, stumbling backward. "May it bring you power. You can claim it's clean, can't you? I loathe my life, my pain torments me; I need ask no mercy, for I know I'll get none. I'll go now and kill myself, for who can I turn to? I'll go and kill myself—"

He bolted from the stage. The drums beat, and roared to a racket; the stage grew dark, and in the dark the coins gleamed on the floor.

"Come now, Sir Pilate," chirped Caiaphas, "what are we going to do with this money here? Can't let it lie about."

"He's slung it, we'll save it!" trilled Annas.

"Quick, take it to the treasury!"

But Pilate said no. It was tainted money, the price of blood; he preferred to buy "a spot of earth" with it, to give burial to pilgrims and criminals. "What do you think of that, Sir Caiaphas and Annas?" he asked.

"Exactly as you like, my lord."

This sounded like a virtuous idea, even one handled with diplomacy. But the York Pilate could not manage virtue. Instead, he had to make his little purchase by trickery. Just at the opportune moment, when the money was in his hands, there came a knock at the door. A squire had come to pay his respects. He bowed deeply to the governor, doffing his feathered hat, calling him "gayest on ground" and "loveliest of limb," and revealed he had a piece of land to sell. Pilate's first question, having brushed the flattery aside, was typical: "Is it freehold?"

It was. And within a few lines, Pilate had boldly and charmingly stolen it. It was a time-honored trick. He asked to look at the deeds, on several rolls of parchment tied with ribbons and dangling with seals, and then refused to hand them back. "I'll keep these quite safe," he told the squire. "Take yourself off. I own it now."

The man stormed out, wild, sending them all to the Devil; and Pilate, with the deeds, smiled a beatific smile. He had got hold of Calvary, and he had some good ideas for it. "This is all very satisfactory," he told Annas and Caiaphas. "We've made a proper purchase, gentlemen. I'm going to call it the Field of Blood." His eyes gleamed, and he snapped: "That's an order!"

"Very nice, sir," babbled Annas and Caiaphas. "We'll call it whatever you like. Must go now."

"Must go now."

"Must do something about that lewd lad . . . that gadling, that dod-
derer . . . put him to death, you know."

Pilate raised his cup to them. "Walk on then, with a vengeance!"

Judas ran through the streets. He barely saw where he was going for the
rain and tears that filled his eyes. The dogs barked at him, or turned tail
and slunk away; slops from high windows splattered on his shoulders. In
an Anglo-Saxon Apocryphal Gospel he reached his own house, threw
himself at the flimsy door and screamed as he entered: "Give me a rope!"

His wife was by the fire. Over the hot coals she held a pan with a
cockerel roasting in it. She said, "What do you want a rope for, my love?"

"To kill myself for betraying my master for Pilate to put him to
death; because he'll rise again on the third day, and then woe betide us!"

His wife, shaking the pan on the coals, merely laughed. "What a
thing to say. That Jesus is as likely to rise again as this cock I'm roasting
on the fire is likely to crow."

And immediately the cock spread its wings. The wings rose out of
the pan among the flames, shining black and green feathers, in a great
fan that filled the room; and the cock raised itself on its silver spurs,
threw out its breast, and crowed.

Judas seized a halter made from a rope and ran from the house. In the
Gréban play four townsmen saw him. "There goes that Judas again, the
dirty villain!" remarked one.

"Drunk again."

"Drunk again."

"Fetch the constable!"

"Leave him alone," said the first. "Let him get on with it."

Satan came strolling along the street. "Poor Judas," he exclaimed,
"our long-lost brother! We'll help him put himself away. Let's find him
a holly tree, where he can hang himself against a blood-red sky. Who can
help him? Ah, Despair, step forward!"

Despair introduced himself to Judas; and they shook hands.

Some say he hanged himself on a tamarind tree. That tree was formerly tall and beautiful, but after the hanging it became short and
worthless. Or he may have hanged himself, as Mandeville said, on an
elder tree growing by the pool of Siloam: Shakespeare's "stinking elder

grief," with its burden of dark fruit. When he dropped to the ground, his blood spread over it: the true Field of Blood.

The cockerel overflew him. Its wings were the onset of night itself, its spurs and eyes the stars. The cockerel was the bridge between the night of the arrest and the morning of the Resurrection: it marked the end and the beginning of the world. Its cry humiliated Peter as he sat in the tavern, reminding him that he had denied Christ and that the movement had fallen apart; but it also accompanied the women as they made for the tomb at dawn. Night fell, the cock crowed, the day appeared. This bird was no spectator, but an agent in the story; this bird might indeed believe, as the children's poem has it, that his crowing made the sun rise.

Was the cockerel Christ? Yes, at one level. But at another, this boastful creature, with his rasping voice, was much closer to the medieval image of Christ's executioner. It was not Christ who strutted through Jerusalem in boots, spurs, sword and glittering brocade. Christ was the victim, unassuming as a sparrow. Only Pilate ceaselessly reminded his hearers of his power, his standing and his golden hair, the refrain of an inveterate preener.

The hour was *gallicinium,* second cockcrow, the fourth and last watch of the Roman night. Over Jerusalem, shrill as a military bugle, the Roman eagle flung his golden wings. Cocorico! *Judicetur!* Let Christ be judged!

Chapter 5

THE GREAT
EQUIVOCATOR

The intriguing thing about Pilate is the degree to which he tried to do the good thing rather than the bad. He commands our moral attention not because he was a bad man, but because he was so nearly a good man. One can imagine him agonising, seeing that Jesus had done nothing wrong, and wishing to release him. Just as easily, however, one can envisage Pilate's advisers telling him of the risks, warning him not to cause a riot or inflame Jewish opinion. It is a timeless parable of political life.

It is possible to view Pilate as the archetypal politician, caught on the horns of an age-old political dilemma. We know he did wrong, yet his is the struggle between what is right and what is expedient that has occurred throughout history. The Munich Agreement of 1938 was a classic example of this, as were the debates surrounding the Great Reform Act of 1832 and the Corn Laws. And it is not always clear, even in retrospect, what is, in truth, right. Should we do what appears principled or what is politically expedient? Do you apply a utilitarian test or what is morally absolute? . . .

Christianity is optimistic about the human condition, but not naive. It can identify what is good, but knows the capacity to do evil. I believe that the endless striving to do the one and avoid the other is the purpose of human existence. Through that comes progress.

TONY BLAIR, interview in the *Sunday Telegraph,* April 7, 1996

I.

IT WAS DARK WHEN HE AWOKE. At the first cockcrow, at that time of year, the moon was often up and shining. At the second cockcrow, the *gallicinium,* night still hung in the silent trees. It must have been around four in the morning. A servant roused him, lighting the fire and opening the shutters to reveal the pale beginnings of the sunrise. The third legion in Syria had once adopted the local practice of saluting the rising sun; it had brought them luck in battle. The *Acta Pilati* imagined that Pilate, too, would have saluted it; later that day this account had him washing his hands "before the sun," the god of purification. Most later writers have liked to think that he ignored it, eyes screwed up, head aching from the fun of the night before; and that it was in this state, hungover and resentful, that he embarked on the day that was to seal his place in history.

In fact, it was not unconscionably early for him. Back in Rome it was not unusual for clients to get up and dress in the dark, in order to be the first to pay their morning respects to their patrons. Lawyers, too, started the court day at dawn, so that by three in the afternoon the business day would be over. Horace in one of his letters rejoiced in this arrangement: "At Rome it was long a pleasure and a habit to be up at dawn with open door, to set forth the law for clients." Others, to be sure, took a different view. Martial wrote that one of the chief delights of going to the country was that "the pale defendant will not break your sleep, and you can dream all through the morning." But Pilate's dreams had fled already, and the pale defendant was approaching.

There was not much dressing to be done. He had probably slept in his undertunic, as was the custom in cold weather. His shoes were by the bed; a servant put them on him and laced them. This was the first essential. To walk around barefoot was slovenly, and the marble floor was cold. He splashed his face, washed his teeth, passed water in a brass pot held by a slave, made sure his nails were clean. His official tunic with its broad purple stripe (a stripe that still smelled vaguely of shellfish dye) was put on him; a fresh toga was placed over his head and carefully arranged on his shoulders. He drank perhaps one glass of water, chewed a piece of bread. If he felt his breath was bad, he could pop in a freshening pastille; in later years, Cosmus' was the recommended brand. Then, seated in a chair by the window, he gave himself over to the attentions of his barber.

The light was still dim; too murky to see his stubble by and perhaps too bad to read, if he had wanted to try. Lamps would be lit to illuminate the scene. The razor scraped across his chin, his cheeks, the nape of his neck. Water dripped in the basin. A little aromatic oil was smoothed across his hair. All this was perfectly normal, routine. Yet it was not just another day in his life. There were perhaps a hundred thousand people in the city, three times the normal population, and he was in the midst of trouble. The judgments he had to make would be easy at one level but vexed at another, when he had to consider how the crowd would react. He was keeping order like a soldier, but he had to be careful like a politician, and he was not good at this.

It was—to take one of the possible dates at random—the sixth before the Kalends of April. This was not in itself inauspicious. The unlucky days were those that immediately followed the Kalends, the Ides or the Nones; these, and some others, would be marked in his calendar with the letter N as *nefastus,* unlawful. On those days, in Rome, the courts could not open. Other days were partly lawful: on NP days (*nefastus parte*) the morning was unlawful, but if the gods were propitiated with sacrifice the afternoon could be used for court business; on EN days (*endotereisi*), hearings were allowed in the middle of the day. There remained the days, like this one, that were reminders of previous troubles. It is probable that the dates around Passover were already marked in his calendar with the special dots or seals proclaiming them unlucky, *auspicio malo.*

At such times, even an unsuperstitious man might start to look for auguries and signs: the wavering flight of birds, water spilled on a table, the left shoe put on unluckily before the right in the dark. If a man of great power were about to appear, palm trees would spring from cracks in the paving stones, put out suckers and draw wild pigeons to nest in their branches. Yellowing sprays of ilex or laurel suddenly revived. Eagles perched on the roofs of houses, or were seen flying where they had never ventured before. They fought with crows and defeated them. Some even swooped down to take food, as one had snatched a piece of bread from Augustus while he dined in a wood at the fourth milestone on the Campanian Road; after soaring to a prodigious height, it dived down again and returned it to him. Before the fall of Sejanus, crows had flocked around him and cawed as he took the auspices, and a weasel had darted through the crowd outside his house. Perhaps omens of this sort had already been spotted in Jerusalem, and Pilate, too busy, had missed them.

Even good omens had to be received correctly. A sneeze had to be greeted with "Salve!" "Good health!"—Tiberius insisted on this, even when out in his carriage. A sputtering lamp had to be calmed with a few careful drops of wine, an empty eggshell pierced or crushed as soon as the egg had been eaten. A bad omen—even one as slight as a misformed cloud, a dropped glass, a horse stumbling—called for certain precautions. To ensure your physical safety you could touch your hand to your heart, murmuring "Salvum sit, quod tango," "May what I touch be safe." You could rebuff the evil omens by saying "Longe a nobis," "Be far from us," sprinkle wine under the table, or change the rings on your right hand. If you were at dinner, you could kiss the table; at home, you could kiss the shrine of the household gods, wishing all the while for the horror to stay away.

Pilate that morning would probably have stood before the shrine anyway, with his head covered and with as many members of his household as he could gather, to pour out the wine and make the morning invocations. This was how the business day started. His statuettes of household gods would probably have traveled with him from Caesarea, as Aeneas' gods journeyed with him from Troy to Latium. And they would have included a little bronze or gold Tiberius, perhaps the one to whom Pilate directed his most earnest prayers. It did not need to take long: "Bene nos, bene te, pater patriae, optime Caesar," was the brief and acceptable form. He would touch the altar as he prayed, or lift his arms, palms upward; the burning grains of incense crackled in a bowl. Servants, or children if he had any, might deck the little statues with flowers clumsily knotted together. He could give an extra touch to Apollo, the god of good luck. And perhaps all that would be enough to keep him safe.

He was probably forewarned of the delegation that brought Jesus to the palace. Since his first question to the chief priests, inquiring about the charges, was a formal one, it did not necessarily mean he was ignorant of the case. When Paul was tried before Felix and later before Festus, the Roman governor on each occasion asked the accusers to bring their complaints to him beforehand. This was how the medieval writers imagined the case of Jesus was handled.

In the York play, Annas, Caiaphas and a Jewish doctor come to Pilate complaining about Jesus before Judas has even thought of selling him. Pilate agrees that "if that wretch in our ward has wrought any wrong," he will act. But he feels they are too angry, doesn't quite understand. "Isn't he the one you said would come down to help you?" he asks. This prompts an exasperated remark from Caiaphas: "Ah, please, sir, shut up."

On the evening before the trial, according to the fourth-century fantasies of the *Acta Pilati,* Pilate sat up late discussing the case of Jesus with Caiaphas, Levi, Nephlahim and the rest of the chief priests. Together, they were drawing up a charge sheet against him; or rather, the priests were arguing the charges among themselves, while Pilate sat in bewilderment. He was still unconvinced of the danger of Jesus, and the priests were furious at his obtuseness. "Well, then," they cried, "we beseech your Majesty to summon him here before your judgment seat and examine him properly. Then you can find out yourself whether what we are saying is true or not."

"Tell me: how can I, a governor, examine a king?" asked Pilate.

"We're not calling him a king. That's what he says of himself," said the priests.

Pilate decided to summon Jesus. He called a messenger and ordered Jesus to be brought to him, "but with gentleness." Then, taking off his own cloak, he handed it to the messenger. "Go and show this to Jesus," he told him, "and say, 'Pilate the governor asks you to come to him.' "

The messenger went out and, when he found Jesus, knelt and worshiped him. He spread Pilate's cloak on the dusty ground, one more robe on the Messiah's path of triumph, and invited him to dismount and come to the *praetorium.* "Lord," he said, "walk on this robe and come this way, for the governor calls you."

Jesus began to follow him. Meanwhile, the Pilate of the *Acta* waited in the *praetorium.* In the center stood the judgment seat; around the walls, the golden standards. Pilate had removed them from the public gaze to display them here, as if in a private sanctuary. Sometimes they were fixed to the walls; sometimes, as on this day, each was held by an unmoving guard. The early sun gave them the barest illumination. And among them, furious, stood the chief priests. The *Acta* and the medieval plays, heedless of the laws of ritual impurity, always put the priests right in with Pilate, even letting them give him elementary Hebrew lessons, while they waited for Jesus to appear. They had much to upbraid him about. "Why did you send a messenger to get him?" they cried. "That messenger spread your robe on the ground and let him walk on it like a king! Why on earth do you think him worthy of an honor like that?"

As Pilate tried to explain himself, there was a commotion at the door. The guest, or rather the prisoner, was arriving. Pilate tensed himself instinctively. But then, all of a sudden, something else happened. The standards along the wall bowed down, a long rippling wave of white and gold crested with brass. They made obeisance right to the floor, coiling like bright snakes from the arms of their astonished handlers.

The banners bowed down in the York play, too, and Pilate leaped from his seat. He was terrified. "What the hell are you doing?" he cried. "You're bowing to this wretch? Are you mad? Put them up again!"

"Sir, we had nothing to do with it, sir!"

"The standards bowed themselves, sir! We couldn't hold them—we tried—"

"Take the prisoner back," ordered Pilate, in a cold fury. "And put the standards up again. Now"—he snapped his fingers for a centurion, who came running—"I want six men to every standard. I want you to hold them here, right in front of the judgment seat. If they bend one hair's breadth when the prisoner is brought in, I swear by the safety of Caesar that I will cut off your heads. Is that understood?"

"Sir."

The reinforcements crowded in, six to each standard, their bodies contorted like wrestlers at a fair. The York Pilate did a tour of inspection, shaking the standards himself; they did not bend.

"I'm holding mine straight as a line, sir!"

"If mine goes the wrong way, you can hack off my hand, sir!"

"All right, you boasters. Don't pull any fast ones on me."

Pilate returned to his chair. He stared for a while at the monoliths before him. Then he snapped his fingers for Jesus to return. The messenger did exactly as he had done before: he spread Pilate's cloak on the ground and, with many entreaties, persuaded Jesus to walk on it. The two entered the *praetorium* again. At that moment, the shafts shook;

the standards shivered, as though the muscled arms of the guards were no more than gossamer threads; and again they bowed to the floor, from which no man could raise them.

Something happened to Pilate, too. Involuntarily he rose from his chair. He found himself standing, slightly distant and light-headed, as if in a dream of devotion. And he could not speak.

"What's up, sir?"

The centurion was holding his arm; the moment was over. Pilate murmured, sitting down again, with a nervous little laugh: "Didn't really mean to do that. It was out of my power. I just felt I had to worship him. Something like that . . . I never saw something like that before."

"We couldn't think what had got into you!" Caiaphas laughed. "Reverencing that ribald."

"I couldn't help it, I tell you. It was out of my power. . . . But listen, listen. I think he should go away. I'm afraid to offend him . . . really."

Astonished, the Jews ignored him. The hall was cleared, but the standards were left against the wall. Pilate had promised bloodshed if they bowed again, but it seemed that everyone had been traumatized enough; and he had forgotten the logic of his order.

Besides, the prisoner stood before him.

II.

Pilate presided that day, as always, "with power," *cum potestate.* He was the emperor's agent, invested with full civil, military and criminal jurisdiction. He did not judge all cases: the Jews had been left with considerable autonomy. But he had the power of review, and in general the more serious the charge, the more likely he was to handle it. This was true even in religious cases. Later, in the early 60s when Albinus was governor, Jesus the son of Ananias went berserk and ran through Jerusalem screaming of "voices" coming out of the west and the east; the priests took him to Albinus to get him silenced, as if this were their only hope.

This would not have made the governor comfortable. When the Jews brought Paul to Seneca's brother Gallio, proconsul of Achaea in 51–52, and accused him of "making men worship God contrary to the law," Gallio instantly cut them off before Paul could open his mouth. "If it were a matter of real wrong or wickedness, you Jews," he said, "it would be reasonable for me to involve myself. But if it is a question of words and names, and of your law, deal with it yourselves. I will be no judge of such matters." And he drove them away from his judgment seat. Some Greeks then approached him as he sat there and, in front of his chair, beat up the chief ruler of the synagogue. "But Gallio," said Luke, "cared for none of those things." They should never have brought the case to him and, if they lynched someone at the end of it, he could not be less bothered.

As he walked through the palace, Pilate probably felt much the same. He, too, would suspect that at least some of the charges that morning arose from "words and names": from those strange Messianic slogans that had been shouted out when Jesus entered Jerusalem. And this may have been why the Gospels show him initiating no proceedings on his own account, but waiting—with no great enthusiasm—for the case to be laid at his door by the Jewish priests.

Insofar as there was a Roman charge at issue here, it was *maiestas* again. In the case of noncitizens, this was automatically punishable by crucifixion. It was also an exceedingly broad charge ("an ambiguous term," Cicero called it), which vaguely included any act prejudicial to the interests of the Roman people and admitted no easy defense. Had Pilate been commanding troops in the field, no procedures would have been necessary: he would have disposed of the matter with his *ius gladii,* summary executions and crucifixions without trial. Both Philo and the Samaritans later accused him of partiality for acting this way, and he may well have had a soldier's instinctive liking for it. A strong body of opinion still holds that the trial of Jesus was not a trial at all, just a farce: Pope John Paul II has condemned it as "an illegitimate tribunal." But Jerusalem, for all its difficulties, was not a battlefield. Correct form had to be followed. And since the city was bursting with dignitaries who could report to Rome any high-handed action by the governor, Pilate had an extra motive for being careful.

By all appearances, the trial of Jesus was correctly conducted according to the rules of *cognitio extra ordinem,* the criminal-justice procedure commonly in use in provinces like Judaea. *Extra ordinem* meant there was no need to follow the law books word for word; Pilate could use his own discretion. The wrongness of the verdict—if indeed it was wrong—did not make the proceedings themselves illegitimate.

A trial of this sort was abbreviated, closer to a simple hearing, as befitted noncitizens who had no rights before the law to speak of. There was no need, for example, for a written version of the accusation. Nor was there a jury, as there would have been in Rome; Pilate was both the judge and the jury. But there still had to be a formal *accusatio,* or statement of the charge; a *cognitio,* or inquiry into that charge, either by a panel of justices or by the governor himself; statements from witnesses; and some opportunity (typically, three chances) for the accused to defend himself before sentence was passed. It was possibly routine procedure for a governor to accept charges brought by other authorities without further inquiry, but not in a case involving the death penalty. As the governor Festus proudly explained to the Jews, "It is not the manner of the Romans to deliver any man to die, before he who is accused has faced his accusers and been able to answer for himself concerning the crimes laid against him."

In this case, the case of Jesus the Nazarene, the Sanhedrin had already made their own preliminary inquiries of the largely silent suspect. (Luke records: "Are you the Christ? Are you the Son of God?" And then Caiaphas' despairing exclamation, "What need have we of further evidence?") As a result of these, they had decided that Jesus should die for blasphemy. Mark's Gospel says they also tried to gather witnesses for Pilate's trial, but—in a portent of what was to come—most of those witnesses had disagreed with one another, and even those who remembered Jesus' remarks about destroying the Temple garbled them, and got them wrong.

In the gray light, groggy with lack of sleep, the small group of elders and priests now toiled up the hill to the governor's palace. Writers used to imagine the *praetorium* as part of the Antonia, the Roman military headquarters: a grimly utilitarian place. This background, with soldiers armed and waiting, added to the underlying brutality of the trial. Filmmakers made good use of it, imagining an empty, echoing interrogation chamber of bare stone containing a chair and, incongruously, an executive's desk with inkstands. But the judgment hall was almost certainly in Herod's palace: a luxurious, even surreal, setting of mosaic pavements, white marble balustrades, softly sweeping servants and the intermittent fluttering of doves. To the east, over the city, the sun was rising.

The scene that followed is given differently in each Gospel. It is impossible to tell how much history is preserved there. The Gospel accounts, and John's in particular, are theology rather than history: the writers wished to show the clash predicted by Jesus between the powers of darkness and the powers of light, between Truth and men, like Pilate, who would never grasp it. The evangelists were not interested in characterizing the governor. The four Pilates of the Gospel trial differ mostly in what they do, not in what they are, and they differ in what they do because they react to the widely varying characters given to Jesus. The Pilate of Mark and Matthew is abrupt and practical because the Jesus of Mark and Matthew, the suffering servant, has nothing to say to this ruler who must brutalize him. The Pilate of Luke, a desperate conciliator, seems to take his cue from Luke's healer-Jesus. The Pilate of John is both brimming with arrogance and touched by anxiety, because he is dealing with a Jesus who is patently king and patently God. The governor probably spoke very few of the words the evangelists, and John especially, gave him. It was what he symbolized that mattered.

Yet for generations the tortuous Gospel accounts of the trial were broadly accepted as historical and true: so true that the words of the chief players remained unaltered even by the medieval playwrights, who altered everything. They reveled in the story of the Roman governor who could not decide between right and wrong, truth and falsehood: because Pilate, in this case, was all men. And other ages have followed them. The stilted "conversations" between Pilate and Jesus have been treated as the most sacred of sacred texts, and every scholar has found a sort of thrill in retranslating them, sucking the juice out of them, uncovering every possible nuance of meaning. It was the Victorians who rejoiced to discover that when Pilate appeared to say the same thing over and over again, it was in fact never quite the same; and from those tiny differences sprang a whole psychology of doubting.

In striking contrast, Josephus in the "Testimonium Flavianum" makes it all seem practical and simple. "Pilate condemned him to the cross upon indictment of the first-ranking men among us." No hesitation, no deviation. This may well have been what the real trial of Jesus was like. Perhaps—as many suppose—the Gospel-writers invented a vacillating Pilate only to make the Roman judge more sympathetic and the Jews worse. They had a reason for doing so, to make the vulnerable new religion more palatable to the empire. If they could not get around the fact of the Roman execution carried out by Roman troops, they could at least make Pilate waver and wonder until his hand was forced by the Jews.

There is plenty in that, as we shall see later. But the Pilate of the Gospels is not just a Roman judge whose character must be softened for political reasons. That is almost the least of the roles he plays. He is also a symbol of the state, the secular power, the material world, ignorance and darkness. He is all men facing, considering and ultimately rejecting Truth. That is why, though many modern scholars favor the kangaroo court and the instant death sentence, people continue to cling to Pilate as the great equivocator. Like an audience at a show, they love to watch him teeter, struggle, almost save himself, and fall. In some sense, they feel they are watching themselves.

Only John began the trial as it needed to begin, with Pilate emerging from the *praetorium* to meet the Jewish priests. Armed soldiers, attendants and secretaries were probably with him; a trial had to be recorded. The backless wooden chair, the seat of judgment, was carried outside too. There was also, perhaps, an interpreter. Although it often seems, and some scholars assume, that Pilate and Jesus spoke Greek to each other, the trial of Paul suggests that governors might stick to their safe judicial Latin, and that Latin-speakers might even be retained to make the case for the plaintiff. Theologically, it made no difference: the interpreter could be forgotten. Both Jesus and Pilate were symbols, speaking symbolic words. The actions, too, had their symbolism, including Pilate's agreement to step outside into the bracing morning air to range himself with Christ's accusers.

This was in any case required of him. The priests could not enter the *praetorium,* or indeed any Gentile building, before the Passover unless every crumb of leavened bread had been scrupulously removed from it. So Pilate had to come to them. In no other city of the empire would a governor have had to submit himself to this indignity. But Pilate, "with his Roman smile," as one Edwardian writer put it—that imperial smile of haughty condescension—came out to accommodate them. Moreover he came early, so that the bloody work of punishment, if punishment were necessary, could be finished before the festival began. Later on in John's Gospel he even mentioned the name of the feast, a word one can hardly imagine falling from his lips: *to Pascha,* Passover. These concessions suggest that, over his years in Judaea, he had begun to learn something. It was perhaps no humiliation after all, for him or for Rome, occasionally to be polite.

The whole Sanhedrin, if it came, would consist of seventy people, with Caiaphas to the fore and the aged Annas possibly in a litter, concealed by a curtain. It is usually assumed that Caiaphas—Pilate's man—was the spokesman. The actual delegation seems to have been just numerous enough to accompany the prisoner Jesus. As for him, he may have been led on past Pilate into the hall, or brought forward to face him; no one knows. He was, at any rate, bound and already battered, with a rope around his neck. This was the way captive kings of barbarian tribes were led through Roman in triumph; Pilate would have laughed and cheered such spectacles before. If his eyes rested on the bound king this time, they might well have registered only that he looked a mess: there was no point in gazing longer at a spectacle that was distasteful. So Pilate proceeded immediately to business, asking, "What charges do you bring against this man?"

This was the routine but necessary beginning to any Roman trial. The response was expected to be equally formal. When Felix asked the question at the start of Paul's trial, the answer (from a Roman orator retained by the Jews for the purpose) was wrapped in honeyed obsequiousness: how much the "most noble" governor was appreciated, what worthy deeds he had done, how deeply the Jews hoped that their "tedious" words would not take up too much of his time. In Pilate's case, according to John, the response could hardly have been more different. The Jews were offended at the implication that they might have brought an innocent man to the *praetorium.* They flung out an insulting answer: "If he wasn't a malefactor, we wouldn't have brought him to you."

Pilate, stung, immediately lashed back: "Take him yourselves, and judge him according to your law."

This was a bad start, the old contemptuous battle lines redrawn: the Roman hating to be used as some unthinking rubber-stamp, and showing it by acidly reminding the Jews how little ground their law actually covered. But it was also a strange beginning, because Pilate and Caiaphas relied on each other, were used to each other and had plainly worked out some mutually beneficial civility over the years; and yet here they were, instantly with their hackles up.

Both sides then seemed to take a breath and start again. The chief priests needed Pilate's help; there was no point in offending him. In Luke's Gospel they delivered their verbal report, as required, wording the charges with care to make sure he understood the hefty political danger behind them.

"We found this man perverting our nation, preaching revolution, forbidding people to pay tribute to Caesar and saying that he is Christ, a king."

Luke's chief priests obviously thought these points conclusive, and were not prepared for Pilate to hesitate. They had even made things easy by explaining to him what the word "Christ" meant. They now expected a simple confirmation of their sentence, but the governor was not inclined to go so fast. He seemed to want to go through the forms, find out a bit more, handle the official questioning himself. This was the usual form with the abbreviated *cognitio* he was conducting. In any case, he was not about to be swept into anything. If he felt himself under pressure he was quite likely to resist, almost willfully, doing what the Jews wanted. It was the old game again.

Besides, the claims made by the priests would not necessarily have impressed him. The first point about "perverting the nation" and "preaching revolution" was possibly true; he had probably heard of the teachings, the wild crowds, and he could associate Jesus with the troublemakers he had arrested. The second point, forbidding people to pay tribute, seemed to be a lie; as far as Pilate knew, Jesus had supported him in this, strange as it was. The third point, the Christ point, was odd and intriguing; it smelled of *maiestas.* It was also highly dangerous; for if Pilate was being asked to execute a king, a popular leader of the people, it might provoke more violence. This was the point he seized on.

By some motion, from him or from the priests, Jesus was brought forward. (Felix beckoned Paul; Pilate probably beckoned Jesus.) They had not looked at each other in this way before, in the direct glance of conversation. But Jesus may not have returned the governor's stare.

Pilate asked: "Are you the king of the Jews?"

"You said that."

All the Gospels record this exchange in almost the same words; it is virtually all they agree on. Jesus had given the same reply to the chief priests when they had asked him if he was the son of God: "*You* say that I am." It was a cool and disturbing answer. It had driven the priests mad; they took it for insolence. Pilate did not seem to. The two men were feeling each other out. The old commentators, dissecting the Greek form of Pilate's first question—"Sy ei o Basileus ton Ioudaion?"—found in that "sy ei" tiny traces both of pity and surprise. He did not quite know what to expect from Jesus. Certainly, this king did not look the part. In the York play, Pilate tells Jesus not to be frightened; in the Gréban play he calls him "the most piteous sight I ever saw." The sense was probably more straightforward: a simple question, without coloration, to which he expected a simple yes or no. He did not get it.

Meanwhile, the high priests continued their accusations. They spoke of Jesus teaching and stirring up the people from one end of the country to the other. In the *Acta Pilati,* the priests made great play of the charge that Jesus was a bastard, that his birth had caused the Massacre of the Innocents, and that his parents had had to flee to Egypt, because they were "ashamed of themselves before the people." In the York play, the priests' arguments with Pilate over Jesus go on so long that Pilate is reduced to snapping at Annas, "Sir, have you done? Then sit down and shut up."

Amid all the hubbub, Jesus stood there silently. Matthew says "He answered never a word to him," implying (as his Gospel bears out) that Jesus never spoke to Pilate, beyond that offhand first answer. This silence was theologically important: the silence of the suffering servant as predicted in Isaiah, or of the God who does not want to reveal himself to men. But Pilate expected and required an answer. That initial "You said that" was not quite the plea of guilty that he needed. Jesus did nothing to build up the tally of accusations, but nor did he offer a defense that Pilate could use. He had to confess to the whole indictment, or else contest it with facts that Pilate could verify. He did neither.

The Pilate of Mark and Matthew asked at last, "Have you nothing to say? See how many charges they bring against you."

He was trying to be fair, almost kind, and encourage Jesus in a defense of himself. Still Jesus said nothing. Pilate, too, said nothing, or nothing that is recorded; he was apparently lost in astonishment. The Greek word *thaumazein,* used by Mark, means to be surprised or astounded, as by an angel in a tree: among the usual branches, the routine leaves, creeping feathers of fire.

At last, Pilate said: "I find no fault in this man."

He said this in Luke and John. In Matthew and Mark he put it rather differently, challenging the chief priests to tell him what wrong Jesus had done. The later the Gospel, or the more derivative, the more the writers—anxious to get this Roman on Jesus' side—pressed Pilate to declare him innocent as early and often as possible. But it was not psychologically or judicially impossible for Pilate to have said it, even if his heart felt nothing. To side with Christ peremptorily, even cynically, would have had its attractions. Besides, he may have hoped to end the business there. The morning was cold; they were standing outside; the defendant was offering no defense; the crimes alleged were trivial or didn't seem to stand up; and the crowd was growing by the minute. But the priests persisted. They probably repeated their remark that they had not brought Jesus to him for nothing; he probably repeated his initial comment that they could take care of him themselves (with the heavy implication that they could screw themselves, too). But then, at some point, the priests made their clinching argument: "It is not lawful for us to put a man to death."

It was the first time death had been mentioned; and not merely mentioned, but offered to Pilate explicitly as the action expected of him. Here was the real point of the exercise, laid out in the open. *We can't kill him, but you can.* Under Roman rule, the Sanhedrin had ceded to the governor all power of life and death. They could pass sentence in a capital case, but they could not carry the sentence out. Even in blasphemy cases, all they had reserved to themselves was a type of lynch power. A proper judicial sentence of death, properly carried out, required Pilate's permission. So, in this case, the odium of dealing with death on the high feast day could be transferred to the hated heathen governor: unless, of course, he did not want to be their executioner.

Some medieval writers were sure he did not want to be, despite his usual brutality. At the mention of the death sentence in the Chester play he bursts out, in his broad northern accent, "What the devil of hell does that mean?" In the *Acta Pilati,* as in the York play, he tries to get to the bottom of things. He asks a group of pro-Jesus witnesses, "Why do they want to kill him?"

"They're jealous of him, because he heals people on the Sabbath."

"So for doing something good, they want to put him to death?"

"That's right."

So Pilate, faced with death, hesitated. Any Roman official might have done the same. Even slaves (and Jesus, standing before him, had the status of a slave in his eyes) were owed a proper hearing in such circumstances. Juvenal pointed this out in his mock dispute between a husband

and his wife, hysterical because of some slip-up in the hairdressing or wardrobe department:

> WIFE.   Crucify that slave!
> HUSBAND.   But what is the slave's offense
>   To merit such punishment? Who has brought charges against him?
>   Where are the witnesses? You must hear his defense; no
>   delay can be too long when a man's life is at stake.
> WIFE.   So a slave's a man now, is he, you crackpot? All right, perhaps
>   he didn't do anything. This is still my wish, my command. . . .

Jean Michel's fifteenth-century *Mystery of the Passion* had Pilate making this point, too: "You're forgetting what danger a judge can get into when he condemns an innocent man to death. You've got to weigh up such a death properly, put it in the scales. It's no small thing, the death of a man."

So Pilate seems to have hesitated. And something else was in play, too. John adds, at this point, that the priests' remark about legality and death was made "so that the sayings of Jesus might be fulfilled, signifying what sort of death he would die." He had to die, of course, on a cross. Only Pilate could put him there. The prophecies had found their mark, and forces more complex than the outrage of the Sanhedrin were clearly pushing Jesus and Pilate together. The *Acta Pilati* adds, after the Jews' statement of their own powerlessness, a rawly pertinent question from the governor: "Has God forbidden you to kill, and allowed me?"

He received no answer. So in John's Gospel, Pilate, as if to clear his head—or perhaps in the hope of getting a proper confession at last—cut off the conversation with the Jewish leaders, turned his back on them, beckoned his prisoner, and shut himself up in the judgment hall with Jesus.

III.

At last they were alone. It was quieter inside the *praetorium,* and the light was softer. F. W. Farrar, writing in 1850, imagined that they did not simply step inside a doorway, a few yards from the Jews. He surmised that Jesus was led "up the noble flight of stairs, over a floor of agate and lazuli,

under the gilded roofs, ceiled with cedar and painted with vermilion."
There is no reason why they should have gone so far, but part of Farrar's
assumption is correct: they would have stood in a room that was sumptuous, in which the marble and gilded furniture would have convinced
some men that they were now in heaven.

They would still have been on grotesquely uneven terms, Pilate in
the full sweep of his authority, Jesus haltered with ropes. Yet John made
them equals, trading points as one power to another. Nor were they truly
alone: no Roman trial, whatever its peculiarities, could be held in secret,
and Pilate's guards and attendants would have stayed with him. Yet John
presented them as two men in a room face-to-face; and, at least for a few
minutes, they tried to have a conversation.

John's Gospel provides three moments when Pilate, in effect, retires
from the trial. On two of these occasions he leaves to question Jesus more
closely, and on the third he appears to distance himself, opting out of
mocking him. There is dramatic method in this. What John provides is
space for relative quiet, dialogue and contemplation. In the other
Gospels the trial moves almost too briskly, like a public auction; Pilate
interacts strenuously with the Jewish crowd, but with Jesus he has no relationship at all. John gives him the chance.

There was also more to it than that. The act of going into the *praetorium* and closing the door was highly symbolic. Jesus told his followers
to pray like this, in the secrecy of their own chambers. There they, too,
were to be face-to-face with God. Yet any act of retirement might have
done as well. The essential was to withdraw from the world and from dis-
traction. Romans, too, understood the importance of this act, even the
possibility of divine encounters. As Seneca wrote to his governor friend
Lucilius:

> If you have ever come upon a grove full of ancient trees that have grown
> to an unusual height, shutting out a view of the sky with a veil of inter-
> twining branches, then the loftiness of the forest, the seclusion of the
> spot, and your wonder at the thick unbroken shade in the midst of open
> spaces, will prove to you the presence of deity. Or if a cave, made by the
> deep crumbling of the rocks, holds up a mountain on its arch, a place not
> built with hands but hollowed out into such spaciousness by natural
> causes, your soul will be deeply moved by a certain intimation of the ex-

istence of God. We worship the sources of mighty rivers; we erect altars at places where great streams break suddenly from hidden sources; we adore springs of hot water as divine, and consecrate certain pools because of their dark waters or their immeasurable depth.

If you see a man who is unterrified in the midst of dangers, untouched by desires, happy in adversity, peaceful amid the storm, who looks down upon men from a higher plane and views the gods on a footing of equality, will not a feeling of reverence for him steal over you? Won't you say, "This quality is too great and too lofty to be regarded as resembling this petty body in which it dwells. A divine power has descended upon that man"?

John's staging of the scene underlines this confrontation. In the inward place, the grove, the cave or the *praetorium*, stands Jesus, who is the truth and the light; outside are the Jews in the darkness of their ignorance, refusing to enter. Between the two walks Pilate, constantly in and out, struggling to decide where he wants to be: in the howling darkness with those who do not believe, or in the holy and unsettling embrace of God. It will take the whole length of the trial for him to make his choice. With Jesus, and for the truth, or against them. This may have been a scene that was recorded and remembered; more probably, it was a scene that John found theologically irresistible, in which Jesus and Pilate, light and darkness, explained themselves to each other.

It is a strangely compelling dialogue, all the same. It has the ring of real conversation between two men who find each other mystifying: polite defiance on both sides, a refusal to give ground, and a procession of non sequiturs in which questions and answers do not quite fit together. No man wishing to write propaganda would produce a piece of dialogue like this. It has its uses, too, for the logical structure of the trial, explaining some of the more abrupt and curious actions attributed to Pilate in the other Gospels: in particular his assertion, only minutes into the trial and on no evidence at all, that he found no fault in Jesus, and his subsequent efforts to avert the fate that was bearing down on both of them.

The nineteenth-century commentators considered this scene crucial. It was, they thought, the first of several occasions in the trial when Pilate ("a man doubtless of corrupt principles and irreligious life") was touched

by the divine despite himself. Caught in such proximity, looking into
the eyes of Jesus and listening to his voice, the governor—they felt
sure—encountered for the first time the ineffable sweetness of God. He
could not have been indifferent to this. Jesus, after all, was a man who effortlessly drew crowds, whom even the mad and blind could recognize as
a spiritual force: "I know who you are, God's holy one!" an epileptic
screamed. Lepers, noblemen, women, rulers of local synagogues, knelt at
his feet and worshiped him. There seemed no reason, then, why a Roman
should not have been affected, however proud and intransigent. In John's
Gospel, Pilate's soldiers in the arresting party had already fallen to the
ground before Jesus. Perhaps it was not mere propaganda that the words
appeared again and again in the trial, "Pilate marveled."

The brevity of the conversation was misleading, therefore. It must
have started something. Those who believe in Jesus have always seen
small epiphanies strewn all through the trial, especially in John. However obtuse or thuggish Pilate is—however obtuse or thuggish ordinary
men and their rulers are—there comes a moment when God, or the notion of goodness, disturbs him. There comes a point when he can choose
the higher or the lower path, the virtuous action or the sin; and he
pauses. Redemption is held out to him, and the question is whether he
will notice it in time before he plunges into darkness.

Even the modern playwright Dennis Potter, who rewrites the trial
completely, preserves a moment of epiphany. It comes after Pilate has
tauntingly reminded Jesus of the commandment to "love your enemies."
"What about me?" he asks. "Do you love me?"

Pause. Jesus looks at him steadily. Pilate's chuckle dies away uncomfortably

JESUS.   Yes, Pontius.
*Pilate slaps out at him in humiliation. And then suddenly covers his face in a
    gesture of shame*
PILATE.   I'm sorry, that was not necessary. That was not necessary.
JESUS.   Don't be afraid.
This really frightens Pilate
PILATE.   *What?*
JESUS.   There is no need to be frightened. *Pilate steps back in alarm. He
    shouts out in bewildered anger*
PILATE.   Take him away! Take the idiot away!

Standing in the *praetorium,* planting the barricades of his awkward questions, Pilate becomes the prototype of every uncertain man or woman forced into a dialogue with God. He asks, only half-believing that he will ever get an answer. What comes back is elliptical, disturbing; but for a moment the heart has been laid open.

"Are you the King of the Jews?" he asked again.

"Are you saying that yourself, or did other people tell you this about me?"

It was the same question, with almost the same answer; except that the formulation was gentler, as if Jesus were addressing a child. It was an appeal to Pilate's conscience, a suggestion that the conversation could go in a different direction. But John's Pilate, completely missing the point, thought he was being put down. And that was exquisitely insulting.

"Am I a Jew?" "Meti ego Judaios eimi?" He snapped it out in fury. Was he one of that tribe, bearded, atheist, fanatical, *circumcised?* All his Roman dignity burned in his face.

After an almost audible swallowing of temper, he went on: "Your own people and the chief priests have delivered you to me. What did you do to turn them against you?"

The answer should have been straightforward. Instead, it was bizarre.

"My kingdom is not of this world. If my kingdom were of this world, then my officers would be fighting to stop me being delivered to the Jews. But my kingdom is not from here."

What could Pilate make of this? The remark came out of the blue. But the last phrase would have snagged his attention: *not from here.* A man might say that casually in the street, and you would not necessarily follow up. Not from here, not from Judaea: a foreigner, therefore. The empire was full of foreigners and petty kings. That much distance was manageable. You might go farther still, toward the end of the world the empire covered or geographers knew, petering out in wilderness and forests and ice. But Jesus had gone farther even than that. He had described a kingdom not of this *kosmos.* Not of this world, not of this earth; not of this universe. Pilate was asked to consider a realm without palaces, armies, temples, roads or the Imperial Post; a place in which Caesar's soldiers had no purchase, and in which invisible officers did not try to stop their master being arrested in the street.

That in itself suggested something else. If the officers of Jesus were not fighting, this meant he expected, or possibly even wanted, to be handed over to Pilate. He didn't care. Perhaps he wished to be handed over to further his purposes. Perhaps he did not want to be saved because death was of no consequence to him; or because, on the contrary, he craved it and embraced it. Such notions were fairly otherworldly too.

The question the governor should have asked next was obvious: "So where are you from, if you are not of this world?" But it did not occur to John's Pilate then; only later, when he had missed his chance. For the moment, he seemed too baffled to pursue it. Out of the vast cloudiness of the answer he had been given, Pilate plucked the only solid grain: Jesus' apparent admission that he was a king after all. He seized on the question that was the least interesting to pursue but the safest, the sanest, to ask.

"So," he said, "you *are* a king, then?"

The tone was one of doubtful surprise, bordering on scorn. You, with your bruised face and blackened eyes, your dirty robe, you're a king? The question should have made him laugh; Jesus' answer should have assured him that, in practical terms, Rome had nothing to fear from him. But the doubt was also, perhaps, a fear of the altitude from which this peculiar man might have fallen.

"You said it," Jesus told him.

That answer again. And its subtext: There really isn't much point discussing such things with you. There's no common ground between us. There's nowhere to go here.

Then, unexpectedly, Jesus went on: "This is what I was born for, and this is why I came into the world, to bear witness to the truth. Everyone on the side of truth listens to me."

Pilate retorted: "What is truth?"

The words linger. In fact they have never ceased to echo, and they have received a slightly different interpretation from almost every scholar who has considered them. Had they been uttered in the middle of the exchange and been answered, they would have had far less impact. But John's Pilate threw them out, and immediately left the *praetorium* and returned to the Jews to announce that he could find no fault in the man he had been talking to.

It is an odd moment, marked in John's original Greek by an abrupt ending to the paragraph; the words are literally left dangling. It is also a moment of acute disappointment. The conversation has been getting interesting, even extraordinary. Pilate has been fed neat Christian doctrine, baffling and astonishing: we imagine it might have the same effect on him as a shot of whiskey on a child. First, he has been asked to apply his conscience ("If he had a conscience," so many have chorused) to the meaning of the charges against Jesus; then he has been asked to consider the nature of universal truth. This was bound to be too hard for him; and so, though the world has come to hang lovingly on this exchange, he cut the conversation off.

The writer of the York play thought he could improve on John's performance. After Jesus' remarks he has Pilate saying, with all the shortness of a Yorkshire pork butcher, "That sounds like the truth to me," and rounding on the chief priests, whom he accuses of lying to him and trumping up the charges. He then falls to wondering where Jesus got such language and such imagery from: "Perhaps his father traveled, and saw wonders, and told him about them." Annas corrects him: "No, no, sir, he's a workman. He's got no subtlety in him."

The writer of the *Acta Pilati* also carried matters on a bit further. When Pilate asks, "What is truth?" Jesus answers: "Truth is of heaven."

"Is there no truth on earth?"

"Well, just look at how those who speak the truth are judged by those who have worldly authority!"

In other words: Look how you are treating me. But in a slightly different version of the *Acta*, Jesus adds another, devastating phrase: "*I am the truth.*"

He had said as much to his followers, of course. Would he have dared to say it to Pilate? It is not completely outside the bounds of possibility. Yet Pilate's most famous remark gains that tremor of authenticity precisely because nothing follows it. Augustine supposed he left because he had suddenly remembered the custom of releasing a prisoner on the feast day, and did not want it to slip his mind before he could mention it to the Jews. John Chrysostom in the fourth century (joined by Aldous Huxley in the twentieth) thought that Pilate, though he had been in earnest for a minute, did not want to waste his time in the thousand idle disputations his question could give rise to; he had serious work to do. In other words, the conversation was disrupted by a technicality.

But disrupted or not, what did he mean? Was he simply, as a well-trained Skeptic, giving the proper and acceptable Skeptics' answer? It seems unlikely. A true Skeptic would have shown none of Pilate's agitation. Believing that nothing was good, nothing bad, nothing false and nothing true, he was meant to have reached a state of quietude. He was beyond choice, beyond decision; his judgment was suspended. Pilate in the trial presented completely the opposite picture. He wanted to make his own decision over true or false, right or wrong, but the choice confounded him. It would not have been the first time in his career.

Perhaps his words suggested sheer world-weariness. In the preface of his *History of Rome,* Livy described "the process of our moral decline . . . the sinking of the foundations of morality . . . then the final collapse of the whole edifice, and the dark dawning of our modern day when we can neither endure our vices, nor face the remedies needed to cure them." Or Pilate's words could have summed up the flippancy of decadent Rome, in which good and evil, true and false, were mere dishes—as Seneca said—to be sampled by idle young men in the eating houses; where, instead of chewing the rough bread of wisdom, they dined on filleted mullet, boned chicken and rare mushrooms, sated on the riot of flavors until they could no longer distinguish them. Bacon's famous passage about "jesting Pilate" who "would not stay for an answer" captures this mood: "Certainly there be, that delight in giddiness; and count it a bondage to fix a belief; affecting free-will in thinking, as well as in acting." Pilate's moments of giddiness—they seemed to be in his character, erupting even at serious junctures—only emphasized how stuck he was, unable to choose and unable to move.

Pilate's Greek, as relayed by John, gives a tiny clue as to what he may have meant. The word he used for truth, *aletheia,* was not quite the construction *(i aletheia)* Jesus had used. Jesus was speaking of absolute truth; Pilate seemed to mean a truth that was narrow and particular. Jesus was referring to a truth that was overpoweringly different: as different, Polybius had once said, as when a galley rower, trained on skeleton ships on dry land, suddenly felt in the live ocean the pull of the oar and the craft's response.

Possibly Pilate could have grasped just a thread of that. But because he was not open to metaphysical explanations, as Jesus gently inferred, the only truth he could understand was the sort a judge was confined to: facts, assertions, the evidence of eyes and ears. How could Jesus imagine (this was Martin Luther's interpretation) that airy speculations about truth would help him out of this particular legal mess? And, most of all, *how did he know?* Most scholars see the remark as a challenge, thrown out by a man of the world who thinks the other fellow has no idea what he is talking about. It was much like Festus' remark after Paul had proclaimed Christ's death and Resurrection: "Paul, you're beside yourself; too much learning has made you mad."

If John's Pilate thought Jesus was mad, this would explain his precipitate exit. After all, he left the *praetorium,* according to John, not to announce Jesus's guilt and execution but to declare his innocence. A madman would not be worth bothering with any longer; they could all go home. Yet there is another possible explanation, short of a conviction of lunacy. Pilate had asked a question that departed abruptly from his one-track interest in the inquiry. That question threatened to engage him in Jesus' argument, on Jesus' terms. This was disturbing; it was the beginning of complicity. Therefore Pilate no sooner asked the question than he dropped it, and left at once to cover his embarrassment. His remark was not just the symbolic statement of a man who could not see God before his face; it was the statement of a man who has had an intimation of the truth but is too afraid, or too self-preserving, to go on.

It is a possibility. There are a dozen possibilities. And whichever way it happened, in John's Gospel, Jesus was left formulating the answer into the empty air.

IV.

By this point in the trial, Pilate seemed desperate to be released from his duties. According to the Gospels, he tried to wriggle out in three different ways. In John, his first device was to go outside, back to the chief priests, and say: "I find no fault in him at all." By this time, however, it was not just the priests who were waiting for him, but a crowd of ordinary people. From this moment on, the trial ceased to be small-scale and conversational. It became an exercise in crowd control, conducted at full volume and with increasing urgency on both sides.

When Pilate declared Jesus innocent, the crowd seemed to take it badly: so badly that he couldn't just leave it there, order the prisoner released and expect them to disperse. He had to do something else. In his long experience of getting stuck with resentful Jewish crowds, he knew there was a simple way out somewhere. There was always some trick, some deception that would work. And in his long experience, he also knew that he could never seem to find what it was.

What he appeared to be searching for was a third way: not to kill Jesus, not to release him, but to take a middle course. The other choices were too extreme, too hard. They involved a commitment he did not want to make. Pilate was, after all, a politician: he wanted to preserve his skin and please his audience and, somewhere down the line, try to do the right thing.

His Samnite forebears had agonized over a middle course on a much larger scale. Livy retailed the semi-mythical story. When Gavius Pontius trapped the Roman army at the Caudine Forks, he was so delighted that he could not think what to do next. He sent a messenger to his aged father, Herennius, the man who had talked to Plato, to seek advice.

"Dismiss them unhurt," his father said.

Gavius rejected that.

"Kill the lot of them, then."

Gavius rejected that, too.

He asked his father to advise them in person, and Herennius was brought to the camp in a wagon. There, like the dogged old man he was, he simply repeated his advice. Spare these men, and they would make powerful friends; kill them, and the Romans would be weakened for a generation. There was, he said, "no third plan": "tertium nullum consilium esse."

But Gavius and the other Samnite leaders demanded one. What would happen, they asked, if they took a middle course? If they let the Romans go unhurt, but imposed terms on them? Herennius was dismissive. "That's a policy," he said, "that neither wins men friends nor rids them of their enemies."

They sent the old man home. Gavius Pontius then went to the Romans with his middle way: he offered them their lives, and peace, but each of them would have to pass under the yoke, unarmed and wearing only a tunic. This was such humiliation that the Romans could scarcely bear it. They passed under the yoke while their enemies reviled them, and then lay down in the Capua road in nakedness and tears.

Yet they had their revenge. As Herennius had predicted, the middle

way won the Samnites no friends, but forged so dishonorable a peace that
they and the Romans were soon at war again. Before long, they too were
defeated and sent under the yoke by the crowing Romans, with Gavius
Pontius among them. He was later led in triumph and beheaded. His
wonderful compromise had come to nothing.

"They had let slip the chance both of doing good and of doing
harm," Livy wrote. History proved that equivocation did not work. A
man should either do good or bad, but not waver between them. Pilate
ignored this simple lesson of history. He wanted his schemes, his escape
routes; there was surely some way out.

His best idea came in Luke's Gospel: he would wriggle out by passing the buck. The chief priests were still accusing Jesus of preaching
"from Galilee to this place," and Pilate's ears pricked up at that. "Is this
man a Galilean?" he asked.

When Felix heard the case of Paul, his very first question was where
the man was from. This was the obvious point to establish before going
any further. It was strange, perhaps even incompetent, that Pilate left the
inquiry so late. If Jesus was a Galilean, Herod Antipas could judge him;
the matter would be out of Pilate's hands. And Herod, conveniently, was
also in Jerusalem for Passover.

So Luke's Pilate, having made his inquiries and satisfied himself that
this might work, sent Jesus across to the tetrarch at his lodgings in the
old Asmonean palace, on the other side of the city. It looked like a diplomatic gesture, almost a present. If he did this, it was the first such spontaneous act ever credited to Pilate. In effect, he sent Herod something he
knew he was intrigued by (even, in one medieval French drama, recom-
mending the "great games" Jesus knew how to play), and divested himself in the process of a prisoner who was becoming difficult.

It didn't work. Jesus refused to answer Herod's eager questions about
his miracles, let alone perform any, and after a brief session of abuse and
mockery he was sent back to Pilate. But Herod seems to have appreciated
the thought behind the gesture. He and Pilate had been enemies, Luke
said. That enmity might well have sprung from the business of the votive shields and the "sneaking" letter to Tiberius, or from Pilate's slaughter of Galileans (also mentioned only by Luke) in the Temple courtyard.
Now, however, they were "made friends together," by a sort of grim
telepathy, on opposite sides of swarming Jerusalem. By the end of the

morning, according to the second-century *Gospel of Peter*—the earliest noncanonical account of the Passion—Herod was calling him "Brother Pilate."

The prophets had foretold such a day when the rulers of the world would unite against Christ. Perhaps Luke was just inventing to fulfill the prophecies; or perhaps he had a source at Herod's court, who fed him an exclusive. The scholars disagree. It occasionally happened in criminal trials that a prisoner was sent from the *forum apprehensionis,* where he was caught, to the *forum originis,* the place he was from, though this was not obligatory. And Pilate had a motive for trying to please Herod; he needed his help against Herod's nephew, the Roman-educated nationalist Agrippa. Agrippa, in Rome, was planning to assume the kingship of Judaea. He had an interest in painting an unflattering picture of Pilate's administration, and he was, at that moment, much closer to Tiberius than Pilate was. The governor badly needed the tetrarch of Galilee to be his friend. That much is certain.

All the same, Jesus was returned rather quickly, and he was not returned as he had been sent. He came back dressed up in a festival robe that was "gorgeous," or "shining white." Herod seems to have meant to dress him like a fool, but a white robe would have had all sorts of connotations for Pilate. A man in white, the good luck color, could be a candidate for election or a proper claimant to a crown; he could be one of those heroes in history or literature whose greatness of soul clothed him in radiance. Tacitus mentioned that the tribunes—so, probably, Pilate himself—wore white robes when they went before the eagles into battle. The spectacle, then, might have been unsettling. The Gréban playwright imagined that Pilate was furious to get Jesus back: "By all the thunders of Almighty Jupiter!" he cried to his attendants. Luke's Pilate took it more calmly. Standing beside Jesus, facing the chief priests, he made his longest and most eloquent plea for him.

"You brought this man to me as one who was stirring up the people," he told them. "Well, look, I've examined him in front of you and I've found him completely innocent of the things you accuse him of. Herod found no fault in him either, for I sent the case to him, and nothing worthy of death has been imputed to him. So I'm going to chastise him and let him go."

This, in effect, was Pilate's sentence of acquittal. But there was a fatal flaw; he had not proved Jesus innocent, because Jesus had offered no defense. There was therefore no reason why the chief priests should accept it. Pilate could have taken the line that this was unimportant; Mark claims that he was well aware that their case against Jesus was based on envy. But here he apparently made a terrible mistake, an attempt at political cleverness—even, perhaps, another attempt at diplomacy—which threw the case open to the judgment of the mob. He remembered, or was reminded, all the Gospels say, that there was a custom of releasing a prisoner on the feast day.

Such a custom is not substantiated anywhere else for Judaea, but it is not implausible. At Roman festivals, provision was usually made to show mercy to criminals and pity to the executed. At the Lectisternia and the Bacchanalia an amnesty was offered, and this was also done at the new emperor's accession. When Albinus was replaced as governor of Judaea a little after Pilate's time, his last act of kindness was to release all those who had been arrested "for trifling matters," in exchange for cash. ("So the prisons were emptied," says Josephus tartly, "and the country was filled with robbers.") The two trials of Paul show both governors "eager to do the Jews a favor" by, in the first instance, keeping Paul bound, and, in the second, offering to try him on Jewish charges: in other words, by treating Jewish malcontents just as they thought the Jews wanted. There also exists the evidence of a papyrus in Greek from Egypt, in which a Roman prefect says to the accused: "You deserve to be scourged for the crimes you have committed, but I grant you to the crowd."

Nothing is recorded elsewhere to suggest that Pilate's gesture was a "custom." It is therefore possible that he had introduced it on his own initiative. If so, it showed an uncharacteristic insight into Jewish sensibilities: releasing a prisoner from bondage at Passover, just as the Jewish people had been released by God from captivity in Egypt. In Luke and John, Pilate talks of this as a Jewish practice ("You have a custom"), but in Mark and Matthew it seems to be the governor's idea: to release one prisoner, whomever the Jews wanted, at the Passover or at "festival time," was something Pilate had "always done for them" and which the crowd noisily demanded that he should do again. Mark suggests that the people had come expressly to ask for that, not merely to observe a trial; and it is possible that at least some came in the hope that Jesus might be the man released. This puts a slightly different complexion on the scene, and on the dilemma that resulted. Perhaps it was not Pilate who made the suggestion of a choice to the crowd, but the crowd which made the suggestion to him.

Yet when all is said and done, the oddest part of the story is not the notion of a judicial reprieve. It is the idea that Pilate should have ceded his authority to the whim of the crowd. He had armed troops at his disposal—dozens stationed in the palace alone, more in the Antonia—and, in this case, absolute power to act. He had no need to let the crowd choose who would live or who would die. That was his job. Philo made his point with venom against Flaccus, the prefect of Egypt, who failed to stop the pogrom of 38 in Alexandria: "When the governor of the country, who, if he wished, could have suppressed in a single hour the tyranny of the mob, pretended not to see what he saw and not to hear what he heard, but allowed them to wage war unrestrainedly, he wrecked the peace."

Besides, Pilate would have been imbued with all the snobbery and distaste that Romans in high places felt for the mob. The people, the *populus,* sometimes had reason on their side; the *res publica,* after all, was the expression of the popular will in lasting laws and institutions. But even the Roman people needed to be led by Caesar and represented by the senators. Left to their own devices, they were just the drunken mob who took to the streets at Saturnalia; or the crowd who stayed in their seats through the intermissions at the shows, singing and skipping lunch in the hope of seeing throats cut. They were the *turba* who surrounded a man to distract him from every good purpose, the goat-reeking mass of bean- and chestnut-eaters pressing around his litter in the market. Seneca wrote that the ordinary crush of the streets disturbed him and seemed to change his character. He felt that even Socrates and Cato might have been shaken in their moral strength by mingling with the crowd.

A Roman citizen facing the death penalty could, by the Lex Valeria, make an appeal to the crowd for his life. This apart, you did not ask such men for their opinions. The *Law of the Twelve Tables,* which Pilate, as a magistrate, was meant to have read, made this quite clear: "Vanae voces populi non sunt audiendae, quando aut noxium crimine absolvi, aut innocentem condemnari desiderant": "When they want to absolve a heinous crime or condemn an innocent man, the crowd's empty voices must not be listened to." But then, as Cicero had lamented some years before Pilate was born, "no one learns that law nowadays."

Besides, the crowd was unteachable. With a small group of men you could talk rationally; but the crowd had to be harangued at maximum volume, with sweeping gestures, and in the process all subtlety of thought would disappear. You threw out trinkets, just as coins and bread rolls were tossed out at the games, and watched as the audience fell on one another to seize them. Only the most primitive ideas could get through; ideas requiring a yes or no. You roared into the answering roar. There was pleasure in it sometimes, the pleasure of rapturous applause on a grand scale. But even Caesar, when he heard it, would feel curiously weakened and afraid that the fawning throng would turn on him.

Perhaps Pilate thought he could keep control. After all, he was trying to release Jesus, and the crowd liked him, didn't they? They had made him their king, hadn't they? Despite what the priests said, perhaps governor and crowd were unexpectedly on the same side. Perhaps he saw himself in a play, one of those tragedies in which the leading actors wore *togae praetextae* just like his own, and in which the crowd was the Chorus, "siding with the good and giving friendly advice, swaying the angry and cherishing the righteous," as Horace said. Perhaps, after all, his choice could be offloaded on to them.

In Mark and John he tried, however clumsily, to get the crowd behind him. "Would you like me to release the king of the Jews for you?" he inquired of them. But that leading question got him nowhere. His offer was quickly flung back in his face, contempt returned for contempt: "No, not this man! Barabbas!"

Joshua (Jesus) Barabbas, if he was not invented, seems to have been a bandit and an outlaw. John calls him "a robber," although Matthew says he was "a notable prisoner," suggesting that he might have been high-born. His name translates as "son of a distinguished father." Whatever his lineage, he was apparently guilty both of sedition, the crime which the priests were trying to fasten on Jesus, and of "murder committed during the insurrection." He had probably been flung into jail a few days before, roughed up after the disturbance in the Temple compound. A couple of other *lestai* were locked up with him, presumably to await execution when Pilate arrived from Caesarea. They became the two thieves (in medieval tradition, Gestas and Dysmas) who were crucified on either side of Jesus. The Romans sometimes preferred not to kill such people immediately, but to make a spectacle of them at a time of general holiday.

The evangelists implied that Barabbas was well-known as both a patriot and a troublemaker. This was not a man who ought to escape death. His criminality was obvious, as was his defiance of the Roman occupying power. To pardon him would be an extraordinary concession by the governor. Pilate would be in the deepest trouble with Tiberius if he ordered Barabbas to be released.

Yet he plowed on. In Matthew, to make the choice clear, Pilate spelled it out to the crowd. He also turned the decision over to them entirely. "Which of the two do you want me to release to you?" he asked. "Barabbas, or Jesus who is called Christ?"

These were outlandish words for a Roman to have uttered, if he ever said them. But what was he thinking by offering this choice at all? Hans Kelsen, an Austrian-American jurist and philosopher whose writing spanned most of the twentieth century, thought this was a wonderful show of democratic sensitivity: untroubled by absolutist notions of what was right or wrong, Pilate simply acquiesced in the will of the popular majority. The German theologian Martin Niemöller disagreed. In one of his last Passion sermons, preached in Berlin in 1937, Niemöller fingered Pilate as a simple coward: a man who handed the choice to the Jews because he preferred not to make it himself. They, not he, would decide whether Jesus or Barabbas died. But, as usual, Pilate omitted something from his perfect scheme: he was still the hangman, and so could not excuse himself from making the same choice. "No man," said Niemöller, "has the right to put this question to other men without giving the answer himself."

And Pilate had, in fact, given his answer. By asking the question "Jesus or Barabbas?" he had already rejected the claims of Jesus. By placing the two on the same level, he had ranged himself with Christ's enemies. This choice was in fact a failure of nerve: failure to commit himself to the defense of a man in whom he had found no crime. Niemöller, preaching in Nazi Germany with the storm troopers closing in around him, saw Pilates everywhere. "In these days and weeks," he said, "it seems dangerous to vote or to work openly and unequivocally for this Jesus, and human foresight and shrewdness may more than once give us the tempting counsel to imitate Pilate and to leave the decision to others. 'Do choose for yourselves; you are free, you know, to decide whether you will have Barabbas or Jesus, of whom it is said he is called the Christ.' "

So, in the Gospels, the crowd chose Barabbas. They are presumed to have decided so quickly because the chief priests, like cheerleaders, whipped them up. There is never any hint of the crowd splitting into factions; the Gospel writers give them one loud hectoring voice. Some commentators suppose they did this to spread the supposed guilt of the Jews evenly and universally; there were no dissenters. Later embroiderers of the New Testament, writing in the same broad climate of distaste for the Jews, begged to differ. They did not forget that the crowd had recently been on Jesus' side. It did not make sense, they insisted, that no one had tried to defend him.

In the *Acta Pilati,* different factions in the crowd clamored loudly for Pilate's ear. Nicodemus spoke first. He pushed himself forward with the request "Might I have a few words, Governor?" and recommended that Jesus be dismissed without punishment: "If what he does comes from God, it will stand. If it's merely human, it will come to nothing." He reminded Pilate that Moses had performed proper miracles, but that his imitators had performed tricks and cures that had not received divine approval; and so they had perished, along with their followers. God himself would save this Jesus or damn him. Pilate could let him go.

Jesus' opponents refused to accept this. "You're his disciple!" they shouted. "You're making a plea for him!"

Nicodemus countered: "Is the governor his disciple too? He's making a plea for him, isn't he? Even though Caesar appointed him?"

Another supporter of Jesus then leaped up, describing how Jesus had made him walk after thirty-eight years of lying in his bed. "Ah, but ask him what day he was healed on!" cried the opponents to Pilate.

"What day were you healed on?"

"The Sabbath, sir."

"Ha!" shouted the opposition. "Didn't we tell you that he heals and casts out demons on the Sabbath?"

"I still don't think he deserves death," said Pilate. "Even for that."

"Then tell us, Governor, if someone blasphemes against Caesar, should he die, or not?"

"He deserves to die, yes."

"So how much more should he deserve to die, if he blasphemes against God?"

Pilate was silent. But the opponents of Jesus went on, insistent and insatiable: "He said, 'I can destroy this temple and raise it up again in three days!' "

"Which temple?" Pilate asked.

"The one that Solomon labored to build for forty-six years; he says he will destroy it and build it again in three days!"

"I don't want to kill him," Pilate insisted. "I don't think he deserves to die."

Supporters of Jesus were now starting up all over the crowd, waving for the governor's attention. One cried: "I was blind, and he put his hands on my eyes, and I saw." Another cried, "I was bowed down, and he made me straight with a word." The woman with the issue of blood tried to speak, but the anti-Jesus lobby cut her short: women's evidence did not count. Then came another shout, louder than the rest: "This man is a prophet, and the demons are subject to him!"

"So why," asked Pilate wearily, "aren't your teachers subject to him?"

"We don't know."

The Pilate of the *Acta* sat down in the judgment seat. He still did not know what to say. But as he sat there, he felt a whisper in his ear. An attendant murmured, "Message from your wife, sir."

"Not now."

"She says, 'Have nothing to do with this just man, because I've suffered many things today in a dream because of him.' "

Pilate looked up at the priests and the elders. He said, "You know that my wife is a worshiper of God, and prefers to adhere to the Jewish religion, along with you?"

"Yes," they said. "We know."

"My wife says, 'Have nothing to do with this just man.' She's had a terrible dream about him."

"Didn't we tell you he was a magician?" cried the elders, laughing. "Now he's sent a phantom of dreams to your wife."

. . .

It is the most fantastical element in the trial. In the Gospels, only Matthew includes it. For one verse in the New Testament Pilate's wife is given, through a messenger, a voice. She warns her husband to bear in mind the innocence of Jesus, revealed as she was sleeping. She then disappears, as swiftly as she has come. Everything else in the trial may be dimly plausible, but not this; not the dreams of distracted women.

Yet credulous souls supposed it happened, and that it affected Pilate; and the were right to some extent. If a dream seemed to carry a message in it, Pilate would not have discounted it. This was by all accounts a vivid morning dream, the sort that roused the sleeper, slightly nauseated, to the shock of daylight. Dreams seen after midnight were taken as true. And they were not to be ignored: even the dreams of spring, which Augustus had found "frivolous and frightful." Heaven still sent them as gifts and warnings. Caesar once dreamed that he was making love to his mother and that she was submissive to his embraces; it meant that he was going to be the master of the earth. On the night before the Ides when he was killed, his wife, Calpurnia, dreamed that the pediment of their house was crumbling and that her husband lay stabbed on her breast, his blood soaking the sheets; as she started up, the doors of their room flew open. That same night, Caesar himself dreamed that he was soaring above the clouds and joining hands with Jupiter.

The career of Augustus was also filled with presentiments and dreams. He took every one of them seriously, for his life had been shaped by them even before he was born. His mother, Alia, dreamed that she had made love to Apollo in the form of a snake; when she woke, the mark of the snake was on her body, and no amount of washing could remove it. Before she was delivered, she dreamed that her womb stretched to encompass the earth and the stars, and her husband dreamed that she gave birth to a beam of sunlight. Quintus Catulus dreamed that Jupiter chose the boy Augustus out of a group playing around his altar, blew him a kiss and wrapped him to his bosom in his cloak; Marcus Cicero dreamed that Augustus was let down from heaven on a golden chain and was handed a whip by Jupiter as he stood at the door of the Capitol.

Specters who appeared in dreams might have nothing to do with the gods directly, but only with private disaster. Valerius Maximus, in his

Memorable Doings and Sayings (a highly popular work around the time Pilate left for Judaea), ran through several examples. After the battle of Actium, Cassius Parmensis dreamed that a huge man came into his bedroom, black skinned, with a disheveled beard and straggling hair. "Who are you?" he cried. "Kakadaimon," the man howled, "your bad demon." Cassius yelled for his slaves, who said they had seen no one enter. He went back to sleep and saw him again. This time he called for light and kept his slaves with him; the demon did not reappear, but Cassius was sentenced to death by Caesar shortly thereafter. The Roman knight Aterius Rufus also foresaw his death in a dream, in which a gladiator pierced his breast with a sword. At the show the next day he told his friends, who were sitting in the next seats; but they laughed the dream away and made him stay. The gladiator of the dream then entered the arena, chased his rival into the knights' seats, and, lunging at him, killed Rufus instead, just as he had been killed in his dream.

Rufus could not have escaped this dream. It was his fate. But if one of his friends had dreamed of his death or his disgrace, Rufus might have been able to deflect it by propitiating the gods. A friend constantly dreamed that bad things would happen to Martial; as a result, Martial complained, he had no more wine, pigs or frankincense left to sacrifice to keep his fate at bay. "Either stay awake, Nasidianus," he wrote furiously, "or dream about yourself!"

What form could Procula's dream have taken? Had Jesus appeared in her room, bearded and loud, or dangling from a golden chain, or in easy familiarity with the gods? Had something suggested that his death might be important? Perhaps he had appeared to her with that strange intensity that characters acquire in dreams: his face sketchy, almost misty, but his body charged with energy and even with eroticism. He might have entered softly, in the white robe of the hero, persuading her of his holiness with a mere gesture or a glance; or in a blaze of extraordinary, embarrassing involvement, as when the gods descended to the couches of common mortals.

Nineteenth-century popularizers were convinced that Procula had dreamed of Jesus, his face appearing with all the sad-eyed solemnity of the lithographs that lined their halls. They imagined that she had gone to bed late, kept up by the odd noises downstairs: deputations, the priests' demands for help in arresting Jesus, the clanking departure of the cohort toward the garden of Gethsemane. She was interested in this man

already, they surmised, already haunting the outer courtyards of the synagogues. It was no wonder he featured in her dreams. But medieval writers dismissed all that. They believed that Procula had dreamed about the
Devil.

The terrifying scene was set. There she lay, center stage, in the half-
dark. In the Gréban play Satan tiptoed up to her, softly twitching the
curtain so that she moaned and moved in her sleep. "No, don't wake,
dear," he whispered. "I won't ravish you . . . or, at least, only through
your ear . . ."

Procula moaned again.

"Your husband holds sway over the life and death of a holy and
saintly man. His name's Jesus, who calls himself Christ. . . . You must
make sure your husband doesn't pass sentence on him, for if he does
you'll both be utterly destroyed."

Procula cried out in her sleep, covered her ears.

"Don't fret!" whispered Satan. "I'm such a gentleman. . . . I won't de-
flower you of anything but your peace of mind. . . . Just remember what
I said! Tell your husband!"

He blew her a kiss and let the curtain fall. In the Coventry play he
did the same, "making no din," but this was out of character. In most
other plays the Devil could creep up on Procula only because she, like her
husband, was a drunkard, and her sleep was deep. Everyone else could
hear Satan as he erupted on the stage "in most horrible wise," hairy, obscene, red-bearded, to make his case. He was the king of hell, commanding thousands of demons, mixing up the brimstone in great brass vats.
But he was worried about Jesus and his miracles. He had worked out a
clever plan to get him; he had made the cross ready, "with three nails to
tack him with"; but perhaps after all it was not a good idea to entertain
this wonder-worker in his kingdom. What if he defeated him? What if,
as his demons fretted, Jesus "burst the power of hell asunder"? It was better, after all, to save him, to make sure he didn't die, so that redemption
was thwarted and hell was left alone. The York Satan made the same
point about this "gentleman Jesus":

> By any sign that I see, this same is God's son.
> If he shall be slain, our solace shall cease.
> He will save man's soul from our hand,
> And ravage our realms all around.

As far as Satan was concerned, to work through a woman was not only sound psychologically, but neat theologically. As one woman, Eve, had brought death to man, so another would make sure that Satan retained his *imperium mortis,* his death grip on the world. And so he crept up to embrace Pilate's wife.

She was terrified. The Gréban Satan, however smilingly, said she would be destroyed; the York Satan snarled that she and Pilate would lose all their power and riches; the Coventry Satan, through whose diatribe she seemed to have been snoring, screamed that they would both go to hell unless they obeyed him, and filled her dreams with "wildfire and thunderblast." In every case she leaped out of bed, pulling the golden drapes down and around her to cover up her nakedness. The York Procula sent her grumpy little son to tell Pilate ("Oh, *what?* I've got to go *now?*"); the Gréban Procula sent her maid, nicknamed Fluff, who had fallen in love with the dark, handsome, cloven-footed man she had just encountered on the stairs. Only in the Coventry play did Procula herself burst in on Pilate, "her skirt and kirtle in her hand, like a madwoman." But however the message was relayed, Pilate received it seriously. Where necessary, he calmed Procula down, but he did not discount what she told him. On the contrary, as in Matthew's Gospel, his wife's dream pushed Pilate as far as he had yet dared go toward sparing Jesus.

We think of this as an attempted act of mercy: Pilate's good angel, in the form of his wife, prompting him to spare an innocent man. The medieval writers proposed a more complicated theology. It was the Devil that pushed Pilate toward mercy, to upset the plan of salvation. But the demands of divine justice were that Jesus should die; Pilate could not decide otherwise. Although it might be true, as Gerard Manley Hopkins wrote, that Jesus "did not entrap Pilate, Caiaphas and Satan into crucifying him; . . . on the contrary he was all the time giving graces which his enemies might have used," those graces always seemed weaker than the roar of the mob and his own silence. At various times in the trial, according to all sorts of interpretations, Pilate was tempted by the notion of being both virtuous and brave. But his good angel, brutal and effulgent, was on the other side.

There was no resolving this contradiction. The theology itself was in confusion. The judgment Pilate was to make would be wicked and damnable, but it would also be liberating and essential. In the centuries that followed, the day of his decision would be cursed: wine would turn sour, washed clothes would never be clean, baked bread would smear the oven with a trail of bloody crumbs. Yet this would also be the Friday that men called Good.

The Gospels suggest dilemmas enough, in any case. Pilate needed no added complications from his wife. If she was really there in Jerusalem, as Matthew says she was, her role was to keep away from the courtroom; the nearest she could get was to sit behind a curtain, hiding herself from the men's world. Pliny's wife was the ideal. "How full of solicitude she is," he wrote, "when I am entering upon any cause! How kindly does she rejoice with me when it's over! When I'm pleading, she stations messengers to tell her from time to time what applause I'm getting, and how the case is going." Procula, by contrast, had drawn Pilate's awful situation in the starkest terms. For if Jesus was just, and Pilate condemned him, he would offend the gods and the reputation of Rome. Yet if he did not give the crowd what it wanted, things might get out of hand and he might be reported to Tiberius and lose his job; or worse.

Pilate's dilemma expressed itself in physical agitation. He kept getting up, pacing around, going into the *praetorium,* coming out again. Such turbulence had no place in a trial; if the crime was serious, Pilate should have judged it sitting utterly still on his *sella curulis,* the sacred symbol of justice and of his office. And such turbulence was the very antithesis of the Roman public speaker, who was supposed to rise "like the morning star from the eastern waters" and, before he uttered even a word, stand rapt and motionless before his audience. Instead, Pilate resembled the dreadful Verres, once pro-praetor of Sicily, who had a reputation for taking money to decide cases. In one, Verres had to decide whether to take a small bribe to acquit a just man, or a large one to condemn him. He could not decide. "He turned himself every way," said Cicero, prosecuting: "not only in his mind but also in his body; so that everyone could plainly see that fear and covetousness were contending together in his heart. There was a great crowd of people present, and profound silence, and eager expectation which way his covetousness was finally going to find rest. His attendant was constantly stooping down to his ear. . . ."

Pilate would not have been alone either, though in the Gospels it seems as though he is. There would have been people stooping down to whisper to him, too, as he sat in his chair, or walking at his shoulder as he paced about. An early apocryphal version of the trial suggests another parallel to Verres: that the Jews were offering Pilate money to give the decision they wanted. But the evangelists would not have missed that routine Roman weakness.

Luke's Pilate asked the crowd: "What shall I do with him?"

"Crucify him!" they shouted back. What else was a Roman governor good for? How else did he amuse himself?

"I can't find him guilty of anything. Nothing he has done is worthy of death. So I'll flog him and let him go."

"No!" they yelled. "Not this one! Let Barabbas go! Crucify this one! *Crucify him!*"

"*Why?*" asked Pilate. He, too, was shouting at top volume now; Luke says that "he cried out in addressing them." "What wrong has this fellow done? I've found no cause of death in him."

He threw out his offer again. The Greek suggests that he was as emotional and insistent as they were, but the repetition did not suggest resolve. It suggested a man who needed to convince himself that anything he did could work at all.

"I will flog him and let him go."

Cicero had something to say on this.

> Now when we meet with expediency in some specious form or other, we cannot help being influenced by it. But if on closer inspection we see that there is some immorality connected with what appears to be expediency, then we should not necessarily sacrifice expediency, but recognize that there can be no expediency where there is immorality.
>
> For if there is nothing so repugnant to nature as immorality (for nature demands right and harmony and consistency, and abhors their opposites), and if nothing is so thoroughly in accord with nature as expediency, then surely expediency and immorality cannot co-exist in one and the same object.
>
> Again: if we are born for moral rectitude and if that is either the only thing worth seeking, as Zeno thought, or is at least to be esteemed as infinitely outweighing everything else, as Aristotle holds, then it necessarily follows that the morally right is either the sole good or the supreme good. Now, that which is good is certainly expedient; consequently, what is morally right is also expedient.

Thus it is the error of men who are not strictly upright to seize upon something that seems to be expedient and straight away to dissociate it from the question of moral right. To this error the assassin's dagger, the poisoned cup, the forged will owe their origin; this gives rise to theft, embezzlement of public funds, exploitation and plundering of provincials and citizens; this engenders also the lust for excessive wealth, for despotic power, and finally for making oneself king even in the midst of a free people; and anything more atrocious than such a passion cannot be conceived. For with a false perspective they see the material rewards but not the punishment; I do not mean the penalty of the law, which they often escape, but the heaviest penalty of all, their own demoralization.

Away, then, with questioners of this sort . . . who stop to consider whether to pursue the course which they see is morally right or to stain their hands with what they know is crime. For there is guilt in their very deliberation.

Did that help?

(Should Cicero have begged Antony's pardon?)

(Should the Spartans have fled when they were sent against Xerxes?)

(Should Alexander have sailed the ocean?)

V.

In art and tradition, Jesus was hidden for the scourging. He was taken into an inner room of the palace, even into the basement, and whipped by soldiers in the half-dark. Yet scourging was a public punishment. In Rome it was done in the Forum itself, in front of the crowd and in front of the judgment seat, before which the victim was flung at the end. In Judaea, at least in Florus' time (a few years after Pilate), it was done precisely where Pilate was now sitting, in front of his chair.

Like crucifixion, scourging was illegal—though not unknown—for Roman citizens, because it was a punishment of slaves. The official order for scourging was "I, lictor, colliga manus": "Go, lictor, tie his hands." If there were no lictors (and the Gospels imply that Pilate had none), ordinary soldiers or even household servants did the job instead. The scourging was done either with the lictors' rods—switches of elm—or with leather thongs tipped with fragments of lead and bone.

This torture was not a legal requirement. It was merely a custom grown solid with repetition, and the severity of the treatment depended on what was meant to happen next. If the victim was to proceed directly to crucifixion, the scourging was relatively light to preserve his strength. If the judge intended to let him off with a flogging only, it was as brutal as he thought necessary. Matthew and Mark take the view that the scourging, as was normal, immediately preceded the Crucifixion, and was therefore the preliminary to death. John supposes that Pilate, still struggling with his conviction of Christ's innocence, meant the scourging as a gesture of appeasement to his accusers, and perhaps as a last attempt to extract a confession by torture. When Paul was arrested by the Romans later, the chief captain ordered that he should be "examined by scourging."

Luke, too, suggests that this was the way the governor's mind was working. According to these writers, Pilate intended to reduce Jesus to a figure of pity who might be spared by the Jews. It was typical Roman thinking: in the Roman law courts an accused man would deliberately dress in black mourning clothes, grow a straggly beard, neglect to wash, in order to incite pity in the jurors. Pilate was the only jury here, but the crowd seemed to be competing with him; so, in a formula that has since become ever more useful to politicians, he scourged Jesus to save him. He had found his middle course.

To say that Pilate "took him and scourged him," as the Gospels do, is not a misstatement. Although he did not do so with his own hands, he would have attended and supervised. Having given the order to start, and knowing just how far he wanted this to go, he also had to give the order to stop. He therefore sat in his judgment seat and oversaw what was done: the stripping of Jesus to his loincloth (he would have been prudish, like most Romans, about nakedness in criminals); the tying, in a half-bent position, to a pillar; the exact loss of blood, the progress of exhaustion. Perhaps he counted aloud, as people counted at the gladiator shows, the precise number of strokes as they fell. *Unum, duo, tres, quattuor.* In the process, he may have found himself watching for stranger signs, despite his position of judicial indifference: for blood the color of resin, for skin that did not break, for bruises of peculiar regularity, that might have confirmed the claims of this man to come from some otherworldly place. The veins of the gods were supposed to run not with blood but with ichor: Alexander had once damped down the idea that he was divine by remarking, when he was wounded, that only blood was flowing from him. In the case of Jesus, too, the blood and the weariness were human.

The medieval plays made much, even too much, of the scourging scene. They dwelt with appalled fascination on the thought that men could actually whip, and then mock, the Son of God. Yet they faced a dilemma: for though Pilate was deeply involved, indeed responsible, they still needed to keep him slightly distant and sympathetic. So while the brutality of the soldiers never wavered, Pilate's did. As during the trial itself, he vacillated from confidence to sadism to sudden horror at what he was doing. In one French play, he even let Jesus in on his ruse to save him: "Jesus, don't worry about these people. You'll be all right."

In the York play, Pilate gives the order as tersely as one would expect: "Right, men, get this straight. Strip him, make him bleed, and beat him black and blue. Wring him till he weeps." The soldiers then set to work, glorying in the job, and remarking that they would go even further "if it wasn't for Sir Pilate." At that point, they stop and look at the governor. He gets up and comes over to inspect the work, holding his robe out of the blood.

"You, man," he says to Jesus. "Why do you suffer all this and never ask us for mercy? Isn't that an arrogant way to behave? You ought to be humble. We're the masters here. If men call you a king, tell us why. Tell us why the Jews want to kill you. Inform me. I want to know."

He searches the swollen face; but Jesus will not answer.

"He's going to faint or something, sir."

"Yes, we'd better not kill him, had we, sir?"

"Inform me!" Pilate shouts.

"Sir, I've got a great idea. He called himself a king, so let's make him one! Let's sit him here in this chair, really comfortable, as if he was in his own hall, and then we'll crown him with nice brambles, give him a lovely purple robe—"

"Do it," says Pilate. And leaves them.

The mockery then begins: the robing, the crowning, the hailing. The silly soldiers prick their fingers on the thorns, admire the blood, make up songs.

"Hail, doughty dumb duke!"

"Hail, lord with no land!"

"Hail, fool with no force!"

"Hey, harlot. What about a bit of thanks to all of us who are working so hard to worship you?"

Just as things are getting out of hand, the door flies open. It is Pilate. He storms in, flinging the men aside. "No more!" he cries. "No more! No more!"

They fall back, stunned.

"Are you men of stone? Leave him alone!"

"But sir—"

"Stand aside! Leave him alone!"

In the silence that follows, Pilate walks up to Jesus, his face slack with regret; and it seems for a moment as though he might touch him.

"Ah, look," he murmurs. "He blushes all blue."

If the mockery happened this way, in the middle of the trial, Pilate probably watched. John gives no indication that he left the scene; he only implies that he took no active part in it. This made him no less culpable. After all, he allowed it, even if he did not order it explicitly. In Matthew and Mark, where the scourging and mocking happened at the end of the trial, he had already left. Matthew's Pilate had washed his hands of the whole affair.

In the vast hall of the palace ("the common hall," Matthew calls it), the whole cohort supposedly passed before Jesus. Hundreds of soldiers each kneeled and saluted him, some spitting and slapping his face. A man who wished to show himself superior to military roughhousing would take no part in this charade; a man who liked the ritual humiliations of the Roman shows, or who wanted to be one of the lads, might enjoy it. We do not know which of these types Pilate was. Possibly he was either, as the mood took him. Those who endorse John's account have usually imagined that he left the soldiers to it. But perhaps, after all, the distancing was only in his head.

According to John, Pilate scourged Jesus although he thought he was innocent. Then, still thinking him innocent, he let him be mocked by his men. Assuming that this is how things were, would it have troubled Pilate's conscience? Or, to put it more brutally, did he have a conscience that could recognize when it should have been troubled? Probably. As a Roman, he understood the concept. In all the incidents of his life that are reported, violence or willfulness or intransigence was followed by a glimmering of conscience, a shadow of repentance. Something or someone seemed to whisper to him then. Perhaps it was his *genius,* the guardian spirit who ruled his birth star, imploring him to keep on a straight track. *Genii,* though divine, were attached as if in cages to each man's life; only death could free them. Their murmur told him not to do what he should not, and reminded him how brief life was. When a man sinned, the face of his guardian spirit changed from white to black like the demon of Cassius Parmensis; and although he could propitiate the spirit with flowers and wine, only virtuous action could restore its brightness. On every birthday he became pure again by offering, in sacrifice to the spirit, the birthday wreaths from his forehead and the honey cake from his table; and also by making resolutions to be good.

A man who revered the gods, or even one single Providence, kept a natural guard over his conduct. He might be more lax if his sense of the gods was routine or distant, or if his most intense devotions were reserved for a man who could not see him. But there remained, as Seneca put it, "his own rules." If Pilate watched the mockery, as John suggests, it may still have been with some of that tortuous examination of the rules or of his conscience which, in other incidents, he plainly had to carry out in public.

At last, he must have stopped the horseplay. Another wave of the hand, or a snap of the fingers. And then the prisoner was brought over. The nineteenth-century writers endlessly pictured and colored this scene. Jesus was wedged between two guards, barely standing. The cloak was askew on his shoulders, the crown of thorns lopsided on his head. Blood was drying on his face; his beard was crusted with it. Pilate, they imagined, looked at the face for a while. He searched it for whatever information it could give him, but it reflected only his own deliberate humiliations. No information, no confession. Ludicrously, some writers thought, he may have tried a small smile of encouragement, as if to say, This is your chance, I'm helping you now. But the smile wavered, his eyes pricked, and he turned away exasperated by his own weakness.

He walked out again to the balustrade. In most ages, the scene that followed—though only John described it—was the emotional peak of the trial. Pilate, having reduced Jesus to the most pitiable sight imaginable, would now present him to the crowd. He had brought him to the point where even he, Pilate, couldn't bear to hurt him anymore. The judge had become the advocate, and, as Farrar wrote, "with all the strength of a feeble pride, and all the daring of a guilty cowardice, and all the pity of which a blood-stained nature was capable, did strive to deliver him."

Once more he faced the crowd. In one Edwardian lithograph of the scene he leans right over, throwing out his left arm, almost airborne in his attempt to persuade them. "Look," he shouted, "I'm bringing him out to you, to let you know that I find no fault in him!"

Jesus was brought out, still in the cloak and the crown. He stood beside the governor now, the unbearable, piteous, ludicrous figure; Pilate could smell his unwashed skin. Medieval and Renaissance painters of this scene put the two men apart, with Jesus almost in the crowd and Pilate, flanked by aides and advisers, still discussing legal strategy in the background. But Christ's nineteenth-century biographers liked to have them close. Some writers imagined he took Jesus by the hand, the first pagan touch that was not meant to cause him pain; or that, like some thoughtless election-winner, he seized and thrust aloft the arm of his rival. But whatever he did, John's Pilate also cried out: "Behold the man!"

What on earth did he mean? Sentimentalists thought the strangeness of the phrase was easily accounted for: Pilate, almost in tears, blurted out any brief form of words that would do as a public statement. His magisterial reserve had melted away. It was replaced by the great phrase the Victorians found so thrilling, "Ecce homo," words that implied man but meant God, and which even suggested adoration: although most writers accepted that Pilate himself was highly unlikely to have thought that, and may indeed have been scarcely aware of what he was doing.

John gave the words in Greek and not Latin, in any case; and "Ide, o anthropos!" could carry a variety of meanings, from "Look at this poor fellow," to "What a figure of a man is this!" According to John (and again, only John) Pilate had last used the word *anthropos* at the very beginning of the trial, when he asked "What charges do you bring against this man?" So perhaps it was more neutral, even legalistic; or perhaps John was putting the word in Pilate's mouth to make some point about glory and divinity in human shape. Only John—or Pilate, if he spoke those words—knew exactly what he meant to say.

Yet the time for introductions was short. Immediately the crowd screamed back, "Crucify him! Crucify him!"

Pilate seems to have been stunned by their reaction. Despite his brutal scourging of a man whose case was, at best, uncertain, the crowd did not pity the victim at all. In fact, he seemed to have made things worse; for whereas before, in John, the crowd had only wanted Barabbas, they were clamoring now for the cross. His ruse had failed. He was beside himself with humiliation and anger.

"*You* take him yourselves. *You* crucify him. I find no fault in him at all."

A ridiculous thing to say. I find him innocent, but yes, kill him. Your immorality and illegality are fine with me. I'm only a Roman judge, what do I know? Or even more ridiculous: *You* crucify him. The Jews could not crucify anyone. He meant, If you are so eager to kill him, go ahead. Don't make me do it. Like so much that day, it came out idiotic and wrong. Even his insults didn't work: his anger and his flippancy alike evaporated uselessly above the seething heads.

He kept on saying, according to John, "I find no fault in him. I find no fault in him." In the original Greek the *ego* is always at the start of the phrase, suggesting that whatever the priests and the crowd might think, he proudly and passionately disagreed. But the crowd went on howling like the sea in a gale, as Virgil described that sea that wrecked Aeneas: violence brewing in great clouds, the "mass-mind boiling over" like the spume of terrific waves. And he couldn't calm them; because the only man who could calm such a sea or such a crowd, Virgil continued, was someone "whose goodness of heart and conduct / has won their respect."

So he stood there, with Jesus beside him.

The elders said: "We have a law, and by our law he ought to die, because he made himself the Son of God."

VI.

Pilate's answer should have been easy. The Jews' religious law had nothing to do with him or with Rome. It was their affair. They could take Jesus away and stone him for blasphemy if they wanted to; they could leave him out of it. But, according to John at least, that is not what happened. Pilate, instead, became "more afraid."

No particular fear had been registered in him before. He had been obtuse, offhand and surprised; he had tried, in his usual way, to slide from one clever scheme to another. Now, apparently, he was afraid. Real fear was something a Roman man tried not to show; rather than show it, he would pull his toga across to hide his face from others. In John, Pilate's fear was not quite like that. It was an increasing anxiety that he could not postpone much longer his decision for the truth or against it. Now the stakes were mounting: he had to find out whether Jesus was the Son of God or not. It was an area in which he had no judicial competence, but he approached it with a petrified fascination: similar, perhaps, to what Felix felt when Paul instructed him in the notion of faith in Christ, and Felix "trembled."

Instead of answering the chief priests, John's Pilate went back inside the *praetorium* and beckoned Jesus to follow him. Once again, to all intents and purposes, they were alone. They could continue their earlier conversation, about kingdoms not of this world. But it had taken a different turn. It had gone deeper. When they had last spoken, they had struggled as far as "truth" before Pilate balked. He had not wanted to go on. Now, consumed with worry, he thought he ought to try.

The question Pilate asked was "Pothen ei sy?" "Where are you from?"

It was not meant literally. He knew as well as Jesus did that he came from Nazareth, in Galilee. It was a composite question. S. T. Bloomfield's *Recensio Synoptica* of 1826 translates it as "What is your origin? what are your parents? [That essential Roman question: establish the tribe and class.] terrestrial or celestial? merely human, or divine? or mixed?" All in three words, which might best be translated in English as: "Who are you?"

Behind that question lay every unsettling, half-grasped phrase John's Pilate had heard that day. *Not of this world. Not from here. I came into this world to bear witness to the truth.* And now, *Son of God.* Pilate did not take chances with gods. This was why he let the Jews worship theirs, although he could neither respect nor understand a deity that was singular and could not be depicted; this was why he honored his own with a fervor that got him into trouble again and again. That was the Son of God he would have thought he knew: *Caesar, divi filius.*

And what of the rest? Whether or not he gave credence to the whole catalogue of characters, he had known since childhood exactly what the gods were like. Bearded Jupiter with the lightning in his pocket; sandal-winged Mercury, blue-eyed Neptune; blond Minerva in her helmet, the goddess he had prayed to as a schoolboy to get his exercises right. Even in a Roman's dreams, as Cicero said, these details were unvarying and particular. When Pilate thought of Juno, the mother of the gods, he saw her in her goatskin and upturned slippers, with a shield and spear; he saw Venus as a woman whose skin was soft as roses and whose hair breathed out ambrosia, even when she disguised herself as a hunting girl, in high soft boots, among the mountains of North Africa.

For the gods did come down among men, at least in the stories he knew. At the founding of Italy they had done so constantly, as well as before it. They had lain with mortals and produced more gods, and sons of gods; but like humans, like this Jesus, they had sometimes been re-buffed, or had wept in frustration. Propertius recorded that even Jupiter had cried with disappointment once, a man rejected: "deceptus quoniam flevit et ipse deus."

As Justin Martyr has pointed out, Jewish prophecies of the suffering Christ were easily confused with these tales. The sons of Jupiter— Mercury, Aesculapius, Hercules, Dionysus—had suffered on earth like men, fighting, torn to pieces, oppressed with labors, struck by lightning. They were taken up to heaven but then, scarcely settled among the stars, they returned again. Castor and Pollux had been sighted, two young warriors on white horses, fighting on the Roman side at the battle of Lake Regillus; Castor's horse had left a footprint in the rock. And often, Cicero added, "the sound of the voice of the Fauns, or the apparition of a divine form, has compelled anyone who is not simple-minded to admit the real presence of the gods."

The sons of gods could always be detected, or almost always. As soon as Aeneas, the son of Venus, approached Dido, the queen of Carthage, she knew that he was half-divine: he stood there "in an aura of brilliant light, godlike in face and figure." Even his small son revealed, when necessary, the touch of the gods: a halo of gently flickering fire among his curls. Al-though these beings might be broken, they still shone, as when the head of the murdered Orpheus sang in the crimsoned river that carried the rags of his body away. If Pilate probed deeper into this man Jesus, he too might find this light: a light that would seem to open a crack in the dome of the sky and let through an icy filament of air.

He could have ignored it. But it was dangerous to ignore the gods; it could bring havoc, ignominy, bad luck. They could adopt the most ludicrous disguises, from hissing snakes to toothless crones; even, perhaps, an irritating Jew in a lopsided crown. When Dionysus descended to earth, he dressed in a deerskin with a wreath of ivy on his long blond curls. It did not seem much of a disguise, but Pentheus, the king of Thebes, still failed to recognize him; he took him for another troublemaker, an impostor, leading the women into the hills to do their obscene dancing. When he had him arrested at last, and they stood face-to-face, he found himself marveling at the brightness of his hair and the whiteness of his skin, the faint thrilling perfume of wine on him. He had scorned and condemned this man but now, suddenly, he wanted to know. He wanted to know who he was.

John's Pilate was now in the same position. Across the chasm of incomprehension he extended, like Pentheus, a tentative hand. He could be informed, he could keep a secret, he could be an accomplice. And he asked the same question as Pentheus, in the same words: "Where are you from?"

But Jesus would not answer him.

The question hung between them. The non-answer seemed to say: If I told you, you would not understand. I'm weak, and it's too complicated. You had your chance earlier, and you threw it away. Remain in your ignorance; I don't want your commiseration.

Pentheus had been there too.

PENTHEUS.   What form do they take, these mysteries of yours?
DIONYSUS.   It is forbidden to tell the uninitiate.
PENTHEUS.   Tell me the benefits that those who know your mysteries
        enjoy.
DIONYSUS.   I am forbidden to say. But they are worth knowing.
PENTHEUS.   Your answers are designed to make me curious.
DIONYSUS.   No: our mysteries abhor an unbelieving man.
PENTHEUS.   You say you saw the god. What form did he assume?
DIONYSUS.   Whatever form he wished. The choice was his, not mine.
PENTHEUS.   You evade the question.
DIONYSUS.   Talk sense to a fool and he calls you foolish.

Pilate had reached the same point with Jesus, the same slap in the face. It was a rebuke, certainly. But Henry Liddon, a Victorian clergyman, interpreted the slap as kindness. This was a child Jesus was talking to, the child to whom he had said, "Are you saying that yourself, or did other people tell you that about me?" He had to be careful how much he told Pilate. To hand him something sacred and transcendent would be foolish; he would only drop it or misuse it. "Do not give what is holy to dogs," Jesus had said once, precisely meaning to Romans. Don't let them break it, even if they beg you for it. Beware those eager, slipping, dangerous fingers. "We should all of us agree," Liddon went on, preaching in St. Paul's in 1881 as anarchist bombs exploded in Moscow, "that there are just now people up and down Europe who are none the better for knowing something of the properties of dynamite; and a wise and kind father would not begin the education of his little boy by showing him how to fire off a loaded pistol."

So John's Pilate was not handed the loaded gun. It was held silently away from him, locked up where he could not see it. He reacted accordingly. "Won't you speak to me? *To me?* Don't you know that I have authority to release you and authority to crucify you?"

The answer to being hurt and humiliated was his usual one: to draw himself up like a wounded animal to the full height of his powers. The word he used for "authority" was *imperium, exousia* in the Greek, the numinous power he drew from Tiberius himself; there could be nothing more impressive. He was also falling back on legal jargon, as officials tend to do in moments of crisis. Yet his question had not merely been a judicial one. It was also a question to which he wanted an answer as a man.

So Jesus replied. His words were both tender and extraordinarily defiant: "You have no power over me at all, except what was given to you from above; therefore he who delivered me to you has the greater sin."

The words were fairly mystifying, and their conjunction more so. In John's Greek, each noun and verb carries several meanings. What comes through is a strange, almost thrilling, clash of egos. The word *emoi,* "to me" or "against me," was thrown out by both men at the start of their remarks: in answer to Pilate's literal "*To me* won't you speak?" Jesus in effect replied, "*Against me,* you're powerless." This *emoi* is so emphatic that it is, in itself, almost an admission of kingship. Pilate was unlikely to have missed it.

Yet the word "sin," *amartia,* is the one that lingers. *Meizona amartia,* greater sin. That apparently belonged to Caiaphas, the one who had delivered Jesus to Pilate; or, as medieval writers thought, to Judas, the one who had betrayed him. But Pilate, too, was among "the sinners" into whose hands Jesus had predicted he would fall. Caiaphas had delivered Jesus out of envy; Pilate was prepared to kill him out of fear, or even out of habit. In the exercise of his authority he had killed men before, and this marked the beginning of his downward slide. As Gerard Manley Hopkins noted, "If you will murder man you may come, as Pilate did, to murder the man who is God."

Jesus' notion of sin was not clear, however. Something was lost in translation. A Roman sin was a crime, a mistake, an aberration—from a slip of the pen to a cut throat. Sins were deeds done, and could be counted. You could fall into one sin or into many, as Cicero put it, "in peccata incidere," as into a swarm of bees; but there was no general state of sin into which a man could sink, as in quicksand. Pilate's day-to-day prayers would have carried no notion of sin or of forgiveness; it was success and safety he prayed for. To the extent that he had made mistakes, his sins that day were obvious. He had vacillated; he had turned the decision about Jesus over to the crowd; in Socrates' words, he had committed sin by failing to know what was false and what was true. But he had not entered—could not imagine entering—that pervasive sense of sin that Jesus was implying.

Socrates may have haunted him in another way. At that trial, too, the accused man had become the man in charge. Socrates knew he was more virtuous than the Athenians who had gathered to condemn him for corrupting their sons. The Oracle at Delphi had pronounced him the wisest man in the world; and he had a "sign of God" in him, a divine voice of restraint that held him back from what was unwise or wrong. It was from this height of God-touched assurance that Socrates spoke at his trial: "not a supplicant or a witness, but the master and lord of his judges," as Cicero described him. And here, in Jerusalem, something similar was happening. The tables had been turned. It was Pilate, not Jesus, who had to acknowledge his guilt and struggle to save himself. Pilate had found no sin in Jesus, but Jesus had found sin in him.

Jesus had also told him something else. He had said that Pilate's power came "from above," or "from the top." He could have meant the emperor—that would have been Pilate's instinctive understanding—but perhaps he meant something higher still. Most scholars agree that the word meant "from heaven," or "from divine power." John's Pilate had nothing to say to this, suggesting eloquently that he couldn't fathom what Jesus was saying; but nor could he deflect it with one of his flippant remarks. The Gréban play gave him a reply of sorts:

> *Well, I don't know what you're getting at.*
> *Who can be greater than the Emperor?*
> *He is Apollo, Jupiter and all the gods in one.*
> *What other Emperor could have a power like that?*

Silence may have been the best reaction, for what Jesus was saying was extraordinary. He was telling Pilate that his role was not fortuitous. Divine Providence had put him there. Pilate's power over him was God-given; Pilate himself was God's vice-regent, perhaps even his instrument. Beyond the brotherhood of humanity, which Pilate may already have sensed, they were in some unfathomable way brothers in heaven. And Jesus, who knew what God's will was, was suggesting that Pilate, too, might come to understand and advance it. He too could be good; he could be the *candidatus* in his shining robe, ready for the wreath of divine favor to settle on his glowing hair.

But what did God, or the gods, demand of him? It was still unclear. In the *Acta Pilati* Pilate called Jesus into the *praetorium* to ask a different, almost hopeless question: "What shall I do with you?"

Jesus answered, "Do as it has been given to you."

"How has it been given?"

"Moses and the prophets said that I would die and rise again."

This was the clearest expression of Pilate as God's agent, but it led in an impossible direction. It asked him not to save Jesus, but to kill him. In the *Acta Pilati* the chief priests, eavesdropping outside, interrupted the conversation before Jesus could explain further; and Pilate continued to believe that he could not, should not, put Jesus to death. Virtue could lie only in the act of salvation.

In John's Gospel too, Pilate apparently made the same decision: to save him. Whereas before, in the literal sense of the Greek, he had merely been "willing" to release him, he now "sought to," earnestly and zealously. If the Jews overwhelmed him, he could call the troops out of the Antonia and suppress the unrest in the usual manner; he would worry later about precisely how to explain events to Tiberius. The force of the sword was the force of right. Blood would flow in the streets again, but Rome would not be party to the execution of this innocent prisoner who was touched by God. In the name of righteousness, certainty, even happiness, he went back out to the crowd.

This was what Seneca was to call "the adventure of being good":

> He that judges right, and perseveres in it, enjoys a perpetual calm; he takes a true prospect of things; he observes order and measure in all his actions; he has a benevolence in his nature; he squares his life according to reason, and draws to himself love and admiration. Without a certain and unchangeable judgment, all the rest is pure speculation.
>
>   . . . If you could only see the mind of a good man . . . the beauty and the majesty of it . . . would not a man bless himself at the sight of such a thing, as at the encounter of some supernatural power?
>
>   . . . What I do shall be done for conscience, not ostentation. . . . I will look upon the whole world as my country, and upon the gods as both the witnesses and judges of my words and deeds. I will live and die with this testimony: that I loved good studies and a good conscience; that I never invaded another man's liberty, and that I preserved my own.

It was thrilling; but it couldn't last. In an instant it fell apart. All it took was one phrase, shouted out of John's mob and then picked up in a merciless chorus: "If you let this man go, you are not Caesar's friend. Whoever makes himself a king speaks against Caesar!"

It was the Jews' last gambit. They had tried "evildoing," but Pilate had refused to accept their allegation. They had tried "king of the Jews," surely seditious, but Pilate had dismissed it. Next they had tried a religious offense, but this had made Pilate even more unwilling to act. Now they had found a real nerve: the governor's private fears. And whatever else may have been imagined in John's Passion story, this part rings true.

Tiberius was known to hoard every scrap of insult, retailed from whatever source: "whether it was a slave denouncing his master or a son his father," as Dio Cassius said. Every slighting remark was investigated, and even secret ones were published, embellished with Tiberius' own inventions. Since the death of his son Drusus by poison in A.D. 23, he had never hesitated to kill or exile people even for fictitious reasons. And by the time of the trial Pilate may also have had indelibly before him the example of the fall of Sejanus, the closest imperial friend of all: a man who had dangled in unbearable suspense between the emperor's love and his abuse.

For John's Pilate the situation was now quite clear. The chief priests had condemned Jesus. They wanted him to die. They now had the people on their side, and the people would riot if he did not give them what they wanted. Moreover, they would tell on him. Here his past missteps and miscalculations came back to haunt him: for even if he wanted to be merciful in this case, he dared not be if it would lead to a blistering report to Rome of everything else he had done. "The nemesis of his past wrongdoing," as Farrar wrote, "was that he could no longer do right."

Tiberius had perhaps already received unfavorable reports of him. Would he tolerate more? Did Pilate have any stock of goodwill left? If he had, was he really going to hazard it, and with it the lives of hundreds of Jews and Romans and others, on the fate of one peculiar preacher? One man's life could never be worth that. If he let his soldiers loose on people, he would be called a butcher. He might lose Judaea. The crowd was already on the edge of tumult, and he was getting nowhere in his efforts to persuade them. Besides, he was not there in Judaea to pursue celestial fantasies or to sift the philosophy of those he sentenced. He was there to preserve law and order in the name of Rome.

If Pilate thought Jesus guilty, the trial came down to this: a contest between defiance of the state and assertion of the state's authority. If he thought him innocent, it came down to a contest between the rights of the individual and the safety of the state. Even if Pilate was troubled by his prisoner, there was therefore no question which path he should take. The judges of Socrates had been in the same position: faced with a man whose crime was merely his teaching, in a society where different opinions were ostensibly respected, they nonetheless condemned him for turning young people against "the gods of the city," which represented the whole apparatus of the state. The law—Pilate's law, their law, our law—stands in extremis always on the state's side.

When Bulgakov's Pilate came before the Russian public, in 1966, it was this dilemma that intrigued the critics. Pilate was seen as a model of the spineless provincial bureaucrats of Stalinist Russia: a man who would reverence the distant tyrant, put up his tinted portrait and drink his health in cheap vodka, while all the time suppressing his conscience. To save the dissident Jesus—to save Pasternak or Solzhenitsyn—was too much for him. Some Russian reviewers thought such moral cowardice could never be justified. Others disagreed. Personal morality, they wrote, could never replace civic duty as a basis for ethical behavior in a socialist society. And a man's civic duty was to preserve the social order and promote the ideology that underpinned it. So Pilate was right: he had, in effect, nobly and firmly subjected the promptings of his conscience to the tenets of the Communist Party of the Soviet Union.

The Victorians, too, debated over many years whether Pilate was right to crucify Christ. John Stuart Mill, in his essay *On Liberty* of 1859, contended that the judges of Christ—both Jewish and Roman—could not possibly have been justified, because they had tried to stifle freedom of conscience. Like the judges of Socrates, they had simply done wrong; even allowing for the temper of the times, they had to be condemned as guilty. It was impossible, Mill argued, to find a principle that would justify them.

James Fitzjames Stephen, an eminent lawyer, took up the challenge. In the course of a sweeping attack on Mill in his book *Liberty, Equality, Fraternity,* published in 1873, he argued that he could certainly find "a principle that will justify Pontius Pilate." Pilate's paramount duty, he went on, was not to preserve anyone's freedom of conscience, or even liberty in the abstract, but to keep the peace. "Therefore, if and insofar as he believed in good faith that what he did was necessary for the peace of Palestine, he was right."

Stephen admitted that the word "right" was problematic. Perhaps it could not be applied to political decisions at all, for much of what politicians did for the public good would never pass muster with "an omnipotent, omniscient and perfectly benevolent man." Ideas of right and duty had to be limited to allow for human weakness: for men, like Pilate, "stuck like limpets or spinning like weathercocks." The main problem, though, as Mill and his supporters argued back, lay in that phrase "in good faith." The Gospels implied both that Pilate knew Jesus was innocent (understanding that the Jews had delivered him "out of envy") and that he said so, several times. No judge could justly condemn an innocent man, no matter how compelling the reason.

But suppose, Stephen continued, a British officer in the Punjab found himself compelled to order the execution of a native preacher who was gentle enough in himself, but whose preaching was "dangerous to the English power"? What if he had by his side, virtually governing in association, a native ruler who was not only supporting but actively encouraging his decision to execute? Back came the answer from J. Taylor Innes, a practicing barrister, in *The Trial of Jesus Christ,* published in 1899:

> If done judicially, it would be a judicial murder. If done administratively, what ought it to be called? . . . I believe that few British officers who considered [such an act] would, as the result, think themselves compelled or even entitled to do it.

As for the officer who examined a "Guru or Imam" and found him innocent, but thought he would whip him anyway, and ordered his execution out of a sudden panic about his own promotion, "suppose that the story came out fully on his arrival in London, in how many drawing rooms would he be received?"

Yet Pilate had his own moral standards, of which the highest were the preservation of the emperor and the Roman peace. Stephen imagined him unconscionably stirred by the sight of his sentries standing guard in the Temple porticoes, "as [the Englishman's heart] beats high as he looks at the scarred and shattered walls of Delhi or at the Union Jack flying from the fort at Lahore." What words of Virgil, "as new and fresh as the best of Mr Tennyson's poems to us," as imperially proud and sentimental, must have come home to him then?

> *Tu regere imperio populos, Romane, memento*
> *(Hae tibi erunt artes) pacique imponere morem,*
> *Parcere subiectis et debellare superbos.*

In Dryden's translation:

> But Rome, 'tis thine alone, with awful sway,
> To rule mankind and make the world obey,
> To tame the proud, the fettered slave to free—
> These are imperial arts, and worthy thee.

Wasn't he right to kill someone who threatened this *pax et imperium,* however indirectly? Yes, Innes answered, he would have been; but it was crystal clear from the Gospels that he had killed Jesus mostly to preserve himself.

That was how it appeared. In John the crowd reminded Pilate, who had been touched for a moment by the light, what his job was, who his boss was, where his reputation lay. And so he capitulated. In all the Gospels, his fall was sudden. He seemed to throw up his hands; some modern writers even imagine him drowning. Bulgakov's Pilate, grieving that he has lost something even though he scarcely knows what it is, feels himself dragged down by seaweed in a purple mass of water. The Pilate of Romano Guardini, a German-Italian writing in 1956, "is sucked into the depths of the powers of darkness, into a confusion so dark and deep that he is no longer sensible of the gruesome and ignominious folly he is committing."

The chair of gilded wood or ivory still waited for him, set on a raised and tessellated pavement. He was out in the open air like a master of ceremonies at a show, with the same thin, wandering acoustic and the same ungrateful audience to address, whose only thought was blood. Well, he could do blood, too.

In John, he summoned Jesus out again for the last time and sat down in the chair of judgment.

"Look, your king," he told the crowd. It was not a bitter or a mocking announcement. He was on his official platform now, obliged to be serious, and he wanted to make the Jews consider what they were asking him, a Roman, to do.

"Away with him, away with him!" they screamed. "Crucify him!"

The endless repeated commands would have been enough to make him balk, as usual. "Shall I crucify your *king?*" he asked, with a trace of mockery now. But the chief priests and the crowd mocked back: "We have no king but Caesar."

In John, this was the end. As soon as the crowd proved it was implacable, Pilate handed Jesus over to be executed. Mark and Luke said the same, and Mark suggests there were no qualms about it: "wanting to please the people," Pilate set Barabbas free and abandoned Jesus. But in Matthew, before he did so, he called for water.

A servant brought it. This would have taken time; it was not a normal request in the middle of a trial. And so Pilate sat there, waiting. Traditional paintings show the servant, when he returned, kneeling to offer the bowl to the governor. It was almost noon, but he did not need water to refresh himself. Instead, he washed his hands, smoothing the water with ritual slowness over the palms and backs and between the fingers. The verb Matthew uses, *aponiptein*, means "to wash off from"; though dirt or blood was not there, it was vividly imagined. Then he took a towel from the servant and dried his hands again.

It was no part of a Roman trial for the judge to wash the blood guilt from his hands. If a sentence or the prospect of a sentence bothered him, Pilate could adjourn the trial to the judgment hall back in Caesarea (where Paul was tried by Felix), or refer the case to his provincial superior. If the case concerned a Roman citizen, he could even refer it to Rome. Sometimes, before they pronounced sentence, Roman judges would turn to the east or to the sun to declare their own innocence. That was as far as they could go.

The Jews, however, believed in the washing away of blood guilt. In Deuteronomy, when a man was found murdered within the boundaries of a city, the elders of the city were ordered to sacrifice a heifer and to wash their hands over it with the words, "Our hands have not shed this blood." Isaiah, too, had emphasized the redemptive power of washing. "Wash yourself," he wrote,

> *make yourself clean,*
> *put away evil from your souls,*
> *learn to do well,*
> *judge for the fatherless and justify the widow,*
> *and come, let us reason with the Lord:*
> *and though your sins be scarlet, I will make them white as wool;*
> *and if they be red like crimson,*
> *I will make them white as snow.*

Matthew's Pilate, with his washing, would have caught the crowd's attention. Perhaps they would have grown quieter and watched him until, at last, he raised his eyes and looked at them.

"I am innocent of the blood of this just person," he told them. "It's your affair."

The formulation seemed to echo the words from Deuteronomy, as if he meant to make a point by it; as if, despite himself, he had adopted a local custom that seemed ideal for the circumstance. If this was so, the crowd picked up the reference at once and, almost debonairly, threw back the response: "His blood on us and on our children!"

Yet the idea of Pilate appealing to Jewish sensibilities, to the point of adopting Jewish ritual, is almost ridiculous. It would have been completely out of character. And so another theory holds that what Pilate did—if he did it at all—was not Jewish, but Roman. Among both the Greeks and the Romans it was customary for a man who had involuntarily committed a crime, such as homicide, to purify himself with water to expiate the offense. Of course, no sophisticated man believed that real guilt could be washed away by water: "A stain on the soul cannot vanish for a long time, nor be washed away by any rivers," Cicero wrote. Ovid agreed: it was something the forefathers and the Greeks had believed in, but modern men did not. He described how Alcmaeon, after murdering his mother, had gone to the River Achelous with a prayer to be rid of his sin; and the river god had purged him. But "it's too easy to suppose, as you do," he wrote, "that those sad crimes can be carried away by water."

Nonetheless, the notion that sin could be washed away remained. Germanicus, faced with mutiny on the German frontier in A.D. 14, cried out to the spirit of Augustus in heaven to "come to these soldiers of yours and wash clean this stain." From day to day, too, a Roman would use water to proclaim that he was pure. Holy water—ideally, living, flowing water—could be used for private consecration, as Aeneas used it at the entrance to the Elysian Fields, or for ritual purification, as when priests—or magistrates, like Pilate, acting in place of priests—poured water over their right hands before the act of sacrifice. The most important prayers of the day, the morning invocations, were made with ceremonial washing of the hands. In all probability, this was how he had started his own day.

So Pilate had no need to imitate the Jews. He understood this ritual in his own heart, as part of his own practice. His offense was now apparent: he was consigning Jesus to that dim part of the Underworld inhabited by those condemned on false charges, between the mewling infants and the sad suicides. Perhaps he felt moved by his own predicament to the point where some gesture of abnegation had to be made. It was the equivalent, compressed and in miniature, of stripping off his clothes and diving into the sea.

Indeed, the sea might have purged him. Its waters were a potent soup of every medicinal virtue of the lakes and rivers that ran into it: of salt, alum, niter, bitumen and sulfur. Dissolved within were the waters of Campania, which cured insanity; the waters of Aenaria, which cured the stone; the freezing waters of Cutilia, stiffening the sinews and the stomach; and the warm springs of Albula, which closed up wounds. If you swam far enough you would find traces of Thessalonian springs that turned black to white and white to black; and of the twin fountains of Boeotia, producing respectively remembrance and forgetfulness.

Not all water healed. The Red Fountain of Ethiopia brought delirium. The dark waters of Avernus, like those of Asphaltites, which Pilate himself had looked on, perhaps touched, perhaps tasted, swallowed both leaves and birds. In Macedonia, the Lake of Insanity became salt and bitter three times a day, and crawled with white serpents twenty cubits long. The waters of the Styx brought death at once; those of Leontium killed after two days. At Tempe in Thessaly, out of a bank overhung with wild carob and purple flowers, a small stream trickled that corroded copper and ate the flesh of men.

But the water Pilate took was pure. It had flowed, perhaps, from his own aqueduct into the cisterns of the palace. This was water you could drink at once, dipping in a beaker to sip the essence of the snows on the mountains of Hebron. It was his own unwanted gift to the city of Jerusalem, civilization and power and peace in liquid form; and its power now included the promise of renewal. The soft touch of rain, the healing wave of the sea, the cold rush of the morning drink through the drowsy pores of the body, all carried the dross of the past away. A man could start again. Desperately, half-wittingly, Matthew's Pilate plunged his hands in the cleansing mercy of God.

VII.

He goes on doing so. His gesture has never ended. It turns up in the stone-flagged passage of a castle in Scotland, where a wild-haired woman wrings her hands in imaginary water for hours at a time. It echoes in

tsarist St. Petersburg, where in a shattered fourth-floor apartment Ras-
kolnikov, his murders done, scrubs away the blood with a hard piece of
soap and water in a pail. It lingers in the bathroom of the grandest hotel
in a gray river port in northern Argentina, where the adulterous Dr. Plarr
of Graham Greene's *The Honorary Consul* washes his hands, gazes at his
face in the mirror and thinks, I am like Pilate.

Political cartoonists still rejoice in it. Only the face of the hand-
washer needs to change. Margaret Thatcher, nose in air, washes her hands
of the Westland arms sales affair; Ronald Reagan cleanses himself of the
Iran-contra scandal; Mikhail Gorbachev, confronted with a limp victim
of heavy-handed policies in the Baltics, nervously seeks a bowl of water.
These, too, are like Pilate. They are even dressed like him. They sport
togas, laurel wreaths and sandals from which their toes protrude ludicrously; minions hold brimming bowls of water. Henchmen surround
them, and the media crowd in with cameras to record the ritual ablu-
tions. Sometimes the leaders look defiant, splashing the water with abandon. More often, the expression is hapless and ashamed. Try as they may
to wash the guilt away, it stays.

In nineteenth-century France, Proudhon declared that, "like Pilate,"
he had washed his fingers of the germ of the Second Empire. He was possibly the only official ever to boast of the comparison. All through the
Middle Ages and the Renaissance, as in the modern world, Pilate's hand-
washing was taken as an act of culpable buck-passing. His double was
understood to sit on the bench of every weak judge surrendering to injustice, and at the desk of every official, or general, or priest of the church
who saw atrocities or scandals and ignored them. The fourteenth-century
Book of the Passion put it as well as anyone:

> *He washed his hands before their eyes.*
> *He could have done better, but—surprise!*
> *He'd rather please them with a fudge*
> *Than be a just and upright judge.*
> *You see that everywhere today,*
> *In every court, it's sad to say.*
> *The godly poor get screwed again,*
> *The wicked rich escape the pain.*
> *And right gets shafted—what a shame!*
> *In every country it's the same.*

The washing of hands is almost the only Passion scene that is found on sarcophagi or in the catacombs. The earliest reliefs and drawings show how the gesture was seen as futile, even then. On the sarcophagus of Junius Bassves, from the mid-fourth century, Pilate stares away from Jesus as the servant prepares the water. He cannot look him in the eye. Another sarcophagus in the Lateran Museum shows Pilate turning away in embarrassment, searching for the water, as Jesus tries to talk to him; above him hangs a laurel wreath, symbolic of Jesus' victory over his judge. Pilate knows—or almost knows—who Jesus is, but he turns away, washes his hands, and condemns him. The fact that he has doubted does not absolve him, but merely makes things worse. The ritual of cleansing is started, not completed; the blood sticks.

Is it right that it should? From the Gospels onward, the question of who had killed Jesus was made complicated. Matthew's Pilate had recused himself, and elsewhere in the Gospels there were hints—for those intent on seeing them—that Jesus was delivered to the Jews to be executed. "He handed Jesus over to them to deal with as they wished," Luke wrote.

In the centuries that followed, even up to the twentieth, Christians wishing to blame the Jews seized on this single sentence. They include some of the most venerated men of the Church: Augustine, Aquinas, Chrysostom. Even if they conceded that Luke's grammar was ambiguous, they could nonetheless point to the pressure put on Pilate by the chief priests and the crowd. All the Jews, they argued, had killed Jesus. They had even, in Matthew, explicitly taken his blood on themselves and removed it from the Romans. And they had reaped the whirlwind. Every misfortune that subsequently befell the Jews—from the destruction of Jerusalem to Auschwitz—carried an echo of that invented blood pact from the trial.

Yet the effect of blaming the Jews was not always—or even often—to exonerate Pilate. The evangelists knew, as their readers knew, that crucifixion was a Roman punishment, and all of them (including Luke) described it as carried out by Romans. Roman soldiers were at the foot of the cross; Pilate wrote out the public charge sheet. Each evangelist stressed, as was politically important, that Jesus had been found innocent of any offense under Roman law. But if that was the case, what was Pilate? At best, spineless, and at worst a murderer.

To the unprejudiced reader of the Gospels—but also to plenty of prejudiced ones, from the Middle Ages onward—the conclusion is inescapable. As Luke said in Acts, all the rulers of the age ganged up against Christ. The Jewish priests may have been instigators, the crowd persuaders, but it was the Roman governor who killed him. In the end, Jesus did not have many executioners. He had one.

Pilate could have refused to sentence Jesus, but he did not refuse. This was probably not because he found Jesus guilty, but because he could not prove him innocent; and Jesus was no help to him. The Pilate of Dorothy L. Sayers weakly summed it all up:

> *I do not think there is any way out of these problems;*
> *One is always at the mercy of events and the world situation;*
> *One takes the thing as one finds it and makes the best of it;*
> *I do not believe there are any ultimate standards.*

Not all his critics thought Pilate was so helpless. Luther described him, not without irony, as "a more honest and just man than any papist prince of the empire":

> I could name many of these, who are in no degree comparable with Pilate; for he kept strictly to the Roman laws. He didn't want an innocent man to be executed and slain without a hearing, and he availed himself of all just means to try and release Christ; but when they threatened him with the emperor's disfavor, he was dazzled, and forsook the imperial laws, thinking, it's only the loss of one man, who is both poor and condemned; no one is supporting him; what hurt can his death do me? Better that one man should die than that the whole nation should be against me.

The modern politician might call this pragmatism. Pilate had taken the middle course. Yet some nineteenth-century commentators thought this temporizing was the worst thing about him: much worse than simply condemning Jesus and having done with it. Pilate, in their eyes, lacked both the courage to be good and the boldness to be bad. Goodness would have saved Jesus; badness would have sent him straight to the cross; but vacillation, Pilate's middle way, led to the protracted torture of multiple interrogations, mockings and scourgings. They led to the unnecessary reed and crown of thorns.

In the fifth of his Lent lectures in 1835 at the church of Holy Trinity in Chelsea, the Reverend Henry Blunt summed up the governor:

> There was indeed, as far as we can see, nothing remarkable in Pilate; he was one of the most common characters to be met with in passing through life; a timid, time-serving man, with just conscience enough to make himself uncomfortable, and with just integrity enough to ruin the best of causes, and even to increase, as he obviously did, the sufferings of Him whom he desired to save.

And so it may have been.

At the solemn moment of sentencing, in a normal trial, the curtain behind the tribunal was drawn across. The judge would then announce, as a preliminary, that he was conceding nothing "to bias or entreaty." Those words might have stuck in Pilate's throat, if he had tried to say them. But no proper sentence was recorded in the Gospels. The *Acta Pilati* imagined a long one: "Your nation has accused you, and you have proclaimed yourself a king. That is why I have decided that you shall be flogged according to the laws of the pious emperors, then hanged on a cross in the garden where you were taken. Dysmas and Gestas, the two robbers, will be crucified with you."

What must have happened would have been decidedly briefer. Pilate ordered Barabbas to be released, condemned Jesus, and saw to it that the record was changed. This was known as "turning the pen": reversing the stylus to erase from the wax tablet the sentence of acquittal that had probably been written there before, and writing a sentence of condemnation. When the blunt end of the stylus had erased a line of words, it was sometimes possible still to read them under the new ones; and even if they were illegible, the "fresh wounds" of the erasure still showed through. You could catch embezzlers that way, as well as judges whose timidity had got the better of them.

Nineteenth-century writers, anxious for one last confrontation between the two men, imagined that the governor's last words were addressed to Jesus directly. They wanted him to look into his eyes—those divine eyes—and say, in his best judicial Latin, "Condemno. Ibis in crucem." He was more likely to have said, in Greek to his soldiers, "Stau-rotheto," "Let him be crucified." Maybe, if the trial was as grueling as it has been painted, there were no words at all.

It was only another day in his life. It was just a bad morning, like any other bad morning, in a man's long struggle to keep to some sort of moral path. As one Edwardian cleric said, "He was tempted as we are tempted, fell as we fall, and might have overcome even as we also by the grace of God may overcome, if we will."

And then he went to lunch.

Chapter 6

WITNESS
TO CHRIST

You never know
Death could still dream
Dream he was alive
Dream he wasn't dead
And shaking his sheets of stone
Disengage himself
And lean out
And tumble from the tomb
Like a child out of bed
(Horror and catacombs)
Fall back into life
You would see it from here
Everything would be put in question
Affection and desolation
And what follows after . . .

JACQUES PRÉVERT,
"Nothing to Fear," from *Histoires* (1946)

I.

IN THE CELLAR of a house in Arnithero, near the city of Aquila in the kingdom of Naples, in the year 1580, a man was digging. We do not know why. We can imagine that the cellar was dark, with damp stone walls; and from the dark of the earth, under the steady blows of the spade, a stone "of marvellous beauty" gradually emerged. Under the stone was an iron box, too heavy to shift, with rusted locks that were quickly smashed open. Inside that box was another, of finest marble; and inside this, neatly rolled up, a yellow document covered with faint and foreign writing.

Several early Spanish romances were "found" in just this way, in costly marble tombs or under floors, unearthed by chance. Yet this was no romance: it was said to be Pilate's sentence from Christ's trial, which had long been rumored to be in Aquila somewhere. A few lines of the sentence, in Hebrew, were said to have been found on a copper plaque that turned up in excavations in the city around the year 1200, in an old vase of white marble. Other lines stated that the plaque was one of twelve copies sent to the twelve tribes of Israel. The vase was placed in an ebony box, and became so celebrated that in the eighteenth century a mere model of it was sold to Lord Howard for 2,890 francs. But the finding of Pilate's "complete" sentence, in the late sixteenth century, caused even more excitement.

Exposed to the light of day—according to the monk who related the discovery, Fray Rodrigo de Yepes—the document turned out to be a piece of sheepskin covered with Hebrew script. At the court of Philip II in Madrid, it was displayed as a curiosity. Courtiers in black, with neat pointed ruffs and beards, poked at it with their long fingers. It was agreed that the piece had its peculiarities: it was not particularly accurate about names of contemporary officials or forms of address. Some queried the signatures, in the same neat Hebrew script, of the leaders of the twelve tribes of Israel. Details that would not have gone unappreciated in

Counter-Reformation Spain—the precise number of wounds to be inflicted, the options of vinegar and lance, the witnesses allowed at the foot
of the cross—had been omitted by the governor. Nonetheless, among the
talk of domestic plotting, of European alliances, of debasement of silver
and the management of the Americas, the Sentence of Pilate circulated
like a piece of treasured samizdat. Many hands translated the Hebrew
original into Spanish, correcting the more manifest errors as they went.
That done, the Sentence was printed and glued into other books. But the
definitive version, according to Fray Yepes, was the one appended to his
own *Life of Christ,* published in 1583.

> In the 17th year of Tiberius Caesar, Emperor of Rome and invincible
> monarch of all the world, and in the two hundred and second Olympiad
> in the 24th Decade. From the creation of the World, according to the
> enumeration of the Hebrews, four times 1187, and from the establish-
> ment of the Roman Empire the year 73, and from the liberation from the
> Babylonish captivity 480 . . .
>
> On the 25th of the month of March, I, Pontius Pilate, President of
> the Imperial Roman Empire within the Palace of the High Court, judge,
> condemn and sentence to death Jesus called by the people Christ the
> Nazarene, and of Galilean origin, a seditious man according to Mosaic
> law and an opponent of the great Emperor, Tiberius Caesar.
>
> I declare and pronounce . . . that his death shall be on the cross, fixed
> to it with nails, as is customary with criminals; because, inviting and
> gathering together many men both rich and poor, he has not ceased from
> making a disturbance through all Judaea, claiming to be the Son of God,
> King of Israel, threatening the destruction of Jerusalem and of the Sacred
> Temple, denying that one ought to pay tribute to Caesar, and in addition
> to this audacity, entering with palms and triumph, together with a sec-
> tion of the people, into the city of Jerusalem.
>
> Wherefore I order my chief Centurion, Quintus Cornelius, to con-
> duct Jesus publicly through the city of Jerusalem, bound and tied, and
> that he be crowned with sharp thorns, and carry his own cross on his
> shoulders, that he may be an example to all malefactors; and in his com-
> pany I desire to be taken two murderous robbers, and they shall go out by
> the gate Golgotha, now called Antoniana: And that they shall take this
> Jesus to the public hill of justice, called Calvario, where being crucified

and dead, his body shall remain on the cross as a spectacle to all wicked men.

We likewise order that no one of any rank, state or condition whatsoever shall have the temerity to interfere with the said judgment which is to be carried out by my order and decree according to the decrees and laws, Roman and Hebrew, under penalty of being in rebellion against Imperial Rome.

[signed]	[notarized by]
The Twelve Tribes of Israel	Notamber (for the Hebrews)
The Pharisees	Sextilius (for the Romans)
The Sadducees	Amasius Chilion

Fray Yepes—for he was most probably the forger—had had fun with this. By calling Pilate *Presidente,* he summoned up an image of the governor of some Spanish province in the Old World or the New: the sort of man who, mounted on a Moorish stallion, would make a tour of his plantations or watch from a decent distance the slaughter of Indians. The signatures of the twelve tribes also had something of this feel: single, primitive names, like the marks of Indian chiefs appended to some charter of expropriation. And at the end, as in any Spanish legal transaction, the notaries came in with their spectacles and sealing wax.

Few thought for long that the document was genuine; but Pilate was such a precious witness that his evidence, if it did not exist, had endlessly to be invented. Any prejudice against his veracity or hatred of him as a man could be set aside in the interests of historical embellishment. Besides, if he had been so close to Christ, how could he have escaped some frisson of conversion?

Pilate's first appearance in the role of witness came in the trial itself. In all the Gospels he kept saying "Look here," *ide* or *idou* in Greek; almost all his remarks to the Jews began with it. Perhaps it was just a tic, a habit of speech, typical of an exasperated man trying to get people in order, but the Gospels were not concerned with that sort of historical detail. By using the phrase in conjunction with "man" and "king" and "king of the Jews," the evangelists were making Pilate do their pleading for them, right to the moment when, in Matthew, he washed his hands of "this just person." In both Luke and John he proclaimed Jesus innocent not once but three times, a highly symbolic number. Matthew also made him the first Gentile to utter the name of Jesus. Tertullian thought these scraps of recognition made Pilate a Christian in his heart, *"iam pro sua consciencia christianus";* the Ethiopians thought they justified his inclusion in their calendar of saints, "because he had confessed to the innocence of Jesus Christ." In the *Acta Pilati,* Joseph of Arimathea proclaimed Pilate "circumcised in heart," and Justin Martyr elaborated on this by saying that Christ "circumcises the hearts of all who are willing with knives of stone."

Pilate also became, in a way, the first priest of the Eucharist of Christ. Christ offered the bread and wine as symbols of his body and blood, but Pilate offered Christ himself. He took him, showed him to the people, proclaimed him and broke him. The first part of the trial, like the first part of the Mass, was the establishment of Christ's claims and credentials. The second part was the sacrifice itself, for which Pilate prepared by washing his hands. Every priest still repeats his action, adding the words which Pilate could not say: "Lord, wash me from my iniquity, and cleanse me from my sin." He repeats, too, as a Roman would have had to, the centurion's mantra of uncleanness: "Lord, I am not worthy that you should enter under my roof." In actions small and large, routine or instinctive, the liturgy of the Church continues to shadow Pilate's performance. This is how ordinary men must deal with a God who is close enough to touch.

Medieval Christians were intrigued by the thought that Pilate had looked on Jesus, that he had talked to him and could have described him. In the eighth century, relic hunters in Jerusalem were shown a painting on the wall of the building that was supposed to be Pilate's *praetorium,* and were told it was a portrait of Christ drawn there on the governor's orders. The guides insisted that Pilate was so fascinated by his prisoner that he had called in portrait painters and had several likenesses done. The only written "description" of Jesus, contained in a thirteenth- or fourteenth-century forgery called the *Letter of Lentulus,* was also supposed to have been drawn up on Pilate's orders as part of the official charge sheet, or a "Wanted" poster before Jesus was arrested.

Some said that Publius Lentulus was a proconsular superior of Pilate's, others that he was a friend; in one case the letter is ascribed directly to Pilate, as part of a report to Rome. The purpose of this forgery seems clear. There were several unflattering portraits of Jesus around, based on questionable versions of the famous passage from Josephus and describing him as small, hunched and ugly to look at; so the early Christians turned to Pilate for a testimony to his beauty. The description ran as follows:

> There has appeared in these times a man called Christ whose name is Jesus . . . whom his disciples call Son of God, raising the dead and healing all diseases . . . fifteen palms and a half in height, with hair the color of an unripe hazel and smooth almost to the ears; but from the ears down slightly darker-colored corkscrew curls, more glistening, and waving downward from the shoulders. He wears his hair parted in the center in the manner of the Nazarenes, and has a copious but immature beard that is also forked in the middle. He has a simple and mature aspect, with blue eyes varying in color and bright. . . .

This was peculiar wording for a report but not so strange, perhaps, for a police poster. Such posters were written in black and red characters on white paper and posted up in public places, and they went into extraordinary detail. In 145 B.C., for example, a slave called Hermon, aged about eighteen, went missing in Alexandria: "of medium height, beardless, straight-legged, with a dimple in the chin, tattooed on the right wrist with foreign characters. He has with him a string purse with three *minas* of gold, ten cowrie shells, an iron ring on which hangs a flask of oil and bath-scrapers, and is wearing round his body an overcoat and a belt." As Hermon's marks were the things he carried, filched from the baths, so the distinguishing marks of Jesus—who carried nothing—may well have been the color and luxuriance of his hair, so strange to the eyes of a Roman.

Yet even if Pilate was implicated in that physical description of Jesus, it was not the vital part of his evidence. That was the *titulus,* or public charge sheet, which had to be written out, paraded in front of the victim or hung around his neck, and placed over him on the cross. Before Pilate could leave the trial behind—go upstairs, sink into his reading chair, cram his mouth with olives, bread and fish—he had to sum up the offenses of the man he had just sentenced.

The *titulus* board that was brought to Pilate was about two feet square, its surface whitened and smoothed with gypsum. The word for this placard was the same as that used in Roman grocer's shops, or in brothels, for the wooden display board that listed the prices of goods. When you looked at such a board you expected a little gilding, a little exaggeration: the best this, the finest that. A prosaic list was disappointing, a sign of a shopkeeper who took no joy in his job. This was a chance to embellish, as well as to have the last word.

A clerk stood by with a bottle of cuttlefish ink and a reed softened at the tip, a larger version of the sort of pen that was used for writing on papyrus. John's Gospel implies that Pilate wrote the *titulus* himself in Latin, Hebrew and Greek. The mystery plays have him writing it, too, in laborious mime, and in the Coventry play he goes so far as to scramble up a ladder to fix his handiwork to the top of the cross. But governors did not write out public notices, any more than they would have chalked up the price of oil or the rate for a Bithynian brunette. Even if he had lowered himself to write the Latin and Greek, Pilate could hardly have managed the odd squared-off characters of the Hebrew, a language of which it is safe to say he knew nothing. The trilingualism may just have been John's invention; and a scribe or even a soldier would have painted the words on the board while Pilate dictated.

How much thought went into it? The Gospels imply that Pilate took charge to the extent of making the board say exactly what he wanted: some variant of "Jesus of Nazareth, King of the Jews." This was deliberately insulting to his Jewish subjects, and especially to the chief priests. He made doubly sure that the insult was not missed by crucifying Jesus between two thieves, as if to say: "Your king, and the whole lot of you, are bandits." There was possibly another joke reference, too, to *latrunculi,* the Roman version of chess, in which the game was over when the king piece was trapped between two robber pieces of glass. At least one commentator imagined Pilate laughing as he thought these ideas up. "Not lacking in witticisms," wrote Oecolampadius in the sixteenth century, "you made a lampoon against Christ."

The lampoon was, in fact, inaccurate. Despite Pilate's multiple leading questions, Jesus had never acknowledged that he was the King of the Jews. Indeed, John's Pilate had been told by Jesus that his kingdom was "not from here." So it is possible, after all, that Pilate had understood nothing of the few answers Jesus had given him. He had simply reverted to the third and last charge brought by the high priests, as if to say, The rest is nonsense.

Medieval scholars and playwrights thought the *titulus* could bear a better gloss. It was Pilate's revenge, they thought, but it was also his confession. It was the moment when Pilate, in effect, acknowledged that this man was a king. In the Northern Passion, the *titulus* is written on a board of palm, the tree of victory and peace; that, says one of the bystanders, sums up what Pilate really meant to write. The governor thus becomes the first in that little procession of Romans who, in the course of the crucifixion, find their eyes suddenly opened to the mysteries of the Christian God.

Most Christians continue to understand the *titulus* this way. No crucifix is complete without the proclamation made by John's Pilate, "Iesus Nazarenus Rex Iudaeorum," reduced as in "SPQR" to "INRI," the four letters of dominion. (Historically, it would not have been abbreviated; it would need to be understood, and besides, Pilate was not a man for abbreviations.) That INRI is flaunted as a banner of victory, a statement of what is obvious and permanent and true to believers: this is the Messiah. Pilate repeats, like a ghostly bureaucrat, in the three great languages of the civilized world of the time, the statement Jesus makes in sweat and blood. He never meant to proclaim the greatest truth of Christendom at all, but, oddly, there he was doing so. As Augustine put it, "It could not . . . be torn from his heart that Jesus was the King of the Jews, but was fixed there, as in the superscription, by the truth itself."

Augustine believed that the cross itself now proclaimed something new, and that this too was the work of "evil men," like Pilate, suddenly made good. The traverse beam now signified the breadth of love; the upright, perseverance toward the goal of heaven; even the depth of the cross in the ground symbolized "the depths of the grace of God, which is beyond human understanding." Not just the *titulus*, but the whole gibbet ordered by Pilate became a means to display the glory of God. The pagan governor could not have done better if he had tried.

Of course, this was not his intention. He had simply passed sentence and had settled on a formula that was neat, obvious and mildly defiant. When it was done, the business should have been over. But John's Gospel says he was not left in peace; the priests came back in fury. In the mystery plays they leaned over his shoulder, jabbing at the board, or rushed in and pointed with indignation to the *titulus* already on the cross; their beards, stiff with glue, stood out sharply from their chins. "This isn't right!" they chorused. "You shouldn't have put 'The King of the Jews,' but '*This man said* he was the King of the Jews'!"

Pilate said, "What I have written, I have written."

"O gegrapha, gegrapha." "Quod scripsi, scripsi." Whether snapped out in Greek or Latin, it carried a clear subtext: Go away, leave me alone. Reduced to the common Roman gesture, he had put up his finger to the Jews.

Christian commentators found another subtext. This was Pilate, the chief witness, repeating his evidence. Not only had he proclaimed Jesus king, unequivocally, but he had meant to proclaim it; he was not to be shifted from this great shining truth. In the trial he might have wavered, but now he was stalwart. He was not going to fiddle even with the form of words. Augustine wondered whether there was not "some hidden voice that sounded through Pilate's inner man with—if one may put it this way—a kind of loud-toned silence, the words that had been prophesied so long before in the very letter of the Psalms, 'Corrupt not the inscription of the title.' Here, then, you see, he did not corrupt it." Pilate had recovered his courage; this was his own good, unalterable confession. *Quod scripsi, scripsi.*

Go away and leave me alone.

They went, at last. It is tempting to imagine his relief, his heady plunge back into his ordinary life. He must have eaten something: bread, sardines, soft cheese, cold meat pepped up with fish sauce. He must have drunk something, probably the usual watered-down wine; though not to the point of stupefaction, for this was still a working day. Then he would have taken his siesta, either on the day couch with his shoes on or properly in bed, in the merciful enveloping arms of his wife. The conversation (we imagine) might have been awkward. "So you killed him, then? You didn't get my message?" Yes, I killed him. The crime was sedition. It was all completely straightforward. There was never any question of what I had to do, apart from not wanting the Jews to bounce me into things. "So that was why it took six hours?" Yes, that was why it took six hours. Six hours, three more troublemakers on crosses. Another productive day in Judaea.

After this, there were probably more cases to hear. By about two-thirty or three, he would have concluded the business of the day and made for the baths. This was the essential winding down, the proper ablution. Perhaps he still felt in need of it. He could let them scrape him, pummel him, bruise him as he lay on the slab; naked too, human too, with only a towel around his shoulders. Then he could slip into the soothing water. Perhaps he plowed ferociously up and down, still feeling his humiliation or his anger; or perhaps he merely lay in the water, watching his limbs float, letting his thoughts drift away. And when he eventually emerged, faintly fragile and glowing, his hair slicked down, it was to find that the sky was dark.

Three Gospels record the "darkness over the face of the earth"; Matthew adds that an earthquake followed. These occurrences may have been symbolic, nature in upheaval at the death of God, but they may also have happened in fact. An eclipse on the likeliest Friday in 33 was recorded in several Mediterranean countries. The second-century *Gospel of Peter* said that people went about with lamps, thinking it was night. Lamps may have been lit, too, in the tall braziers around Pilate's palace, while the air outside turned thick as smoke.

Intelligent men were not afraid of eclipses. Cicero remembered soldiers in camp, always prone to superstitious fears, being instructed by their superior officers—as Pilate would have had to instruct them—that this was no miracle, but something that happened at fixed times and would continue to do so in future. All it meant was that the moon was passing between the earth and the sun. Earthquakes, too, had a rational explanation: trapped winds bursting out of the earth, like a bout of cosmic farting that made even the wells stink. Yet Romulus had died during an eclipse of the sun, as had Caesar, and similar disturbances had attended the death of Augustus in 14: a total eclipse, then the sky on fire, glowing embers that fell in showers, blood-red comets. As for earthquakes, as Pliny the Elder pointed out, "The city of Rome never experienced a shock which was not the forerunner of some great calamity."

Jerusalem, too, was prone to tremors, and according to Matthew this one caused no particular damage to buildings. But the rock tombs around the city were shattered, uncovering their cargo of gray bones, and the great hanging curtain in the Temple (forty cubits high by ten cubits wide, as thick as a hand, woven of gold and purple thread) was torn from top to bottom. This was an earthquake Matthew's Pilate would have felt. Perhaps the lamp stands swayed and crashed to the floor; perhaps a little gritty dust fell from the ceiling onto his hair; or perhaps he merely felt the terror of the solid marble floor not quite steady, shifting under his feet. He may have scarcely dared to look up in case he saw—as a Jewish family seated at dinner had once seen—the whole dome of the roof peel back like a soft fruit, disclosing the sky.

It passed after a while. The day began to lighten without explanation. Fallen objects were picked up from the floor, and Pilate returned to whatever his business was. Tradition says he did not work long, however, before a stream of visitors came in to interrupt him, pestering him about the man he had caused to be nailed to the cross. The Gospels "recorded" most of them, since they wanted both the soldiers and Pilate to bear witness that Jesus had died, been taken down, buried and placed under guard. But only the Towneley playwright described the first visitors to Pilate on that particular afternoon, when the milky dust of the earthquake still hung in the trees and the air: three soldiers, one of whom carried a robe made of cobwebs and moonshine, and woven in one piece.

This was the only personal relic of Jesus that had survived intact. According to the Gospels, his overcoat was cut into four by the soldiers who kept watch at the foot of the cross, but his undergarment had no seam for a knife blade to unpick. Medieval writers took this story further. The Virgin Mary had woven the robe for Jesus when he was a child, and it had gone on growing with him. In one sense, it was his own mystical body; in another it was the magical garment woven for a loved one, as the old song said.

> *I will make you a cambric shirt,*
> *Parsley, sage, rosemary and thyme;*
> *Without no seams or needlework,*
> *Then you'll be a true love of mine.*

When the shirt was made, Mary washed it in the sea and hung it on a withered thornbush to dry. Later, when she went to fetch it, she found the linen gently rising and falling, and the thornbush covered with roses varying from red to white: Passion and Resurrection in one place.

In the Towneley play, after Christ's clothes were taken from him, they did not end up with the soldiers. Pilate had ordered the clothes to be brought back to him, together with the news that Jesus was dead. The soldiers therefore gathered up the overcoat and the seamless garment, which still carried the soft sheen of rose petals and the phosphorescence of the sea, and raced down the hill of Calvary, heading for Pilate's house. All three were wildly excited. As they pitched up, gasping, against the painted sentry box outside the *praetorium,* one complained that he had almost shat in his breeches, another that he had "burst his bollocks" to get to Pilate and put in his claim. Each man wanted the garment badly, because whoever got it would have good luck for the rest of his life.

But Pilate wanted it, too. This was intolerable. He had done nothing to deserve it; soft tyrant that he was, he was at that moment lying in bed asleep. Together, the soldiers swore by Mohammed—the god of all villains and heathens—that they would keep it out of his clutches. That done, they knocked on the door.

Pilate's councillor answered, dressed in the robe of a scholar. The governor was slow to rouse. "Don't call me again, you've called me twice already!" he groaned from his bed.

"My lord!" yelled the councillor again.

"Why do I seem to feel a bit bad today?" moaned Pilate.

"My lord, I entreat you, *get up!*"

"Is it traitors? Plots?"

"Not that I know of."

"Then stop annoying me! Just pick me up, set me softly in my seat. . . ."

But the councillor, grimly pulling away the sheets, had a lesson for him. "They've come about that boy you killed, sir. You'll be in a fair amount of trouble if you killed him and he was innocent."

"Would you mind not mentioning that?" Pilate snapped. "Is there any point in drawing attention to it? Why don't you look up the law about it? And show it some respect, or I'll buffet you fit to kill you!"

"I thought I should mention what I taught you, sir. I wouldn't like to see you go wrong—"

"Have you finished?" screamed Pilate into his face.

"Yes, lord."

"Then get out, for God's sake."

The councillor left, and the soldiers crowded in. They were welcome: they brought the news that Jesus was dead. But Pilate was strangely prickly. When the second soldier gabbled ingratiatingly that Pilate had tortured Jesus "really well," the governor murmured, "Leave the part I played out of it, will you?" And when the third soldier held out the armful of shining clothes, asking "Did you have any hope in your heart of having his gear, sir?," Pilate turned white.

"That belongs to me! I by no means meant you men to have this!"

The soldiers jumped back, clutching the clothes tight. "We got there first!" they cried. But Pilate caught hold of the overcoat and pulled. Desperate, scrambling to be deferential, the soldiers agreed to tear it to shreds, and in the ensuing storm of fabric Pilate was left with the largest piece. He smiled and thanked them.

"He can't get the other coat too," muttered the third soldier.

"Better cut it into four parts, properly," said the first.

But they could find no seam. The second soldier, knife ready in his hand, searched all over it. At last he went to stick the point into the middle of the garment, but Pilate caught his arm. "I command you not to cut it!" he shouted. "You bastards, leave it whole, or I'll kill you!"

The soldiers were shaken. "Calm down, sir, he meant well," they told the distraught governor. "He'd be upset if you killed him, sir."

"All right," Pilate whispered. "I forgive him."

"Wonderful, sir! Thank you, sir!"

The first soldier was still kneeling beside the shining white robe; the folds spread around him like milk. He said, "Shall I save it, sir?"

"I say we cast lots, and the highest wins it."

Nobody trusted this suggestion. Dicing was touched by the Devil (in some French mystery plays, Satan actually taught the soldiers how to play). On the other hand, the third soldier had the three dice ready in his pocket. At least Pilate had no chance to tamper with them. The first soldier imagined they all had an equal opportunity of winning. "He can't cheat us at dicing," he remarked.

Eager and magnanimous, Pilate sat down on the floor. "I like this game!" he cried. "Who's going to start?"

"You first, sir."

"I'll win it with a single throw; just watch!"

He threw thirteen.

"I'm going to win now, for sure."

"Maybe, sir," said the first soldier; "but I might just spoil your joy, if Fortune looks on me."

He threw the dice. "And I've seen Fortune look on great knights just the same!" crowed Pilate. "You've only got eight there, for all your boasting!"

"Eight? What the hell's wrong with me? It must be these dice, the bitches!"

"Well, *you* don't get it," said the second soldier. "Let's see if luck will look on me."

"I hope not," said Pilate.

The second soldier threw, and fell silent. "Mohammed's bones, you've only got seven," the third told him.

"Oh blast, it's short!" said the thrower in despair.

The third soldier seized the dice, blew on them, and threw. "Bitched bones, be as I tell you, or be cursed!"

He threw fifteen.

"There, fellows, just as I forecast! I win it!"

"What?" cried Pilate in scorn. "You whistle, and the moon is waning? Where've you been? You can take your throw back again!"

The third soldier jumped to his feet. "There are plenty of people here, law-abiding people, who can witness that I did nothing wrong. Ask them!"

His colleagues backed him: "You didn't do any trickery that we saw."

"Yes," shouted Pilate, "but I don't play this game puffing and blowing like that! I wouldn't mind if he played straight—"

The third soldier clapped him on the back, smiling. "Calm down, sir. Don't spoil your day."

Pilate sprang from the floor, furious; but before he seized the man he seemed to remember something, and collected himself. He took several deep breaths, straightened up, and settled his chaplet on his golden head. He was princely again. And, being princely, he turned to the winner with a perfect smile.

"Sir," he said. The artificial humility was deeply worrying; the soldiers began to edge away. "Since you've won this gown now, do you suppose you could be enormously generous and good, and give it to me?"

"No, sir. This you won't have."

"Then I'll make you!" Pilate roared. "Cursed you are and cursed you'll remain! What? You think you're free to defy me?"

The soldier grew pale. "Your words go through me, sir," he stammered. "They really do. I—I'd give you three if I had them, sir."

The robe was handed over.

"How extremely kind of you!" beamed Pilate. "Thanks so much."

The soldiers made their exit, grumbling and cursing. Their curses were an elegy on the folly of gambling: how Fortune threw men in the ditch, made them sell their cattle for nothing, emptied the bakers' ovens, and all for "a sweet girl's gift." As they reached the door, the third soldier turned back and said to Pilate: "You should realise what comes of dicing, sir. You'd do better to leave such a vain thing and serve God instead, if you want to know the bliss of heaven. We know that the Lord is the most mighty and the gentlest of all the Jews. We believe he is holy. What do you think of that?"

Pilate stood in the hall with the garment in his arms. He smiled at them. "I think you're wonderful," he said, in a voice that sounded as though he were dreaming, touched by the sun. "Of all the scholars I know, you're the most full of wisdom and subtlety. Every law you keep dutifully. I grant you all power and all the friendship I can give you. *Dieu vous garde, monseigneurs,* and may Mohammed in his castles and towers protect you. Have a good day, gentlemen."

The soldiers disappeared. Pilate remained with his precious burden, bright as light, light as air, soft as petals, winking with the white foam of the sea, and found himself bathed in a benevolence he could not understand.

II.

The purpose of the soldiers' mission had been to tell Pilate that Jesus was dead. In their rage and excitement, the Towneley soldiers almost forgot to do so. But other messengers in other accounts, including the Gospels, brought the message properly, and sometimes in disturbing ways. All had been touched by Jesus, some even converted in a matter of moments. In this state they approached the governor. Their very obeisance must have been troubled and unsteady, for they knew now who this man was whom Pilate had put to death.

According to Mark, the first to appear in the *praetorium*—at some time around four in the afternoon—was not a soldier at all. It was Joseph of Arimathea, who was seeking the body of Jesus for burial. Joseph's credentials were confused. Mark, most plausibly, called him a member of the Sanhedrin, "an honorable counselor, who also waited for the kingdom of God." Yet it is not clear how this religious Jew could bring himself to enter the unclean Roman palace, even in emergency. *The Legend of the High Holy Grail* transformed him into a Roman soldier who had seen seven years' service with Pilate and wanted the body as his reward.

John's Gospel suggested he was a friend of Nicodemus, the secret disciple, who was also to bring the unguents for the burial. In the *Gospel of Peter,* Joseph was called "a friend of Pilate and of the Lord," and some modern writings on the legends of the Grail continue to surmise that he was close to the governor. The fact that he could go in "boldly" to Pilate, as Mark says, suggests either intimacy or authority, as well as reckless disrespect of the governor's fragile temper. But though Joseph "begged" for the corpse of Jesus—the phrase is full of ritual subservience—Pilate could not give him the body at once. He needed to find out how things stood at Calvary, and whether Jesus was indeed dead.

Accordingly, he sent for the centurion who had kept guard at the foot of the cross. This was his second set of orders. In John he had already sent out commands, at the behest of the Jewish priests, that the legs of the victims should be broken with a heavy mallet to make sure they died before sunset. (Again, that necessary acquiescence to Jewish feelings.) The messenger sent to relay those orders could have reported back that Jesus was dead, but the centurion's report was of a different sort. He had watched Jesus all the time, and was therefore in a position to provide as much detail of this death as Pilate wanted.

The scene of the centurion's report takes only a verse in Mark, but it is heavy with implications. This man had heard Jesus call out, "My God, my God, why have you forsaken me?" He had seen him offered the sponge on a stick, noticed the confusion about whether or not he was summoning Elias, and had heard him cry out loudly as he died. In Matthew's account, he saw how at that moment the dusty twilight of the eclipse came down, and the ground shook. His reaction, in Matthew, was to say: "Truly this man was the Son of God." In Luke, he cried out, "Truly this man was innocent." Unlike his superior officer's hand-washing or his sarcastic charge sheet, this sounded like a proper change of heart.

It was not much of a military report, however. It probably required suppressing, though it contained the answers to Pilate's most urgent questions from the trial. So the centurion stood in the *praetorium,* not without anxiety. His conversion was fresh and sharp, his memories of the death still burning; and Mark's Pilate, for his part, also seemed to want to know exactly how events had unfolded. He had a Roman's interest in the mechanics and the minutiae of death. There were always lessons in the way men died, sometimes more than in their lives.

He might have asked whether Jesus had said anything before he died. Last words were important. The centurion would not have understood Jesus' Aramaic, as Pilate would not have done. But part of the chatter at the foot of the cross had been to puzzle out what the crucified man was saying. At one point he cried out a word that even Pilate could have grasped: "Abba," "Father." What had he meant by that? Men in pain cried out for their mothers, not their fathers. But the King of the Jews had called for his father, looking up into the dark sky. He could not have meant the Jewish God, whom nobody could see; it was as if, improbably, he had called for Jupiter, the Father and helper. Iove, from *adiuvare,* "Come here and help me." Do not forsake me. It made sense to call on such a god, with broad arms and a breast so immense that each fold of his robe was like a sweeping beach of deep, soft sand. Yet the word *Abba* suggested more intimacy than that. It was also "Daddy," the word toddlers chirped in the market, a word you would never use to a deity who might strike you.

The faint, strange suggestion was of some sort of family feeling between the man on the cross and the company of the gods; and the next question, the counterquestion, was why they had not helped him. When the servants had gone to the Tiber to drown the newborn Romulus and Remus, the future founders of Rome, they had made the same appeal as they placed the squalling babies in their little boat: "If some god were the author of your being, he would surely come to your aid in so perilous an hour." On that occasion, he had done so. But in the case of Jesus, Daddy seemed to have looked away.

According to Luke, Jesus had added something more. He had said, "Father, forgive them, for they know not what they do." The prayer encompassed everyone by the cross: thieves, bystanders, Romans. The evangelist also clearly implied it went further, over the chief priests and the Jewish crowd, and that it included the governor in his palace. So Pilate had been forgiven, if he wanted to know. This Jesus had loved his enemy, even though his enemy had scarcely left him the breath or the strength to do so. And, having forgiven, he died almost instantly. Far from putting up defenses against death, he seemed to invite it in.

A Roman could only admire this, even in the lowest sort of men.

This was the good and acceptable death, the perfect ending. A gladiator in the ring might have lost every weapon and be staggering in circles— the crowd would be screaming "Habet!" "He's had it!"—but with his last energies he would approach his opponent, one dragging step, two steps, and offer him his breast as if to say, Kill me. I forgive you, kill me, it's necessary. As Jesus had done.

Or, like Cato, he would tear off his bandages. This was the wonderful, heartbreaking story known to every Roman as the example of death determinedly embraced. Marcus Cato Uticensis had been a friend of Cicero's and a supporter of the Republic. In 46 B.C. he had found himself cornered by Caesar's troops at Utica, in Africa. The rest of Africa had submitted to Caesar; there was no way out. On the night before he would be forced to surrender, he laid two things beside his pillow. One was Plato's *Phaedo,* on the immortality of the soul, and the other was his sword. One gave him the will to die, as Seneca said, the other the means. He read the *Phaedo,* and then pierced his breast with the blade. A sample school exercise still exists, perhaps one Pilate, too, had memorized as a boy, describing Cato as "the finest model of how to live and how to die," and ending: "he put into those hands, clean to the last of Roman blood, a sword to plunge into his hallowed breast." But the thrust did not go deep enough; the doctors found him, and bandaged the wound. It was hard to imagine how a man would feel when, ready and resigned to death, the fussing doctors pulled him back from the brink. Cato could not bear it, and as soon as they had gone he ripped the bandages apart. The wound opened, and bled his life away.

Jesus had done much the same. He had rehearsed his philosophy and then, resigned, had gone to the cross. Once there, he barely tasted the sour drugged wine and water that might have kept him alive for longer. He was impatient to die. In the end, like Cato, he almost seemed to race toward it; his final scream was an act of violent liberation. Yet even this indifference to death—if he had truly been indifferent—was not the most beautiful or admirable thing. The most admirable was to lay down one's life to save the lives of others: to be the one man, as Caiaphas said, whose death would redeem the whole nation.

This sort of death, too, would have been familiar to Pilate. Every Roman knew the stories. P. Decimus Mus gave up his life to save the Roman army when it was fighting the Latins, and his son Decius, a military tribune, did the same at the battle of Sentinum against the Samnites, Pilate's own tribe. To die like this was a ritual, with prescribed actions and prayers; it was not an impulse, but deliberate and controlled. A man offered himself to the gods to turn destruction aside. So, at Sentinum, Decius called for the army priest, and the priest instructed him to put on the purple-bordered toga and cover his head. A spear was laid on the ground. He stood on it, touched his finger to his lips and prayed to Jupiter, Mars, Bellona, the household gods and the shades of the dead. Then he girded up his toga with the ceremonial Gabinian cincture, vaulted onto his horse and plunged into the thick of the enemy. It took his friends a day and a night to find his body; when they did, it was covered with missiles and the corpses of his attackers. But the Romans had won the day.

All these deaths had a common theme. The men who died controlled their deaths completely, even how they happened and when they occurred. Pilate had imagined that these matters were in his hands. But Jesus surprised him. According to Mark, it was the quickness of Christ's death that most fascinated Pilate. He was surprised—"astonished," Mark says—that Jesus was already dead when the officer went to break his legs. Was it really that fast? And if so, why? A death from crucifixion might easily take two or three days; Jesus had died in three hours. It was as if, in the words of Tertullian, "he released his spirit of his own accord with a word, anticipating the duty of the executioner." And he had died not just at the ninth hour, as the centurion could have reported, but when the sun went dark and the light, too, died.

Would the centurion have thought that worth adding? An eclipse was far more noteworthy than hours measured on Pilate's water clock. The centurion on Golgotha may have had no idea of the time; but he would have watched the sky. And he knew, as Pilate knew, what sort of men died when eclipses came.

There was no necessity to recount his own ideas. He was only on guard, the most boring job in the world, watching in case the relatives crept up with pliers in their pockets. But if he was asked for any further observations, would Matthew's centurion have dared to blurt out to Pilate what he had already uttered to the empty air, the weeping bystanders and his own half-listening colleagues? However carefully he picked his words, however generalized the language, his eyes would have met the governor's with a pained and disquieting stare: "I thought he was the Son of God, sir."

. . .

Behind the centurion came the lance man, the soldier who had pierced the side of Jesus to ascertain whether he was dead. In the Gospels, only John described the piercing. It may have happened, but it was also symbolically necessary: without it, not enough blood would have been spilled at a crucifixion to carry out the prophecies of sacrifice.

Once his job was done, John's anonymous lance man vanished from the scene. But he reappeared in the *Acta Pilati* with a name, Longinus, which he kept all through the Middle Ages. Medieval playwrights joyfully made use of him, sending him into the *praetorium* to improve on the centurion's conversion. For their Longinus had been blind, or as good as blind; he had dimly glimpsed the scar of the old wound inflicted on Jesus as a child by Judas, and had used it to guide the lance home. In the York play, Pilate had instructed him: "In Jesus' side / Shove it this tide." He had done so, and immediately tumbled to his knees. Out of the pierced side had flowed blood and water, though blood never flowed from a dead man; and the drops, part silver, part crimson, had fallen on the blind man's eyes. Now Longinus walked in to Pilate unaided, his chin lifted, for he could see.

But Pilate did not notice him. Longinus' witness to Christ ("Ah, mercy my succor, mercy my treasure, mercy my Savior; thy mercy be marked in me") was heard by the audience alone. Medieval writers put these soldiers on the stage with Pilate, only to eschew the drama of making them report to him. He seemed preoccupied, distracted, and above all not ready to hear that he had made the worst mistake of his life. The York Pilate remarks to Caiaphas and Annas that "I'm not very happy that he's hanging up there," but that is all. He does not elaborate. As for the Towneley Pilate, he strides in after the trial with a roaring song of triumph:

> Mighty lord of all, *me Caesar magnificavit!*
> Down on your knees you fall, great God *me sanctificavit!*

The *Acta Pilati,* on the other hand, presumed that as the day wore on Pilate began to feel worse. When the last of the witnesses had left, Pilate and his wife were "furious." The servants brought food, but they ignored it. They ate nothing, drank nothing. Procula sat there like a statue, her hands in her lap or sometimes, distractedly, scratching at her pale cheeks. The only thing Pilate raised to his lips, as if they were the only sustenance he had, were his white knuckles and his fiercely bitten thumbs.

At one point he summoned the chief priests. "Did you see what happened?" he asked.

"It was just an eclipse of the sun," they answered. "Of the usual sort."

He knew it was not of the usual sort.

At the end of the afternoon, in the most fantastical accounts, a servant brought in a hexagonal dish of green emerald. It was empty, but the deep cross-cutting of the base suggested that it was full of green light glittering on water. This souvenir had been brought, on Pilate's orders, from the upper room in which Jesus had eaten his last meal before the trial. In this dish the roast lamb of the Passover had been passed around the table. It was now, for the moment, the property of Pilate, shining strangely on his table among the untouched food.

First the magic coat, now the magic dish. No writer imputed any special motive to Pilate for wanting these things. They seemed to come to him like war spoils, objects casually acquired because their owner had been parted from them. Yet he wanted them badly. He was prepared to lie and cheat to get them, or to rifle through the otherwise unremarkable tableware of an ordinary Jewish house. They were evidence of a kind, souvenirs of a kind, but also talismans that he did not want to fall into anyone else's hands. Though he did not understand their power, he accepted that they possessed it, just as although he had never understood the claims of Jesus, he had found himself afraid of him. He needed these objects as one might need the personal effects of a murderer or a magician, the knife, the dried herbs, the jacket with a dust of poison in the pocket, to keep the power locked up.

Yet he did not keep the dish for long. A servant brought a message, as the light faded, that Joseph of Arimathea had returned to repeat his request to take the body from the cross. All the Gospels "recorded" this scene, and all agreed that the interview was short. Mark's Joseph asked for the body, using the word he would have used of a living man. Pilate said he could take it, using the term for a corpse. Joseph was hinting at the Resurrection; Pilate was still a witness to the death. Now he was to be the chief agent of the burial, so that again the words of the Creed could be fulfilled in him: *crucified, dead and buried.* Only one Coptic text suggests that he resisted giving up the corpse, as though, like the coat and the dish, he needed to keep it under his control. That text contained a long appeal by Joseph, every clause of which began with the words "Give me this stranger," as if Joseph meant to play down Jesus while Pilate, for some reason, suspected he might be important.

Pilate was not bound to hand the body over. Corpses were usually removed from the cross on request, but most were thrown into a common pit. The corpse of a man found guilty of sedition was often granted not even that grace, but was left to the crows and the vultures as a final humiliation. In Judaea, the Jews demanded more respect for their dead criminals. This alone may have accounted for the speed of the transaction. The Jews cared, Pilate did not, and unrest had to be avoided. The decision was easy.

Yet some scholars have imagined there was more to it than that. Perhaps the handing over was so prompt because Pilate felt the beginnings of guilt, and wanted to show some respect to Jesus. John's Pilate seemed even to discern that Joseph was a secret disciple who should be "granted" this concession. In that Gospel, Joseph had already discussed the burial with Nicodemus, and Nicodemus had his servants ready with ointment of myrrh and aloes in dozens of alabaster jars. It was abundantly clear that if they took this man down they were going to bury him as a king; Pilate's insulting words on the *titulus* were going to be taken literally. And he made no attempt to question or prevent it.

Roman piety demanded in any case that bodies—even the bodies of enemies or criminals—should be given some ceremony of burial or farewell. At a minimum, three handfuls of earth had to be scattered over them with the prayer "Sit tibi terra levis," "May the earth lie lightly on you." If this was not done, the shade could not be ferried across the River Styx but had to remain among the desperate crowds on the bank, doomed to wander eternally. The worst part of the killings going on in Rome at that moment—the purges of the accomplices of Sejanus—was less that men died than that their bodies were left on the mud banks of the Tiber, uncremated, untouched even by the loving hands of their relations. If you respected your enemy you handed his body over, as Aeneas had handed over the body of the brave boy Lausus to the ashes and the shades:

> *teque parentum*
> *manibus et cineri, si qua est ea cura, remitto.*

It was possibly significant that no cash seemed to change hands. Mark's use of the word "gave" or "presented" suggests that, unusual as it was, Pilate made no charge for this service. Conspiracy theorists take this as a clue of the friendship between Joseph and Pilate, and of Pilate's connivance in the idea that Jesus should be buried splendidly. But it could have meant anything, from *pietas* to profound indifference.

The Pilate of "Joseph of Arimathea," a fanciful medieval poem by Robert de Borron, went a little further. He was happy to give Joseph the body, because he expected him to drag it around the streets of Jerusalem and leave it in some mean place. But when the guards at the cross proved reluctant to hand the body over, he sent Nicodemus to persuade them, and gave him an extra gift for his service. At the end of the interview he picked up the emerald dish from the table and thrust it into Nicodemus' hands. It was no holy relic to Pilate, but vaguely malevolent, like a witching stone. He was almost afraid of it, with its green glittering shine. Perhaps this was something that ought to be swiftly passed on.

Nicodemus handed the dish to Joseph. He took it out to the cross, to collect in it the blood of Christ when he was taken down. The dish that had held the blood of the lamb held the blood of the Lamb again. And Pilate became the first man to seek and find—and lose at once—the Holy Grail.

III.

Once the trial was over, a record was placed in the archive. This was standard, indeed required, practice. No more than a few lines were needed to note the name, charge and sentence. And of course it has disappeared, together with everything else Pilate and his secretaries committed to wax or paper.

If the case was important, a longer version would have had to be sent to the imperial archives in Rome. There is no particular reason why Pilate should have thought that the sentencing of an obscure provincial should have justified further attention. So it is probable that no report was sent; but the early Christians were predictably dissatisfied with this. Pilate, they thought, must have been moved by Jesus and troubled by the signs attending his death. He would now have to scramble both to atone and to cover himself.

Tertullian in the second century took it as fact that Pilate had sent a full report to the emperor, a report so persuasive that Tiberius himself had been convinced that Jesus was divine. Justin Martyr referred to the governor's written record as a matter of course, "from which you may learn the details of the Crucifixion," including the piercing with nails and the division of Christ's clothes. He also claimed that Pilate's own *acta* contained accounts of Jesus' miracles, his healing of the lame and blind and his raising of men from the dead, and told his second-century Roman readers that they could easily consult them. In 311 the Emperor Maximinus apparently caused certain *Memoirs of Pilate* to be forged, circulated and memorized by schoolchildren in order to rebut the claims of the Christians. It is possible, though unlikely, that the basis of this was the real, brief, judicial entry in which Pilate described the simple sedition for which Jesus had been executed.

Yet any real records had probably vanished even by the time of Maximinus; and since they were bound to be embarrassing in any case, the *Acta Pilati* were invented by early Christians to take their place. The existing versions date from the fifth century, but they are mentioned in the fourth, when Epiphianus, in a sermon of 387 on fixing the date of Easter, asserted that the correct date for the Crucifixion was given in the *Acta Pilati* as the fifth before the Kalends of April.

These *Acta,* though they were supposed to be Nicodemus' official record of the Passion events, were not written to resemble judicial records at all. They were a highly colored version of the Passion story, in which the role of Pilate was so far expanded that he became chief actor. They found a wide audience. Not long after their first invention they were translated into Coptic, Slav, Syriac, Armenian and Georgian, finding a wide audience all through the shaggier fringes of the disintegrating empire. As they spread, so their version of Pilate—the regretful intellectual—spread too, at least in quarters where there were no bigger and badder Pilates to compete with.

Yet there also existed, from the second century onward, several official letters or reports the governor was supposed to have written to Tiberius. Here the forgers tried harder to make their documents look officially Roman: beginning with one "written" right after the Crucifixion, on the very day given in the *Acta* for the trial.

Pontius Pilate to Tiberius Caesar, Emperor, Greeting.

Jesus Christ, whom I mentioned in my last letter, has been executed by
the will of the people. I myself was unwilling and apprehensive. By Hercules, so pious and austere a man has never been seen nor will be again.
But there was an amazing unanimity in the request of the Jews and their
leaders that this ambassador of truth should be crucified, even though
their own prophets (who are like the Sybil with us) testified against them.
When he was hanged supernatural signs appeared, and these—in the
judgment of philosophers—menaced the whole world with ruin. . . .

Had I not feared that the people would riot—for they were almost
furious—perhaps this man would still be living with us. Although I have
to say that—compelled by loyalty to your dignity, rather than my own
inclination—I did not strive with all my might to prevent the sale and
suffering of this innocent blood, which was guiltless of every accusation.
It was an injustice, caused by the maliciousness of men, and yet, as the
Scriptures say, it will destroy them.

The fifth before the Kalends of April.

As forgeries went, it was quite good. The groveling tone, and the attempt to pass the buck, were both plausible; the Sybil was a nice touch.
That "By Hercules!" perhaps went a little far: as if a Victorian governor
writing to the Foreign Office were suddenly to say, "Damn it all, what a
fine fellow he was!" And perhaps there was not enough detail for the letter to be truly persuasive. Lick the pen, roll up the sleeves, try again:

To the most potent, august, divine and awful Augustus [sic] Caesar, from
Pilate, the administrator of the eastern province, greeting.

I have received information, your excellency, which fills me with fear and
trembling. For in this province which I administer, my lord, according to
the command of your serenity, one of whose cities is called Jerusalem, the
whole multitude of Jews delivered to me a man called Jesus, and brought
many accusations against him, but they would not convict him of anything. They charged him with one heresy in particular: that he said the
Sabbath was not a day of rest, and was not to be observed by them. For he
performed many cures on that day, and made the blind see and the lame
walk, raised the dead, cleansed lepers, healed the paralytic who were

wholly unable to move their bodies or brace their nerves, and gave them power to walk and run, removing their infirmity by his word alone.

There is another very mighty deed which is strange to the gods we have: he raised up a man, Lazarus, who had been dead four days, summoning him by his word alone, when the dead man had already begun to decay, and his body was corrupted by worms and stank like a dog's; but seeing him lying in the tomb he ordered him to run, and the dead man did not hesitate, but ran out of his tomb like a bridegroom out of his chamber, and the tomb was filled with sweet perfume. Moreover, he approached men who were strangers and clearly demoniacs, who lived in deserts and devoured their own flesh and wandered about among cattle and creeping things, and caused them to live in cities in their own houses, and by a word rendered them rational. He caused men who were vexed by unclean spirits to become wise and honorable, and he sent the demons that were in them into a herd of swine and pushed them into the sea and drowned them.

And again, there was another man who had a withered hand and lived in suffering, and had neither the shape of a man nor the symmetry of a body; and he healed even this man with a word and made him whole. And there was a woman too, who had had an issue of blood for a long time, and whose veins and arteries were exhausted, and the joints of her bones stuck out and shone through like glass, so that all the doctors of the district had dismissed her without hope and had not relieved her; but as Jesus passed by she mysteriously received strength by his shadow falling on her from behind, and touched the hem of his garment; and immediately, at that very moment, strength filled her exhausted limbs, and as if she had never suffered anything she began to run along toward Capernaum, her own city, and she reached it within six days.

That is how these things happened. But the Jews reported that Jesus did these things on the Sabbath; and I saw greater works of wonder done by him than by the gods whom we worship.

But Herod and Archelaus and Philip, Annas and Caiaphas, with all the people, delivered him to me to put him on trial. And because many people raised a tumult against me, I commanded that he should be crucified. I scourged him first, though I found no cause in him for evil accusations.

Now when he was crucified darkness came over all the world, and the sun was obscured for half a day, and the stars appeared, but no lustre was seen in them; and I suppose your excellency is not unaware that all over the world they lit their lamps from the sixth hour until the evening. And the moon, which was like blood, did not shine all night long, although it was full, and the stars and Orion made lamentation. . . .

The forgers went on trying. The more words they wrote, the less Roman and rational Pilate became; and the more medieval, credulous, open-mouthed. He walked among wonders and recognized the prophets, as if he himself were one of the shattered Jewish crowd. And although he was writing at his desk, supposedly in cultured detachment from it all, it was clear that he bent over his writing like a medieval clerk, eyes wide and head to one side, while outside the window hung stars with faces on the flat blue backcloth of the sky.

Yet the faint possibility remains of some explanation to headquarters. Pilate had got himself into a very public difficulty, at a time when the city was full of foreigners who could carry rumors home. The Jews had hinted at telling tales to Rome, and the release of Barabbas may have required justification. Dealings with Tiberius were so sensitive that self-protecting cover letters, even for small incidents, might have been essential.

Emergency letters could be scribbled on anything, even the backs of old ones, if you were in camp and paper was scarce. But a letter to the emperor, no matter how urgently self-justifying, had to be written with maximum formality. The best pen was chosen, one with decorative bronze leaf or wire chased into the iron shaft. Ink was freshly compounded from carbon, gum arabic and water. The writing paper, made of papyrus, was smoothed down with ivory and pumice until there was no risk that the pen would blot on surface imperfections. Augustan paper, the best kind, was still perilously thin, snagging the nib and showing through any writing on the other side.

Secretaries usually wrote Pilate's letters, but a letter to the emperor might be an exception. He might try to do it himself. The cursive script of men who were usually too grand to write for themselves was often spidery and wobbly, with the letters—trailing "s"s, open Greek "e"s, languid left-leaning "d"s—set nervously apart from each other. Pilate's anxiety to please would have been apparent in every stroke, as if he were once again the child with his slate, terrified that the wet rope would lash across his back.

When the letter was written it was rolled up, tied and sealed. A stick of wax was melted over a candle flame; the blob of hot wax was applied to the tie. Pilate would have taken the gold signet ring from the fourth finger of his left hand and pressed it into the wax. We do not know what impression it left there. Pliny's signet ring was engraved with a four-horse chariot, Tiberius' with his own profile; it was common to have animals or gods. If you did not want the engraved stone to be damaged by the wax, you moistened it first with your lips, an action that became as swift and unthinking with repetition as licking a finger to turn a page. When replaced on the finger the ring was still warm for a moment, like the tightening flush on a man's face when he knows he has written an account that is just a little colored, just a little false.

In Pilate's mind, the sealing of this letter might have sealed up the case of Jesus. He should never have had to think about him again. But in the subsequent dramatizations of his life, that letter to Tiberius merely marked the beginning of the biggest dramas of all.

IV.

Pilate was officially the chief witness now. He had declared Jesus king at the trial and on the cross. He had recounted his wonders to the emperor himself. As the first of the relic seekers, he had gathered up souvenirs: the magic coat, the Holy Grail. With elaborate care, he had made his soldiers prove that Jesus was dead. Next he was required to lay out the most thrilling evidence of all: that he had risen, and lived.

First, like the magician's partner, he had to lock the box to make escape impossible. Each catch had to be fastened, each bolt thrust home, the audience positioned to watch for trickery. And trickery was expected. In Matthew's Gospel the chief priests came to Pilate on the Saturday morning, suddenly unafraid of being defiled by meeting him on the Sabbath. "Your Excellency," they said, "we remember that that deceiver said, when he was still alive, that after three days he would rise again."

Possibly Pilate remembered. Such things could be expected of Messiahs: they never died, never lay down. Others came back in the same clothes.

"So, sir," Matthew's priests went on, "order the sepulchre to be made secure until the third day, or else his disciples will come by night and steal him away and tell the people he's risen from the dead, and the last error will be worse than the first."

Pilate could see there was a grain of sense in this. If he could prevent the growth of a dangerous cult based on the rising of a man from the dead, he ought to do so. Archaeology, too, bears this out. In the nineteenth century an imperial edict was discovered in Nazareth, inscribed in Greek on marble and dating from close to Pilate's time, decreeing that tombs should be kept inviolate. Offenders would be punished especially severely for taking bodies out of tombs and putting them in other places. Even if it did not happen in the case of Jesus, the possibility of cultic or political deception was well understood. Matthew's Pilate did not hesitate. "Take a watch," he told the Jews, meaning "Take some of mine"; "go off and make it as secure as you know how."

Tradition says he let them have four soldiers, including a centurion. The word used by Matthew for the troop usually meant men who reported to the governor; later in Matthew's account, they dreaded that they would have to face Pilate afterward. The apocryphal *Gospel of Peter* says that a man called Petronius was their commander. Some scholars, translating the Greek a different way, thought Pilate told the Jews rather haughtily to use their own police force, the Temple guard. But the technical terms used by Matthew (including Pilate's "Echete koustodian") suggest that these were the governor's men, put for a day or so under the orders of the chief priests.

Besides, it was theologically vital that the soldiers should be Roman. It meant that Jesus, in his rising, would overthrow the power of darkness and all the obstacles it put in his way: swords, helmets, shields, the whole might of *pax et imperium.* The soldiers who would sprawl by the tomb in hundreds of later paintings, in the unguarded attitudes of sleep, had to display the weight of the old order. Not only death would be shattered, but also the earthly equipment that dealt out death. Real prisons and real stones, secured with official imperial seals, would be cracked and broken as surely as prisons of the spirit.

Matthew ignored the actual setting of the guard, but medieval writers made the most of it. At nightfall, their Pilate went to the garden to put his soldiers in place. The great storm of the day before, the cracking of the hills, the sun eclipsed, the "mist and great weather" had cleared away. The cross still stood, empty, in the cool unelectric air. In the garden the great trees stood too, becoming their own shadows: the descendants of the trees of Eden, hung with the same golden apples and pomegranates, about to witness the new creation. Pilate walked on a path that showed dimly between them, winding upward. In his long cloak and pillbox hat, he was the only element of agitation.

At his side trotted an attendant with wax in a bowl and a torch to melt it. In the twilight air, the torch smoked. Behind him came the soldiers, a reluctant posse. These were the same men Pilate had cheated of the seamless garment; they dragged their feet and grumbled. "Look here," moaned one, "what the hell's the point of watching him, if he's dead?"

"If they're going to pay me, I don't care what he is. Just give me the money, mate."

They marched on. Eventually, through the trees, came a glimpse of the new tomb, embedded in the hillside like a segment of the moon itself.

Pilate approached it and touched it, as if to defy any magic that lurked there. Then, stepping back, he barked: "Set the watch, men."

"Right, sir! They could set a whole mob on us, and we wouldn't let him out!"

"I could kill a hundred thousand with one hand, sir!"

Pilate beckoned to each in turn. The Coventry and Redentin plays, written for listeners in the English Midlands and on the German Baltic coast respectively, gave these men names that were thought to sound Jewish or heathen, together with exotic armor and big ridiculous weapons. Over these lumpen auxiliaries, Pilate fussed and fretted. Amoraunt, also known as Solomon, he placed to the west with his fine sword Mummink, which could cut through the bolts on armor and lift rings off fingers. Arfaxat, also known as Samson, he placed to the north with his sword, Strike-the-Shield. Cosdram, also known as Boas von Thomas ("My good man Boas!"), the clumsiest of the soldiers, was placed to the east and ordered to be nimbler than usual. He rattled his good sword Klinger in its scabbard, promising to "split the pants" of anyone who came past. Lastly, Affraunt, also called Sasoch, "my faithful knight," was placed to the south. When Pilate had put them in their places, they puffed out their armor-plated chests and saluted him.

"If anyone comes here he's a dead man, sir!" cried Affraunt.

"I'll guard his feet, sir, even if both Jack and Jill come to get him!"
Arfaxat shouted. "He'd rather he had the whooping cough, I tell you!"

"I'm on the right side, and I'll kill anyone who comes!" yelled Cosdram.

"And I'll take the left," said Affraunt; "if anyone comes here, I'll give
him some fearful blows to think about. Have a nice night, Sir Pilate,
don't you worry yourself! We'll keep him safe."

"I only hope he is really dead," the governor muttered.

"Dead as a log, sir! He's not going anywhere."

Pilate called for the melted wax. Along each edge of the great white
tomb he smeared the wax and pushed in his ring. He did so seven times,
symbolically sealing the tomb, like the scroll in the Apocalypse, so that
no one in heaven or earth could break it open—save Christ. "On every
corner I've set my seal," he said at last. "My heart's easy now. No briber
will steal away the body from under this stone. Will he, men?"

"Not likely, sir."

Once more Pilate touched the seals. The wax had hardened; there
was no chink where light could enter. The stone slab would take six men
to lift it. After that the Nazarene would need to wriggle from his graveclothes, gray-faced and tousle-haired, like a snake from its skin; and then
the soldiers would cut him down.

"Right, men," said Pilate. "Be fierce as the wind. Guard the man
well. If you lose him, you and your wives and your children will regret it,
believe me. If you keep him safe, I'll give you gold and silver and steel
helmets. I'll be your friend without deception. Remember this especially: a good deed is never wasted. I'm going home now."

"Sir."

As he walked back, the knights were singing to keep themselves awake.
The *Gospel of Peter* claims they arranged to keep watch two by two, and
pitched a little tent among the trees. In the Redentin play they sang of
gold, and the soft-skinned wife of the German emperor, and of a boat
tossing in the wild sea between Hiddensee and Mone. From time to
time, as they related it later, their throaty carousing seemed to be over-
taken by a note of pure beauty, as if someone had tapped the side of a
glass. But perhaps it was only a bird, ruffled in its night feathers, spilling

notes from a needlelike beak; or the tinkle of a rivulet of water, or the high solemn tone of the stars.

Pilate lay down in his gold bed, but he did not sleep. Beside him his wife did not sleep either. They lay in separate silences, two entombments. He too was wrapped in linen like the Nazarene, head to feet; his body was oiled, as Christ's was, with glistening sweeps of a woman's hand. The weather had not fully settled; there were rattling thunderdrums, weird lights in the dark. Pilate's head ached with wine, and worry, and an intimation of calamity.

Before dawn had broken he heard the soldiers' voices.

"What the hell do we tell him?"

"Tell him the truth. That his disciples stole him from us—"

"There was this terrible earthquake—"

"I couldn't stand. I couldn't sit, even."

"Why the hell did we trust the watchman to wake us? I read in a book once, never put your trust in anything."

"So someone tell me, what do we tell him? That we've lost Jesus?"

Then, dogmatic, Affraunt's voice: "Well, lost is lost! What are you shouting about? Things have gone wrong, but we're innocent, aren't we? Why should we get it in the neck?"

Pilate seized his cloak and went out to them. Fury began to consume him: fury, and terror. "What!" he screamed. "What? What? What are you saying, you bastard? What garbage are you trying to tell me? That he came back to life? When he was dead and in the tomb? What the hell happened here?"

His hands were at Arfaxat's throat. The man babbled about an earthquake, about trying not to sleep but being unable to keep his eyes open; he said he had been held to the ground as if pinned there. Pilate let him go contemptuously, as he might have discarded a cockerel once its neck had snapped.

"What a great set of knights you are. God, what a glittering reputation you must all have. How about going to sit in the corn, to see if you can scare off a raven or two?"

"Sir," said Arfaxat, "please listen."

His voice was bruised and feeble, but something made Pilate give half an ear to him.

"Sir, beautiful angels came down. They came from the highest

throne, and they took the man away from us. We were terribly frightened. I don't know how, but something happened to me. I couldn't see, I
couldn't hear. Look"—for he could sense Pilate's anger again, see the tick
of the vein in his neck—"believe me, sir, it wasn't our fault. There we
were, all lying by the grave. We could see everything clearly, absolutely
clearly. The angels came—"

"Angels," said Pilate blankly.

"Beings came, in great force, in wonderful clearness and beauty. They
shone like lightning, like the snow. They robbed us of our wits and made
us fall asleep. The angels came to the grave, and they took Jesus out. He
was there among them, and they led him to a bright place, singing for
joy all the time. And all this"—here his voice faltered again—"I noticed
in my sleep, sir."

"If you were asleep," yelled Pilate, "then how could you see it? That
can't possibly make sense. When I see something, I'm not asleep! You invented that story, the lot of you, between yourselves. I've a good mind to
put the thumbscrews on you! Get out of here! You're dismissed, and
you're disgraced!"

Then the York Pilate thought again. Caiaphas and Annas, drawn by
the noise, had hurried across to his palace and were sitting on the steps.
"Caiaphas, you're a cunning clerk," said Pilate. "I think we're in danger
of having made a big mistake here. What do you think we should do?"

"Best if no one knows about it, for sure," answered Caiaphas.

"I know what!" piped Annas. "Get your men to spread the word that
he was taken by at least twenty thousand men. Get them to say they were
almost killed. And we'll pay them for their lies out of our treasury."

"Great idea!" cried Pilate. "Now, men, listen well: here's the story.
Ten thousand heavily armed men took him away by force. You tried to
resist, but they would have killed you. That's the story I want told everywhere. And here's a reward of a thousand pounds, in cash. Oh, and—my
eternal gratitude, men. You can count on it."

"We'll tell that tale wherever we go, sir. Night and day."

Pilate put a money bag in each hand, then paced up and down in
front of them. "Wherever you go," he said, "whatever country you're in,
see that no man's the wiser about what we've done. Remember: you
didn't see anything. That sight you saw, forget it. We'll back you up.
We'll tell people it's against the law to believe stupid stories of dead men
rising. We'll make them think it's all lies. Remember the old motto!

So shall truth be bought and sold
And treason shall for truth be told.

Goodbye now!"

The idea of a plot to conceal the Resurrection also originates with Matthew. It seems plausible enough: no one would have wanted the story of a Messianic miracle to spread through the Passover crowd. But Matthew's version of the plot was different. In his Gospel, it was the Jewish priests, not Pilate, who gave the terrified soldiers "a considerable sum of money" to say that the disciples had stolen Jesus in the night while they slept; "and if this comes to the governor's ears, we will put things right with him and protect you." Far from being the inventor of the "stolen body" plot, Pilate was the chief victim of the exercise.

Matthew's chief priests seemed confident that they could do it. All through the trial, they had showed an acute understanding of the governor's psychology. Now they divined that they could run rings around him again. But in exactly what fashion did they hope to "put things right" with him? The soldiers would have been bound to report to him eventually, even if they went to the priests first. Their story, shorn of the "ten thousand armed men" of the Passion plays, suggested unbelievable incompetence. It could hardly have protected them from Pilate's lashing sarcasm, or his temper. What the Jews' proposal provided, however, was an explanation for something that otherwise seemed baffling: how a nervous governor, highly sensitized at that moment to crowd hysteria and the threat of violence, could have missed the news that his difficult victim had disappeared from the tomb and was presumed to have risen from the dead.

For, according to the Gospels, he did miss it. Matthew's mention of the plot that might come to the governor's ears was Pilate's last live appearance. There was no Roman reaction to the Resurrection, though the news of the body's disappearance, and the supposition that Jesus lived, burned through Jerusalem. In Luke, all Jesus' appearances were in or near the city; he materialized in rooms, but he also haunted the roads and the gardens. When two disciples met the risen Jesus a little later on the road to Emmaus, they could ask him: "Are you the only person who doesn't know what's been happening in Jerusalem these past few days?" No, apparently he was not the only person.

Perhaps Pilate had already left, riding back in splendid and indifferent convoy to the haven of Caesarea. Or perhaps the evangelists' imaginations failed them. Again and again, through the Passion naratives, they had made Pilate an unwitting witness to the divinity of Jesus. Here, with the Resurrection, was their chance to make him confirm the most astonishing miracle of all. For some reason, they chose not to.

He could at least have gone to the garden. He could have sent out a search party, treated the case as a simple escape. But the Gospel Pilate did not even show as much interest as that. With so many wild stories floating around, perhaps he thought there was no point. Better to withdraw from the scene, leave the Jews to it. There was, besides, the humiliation of losing face: his own *imperium* had been thrown back at him and counted for nothing.

The notion of men rising from the dead would have struck him first as Jewish fanaticism; yet it was not completely unheard-of. There were similar stories recorded. Men had been found alive in the funeral pyre; some had been claimed as corpses, though they still breathed, by relatives who wanted their money. As you placed the body in the winding sheet you would notice the soft heave of the cloth, a warm moistness when the hand was held over the face. Men had been carried to the pyre and had then walked home and clapped their hands for the servants; or their souls had wandered from their bodies and gone to other countries, only to return and nudge their corpses back to astonishing life. But those were men who had merely been declared dead, not buried. As the elder Pliny put it, "we are treating of the operations of nature, not of miracles."

The Nazarene had been quite dead, of course. Pilate had had the reports to prove it. It was just conceivable that his soldiers had been deceived, and that the man had been taken down still breathing. If the claim of resurrection reached his ears at all, Pilate might have concluded that Jesus was an athlete or a trickster. He might have grudgingly admired his fortitude, like that of the gladiators whose names he yelled and whose winning bouts he argued over. But his reaction, whatever it was, was beyond the imagining of any of the Gospel writers.

The absence of a Roman *imprimatur* does not weaken the Resurrection story for those who believe it happened. Yet it will always be strange. For some early Christian writers, notably in the Coptic church, it was too strange. They insisted on having their Roman witness, *the* Roman witness, to the fact that Christ had risen. In this, according to one Edwardian scholar, they showed "no feeling for the tragic irony of history": the irony that "the greatest event of human history passed unnoticed by the rulers of the earth." But this, of course, did not bother them.

The author of the *Gospel of Peter* sent the centurion, the soldiers and the chief priests racing by night to tell Pilate what had happened. "They were in great agony," he wrote, "saying, 'This man really was the Son of God.' "

Pilate answered in a telling variant of his words as he washed his hands: "I am clean of the blood of the Son of God, but this was what seemed good to you."

The chief priests begged him, implored him, not to let the soldiers reveal what they had seen; if they were to do so, the people would stone them. So Pilate told the soldiers to say nothing. Apart from that, he showed no curiosity, no reaction, as if his mind was deliberately cleansed of the affair. In most of the Apocryphal Gospels of the Western Church, this was his attitude: proud, almost indifferent. The notable exception was the longer version of his invented letter to Tiberius. In this he claimed to have witnessed the Resurrection; and not only that, but the harrowing of hell and the destruction of the synagogues, in one great cosmic theater show from the terrace of his palace.

> On the first day of the week, about the third hour of the night, there came a sound from heaven, and the heavens became seven times more luminous than on all other days. And the sun blazed out more luminously than it had ever shone, lighting up the whole hemisphere. And just as lightning-flashes suddenly appear in a storm, so tall men in beautiful clothes, and of indescribable glory, appeared in the air, an uncountable crowd, crying out, "Glory to God in the highest, and on earth peace, goodwill among men; Jesus that was crucified is risen again; come up from Hades you that were enslaved in the subterranean recesses of hell." And at their voice the mountains and hills were moved, and the rocks were split, and great chasms were made in the earth, so that even the foundations of the earth appeared. And He that raised up all the dead and bound Hades said, "Tell my disciples that He goes before you into Galilee, and there you shall see Him."

And amid this terror the dead appeared rising again. The Jews themselves saw it, and said it was Abraham, and Isaac, and Jacob, and the
twelve patriarchs, and Moses, and Job, who had died (they say) 2,500
years ago; and we saw Noah clearly in his body, as in life. And all the
crowd of men walked about and sang hymns to God in loud voices, saying "The Lord our God, who has risen from the dead, has brought all the
dead to life, and Hades has been spoiled and slain."

All that night, my lord king, the light went on shining. And many
of the Jews died in the chasm of the earth, as they were swallowed up, so
that the next morning most of those who had opposed Jesus could not be
found. Others saw men rising again whom none of us had ever seen. Only
one Jewish synagogue was left in Jerusalem itself, for all the synagogues
which had been against Jesus were destroyed.

Through that terror, therefore, amazed and seized with the most
dreadful trembling, I wrote down what I saw . . . and I have sent it to your
divinity, my lord.

Trembling as he was, this was still Pilate writing as a bureaucrat in detachment. His terror contained no element of remorse, because he had
blamed the Jews for everything. The Coptic writers, however, knew they
could do better with their witness. The Coptic hagiographies of Pilate
(later read by many more people in Arabic translations) enjoyed a huge
vogue in Egypt and Ethiopia from the fifth century onward. Even in the
eighteenth century, a Jesuit missionary reported that these stories were
still being read in churches, and that babies were still being christened
"Pilate" after their reluctant hero. The anti-Semitism of the Copts, who
lived next door to the Jews, makes these tales almost unreadable in parts,
but they are not without interest for their treatment of the governor.
These writers thought they could make him involved and moved; they
could make him approach Jesus, even touch him. They thought they
could make him sorry.

In the *Martyrdom of Pilate,* an Egyptian fantasy of the sixth century,
Pilate quickly noticed the miracles and prodigies occurring around the
tomb of Jesus. He went to his house and prepared a banquet for the poor
to celebrate his joy at the Resurrection, and Procula, even more joyful,
prepared to go to the tomb to worship. When the Jews got wind of this,
they went in search of Barabbas to persuade him to ambush Procula and

kill Pilate. But the author of the *Martyrdom,* one Gamaliel, passed this news to Joseph of Arimathea, who tipped off the governor; and Pilate drew up his troops in readiness.

Procula got up in the night, with her handmaids and servants, and went to the tomb. There she worshiped, spreading precious ointments and perfumes on the tomb itself and on the cross, which was propped beside it. She lit dozens of lamps and burned incense. As the women lingered by the tomb, veiled heads bending and hands upraised, Barabbas and his men attacked them. But Pilate's soldiers fell on the attackers. Barabbas himself was sentenced by the governor to be crucified upside down, his side pierced and his legs broken. The execution took place five days after the Resurrection. It was, Pilate told Barabbas, revenge for "that innocent blood which we have unjustly shed."

Which *we* have unjustly shed. The Copts may have made a saint out of Pilate, but they did not exculpate him. He had killed Christ, certainly; but it bothered him. So in another Coptic fragment—the one that survived the wreck of H.M.S. *Captain*—Pilate interrogated the soldiers from the tomb, dismissed their feeble excuses, threw them in prison, and went back to the garden himself.

It was still early. The bushes of the garden were soaked with dew as he brushed against them, and mist garlanded the trees like the drift that followed an explosion. It hung there, that sense of Him, moving away as he approached it. Early dawn was the time when honey fell from the air; a man out walking then would find himself sticky, under leaves that were dribbled with nectar in the color of the scattering clouds.

He did not go down the winding paths alone. The chief priests and the centurion went with him, at least as far as the tomb, when the priests refused to go farther. They drew back, letting the two unclean Romans go ahead of them. Yet the tomb itself did not suggest uncleanness. The new stone gleamed, and under Pilate's hand the tiny grains glittered like diamond. The air was cool; the heat of the day had not yet warmed the surface of the stone. And the neatness of its displacement, which had left the grass blades and rose petals unbruised beside it, caused Pilate's hand to tremble.

He needed to enter the tomb, too. Perhaps it would contain evidence of a mistake: the corpse somehow shifted into a corner, overlooked. He took the centurion with him to confirm whatever he found, but they were two unseeing men together. The centurion, half-blinded in battle, was now utterly blind in the enclosing darkness. As for Pilate, he was afflicted again with that temporary blindness that had overcome him at the trial. He was once more the man who had failed to see God when he had stood within a yard of Him.

The tomb was filled with astonishing perfume. Before Pilate had gone two steps inside, the air seemed to swarm with all the potions and essences of the apothecary. After he had handed the body over to Joseph, after Nicodemus had performed his own anointing, the women had crept in with their small jars of salve and ointment, and these were the perfumes that surrounded him. The Passion plays listed them: pepper, ginger, cinnamon, new saffron powder from the purple crocus fields of Anatolia, nutmeg, pomegranate and the wrinkled buds of cloves; raisins, garingay, violet-scented sugar, aniseed and cumin; grains of paradise; white ginger; cubes of white sugar as clear as ice; rosewater, olive oil, yellow wax, white wax, honey in the comb. And over all these was myrrh, the golden fragrance wept by Myrrha in her imprisonment under the bark of the unyielding tree.

Pilate was enraptured. "Why is the air so sweet here?" he called to the priests. "Where are these perfumes from?"

"It's just the wind in the garden," they told him carelessly. "The wind blowing through the flowers."

He did not believe them. The three women must have compounded these scents, their long dark hair hanging down past their anguished eyes, the ground littered with little precious boxes and bags and measuring spoons. They had smeared it so thickly on the beloved body that the winding sheets appeared to be stained not with blood, but with drifts of petals and violets and dried jasmine flowers; and the sheets lay as a young man in impetuosity might have hurled them off one morning, stepping out into the glare of the light.

"If he was stolen," Pilate murmured, "the thieves would have taken these graveclothes, too."

"No, no," the priests told him. "Those belong to someone else."

He did not believe that, either. He knew they belonged to Jesus, who had somehow left them. Picking up the winding sheets, he pressed them to his heart and kissed them for joy, as if Jesus were still wrapped in

them. Then, over the holy sheets, in the intoxication of spices and flowers, he bent his head and wept.

The centurion, too, touched the winding sheet. He held it to his eye,
and he saw again. At once he acknowledged Jesus, but Pilate did not do
so yet. He sent for Joseph and Nicodemus, needing to consult with
them. At the same time, the priests informed him that in a well elsewhere in the garden they had found the body of a crucified man. Everyone rushed to the well, where the corpse floated vertically like a white
stone. The priests cried, "Look, it's the sorcerer!"

"Is this really him?" asked Pilate.

Joseph and Nicodemus told him no. The graveclothes had belonged
to Jesus, but this body in the well was that of one of the thieves who had
been crucified with him.

Pilate then remembered that Jesus had said, "The dead shall come to
life in my tomb." He ordered his men to carry the body to Jesus' tomb
and to roll the stone across. The Jewish priests were outraged that a
Roman governor would come meddling to a sepulchre. But as they up-
braided Pilate, a voice from the tomb commanded them to take the stone
away. The body of the thief had risen from the dead.

The pagan governor had, after all, witnessed a resurrection. More
than that: he had helped it to occur. It had happened in the middle of a
scene that seems farcical enough, with stock priests and bumbling soldiers, and with bodies, naked or in shrouds, popping up with the regularity of lovers in wardrobes in a Feydeau play. Yet it was meant to be an
awakening of sorts, even the start of an apology. That was the gist of the
end of the fragment found after the wreck of the *Captain* in 1870, where
Pilate stood in the garden and raised his hands in the praying posture of
both Romans and Christians. He said nothing within earshot of the others, although they swarmed around him. Yet in his heart the phrase of
recognition had already formed: *Oh, my Lord.*

V.

The Pilate of the *Acta Pilati* was never quite so vulnerable. He was angry
rather than sorry, and the evidence he sought was intellectual. Although
it might have been an obvious step to go to the tomb, to inspect the
clothes, to order his troops to check for footprints or the signs of a strug-

gle, he did not do so. Instead he gathered the chief priests and teachers in the Temple, ordered the doors shut, and said: "I've heard you have a great Bible here. I should like you to bring it before us."

The chief priests brought it out. Four of them carried it, two of them struggled to open the great golden clasps. Pilate went on: "I adjure you, by the God of your fathers who commanded you to build this Temple in the place of his sanctuary, not to hide the truth from me. You know everything that is written in this Bible. Tell me if you have found in the scriptures that this Jesus whom you crucified is the Son of God who was to come for the salvation of mankind, and in what year he was meant to come. Tell me whether you crucified him in ignorance or knowingly."

In reply, Annas and Caiaphas immediately asked everyone in the Temple to leave. They closed the doors again. The mood was conspiratorial, the chamber dark; the great Bible lay mutely on the table. Caiaphas, leaning close to Pilate, admitted that they had found among the Jews many witnesses to the Resurrection. They had even found two who had been raised from the dead and had witnessed Christ's harrowing of hell; they had taken written statements. And they had gone back to the Bible, laboring to turn the great creaking pages, to find out what God had to say on the subject. The arithmetical progression, from the creation to the Flood, to the exile, to the building of the Temple, to the coming of Christ, was quite clear: it was (in a slight variant of what Michael the archangel had already told Seth, the son of Adam) exactly five thousand five hundred years. So, yes, this Jesus was the Son of God. But they had not told a soul; and they appealed to Pilate "by your life and health" not to tell anyone either.

Pilate took this news calmly. No anger, no emotion; indeed, no reaction, except to sit down and write an account of everything the two priests had told him, "and to lay them all up among the acts of the Lord and Savior in the public books of his judgment hall." Then he wrote another letter, this time to "Claudius, king of Rome." It was much like his other "letters" for the first paragraph, retailing how the Jews had brought a fearful judgment on themselves by ignoring the fact that "their God would send them out of heaven his holy one who should rightly be called a king, and promised he would send him on earth by a virgin." "This god of the Hebrews," he wrote, "came when I was governor of Judaea" and performed miracles for everyone to see; but the priests had told Pilate that he was a sorcerer, and Pilate had believed them.

He delivered him to death and the body was buried: "but while my soldiers watched him he rose again on the third day." The chief priests bribed the soldiers to say that the body had been stolen, "but, though they took the money, they could not keep quiet about what had happened, and they testified too that they saw him when he had risen." In his closing sentence he tried to explain himself, the only sentence that might have remotely rung true: "I've reported these things to you, most mighty one, in case somebody else tries to tell you a pack of lies."

There was still no conversion in this invention. Pilate had been duped into killing a god, but it was not his god, for all the signs and wonders. It was still "the god of the Hebrews." The execution of Jesus was an administrative lapse, not an error with any cosmic meaning; though it might be inconvenient and even dangerous to have dealt out death to a representative of divinity, Pilate's gods were still in charge here. He was going to clear up this mess, keep it under control. It was the Jews who would pay the price for snubbing their God.

Meanwhile, the Pilate of the Eastern Church had been writing letters of a different sort. In one sixth-century letter, written in Greek, he told Herod Antipas how after the Resurrection he had kept track of Jesus. He followed him with spies as far as Galilee, where he learned that he was preaching. His wife, Procula, had gone up to Galilee to see him, together with the lance man Longinus and the soldiers who had guarded the tomb. They found Jesus sitting in a tilled field, where the lines of rolled brown earth echoed the regular curls of his hair, with a great crowd listening to him; and though they did not dare approach, he saw them.

"What is it?" he asked them. "Do you believe in me?"

They could not answer him.

"Procula, you should know that everyone who has died shall live by my death, which you have seen. You see that I'm alive, though you crucified me. Now, listen to me, and believe in God my father, who is with me. For I have burst the bounds of death and broken open the gates of Sheol."

Procula returned, in tears, and told Pilate. Overwhelmed with grief, he lay on his bed and wept for a while. Then he put on black robes of mourning. Procula took off, one by one, her rings and bracelets, ripped the gold braiding from her dress, and let her hair fall in long tangled tresses. Like this, in their litter, clinging to each other, they went to Galilee. All the way there, Pilate complained: "It's Herod's fault. It was Herod who made me judge him. It's Herod's fault."

Fifty soldiers marched behind them. Pilate and Procula were desperate to see Jesus, but again they hardly dared to get close. They watched him from a distance, from behind the trees, until they summoned up enough courage to take the first steps in his direction. Then, at once, the heavens roared, thunder cracked, the earth moved; and in that moving of the earth came, once more, the perfume of paradise, of roses and cardamom and garingay and jasmine.

Pilate stood still in the middle of the road. He could see Jesus standing and talking to his disciples and, as he stood there, Jesus saw him. Pilate began to pray in his heart, for, as he told Herod, "I knew that this was the lord of created things." Then, unable to look anymore, he knelt, with Procula beside him. Together, they fell on their faces on the hard ground. Pilate managed to cry out, "I have sinned, Lord, that I judged you. I know you're God, the Son of God. I saw your humanity, but not your divinity." And he added, again, wretchedly, "It was Herod who made me do it."

Jesus came across to them, bent down, and took their hands to raise them. As Pilate's fingers intertwined with his, he felt the deep wounds of the nails that he himself had ordered driven through them; and as he dared to raise his eyes to the face, a face misted with his own tears, he saw the scabbed scratches of the crown of thorns.

The hands of Jesus were now laid on his shoulders. "All generations and families shall call you blessed," he told him, "because in your days the Son of Man died and rose again." And with these astonishing words, he left them.

Unfortunately for the pathos of this scene, Herod wrote a reply to Pilate's letter. (This was also sixth-century, also in Greek, with an optional version in Syriac.) He seemed to overlook the blatant buck-passing, for he had a more urgent interest. "Since you're seeing this man Jesus again," he scribbled,

would you put in a word for me? I'm having a hard time at present. Lestonax, my son, is in the last stages of a decline. I've got dropsy myself, and worms are coming out of my mouth. My dear daughter Herodias was playing on the ice and fell in up to her neck; her mother caught at her head to save her, and it was cut off, and the water swept her body away. My wife is sitting with the head on her knees, weeping so much that her left eye is blinded, and the whole house is filled with sorrow.

Please intercede for me, and bury my family honorably. I'm enclosing my wife's earrings and my own signet ring.

—Herod

These fantasies would be laughable if they did not carry a dark undercurrent: the determination of early Christian writers in every branch of the church, whether Greek, Coptic or western, to shift the blame for the Crucifixion from Pilate to the Jews. This could reach grotesque levels, as when Origen in his commentaries on Matthew and John simply pronounces Pilate innocent, and ascribes to the Jews all the cruelties that were clearly inflicted on Christ by the Romans. Once the Gospel embroiderers had lost sight of the fact that crucifixion was a uniquely Roman punishment, uniquely in Pilate's power, they could take Jewish "responsibility" to absurd lengths: even, in the Coptic apocrypha, causing the Jews to crucify Pilate himself as a loathsome "Egyptian."

The reason for these inventions, at least at first, was not simply to hurt the Jews. For at least three centuries after Christ's death, as the new religion struggled to establish itself, it was vital to have a Roman official who would say, repeatedly, that Jesus posed no threat to the empire. Pilate had to be Christ's advocate, even his friend, and this made the Jews the villains. As Christianity became accepted and official—starting with the Edict of Milan in 312, when Constantine recognized it as a *religio licita* throughout the empire—Pilate's fortunes fell into steep decline, and he became a villain in his own right. The Nicene Creed of 381 could state unequivocally that Jesus was crucified under Pontius Pilate, with no mention of the Jews.

Nonetheless, medieval anti-Semitism was still based squarely on the notion that the Jews had killed Christ. Pilate—who has always been used as men want to use him—became a witness to their supposed intractability, their capacity to sow evil in the world. Although there was probably a core of truth in Pilate's reluctance to kill Jesus, it was expanded and embroidered. In invented story after invented story he complained that the Jews had misled him, made him do what he had never wanted to do. He had tried every subterfuge to save Jesus, but they had insisted on his death.

Even twentieth-century anti-Semitism, with its roots in prejudice both political and economic, was not free from that lingering image. Much of the nineteenth- and early twentieth-century literature about Pilate is in German. It could be argued that the Germans (like other imperial powers of the time) had an unhealthy fascination with him. The blond, blue-eyed forest child was not forgotten. If the Germans—or, for that matter, the Russians or the Poles, or any other instigators of pogroms—wished to make a point against the Jews, their case was partly made for them by the struggles of an officer of a "superior" and civilizing power in ancient Judaea. Even imperial and Nazi Germany could not beatify the governor and did not try; but he could still play the role of the besieged Aryan in the dangerous crowd, the upholder of reason against fanaticism, and a witness to the unchanging, unvarying "problem" of the Jews.

All this reinterpretation made no hero of Pilate himself, however. Nor did it really exculpate him. In almost all the Apocryphal Gospels and the mystery plays, as in the New Testament, the Crucifixion was a joint effort by Pilate and the Jews; but the Apocryphal Pilate felt worse afterward. Even the Coptic Pilate was only a saint because of his endless apologies and craven repentance. But this, too, inculpated the Jews: by showing how sorry one killer of Christ could be, it emphasized by contrast how strikingly unsorry the others were.

The idea of Repentant Pilate never caught on in western Christendom. It was too much even for fertile imaginations. But the end of the nineteenth century saw, for a few months, a sentimental revival. The Coptic fragment of his "prayer" at the tomb was published in the *Newbery House Magazine,* a sort of clerical gazetteer, in December 1892. There, among advertisements for communion wine and warm underwear and offers of home loans for two guineas a month, the Reverend Arthur Baker, R.N., indulged himself in some speculation.

> There is surely no-one who would not wish such a tradition [of Pilate's repentance] to have at least some ground in truth. Could there be anything which would add more luster to the triumph of the cross than the con-

version of the Roman Procurator himself? . . . If the story of Pilate's visit to the sepulchre . . . has any foundation in fact, may we not hope that it was something more than curiosity which drew the Roman Governor to the spot, and that at least "He was not far from the Kingdom of God"? . . . Moreover, even if it be assumed that the whole thing is forgery pure and simple . . . the world in the nineteenth century is the richer for a discovery which suggests ideas which, improbable as they may seem to many, must surely be sweet to every Christian mind.

The translator of the scrap for *Studia Siniatica,* Margaret Dunlop Gibson (one imagines her as a formidable woman of serge skirts and thick glasses), fervently agreed. "We cannot but admire the author's truly Christian appreciation of the scope of Divine forgiveness, which could soften even Pilate's heart, and number him with the redeemed."

Despite this, the more reputable sources offered no hope whatsoever. In place of high emotion, vivid letters, silly chatter, speculation, there was only a deafening silence. In the Acts of the Apostles the disciples stayed indoors after the Resurrection "for fear of the Jews." They might have been afraid of the authorities generally, but the Romans and their governor had disappeared from the scene. Jesus had even told his followers to stay in Jerusalem, as if confident that there would be no more executions and no reprisals. And there were none.

This was not the normal pattern of events. As the Pharisee Gamaliel pointed out to the council of the Jews in the fifth chapter of Acts, two previous "prophets" and their followers had been comprehensively eliminated by the Romans. At the time of the census, under Coponius, Judas the Galilean had been executed and his followers sent to the winds. Pilate had only to consult the records to find, under his predecessor Gratus, two hundred crucifixions after one such Messianic eruption. He apparently settled for three, and then handed the matter over entirely to the Jewish authorities.

Why he did so is unclear. The accounts of the trial suggest that he did not like this case and badly wanted to offload it; but once he had judged it as political, and therefore a danger to Rome, he had to keep an eye on it. Tacitus clearly thought it was Pilate's job to nip this "pestilent superstition" in the bud. Moreover he credited him with doing so, at least for a while. But Pilate had not even kept Jesus' supporters and sym-

pathizers away from the scene of the Crucifixion, as might have been prudent. And, according to Luke, the little band of apostles prospered and
grew.

In the forty days leading up to the Ascension the apostles mostly
kept quiet, but after Pentecost they were suddenly out preaching in the
streets and the Temple. Astoundingly, Latin was among their languages:
visitors from Rome apparently heard them and grasped what they were
saying. In the normal run of events, such visitors would also have
touched base in Caesarea. Romans in Judaea tended to flock together, ex-
changing hospitality in this inhospitable land for precious news of the
City. It would have been strange indeed if no one had informed Pilate
that in the streets of Jerusalem people were being fed, in Latin, with extraordinary versions of recent events. According to Peter in his first public sermon, "In accordance with his own plan God had already decided
that Jesus would be handed over to you; and you killed him by letting
sinful men ["outlaws" was more the sense of it] crucify him. But God
raised him from death, setting him free from its power, because it was
impossible that death should keep him prisoner."

Such teaching went beyond being merely insulting to Pilate. It
raised again the disturbing idea that the God of the Jews had made use
of him. It was dangerous, too. Crowds began to gather, saw miracles and
became adherents of the new sect. In one day, three thousand joined the
movement. The sick on their sleeping mats were brought into the streets
of Jerusalem, under the horses of Pilate's attendants and the feet of his
litter bearers, in hopes that the shadow of Peter might fall across and heal
them. Nor was this merely religious impulse. The first question the
apostles asked Jesus in Acts, when they met again after the Resurrection,
was "Lord, are you now going to give the kingdom back to Israel?" Jesus
replied that this was up to his father, but then added that the apostles
would become his witnesses "in Judaea and Samaria and to the ends of
the earth." It cannot have been coincidence that he mentioned Pilate's
patch first, as the place most in need of liberation and enlightenment;
and then, in a phrase the Romans used too, sweeping from the Indies to
the fog-bound Britons, suggested that his teachings would spread and
surge to the very limits of the empire.

Still Pilate did nothing. He left everything to Caiaphas and the elders; and they, though desperately uncertain how best to proceed, apparently never brought a religious case before him again. When Stephen

appeared, prophesying the destruction of the Temple just as Jesus had done, they simply took him outside the city and stoned him.

Again, the writers of the Apocryphal Gospels found the governor's absence disappointing. In the *Revelation of Stephen,* a Greek manuscript allegedly dating from 415, the author insists that Pilate played a part in the death of the first Christian martyr. In his version of the story, the crowd led Stephen to Pilate on a charge of blasphemy. Pilate stood on the steps and shouted, "You made me crucify the Innocent One; why rage against this man? Why gnash your teeth? Are you still mad?"

Having failed to persuade the governor, the Jews took Stephen away to stone him. Meanwhile, Pilate called his wife and two children, and they baptized one another. Having done this, still damp with holy water, they joined the crowd of believers surrounding Stephen and tried to protect him from the stones. Their efforts failed. Afterward Pilate took the body of Stephen and two others who had died with him and put them, in gold and silver coffins, in his secret sepulchre. In the morning he rose early to burn incense before them, but an angel had taken them away. As Pilate cried out to God, "Wasn't I worthy to be your servant?," Stephen himself came in to comfort him.

In truth, Pilate was in Caesarea. There his days unfolded as usual: the morning shave, the afternoon bath, the letters and briefings, the dinner parties. At some point a man called Saul came through the city, under attack by Greek-speaking Jews and on his way to Tarsus. He claimed he was a Roman citizen. Pilate's successors had reason to question his credentials, but Pilate did not notice him. The future St. Paul merely walked under his windows, went down to the harbor, inched across the blue sea, while the governor worried about something else: about who was living and who was dying at home, or about the phoenix that had been sighted in Egypt, its body purple, its neck gold, its tail of blue feathers picked out with rose, making its nest of frankincense and wild cinnamon before its immolation on the Altar of the Sun.

More strangely, the pernicious new superstition crept into Caesarea itself, and Pilate did not seem to notice that either. The date would have been between 35 and 38; Pilate was there until the end of 36, so he could well have been there to notice it, or not to notice. The Acts of the Apostles recorded that there was a deeply religious Roman in the city, a man called Cornelius, who was drawn toward Judaism. He was a captain in what Luke calls the "Italian" regiment, the troop which, by tradition, had been with Pilate in Jerusalem during the trial of Jesus and had carried out the Crucifixion. As their name implies, these were the only Roman soldiers in Judaea. They made up a personal guard for the governor, a regiment of familiar faces and voices among the barely manageable auxiliaries. Cornelius and Pilate were almost certainly colleagues: messmates, perhaps even friends. They would have shared *castrensia verba,* camp slang, but they were already moving apart from each other.

Cornelius was constantly praying to God. He was doing so one day at about three o'clock in the afternoon (dinnertime, on the Roman schedule), when he was suddenly faced with a vision of an angel.

The angel said, "Cornelius!"

His reaction was absolutely instinctive: "What is it, sir?" He would have snapped to in just the same way to Pilate, another vision in white.

The angel told Cornelius to send to Joppa for Peter, and he did so. Peter came quickly to Caesarea, where he found Cornelius' house packed with relatives and close friends who had been invited to meet him. There, in a house that cannot have been far from Pilate's palace, was a crowd of men and women which must have included acquaintances and friends of the governor's; and they were waiting eagerly to hear about this Jesus, this man-God whom Pilate had put to death.

As Peter entered, Cornelius fell at his feet. The emperor was greeted like that; even Pilate could be greeted like that. But Peter helped Cornelius up, saying, "I'm only a man." He explained that although he would not usually consider defiling himself by consorting with Gentiles, God had told him that on this occasion "I must not consider anyone ritually unclean or defiled." He asked Cornelius why he had sent for him. The captain told the story of the angel (he called him "a man in bright clothes"), concluding that "we are all here now in the presence of God, waiting to hear anything that the Lord has instructed you to say."

Peter then preached to them, his first sermon specifically to Romans. Oddly, he assumed that they already knew everything he was going to tell them. "You know the message of God to the people of Israel, the good news of Jesus Christ," he told them. "You know about Jesus of Nazareth and how God poured out on him the Holy Spirit and power.

. . . We are witnesses of everything that he did in the land of Israel and in Jerusalem. Then they put him to death by nailing him to a cross."

They put him to death. Who were "they"? The word was perhaps deliberately vague and diplomatic. Peter may not have wanted to spoil the astonishing moment of conversion, for, as he spoke, the Holy Ghost came down on everyone in the room, Jews and Romans alike. Peter ordered them immediately to be baptized. Perhaps this was done in the baths, or in the fountains in the garden. However it happened, "believers throughout Judea," Luke said, heard of these Roman conversions. It is hard to believe that no inkling of them reached Pilate. He was Cornelius' superior officer, after all. In Cornelius' utterly Roman house in Caesarea, a house perhaps as familiar to Pilate as his own palace, Peter the apostle was breaking bread and prayers were being offered to Jesus the Son of God.

The vivid mythology of "secret crimes" imputed to Christians had not yet been invented. The secret meals and meetings were apparently just that, secret meals and meetings. The dangers of Christianity for the Roman power were not yet evident and, even when they became so, Roman provincial officers felt tentative in dealing with them. Perhaps this would have been Pilate's reaction. Nonetheless, it was becoming clear that a man could not worship the emperor if he believed in Christ; and, if he did not worship the emperor, the glue of the empire would crumble. The earliest encounters of Roman officials with Christians vividly show this growing anxiety: with the difference that Pilate had met, talked to, scourged, killed, but possibly tried to save, the man his own captain now accepted as divine.

Pliny to Trajan   [sometime after 111]

It is my custom, Lord Emperor, to refer to you all questions I feel doubtful about. Who can better guide me when I am perplexed, or enlighten me when I am ignorant? . . .

This is the course I have taken with those who were accused before me as Christians. I asked them to their face whether they were Christian, and if they confessed, I asked them a second and a third time with threats of punishment. If they kept to it, I ordered them for execution; for there seemed no question to me that, whatever it was that they admitted, in any case obstinacy and unbending perversity deserve to be punished.

There were others of the same insanity; but as these were Roman citizens, I noted them down to be sent to Rome.

. . . As for those who said that they neither were nor had ever been Christians, I thought it right to let them go, since they recited a prayer to the gods at my dictation, made supplication with incense and wine to your statue (which I had ordered to be brought into court for the purpose, together with images of the gods), and moreover cursed Christ—not a thing (so it is said) that those who are really Christians can be made to do.

. . . They maintained, however, that their only crime had been this: that it was their habit on a fixed day to assemble before daylight and sing by turns a hymn to Christ as a god; and that they bound themselves with an oath, not for any crime, but not to commit theft or robbery or adultery, not to break their word, and not to deny a deposit when demanded. After this was done, their custom was to leave, and meet together again to take food, but ordinary and harmless food; and even this (they said) they had given up doing after the issue of my edict, by which in accordance with your orders I had forbidden the existence of clubs. I considered it necessary to find out by torture from two maidservants (who are called deaconesses) how far this was true; but I discovered nothing else than a wicked and arrogant superstition. I have therefore adjourned the case and hastened to consult you.

The matter seemed worth deliberation to me, especially taking into account the number of those in danger; for many of all ages and every rank, and even of both sexes, are brought into present or future peril. The contagion of that superstition has penetrated not only the cities, but the villages and the countryside. Yet it seems possible to stop it and to set things right. . . .

TRIAL OF THE SCILLITAN MARTYRS AT CARTHAGE, SEVENTEENTH OF JULY 180
Consulship of Praesens (2) and Claudianus
Saturninus, proconsul, presiding

PROCONSUL: You can win the emperor's mercy, if you return to a sound mind.

FIRST CHRISTIAN: We have never done wrong, we have not lent ourselves to wrong, we have never spoken ill, but when ill-treated we have given thanks; because we pay heed to our emperor.

PROCONSUL: We too are religious, and our religion is simple, and we swear by the genius of our lord the emperor and pray for his welfare, as you should do too.

FIRST CHRISTIAN: If you will listen peaceably, I can tell you the mystery of simplicity.

PROCONSUL: I will not listen to you when you start to say evil things about our sacred rites; you should swear by the genius of our lord the emperor.

FIRST CHRISTIAN: I do not recognize the empire of this world; I serve that God whom no man has seen, nor can see with the eyes of the body. I have committed no theft; if I have bought anything, I pay the tax; because I know my lord, the King of Kings and Emperor of all nations.

PROCONSUL: Cease to be of this persuasion.

FIRST CHRISTIAN: It's a bad persuasion to do murder, and to bear false witness.

PROCONSUL *(to the rest)*:   Take no further part in this folly.

SECOND CHRISTIAN: We have no one else to fear, save only our Lord God, who is in heaven.

THIRD CHRISTIAN: Honor to Caesar as Caesar; but fear to God.

FOURTH CHRISTIAN: I am a Christian, and what I am I wish to be.

PROCONSUL: Will you have a space to consider?

FIRST CHRISTIAN: In a matter so straightforward, there is no considering.

PROCONSUL: Have a delay of thirty days and think about it.

FIRST CHRISTIAN: I am a Christian. *(And with this they all agreed.)*

PROCONSUL *(reading from the tablet)*:   Having confessed that you live according to the Christian rite, and having obstinately refused to return to the custom of the Romans when you were given the chance, we sentence you to be put to the sword.

SECOND CHRISTIAN: Today we are martyrs in heaven! Thanks be to God!

VI.

The worlds might have moved on in parallel, never meeting: the governor in his pretty palace, the Christian groups inexorably multiplying.

Yet one last time, strangely, the tracks crossed. It happened not in Judaea but in Samaria, the northern part of Pilate's province. This was a country most Jews looked down on as rough, volatile and infected by a rogue strain of Judaism, primitive and embarrassing. The Samaritans had a holy mountain, Mount Gerizim, on which they held gatherings and rituals; there was an ancient temple there, four hundred years old, and the site of an altar of stones where, they said, the Ark of the Covenant had rested. It was at the foot of those slopes that Jesus had sat with the Samaritan woman as she scooped water from the well, telling him with country simplicity that "our fathers worshiped on this mountain, but you say that Jerusalem is the place where people pray."

According to Josephus the Samaritans were a credulous lot, and they fell for the tales of a mendacious upstart who told them that, if they came to the mountain, he would show them the sacred vessels buried there by Moses. In the Acts of the Apostles one such upstart in Samaria—very probably the same man—was given a name, Simon. Some assume that this was Simon Magus, the magician. "He claimed that he was someone great," runs the account in Acts, "and everyone in the city, from all classes of society, paid close attention to him. 'He is that power of God known as the Great Power,' they said." The apostles kept Simon at arm's length: although they were converting many in Samaria, and even baptized Simon himself, they soon discovered that his interest in Christianity was skin deep. He thought it was just another sort of magic in which he could be instructed, if only the apostles would accept his money. Indignantly, Peter told him that "his heart was not right," and that he should take his "evil plan" away.

He apparently took it to Mount Gerizim, where the people were entranced. If the Ark had been carried there, and Moses' words had been recited there (by Joshua, as the story said), a cache of holy objects might well be there, too: not only the Ark itself, but the holy oil, the jar of manna, Aaron's rod. Their discovery would have important implications. Once these objects were recovered, the proper worship of God could be reestablished and he would appear as the Cloud of Glory, hovering over his new Temple on Gerizim and compelling recognition even from the pagans.

Fanatical Christian statements did not seem to get reported in Caesarea, but this, in some garbled version, did. And Josephus suggests that Pilate panicked. Mount Gerizim had its associations for him, too: it was where, eighty years before, the Romans had been besieged and cut down by rebel Jews. There was perhaps still honor to be satisfied there, as Germanicus had done in Germany: bones of the dead to be buried, rites to be performed. Perhaps, too, Pilate was uneasily aware that he should have been sharper in putting down the sect that was blossoming on all sides in the name of Jesus. Perhaps he was not inclined to get caught out again.

Josephus implies that Pilate went himself, with a unit of horse and a unit of infantry, to sort the Samaritan business out. Prefects of Judaea did their own fighting. In the battle against Simon the impostor, in Gratus' time, Josephus described impostor and prefect racing on horseback through a defile, "yet Gratus overtook him and cut off his head." Here, in case Pilate had been missing it, was real war.

The Samaritans had gathered, feverish with expectation, in a village called Tirathana at the foot of the mountain. They carried arms. Crowds came to join them, and they prepared to go up the mountain en masse. But Pilate had made good speed. He got there before them, blocked the access road and seized control of the higher ground. It was a typical Pilate maneuver: sneak in, take by surprise, surround, cut off. His troops waited, half-hidden in the trees and the rocks. Their commander-in-chief was among them, once again chafed by a breastplate and half-deafened by helmet flaps, while his horse shifted uneasily in the resinous shadows.

On a signal, they began to move down toward the village. At the same time, the crowd in the village began to storm the mountain. Scrambling and slipping over the rocks, the two sides met, but the contest was unequal. The crowd was repulsed. According to Josephus, some were killed, many fled, and many more were taken alive. The auxiliaries doubtless behaved with the same unmodulated brutality they had shown during the aqueduct riot, though when the battle was over Pilate himself showed some restraint: he ordered the Samaritan leaders to be killed and apparently let the rest go. There were perhaps more crucifixions, though these took time; the sword was quicker. Once the trouble was subdued, the mountain cleared and the village swept for subversives, Pilate and his troop went back to Caesarea. Simon himself—if it was he—appears to have escaped.

The province was quiet again, but that was not the end of the story. The Samaritans complained to Vitellius, who was in charge in Syria, that Pilate had committed murder. They had never had any intention of re-

volting against the Romans, they said. On the contrary, they had gone to
Tirathana to escape Pilate, who had been violently pursuing them. Vitellius seemed to believe this story. The Samaritans had gathered out of religious enthusiasm, not revolutionary zeal, and Pilate had marched on
them immediately, fearing Messianic unrest.

Yet his action had not been extraordinary. When Festus, who was
governor of Judaea under Nero, found people "seduced by a certain impostor, who promised them deliverance from their miseries if they followed him into the wilderness," he sent a force like Pilate's of horse and
foot and "destroyed" both the impostor and his followers. This did not
draw official censure, and Josephus did not even think it worthy of a critical remark. Perhaps the difference was that Festus was new then, and Pilate's cruelty had been felt before. Or perhaps Pilate had begun to sense
that his tour was nearly over, and was starting to dream of the triumphs
that attended the return of officers who had performed spectacular service abroad. He, too, could go out with a bang, averting revolution; he
too could enter Rome in the special chariot, in the *tunica palmata* and the
purple robe, while the people cheered and clapped. Yet it was a far-
fetched dream. As one of Cicero's friends once wrote to him petulantly
from Dalmatia, you could storm twenty towns and still not receive a fa-
vorable mention in the Senate.

Whatever the motivations on either side, Pilate was now in trouble.
Vitellius intervened immediately, as if he had been waiting for an excuse
to do so. He had been in command in the east for about a year, trying to
sort out feuds among the Parthians. His reputation in Rome was scandalous, Tacitus said, and his interest in Syria seemed to revolve around
exporting new strains of fig trees and pistachios for his country estates at
home. But "old-fashioned integrity," surprisingly enough, seemed to
guide his actions abroad. He wanted to make a good impression on his
emperor: not only by sacrificing a bull, a boar and a ram to mark Roman
power on the banks of the Euphrates, but by doing a little cleaning up in
Judaea on his way home.

Josephus records that Vitellius sent a colleague, Marcellus, to look
after Judaea, and ordered Pilate back to Rome "to answer the accusations
of the Jews before the emperor." This suggests a more general set of
charges from the Jews in general, not merely the Samaritans, and about
other things: a list that spanned the years. "He dared not contradict

Vitellius' orders," said Josephus; "so, having stayed ten years in Judaea, he hurried back to Rome."

We have no other sources for the end of Pilate's tour, but Josephus' account seems convincing enough. Pilate had gone too far one last time, and now he was going home. It was only his subjects' word against his, but he put up no resistance. It seems never to have occurred to him to protest.

In the palace at Caesarea, the wall hangings were taken down and the silverware packed in boxes. Once Marcellus was in place, Pilate had three months to put his affairs in order and get home. Although Marcellus was a stopgap and Pilate's case had not yet been judged, it seemed clear that he would not be returning. Governors who were recalled to Rome were seldom acquitted and usually banished; they needed to bring back with them what they could, for they would never be so rich again. After ten years of diplomatic presents, impulse buying and ointment money, there was much to pack away, and much to regret.

His tour had not been a total disaster. Even Philo could characterize those years in Judaea (though attributing them to Tiberius, not to him) as "peace and the blessings of peace." All the same, he was returning as a bad governor covered with disgrace. Philo summed it up: "No lot is so hard as for . . . rulers to be accused by their former subjects; as well might masters be accused by the slaves whom they have bred in their house or purchased with their money."

Before he left, Pilate was obliged to brief Marcellus and to go through the books with him. One set of accounts was left in the province; a duplicate had to be sent to the Treasury in Rome. A list had to be made of losses sustained by his troops or by the enemy in any battles fought, to be delivered to the Senate; street rioting may not have counted. Alongside these, within thirty days, he had to send a list of those members of his staff who qualified for *beneficia,* or special service bonuses. It was a painful duty for a man about to be reprimanded; he may not even have bothered to do it. But he would have made time, as Cicero recommended, to purge his correspondence. One of his freedmen would read through duplicate letters and destroy any that were "inequitable, eccentric, or inconsistent . . . or insulting, or in poor taste, or bad-tempered." Thus he would selectively rearrange the record he left behind him.

In the archive, the rolls were stacked up on the shelves with their identifying tags: accounts, *commentarii*, judicial decisions, arbitration about orphans, estates and the status of slaves: rulings from the time when he had been invested with power. The exercise of that power had demanded a certain discretion, a certain subtlety. Rome did not need to know exactly what deals he had made, what corners he had cut, or what cruelties he had committed in the name of order. Perhaps there had been none that he had not punctiliously reported. Perhaps there had been some that he would always suppress.

People were bound to remember him for something. They would see the Tiberieum standing above the sea, where surely it would stand for centuries. In the markets of Nablus, Nazareth and Jerusalem his coins would go on passing from hand to hand. His aqueduct would continue to snake across the dry hills, bringing clean water for which he might sometimes be thanked. And in the records of his judgments some decision would surely stand out for its usefulness, its perspicacity, its wisdom, before he disappeared forever from the consciousness of men.

Chapter 7

THROUGH BRAKE, THROUGH BRIAR

Survey everything that lies about you, as if it were luggage in a guest-room; you must travel on. Nature strips you as bare at your departure as at your entrance. You may take away no more than you brought in; what is more you must throw away the major part of what you brought with you into life. . . .

Why love such a thing as if it were your own possession? It was merely your covering. The day will come which will tear you forth and lead you away from the company of the foul and stinking womb. Withdraw from it now too as much as you can, and withdraw from pleasure, unless it is bound up with essential and important things; estrange yourself from it even now, and ponder on something nobler and loftier. Some day the secrets of nature shall be disclosed to you, the haze will be shaken from your eyes, and from every side the bright light will break on you.

. . . You behold that light darkly now, with vision that is cramped to the last degree. And yet, far off as it is, you already look upon it in wonder; what do you think the heavenly light will be like when you see it in its proper sphere?

SENECA, *Moral Letters,* CII

I.

HE PROBABLY LEFT JUDAEA in December 36. The sea-lanes were closed; no quick way out. Those who were desperate sometimes dared the sea journey, as the Jewish delegation did in 41 to make their petition to Gaius. Flaccus, too, had "tasted the terrors of the sea"—the sickening swell, the brine in the throat—on his way home from Egypt, also in disgrace, in the early months of winter. For twelve days around the winter solstice nature provided a respite, when the sea calmed down for the breeding of the halcyon birds. They floated on the water, sea-blue themselves, or took to the air at the setting of the Pleiades; their nests, too, floated on the surface, white and vaguely sparkling, woven of fish bones or dried sea foam. The ships stole past them.

Despite this chance, Pilate probably went overland. He would have traveled two thousand Roman miles at a rate of, at most, forty miles a day, through Anatolia and Greece, along icy military roads marked with drab military hostels. In the bitter weather, he would have needed felt overshoes, wool socks and the sort of heavy cloak soldiers had to wear under the British rain. These would have compromised his dignity a little, but perhaps there was not much of that left: only mud, snow, slipping luggage, the frozen breath of horses, and a dull sickness in his heart.

What awaited him, for all he knew, was the sort of treatment that was dealt out in 22 to Gaius Junius Silanus, the former governor of Asia. Silanus' subjects had accused him of extortion and brutality. In fact, Tacitus wrote, he was charged with offenses against the divinity of Augustus and the majesty of Tiberius. Solid accusations, which might have been countered by revenue scrolls and account books, were suddenly numinous and cloudy; defense was almost hopeless. Two members of his staff in Asia joined the case against him, and his slaves were sold to the Treasury agent for examination under torture.

Then Silanus was summoned to the Senate, before the senators and before the emperor. (Pilate would not have seen it, but the *Daily Gazette* would have been full of it.) According to Tacitus, Tiberius himself conducted the questioning. He proceeded threateningly and grimly, his thoughts as usual expressed with what seemed to be enormous effort; it was said that the grimmer he got, the more the words stuck in his throat. Whenever he was not speaking, he stared at Silanus unwaveringly with those large, dark, shortsighted eyes; that too was terrifying. Silanus found that, under the relentless imperial questioning, he did not dare as much as an evasion or a negative answer. That in itself was treason. Besides, the best orators in Asia were employed to argue the case against him. At last, the ex-governor—"an inexperienced speaker, standing alone, in mortal fear"—abandoned his own defense. Before he was exiled, he sent a short letter of complaint to Tiberius. That was not something Pilate was likely to do.

In Rome it was the holiday month of Saturnalia, the month of gambling and cheap presents, when, as Martial put it, "napkins fly about, and thin spoons, and wax tapers and paper, and pointed jars of dried damsons." Pilate's own gifts had perhaps been sent on before him, in hopes of winning or preserving his friendships. They were probably the last smells and tastes of his province: dates from Herod's great palm grove, ointment perfumed with balsam, fine jars of aromatic leaves. Slowly, milestone by milestone, he approached the distant horror and the distant celebration.

The journey took at least two months, perhaps three; he did not reach home until March 37. When he finally arrived in Rome, Philo tells us, the city was not as he remembered it. People were laughing in the streets, dancing. They were dressed in white, with garlands on their heads, and more garlands were draped on the public buildings. All night the torches burned and the flutes played, like wild birds. It was as if Pilate had stumbled on a festival in honor of some new god; or, wrote Philo, as if the age of Saturn had really dawned at last. If he looked around for portents of this change, they were there too: the Circus and the Aventine laid waste by fire, and the houses by the Tiber still flooded with mud and refuse. Quickly enough, the explanation reached him: Tiberius was dead, smothered in his bedclothes at the age of seventy-seven, and the blank-eyed, monkey-haired Gaius was emperor in his place.

Rome was in a paroxysm of relief. Its citizens had poured into the streets, hardly daring to believe that they could laugh again and speak openly. Pilate, who had revered the emperor with the sentimental loyalty of an expatriate, may have felt differently. He may have been devastated. Philo described vividly—too vividly, as usual—how Flaccus, still prefect in Egypt, had reacted to the old man's death. Flaccus had been appointed by the emperor in 31, five years after Pilate, and had looked on him as "his closest friend." When he heard of his death he fell into a deep depression, and wept for days. He wept all the more, Philo said, because he was terrified of suddenly finding himself on the wrong side politically. He was frightened because he had said bad things about Gaius' mother; but the worst came when Gaius put Tiberius' grandson to death, which suggested that closeness to the old emperor was no guarantee of survival. At this point, Philo claims, Flaccus flung himself down on his bed and lay sobbing and speechless, unable to begin to think straight.

Did Pilate weep too? He had missed the purges after the fall of Sejanus, purges in which he might have died himself, and he had heard of the emperor's wanton atrocities only through dry reports. Yet he had still felt the lash of his anger at a distance, and had spent the long journey from Judaea in the knowledge that he moved steadily toward that anger, as the sheep was driven to the altar of sacrifice. In the end, despite his best efforts, the last things Tiberius had heard of him had been unfavorable. As he gazed on the wax effigy of his patron on the Rostrum of the Orators, perhaps still laid in its imperial robes on the state couch of gold and ivory, jostled by images of ancestors and gods, it must have been hard to know whether to laugh or cry.

And at this point—just as Rome, wonderful and awful, filled his eyes again—Pilate disappears from the ancient accounts. Josephus follows him no further. His case disappears, too; we do not know what happened to it. Possibly the death of Tiberius made it moot and it was laid aside. We only know that a few days after the emperor's funeral Gaius made Herod Agrippa king of the territories of Antipas and Philip, an honor for which Agrippa had been lobbying for years, and that a little later he appointed Marullus as the new governor of Judaea. Vitellius, meanwhile, had been clearing things up there. He had abolished the sales tax on grain, replaced Caiaphas as high priest, and regained for the Jews the custody of the holy vestments stored in the Antonia. Finally, as he passed through Jerusalem on the Passover of April 20, 37, he "sacrificed to the God of the Jews." This seemed to mark more clearly than anything the end of Pilate's wave of Romanization. The news would have astonished, even scandalized, the new ex-governor.

Yet despite such signs of a purge of the old ways, Pilate had not necessarily been condemned or even held to account. The death of Tiberius had legally terminated his appointment in any case, just as Rufus' had been terminated by the death of Augustus. In the first pious months of his reign, Gaius freed numbers of prisoners, put an end to charges of *maiestas* and showed no particular eagerness to prosecute outstanding cases. Shortly after that, he fell ill. When he emerged from his illness, only a year or so after his accession, he began to manifest multiple signs of madness: taking up with actors, dressing as a god, dancing at midnight before the Senate. A man without political astuteness could die easily in those days; as easily as the man who unwisely sold hot water during the mourning days for the emperor's sister Drusilla.

Those who survived had to learn a new, craven language. Vitellius, the army commander who had ejected Pilate from Judaea, demonstrated this art in 40—according to Suetonius—when he found himself under sentence of death for no worse offense than being more successful than Gaius. He put on low-class clothes, fell at the emperor's feet, and worshiped him. Eventually, when Gaius claimed one night to be making love to the moon, he asked Vitellius whether he could see her under his jerking body. The splendid Hammer of the Parthians, the Hammer of Pilate, began to tremble with awe. Then, with his eyes fixed on the ground, he answered in a half-whisper: "Only you gods, master, may behold one another."

This is where history left Pilate too, somewhere in Rome, between the moon and the fickle gods.

II.

Again, this was not good enough for the writers of the Apocryphal Gospels. They wanted their witness to carry his work into Rome itself. He had, after all, written all those letters and reports to the emperor, and the emperor must have been curious to know more. Perhaps Tiberius was not quite dead yet; or, if he was, another emperor had taken up his interest in Jesus. It did not matter much who this emperor was, whether Claudius or Vespasian or merely "Caesar," as long as he could play the antagonist to the increasingly hapless governor.

From the second century onward, these tales seem to have multiplied. They survive now on fragments of manuscript that are impossible to date precisely or set in any context, other than popular craving for more than the Gospels provided. One popular story, cited by Gregory of Tours in his sixth-century *History of the Franks,* maintained that Tiberius was so impressed by Pilate's reports that he requested the Senate to recognize Jesus as God. Not surprisingly, the Senate refused. Other accounts described the emperor as fearsomely angry. In the *Anaphora of Pilate,* a Greek text of the sixth century, Pilate was recalled because Tiberius could not believe he had been so crass as to kill a man who might have been useful. Tiberius was grievously ill with a fever, ulcers and nine kinds of leprosy which covered his skin with purple lesions. (In the Anglo-Saxon version, the emperor was Vespasian, who, true to his name, had a nest of wasps in his nose.) News had reached Rome, from sources other than Pilate, that Jesus cured people. Tiberius had already made a request for the holy veil on which a woman called Veronica had taken an impression of the face of Jesus on the way to Golgotha, for he had heard that it could work miracles. When the veil arrived, wrapped in a golden cloth in a box enclosed in a golden cage, Tiberius welcomed it with a trail of silk handkerchiefs spread along the ground. He merely looked at the relic, and at once his skin was as soft and clear as a child's. (When Vespasian looked at it, the wasps immediately dropped buzzing from his nose.) How could Pilate have executed a man whose very image, imprinted on a square of cloth, could be so powerful? What sort of idiot could he be?

Tiberius dispatched a messenger with two thousand soldiers to bring Pilate home. The messenger was called Raab; he was the same man Pilate had once sent to spread his cloak at the feet of Christ. Raab also handed Pilate a letter.

Tiberius, most excellent Emperor of the Romans, to Pilate, prefect of Judaea, greeting.
Since you inflicted a violent and iniquitous death on Jesus of

Nazareth, showing no pity; since you received gifts to condemn him; and since you expressed sympathy with your tongue but, in your heart, delivered him up, you shall be brought home a prisoner to answer for yourself.

I have been most distressed at the reports that have reached me. A woman called Mary Magdalene has been here, a disciple of Jesus; he cast seven devils out of her, and she has told me of all his wonderful cures. How could you have allowed him to be crucified? If you did not receive him as a god, you might at least have honored him as a doctor. Your own deceitful writing to me has condemned you.

As you unjustly sentenced him, I shall justly sentence you, and your accomplices as well. Farewell.

In the thirteenth-century *Golden Legend* and in *The Healing of Tiberius,* a fantastical story from the eighth century, the scene unfolded rather differently. Tiberius assumed that Jesus was still alive and available to cure him. He sent a "great officer" called Volusianus to Judaea, not to get Pilate, but to ask Pilate to hand Jesus over. Volusianus appeared on Pilate's doorstep, asking to see "this physician, Jesus." This put the governor in a tailspin of fright. This man was no physician, he stammered to Volusianus; he was a troublemaker. In any case, could he have fourteen days' grace?

Volusianus agreed. Pilate used the time to send letters to Tiberius and ply him with presents, trying to persuade him to overlook the awkward fact that he had put Christ to death; but these were all caught in a shipwreck and sent to the bottom of the sea. Meanwhile, Volusianus had learned the truth from Veronica: Pilate had condemned Jesus and killed him. She assured him, however, that her veil had preserved Christ's healing powers. Immediately, Volusianus sent four quaternions of soldiers to arrest Pilate and put him in a cage. He was made to confess, publicly, that Jesus was dead and that it was his fault. Naturally, he tried to put it in the best light. "This man you seek despised the Jews and broke Roman laws; so I found him guilty of grave crimes, and I crucified him. Tell my king that." Or, even oilier, in another version: "Tell Caesar that for his honor and to safeguard his prerogatives, by right judgment and by right sentence, I allowed the Jews to crucify a man called Jesus, who was a magician and made himself a king and put himself up against Caesar." Then the three of them, with the veil laid softly in its cage of gold and Pilate bumping in his cage of iron, set off for Rome.

There was yet a third version of this "send for Pilate" scene, and it was kinder; indeed, too kind. According to the Coptic *Martyrdom of Pilate,* the governor's days in Judaea were numbered. Ever since he had begun to worship Jesus, and ever since he had put Barabbas to death, the Jews had decided that this "foreign Egyptian" had to die too. But because they could not execute him themselves, they decided to bribe the imperial messenger either to let them do it, or to do it for them. The messenger therefore summoned Pilate. The governor advised his wife to take the children and leave town, only making sure that she recovered his body and buried it near the tomb of Jesus, "so that his grace may overtake me." But Procula insisted on staying with him. "It is wrong," she said, "that you should love me more than you love him."

Pilate was taken to the emperor's messenger. "Are you Pilate?" he asked. "Are you the one who said, 'There is no hand over my hand'? However did you kill this Jesus without consulting the emperor first?"

Pilate would not answer him. He merely said: "I am prepared to die for his holy name. I have faith that if I die for his name I shall possess eternal life, and you will not impede me from his glory." He was then stripped, flogged, put in chains and thrown into prison. Procula, her head bare and her clothes disordered (a deeply shaming fate for a woman), was thrown in beside him. The Jews shouted, "Pilate, your life is like his, and your lot is his lot!" Pilate answered, "Amen. My life is with him."

In prison, Jesus visited them. He came down from heaven, bathed in effulgent light, and took them in his arms. Instantly, the fetters they wore flowed away like water, and the column to which they were tied bowed down to the ground. Jesus told Pilate that he would be crucified like him and crowned with thorns like him, but that his enemies would be unable to kill him at the first attempt because he would have to be taken before Tiberius. And that was how it happened. The Jews asked the imperial messenger, in exchange for a huge bribe of silver, to let them crucify Pilate. So he hung on the cross for a while, encouraged by Procula to enter heaven as a martyr and a king, before the crowds decided that it would be better if the messenger took him to Rome instead.

In a second Coptic story, Tiberius' only son was strangled by an evil spirit as he washed himself in the baths. He was buried, and his parents mourned him for three months, until the emperor's wife remembered Pilate's reports of a miracle worker in Judaea. Tiberius wrote to Jesus (whom he knew to have risen from the dead) and sent the boy's bones along in a coffin to be placed in the Holy Sepulchre. Joseph and Nicodemus placed them there and waited for three days; on the fourth day, in a magical weaving of flesh over dry bones, the emperor's son came back to life. Pilate was fetched from prison, bowed to the ground with joy, and went to the tomb to see the boy. The emperor's vizier, who had brought the coffin from Rome, apologized to Pilate, kissed his hand and asked his forgiveness. Then the whole party went off to Rome with the newly risen boy, his skin and hair still delicate and bright, to present the miracle to Tiberius.

When Pilate reached Rome, all these dozens of legends—Coptic, Greek, late Latin, Anglo-Saxon—agree that he was taken prisoner at once. Some say Tiberius did not even bother to see him; he simply asked why he had not yet been executed. But it was undeniably more dramatic to have the quaking governor dragged, bound with fetters of iron, into the emperor's presence. It bothered none of these writers that, historically, Tiberius had died before Pilate arrived in Rome. As the emperor most closely connected with Jesus, he was required to be there.

In the sixth-century Greek *Anaphora* the emperor received Pilate in the Temple of the Gods before all the Senate. He was seated on a throne with his army around him "and all the multitude of his power." The moment he saw Pilate, he screamed out: "How did you dare to do such a thing? You most impious man! How could you do it, when you had seen all those signs and wonders concerning this man! Your wicked daring has destroyed the whole world!"

Pilate, standing before the judgment seat, tried his old excuses. "Emperor, I'm blameless in this. The Jews did it."

"What Jews?"

"Herod Archelaus, Philip, Annas, Caiaphas, and the whole lot of them."

"But why did you give in to them? Why did you obey them?"

"My lord, their whole nation is seditious and rebellious. They do not obey your authority."

"Look," thundered Tiberius, "when they delivered him to you, it was your duty to put him in prison and keep him safe, and to send him carefully to me in the safekeeping of my soldiers! It was *not* your business to take the advice of the Jews and crucify him! This man was righteous! He did all those good works! Why, you admitted it yourself when you wrote the *titulus* for his execution, that this was Christ, the King of the Jews!"

Suddenly, all over the temple, the gods crashed down and were smashed to the floor like powder. They fell, pieces of Apollo's tunic and chunks of Jupiter's beard, at the feet of the emperor and his officers. They had tumbled at the name of Christ. The officers were terror-stricken, seized with involuntary trembling; one by one they left the building and crept to their homes. The emperor ordered Pilate thrown in prison and held for further questioning.

On the next day, Tiberius put up his judgment seat in the Capitol. Again, he convened the Senate and ordered Pilate to appear; again the governor, in chains, took up his defensive stand. "Do you see what happened?" cried Tiberius. "You dared to stretch out your hand over the Son of God, you villain, and now look what your wickedness has done! The gods have fallen, and been ground like dust, and have perished from the earth! Tell me, tell me truly: who was that man who was crucified? His name alone has destroyed all these gods!"

Pilate said: "He is the Son of God. The report I sent you is true. Even I have been convinced that he is greater than the gods we worship."

"Why then did you do those things to him, when you knew he had done nothing against us?"

"Because the Jews made me. That's why I did this to him."

Tiberius exploded with anger. His wrath rose "like smoke from a furnace," and he instantly issued an edict to the governor of the East that the Jews should be enslaved. Pilate was spared for the moment, and sent back to prison. Tiberius had more questions to ask him.

The *Anaphora* did not say what those supplementaries were, but the *Martyrdom of Pilate* provided a gentler line of interrogation. This Pilate, after all, had survived crucifixion; he came to Tiberius in a state of ecstatic weakness, bearing the marks of the nails and the thorns. The emperor asked: "Are you the governor Pilate, who crucified Jesus?"

"Yes. It is I, your servant, who stands before you. As to the crucifixion of Jesus, our living God, the Jews did not listen to me, and Annas and Caiaphas decided judicially on his execution."

Inevitably, constantly, Pilate passed the buck back to the Jews. But Tiberius let that go; he wanted to know what Jesus had looked like, "his image, his portraiture, his picture, his majesty, his beauty." Pilate's answer was mystifying. "Oh Emperor, my lord, he was three days in my court, and I did not see what he looked like. Once I saw that he was the color of fire, and once I saw him like a bird flying to the heights of heaven, where an angel spoke to him."

He told Tiberius under questioning about his wife's dream, about the trial, about the virgin birth and the Annunciation. "How long was he on the earth?" asked the emperor.

"Thirty years, sir."

"And in all that length of time you saw that man, noticed the miracles and prodigies he was performing, and never told me?"

"By your life, my lord Emperor, I never saw him in all that time, and I never saw his face except on the day he was crucified."

"Let's get this straight. They delivered him to you, and you didn't remember his miracles and prodigies. In his presence you felt no awe at all, and even the glory of his divinity did not frighten you. How highhanded can you get? *And why didn't you tell me?*"

Pilate could not answer. Tiberius therefore ordered his soldiers to take him away and kill him: "Now I'll do to you what you did to him." But, according to the *Golden Legend,* Pilate almost managed to escape the emperor's wrath. His buck-passing had made no impression, but he had one last trick almost literally up his sleeve. He had not cheated so hard to get this particular relic for nothing.

When he was summoned before Tiberius for the last time, he put on the seamless garment of Jesus. In some German legends, it was only a scrap of the garment that he put on, like an amulet, underneath his clothes. The effect was the same: Tiberius was disarmed completely. Raging as he was, he became unaccountably gentle; he could not savage the man who stood before him, shining and pure and quiet. Instead, he rose to greet him, without a single harsh word. He sent him away with a smile.

The moment Pilate left, Tiberius was furious again. He stormed up and down the room, swearing and calling himself a wretch for failing to show him the anger in his heart. "Pilate is a son of death!" he screamed. "He cannot possibly be allowed to go on living on this earth! Bring him back here! I'll sentence him to death!"

Once more Pilate came to him. He stepped in softly, like an angel, with the seamless garment a shaft of blue-white light from his shoulders to his feet. Tiberius opened his mouth, but could not speak. Again he greeted him tenderly, and his wrath subsided. Everyone stared at him; no one could understand how Tiberius could be so incensed when Pilate was absent and so gentle with him face-to-face. Then someone—God, or a bystander—gave Pilate's game away. Tiberius screamed for his guards; he made them tear the robe from Pilate's back, or, strip-searching him, pluck out the sacred scrap of cloth from beneath his clothes. Instantly, he saw the truth: before him stood an ordinary criminal.

Pilate's long trail of apocryphal witness was bound to end in scenes like this. The killer of Christ would put on Christ, assume his outward appearance, approximate his sufferings. Pagans, too, as St. Paul told the Ephesians, would share in the body of Christ; the withered thornbush would break out in fragile blossoms of divinity. No hagiographer dared to have Pilate publicly baptized, although in the *Martyrdom of Stephen* he baptized himself privately; there was a limit even to invention. By the same token, no one dared to make Pilate's imitation of Christ completely saintly or completely faithful. In his many apocryphal trials, before the Jewish priests and before Tiberius, he sometimes tried to keep a Christ-like silence before his questioners. But his tendency was to whine and transfer the blame to others; so that when he was slapped and reviled, as Jesus had been slapped and reviled, it seemed no more than his sanctimony deserved.

The most daring approximation of Pilate to Christ was to put him on the cross, as the Copts did; to make him, in the supposed words of Herod's men, "die on the cross like your God Jesus." There was a pleasing, brutal symmetry in this. Pilate would be judged as he himself had judged Christ; he had been scourged as he had scourged Christ; his blood had been shed as he had shed Christ's. In short, as Jesus himself told him in prison, "Everything that has happened to you is for the sole reason that you may be saved from the sin of my death."

Yet even the Copts found this scene almost too hard to stage. Pilate's crucifixion at Herod's behest was a farce, with the governor taken twice to the brink, stripped, decked with a loincloth and flogged, before being put back in prison. When at last he got to Golgotha, and the soldiers were about to raise him on the cross, they suddenly realized that Christ's own cross would make a better gibbet; so they ran to the tomb, lugged it out, unfixed Pilate and nailed him up again. This made him more like Christ but also, by closer comparison, less like him. His prayers on

Christ's cross acknowledged his deep unworthiness of this honor; if the Copts were not embarrassed to put him there, he seemed embarrassed himself. His body was "impure," his blood "carnal"; he had "defiled and polluted" the sacred wood on which Christ had hung. He was a hopeless sinner who did not deserve the outrageous glory of dying on the very cross to which his weakness had sent Christ.

And in the end, that glory eluded him. His pending martyrdom was signaled by the sight of two crowns, one for him and one for Procula, descending from heaven, but this miracle so impressed the crowd that they cut him down before he could die. Instead of finding himself, as Procula had fervently predicted, "lighting your lamp at the wedding of your lord Jesus Christ," Pilate found himself manhandled into a hot bath and back into his clothes, in preparation for a trip to Rome to explain himself to the emperor.

The seamless garment, too, made no saint of Pilate. It was simply a trick, a suit of magic clothes. Just as the mystery plays never made it quite clear why Pilate wanted the garment anyway, so the *Golden Legend* never explained his precise motivation for putting it on when Tiberius summoned him. In the legends where the garment was merely a scrap of material, it was clearly a sort of lucky charm. But to wear the whole garment was much more suggestive than this.

A gnostic document of at least the ninth century, the *Hymn of the Soul,* originally written in Syriac, described the descent of the soul to the earth in terms of leaving behind a wonderful robe "set with gems and spangled with gold . . . which they had made for me because they loved me." The soul, traveling through the world, constantly remembered this garment. When the earthly trials were accomplished the robe suddenly appeared again: and this time, the soul could put it on.

> I stretched forth and received it, and adorned myself with the beauty of
>   the colors of it,
> And in my royal robe excelling in beauty I arrayed myself wholly.
> And when I had put it on, I was lifted up unto the place of peace and
>   homage,
> and I bowed my head and worshiped the brightness of the Father who
>   had sent it to me,
> For I had performed his commandments, and he had fulfilled his
>   promise to me.

This, believers know, is the journey of all souls, from the brightest to the darkest. Even a man who is steeped in sin has described the same trajectory, falling to earth to ascend again; even he has come, in Wordworth's phrase, "trailing clouds of glory." Wordsworth also says, a little earlier, "not in entire forgetfulness." The light of perfect goodness is somehow remembered. Plato, too, constantly emphasized the fall of the soul from the sphere of brightness. If Pilate, like Cato on the night he died, had read his *Phaedo,* he too—even he—would have stumbled across this idea.

The legends took it literally. So Pilate, who is still in the *Golden Legend* an unbeliever and a villain, clothes himself in the grace of Christ. He shines and is perfect; his presence touches others like a blessing. Yet he has no notion why. For just a few moments he is the model of the child at baptism or the initiate touched by heaven; he has put on the ritual white robe, the garment of light. But in his confusion and unbelief, the magic—or the grace—slips away.

III.

The end of the governor's life is simply a mystery. He was probably only middle-aged when he returned to Rome, but his career had been interrupted, and it was not clear in what form he could pick it up again. His "biographers," medieval and modern, provide three possibilities. Assuming he faced no penalty for the Samaritan business, he could have gone into semi-retirement, still in Rome but playing no part in public life. Assuming he was sentenced, he could have been sent into exile, in Italy or abroad. Or he could have chosen the common Roman route, and taken his own life to avoid the disgrace of punishment.

His fate was not without theological implications. If Jesus was God, the theory went, Pilate's end should have been horrible; if he had lived on in comfort, Christ's claims were not to be believed. True gods destroyed their destroyers. This was part of the great debate that took place between Origen and Celsus in 248 over the validity of Christian teaching. Celsus, the pagan, argued that if a man had killed a god, he would certainly suffer for it. What had happened to Pentheus after he had mocked Dionysus, cut off his curls, taken away his ivy wand and cast him into prison to "dance down there in the dark"? First, he saw his palace explode in flames, while Dionysus escaped, sinuously, effortlessly, on tiptoe amid the rubble. Pentheus next did what Pilate would have done: called out the heavy infantry, the fastest cavalry, the mobile squadrons and the archers, to hunt him down. But Dionysus got the better of him even then, persuading him to dress up as a woman to observe the Bacchic rites he was so curious about. In his long dress, dazed by divine hallucinations, Pentheus was torn to pieces on the holy mountain by his mother and his sisters.

Yet Pilate had never suffered, said Celsus: "the men who tortured and punished your God in person . . . suffered nothing afterward as long as they lived." It therefore stood to reason that Christ was not divine. Origen contradicted him, but not to say that Pilate had suffered. He maintained he had never been guilty. It was, he said, the Jews who had killed Christ; and their nation had suffered calamity ever since. Pilate, he implied, had ended his days in peace and in obscurity.

Only one of Pilate's biographers, and a very late one, took up that idea with enthusiasm: Anatole France, in his short story of 1892, "The Procurator of Judaea." His Pilate had been exiled, but merely to Sicily, where he lived happily enough as a farmer with his daughter looking after him. There he grew "the fattest ears of corn in the country." Because gout and obesity afflicted him, he would make his way slowly by litter round the cliffs of the Tyrrhenian coast toward the steaming sulfur springs at Phlegra. Yet he lived well, and his obsessive broodings about his career in Judaea took place over lunches of larks in honey in the shade of terraces of roses. In his old age, he did not miss Rome. Nor, in the most famous line of the story, did he recall the trial that had fixed his place in history. He remembered the various slights of the Jews, yes, and the way they had clung to him and badgered him for favors; he remembered silk dresses, dancing girls. But "Jesus? Jesus of Nazareth? I don't remember him."

Philo and Josephus seemed to endorse this view. Neither mentioned any official condemnation or any violent end. Had there been one, Philo would surely have reveled in it, as he did in the lynching of the prefect Flaccus. Yet among both the early and the later Christians, a comfortable retirement for Pilate was not acceptable. Pilate would have to remember Jesus, the early Fathers fretted; he could not do otherwise. Somehow, he would have to pay the price. It was not good enough to say, with Origen, that he was innocent; everyone knew it was the Romans, not the Jews, who had actually crucified Christ. And the Romans themselves believed that guilty men never escaped justice, even if they were not condemned by human judges. There was a sense of implacable pursuit: "not really by the Furies with blazing torches, as in the tragedies," Cicero said, "but by the anguish of remorse and the torture of a bad conscience." These guilty consciences, as Juvenal wrote, kept them in a lather of fear:

> *The mind's its own best torturer,*
> *lays on with invisible whips, silently flays them alive.*

The guilty man could not eat, Juvenal went on. His throat was dry with fear. He choked on his food, spat out his wine. At night he thrashed in his bed, dreaming of his broken vows to deities and altars, and visited by monstrous images of the men he had injured or defrauded. The slightest headache might be a visitation from the god he had offended. And there was no escaping this, no matter how far and fast he ran away.

Yet even the torment of a guilty conscience was not enough if a man was still in his own bed in his own house. Many legends of Pilate preferred to see him sent away. In *The Healing of Tiberius* the emperor exiled him at once to a place called Ameria, in Tuscany. Pilate was often associated with lakes and ponds that were disturbed or enchanted, and even little Ameria had one of these. Pliny the Younger recalled being shown by his wife's grandfather a peculiar round lake that lay at the foot of the hills outside the village. It was pale blue with a touch of green, smelled of sulfur and was considered sacred because the water healed fractures. There were no boats on this lake because it was holy, but instead green floating islands of reeds and sedge that jostled in the wind continually. Sometimes the islands joined together to look like land; at other times they scattered; at times they were so firm, apparently, that cattle wandered out onto them as if on solid land, but at others they drifted, with the animals bucking in terror.

Ameria was disturbing, but it was neither very nasty nor very far. So a persistent tradition, found in the *Golden Legend* and in medieval manuscripts scattered all through Europe, said that Pilate was exiled to Vienne, in southern Gaul on the edge of the Alps. For once, the story was not implausible. The mountain regions of Gaul were just right, Romans thought, for troublemakers from Palestine. Herod Antipas, who had been deprived of his tetrarchy by Gaius not long after Pilate's disgrace, was sent to Lyons with his equally troublesome wife; Archelaus, his half-brother, was exiled to Vienne itself. This town, it was said, drew its name from via Gehennae, the road to hell; Gehenna itself had been the name of the giant public rubbish pit in Jerusalem which Pilate, in better times, could have watched with its web of smoldering fires from the windows of his palace.

Vienne was not quite the end of the world. There were quasi-Roman buildings and bookshops there in which, according to Seneca, Caesar's works were recited. Horace dreamed that after his death he would fly over such barbarian outposts as a swan, and that even "those who drink the waters of the Rhone" would come to read his poems. Among the Roman ruins that remain, several are said to be Pilate's, including a building that locals call his *praetorium,* and a peculiar four-sided pyramid on a base of four arches, eighty feet high, that some suppose to be his tomb. The Rhone itself has tales to tell, but that is to run ahead of the story.

One Latin verse romance of the fourteenth century, traced to Vienne, put Pilate instead in Lausanne, just over the border of modern Switzerland. There his enemies consigned him to a deep, dark well that was to be his prison for at least twelve years. They delighted to think of him sweating there, loaded with chains, his hair a mess and his "pretty feet" crippled and sunk in mud. In the dark he sobbed continually, for he could not escape. Nonetheless, in his more lucid moments he admitted that it was "reasonable" that he should be among the rats, "for the damnable false judgment I made, against truth and God's goodness."

Between Lausanne and Vienne, eventually, he got out and wandered. His story was now in the realm of folklore. In villages and valleys all over Europe people made up his fate, imagined they saw him, linked his name with mountains and pools and bad weather. They still do. Very little of this was written down until, in the late nineteenth and early twentieth centuries, the folklorists made their collections. It passed instead into children's songs and shepherds' superstitions. And behind it all lay the medieval conviction that Pilate could not stay still. He was condemned to the deathless life of those who had taunted God, like the Wild Huntsman, doomed evermore to chase red deer because he had preferred this to praying; like the Man in the Moon, doomed to wander the sky eternally because he had gathered sticks on a Sunday; or like the captain of the

Phantom Ship, who, insisting on doubling the Cape whether God willed it or not, plowed the great seas forever in a vessel festooned with ice.

In the folklore of Europe, every living thing involved in the Passion was made to suffer afterward. The evergreen oak, because it did not resist being made into the cross, became a cursed tree that stained red the axes of anyone who cut it; the once-towering mistletoe, also used for the cross, became a shriveled bundle of parasitic twigs. As for Pilate, some thought he had been branded, literally marked on his forehead with the mark of the beast. His branding burned him; it stayed raw, like a plague sore. People fled away from it, and it forced him to wander through the world in an effort to slough off his pain.

Some men imagined he saw Christ before him all the time, or the shadow of the cross on his path; he could never sleep, never blot out these things. Perhaps he wandered where the broom grew; that, too, was cursed, because it had revealed the whereabouts of Christ in the garden by cracking and spitting out its seeds. Or he caught his robes among brambles, condemned to bear black berries and leaves smeared with red because they had consented to be part of the crown of thorns.

After years of wandering he took to the mountains and, men assumed, lived there in solitary huts in the wilderness. In 1552 Felix Platter passed by one such house on the outskirts of Saint-Vallier in the Dauphiné, "Pilate's house," halfway up a grim hillside, and noted that the governor had lived there "in misery." All over Alpine Europe, peculiar ruins and abandoned houses were given a demonic charge with the claim that Pilate had lived there. He was not imagined as old, for his age had been frozen at the date of the Crucifixion; but he sat there in his toga consumed by guilt and harried by devils, in the midst of the gray woods.

Were there any facts at the base of all this fantasy? It is possible that he was exiled. If his trial took place and he was found guilty, exile was the usual punishment for erring provincial governors. It was mercifully short of death, but its pain was not to be underestimated. A man who was exiled was no longer a Roman citizen; once interdicted "by fire and water," as the formula went, he could no longer wear the toga, and he was presumed to belong only to the provincial outpost where he lived. Unless he was merely *relegatus,* "relegated," as the poet Ovid was in A.D. 8, he also lost his property. And, not least, he lost the City.

Ovid described in graphic terms the misery of leaving Rome. In his grief he forgot to shave or comb his hair, and he was too dazed to choose which clothes or which slaves (a Roman's order of priorities) to take with him. He kept forgetting things, finding hopeless excuses to go back just one more time into his house. Friends put their arms around his shoulders and wept, but he himself felt dead, "as if I was being carried for burial without a funeral." Flaccus, exiled to Andros, used almost the same words: "It's as though I am carrying the corpse that is myself to the sepulchre." Ovid realized that the numbness that held his limbs, paralyzing them as if they had been severed from his body, was his love of his country.

Pilate, too, would have felt this pain. It went with sharp social humiliation: the word *exul* was used as a term of abuse in the Senate, and any contact with friends from home was usually forbidden. On their side, friends were forbidden even to mention the man who had been sent away. For someone who had once been important, the loss of prestige was disabling. According to Philo, Flaccus on Andros used to pace up and down, slap his thighs and clap his hands as if he were going mad; he would cry out, "I'm Flaccus, the recent governor of Alexandria! Ruler of the blessed land of Egypt! Thousands of people respected me! I had infantry, cavalry, naval officers, men of excellence, and crowds of followers escorted me whenever I went out! Was this a phantom, then, and not the truth? Was I asleep, and just dreaming the light-heartedness of those days? Yes, I must have been. . . ."

Ovid makes a sadder and more sober witness. Since the time of Augustus, exiles had been forbidden to go to pleasant places, such as the Greek islands; they were sent to the fringes of the empire, among barbarians with plaited hair and trousers. Ovid himself was sent to Tomis, the modern Constansa, on the western shore of the Black Sea. The place was rocky, almost treeless, and bitterly cold in winter; so cold, he wrote, that the beards of the natives tinkled with ice. Few people spoke Greek, fewer Latin; the beautiful language grew rusty with disuse. Ovid described how, rather than lose the habit of it, he would talk to himself. When he ventured out among the barbarians, past the guard at his gate, he could tell he was being talked about and laughed at; he would defend himself by nodding at them, pretending to understand their language. This fooled no one. Human contact with the natives was almost impossible, and homesickness only grew worse with time. He began to envy Ulysses for eating the lotuses that had made him forget his country: "If only those were on offer," he wrote, "I would give half my life to buy them."

Love of Rome, where his wife still was, tormented him. He imagined himself walking the streets, climbing the steps to the temples, taking down book rolls in the libraries. Lingering like a ghost by the house of Augustus, he could touch the garlands of oak leaves hanging over the door. In his dreams he saw the city below him, "now the *fora,* now the temples, now the theaters sheathed in marble, now every portico with its leveled ground, now the green expanse of the Campus that looks toward the lovely gardens, the pools, the canals . . ." By day he gazed constantly on a medallion of Augustus, Livia and Tiberius that a friend had given him, trying by sheer willpower to make their expressions change from severity to mercy. In words that Pilate would have felt the force of, he explained the holy charge of these images: they were "my eagles, my standards."

Ovid was never to return to Rome. For any Roman, that was punishment enough; but the medieval writers had one last horror for God to inflict on Pilate. He had to die violently.

In one account, after the episode of the seamless garment, Tiberius ordered Pilate to be shut up in a cave while he consulted all the princes and people of the city to decide what should be done with him. As Pilate sat there, the emperor rode out to the hunt through the greenwood, in boots and pointed hat, with his hounds baying at his heels. An old law held that if a condemned man looked on the emperor's face, he would be spared; so Pilate craned his head out from his prison, trying to see him. At the same moment, Tiberius took aim at a hind; but the arrow missed, and tore instead through the window of Pilate's cave. It killed him instantly.

Only one other tradition, the Coptic, had Pilate dying by the violence of other people. In the *Anaphora of Pilate,* Tiberius—not content with Pilate's demi-crucifixion by Herod—decided to crucify him again, and then, for good measure, to behead him for the crime of deicide. In the midst of his torments Pilate asked the soldiers for a respite so that he could pray. He turned toward the east, knelt down and said: "Oh my Lord Jesus Christ who took away the sins of the world, have pity on your servant Pilate and forgive all my stumblings, omissions and sins. . . . I have indeed dared to judge you, just Judge, but do not rebuke me for this sin I have committed, because you are a merciful and compassionate God, and I am a created being, and I dared to say to you, 'Who are you?' "

He asked mercy too for Procula, who was standing beside him: "Pardon us and number us among thy righteous ones." A voice from heaven then reassured him: "All the generations and families of the Gentiles shall call thee blessed, because in thy days were fulfilled all the things which were spoken by the prophet concerning me." Then the executioner cut off Pilate's head, and an angel received it. At the sight of the angel, Procula, overwhelmed with joy, died instantly. It was the fifteenth of June by the old Syriac calendar, the twenty-fifth of June by the new, when Pilate was beheaded. He was laid in the tomb of Jesus, as he had requested, together with the bodies of Procula and their two children, who happened to have died the same day.

The western tradition had no time for such sentimental stuff; it was determined to pile up heaven's vengeance on the governor's head. In the *Golden Legend,* Tiberius ordered Pilate to die by "the basest of deaths," but Pilate forestalled him by committing suicide. ("So, he *did* die by the basest of deaths," the emperor remarked, "since his own hand did not spare him.") Almost all the medieval writers believed that Pilate had died this way, within a few years of his return from Judaea: usually in Rome, occasionally in Vienne in a tower by the Lyons gate, where he had shut himself up to die, and sometimes in the Alpine wilderness. The German Pilate, wandering in that wilderness, came to a pool of marshy brackish water among the pine woods southwest of Lucerne. It must have been the wintertime, for in summer the little lake dried up entirely. He waded out into it, his robes growing heavier, and plunged in like a swimmer. The waters closed over him.

For the early Church Fathers, suicide seemed the only possible end to Pilate's career. "He fell into such misfortunes under Gaius," wrote Eusebius, "that he became by necessity his own murderer and his own executioner; apparently, divine justice didn't spare him long." Eusebius confidently dated his suicide to the third year of Gaius, sometime between March 39 and March 40.

That end was not implausible. Under Tiberius' reign of terror in the early 30s, a mere charge of wrongdoing—even before the trial and sentence—was often enough to make a man retire to his house and there, with pocket knife or poison, try to put himself away. If he was guilty, the gesture was more or less expected. Pliny the Elder recorded a case very close to Pilate's, of a knight recalled by Tiberius from his deputy governorship for maladministration. "In his extreme despair," he wrote— "summa desperatione"—"he swallowed a dose of leek-juice weighing three denarii in silver, and immediately expired without suffering any pain."

No particular stigma was attached to suicide. On the contrary, Cicero called it the noblest of deaths, "the course best adapted to the retention of honor and escape from unendurable sufferings." Horace called it "dying bravely"; Martial recalled his friend Festus, who "closed his sacred life by a Roman's death." The means were known and discussed: cantharides, hemlock, shoemaker's vitriol, the opening of a vein in the wrist, simple self-starvation. Almost no sentimental or patriotic story was complete without the moment when a man put his breast to the sword and, like a lover, leaned on it. The scenes would have been well known to Pilate: the moment when Scipio, in charge of the fleet off Africa and striving to avoid capture, fell on his sword but insisted on a final message to his men, "All is well with the commander!" "Imperator se bene habet!" Or the moment when Gaius Fufius Geminus, accused of *maiestas* against Tiberius in 30, mortally wounded himself before his executioner arrived and, when the quaestor came to the door, showed him the welling blood with the words: "Report to the Senate that this is how a man dies."

Suicide was often a sacrifice that was performed for the sake of others. A man who was exiled could make no will, and those convicted of crimes might leave their families destitute unless they killed themselves. Those who committed suicide had their wishes honored, and their family's reputation was unaffected. (Dio noted that, under Tiberius, most of those who killed themselves left something in their wills to the emperor who had driven them to suicide.) They could also be cremated with full rites, which was crucial. The act was not interpreted first as one of despair, but of calculated courage. Stoics invoked it to show how innocuous death was, how unimportant the dissolution of the body: "not quite such a small matter as whether your hair should be worn evenly or unevenly," as Seneca wrote, but almost. Nor was it necessarily a sign of anomie or belief in nothing. Many suicides doubtless believed they were going into

blackness; but Cato fell on his sword only when he had convinced himself of the immortality of the soul and the prospect of heaven.

So in the popular imagination Pilate, disgraced even if unsentenced,
hounded by his demons, went into his room and shut the door. He lay
down on the couch, not troubling this time to remove his shoes. The Pilate of Kazantzakis' novel *The Last Temptation of Christ* had always worn a
sharpened razor, on a golden chain around his neck, for just this purpose:
for the moment when he became weary of eating, drinking or governing,
or when the emperor exiled him. He had called it, with a laugh, "my
Messiah, my liberator." But perhaps it was with a little knife, as the medieval writers thought, that he nicked open the blue vein in his wrist.
The pain was sharp, then quiet. As he let his arm sink toward the floor,
he felt both faint and warm. The last salutation to the dead would have
crossed his mind: *Aeternum vale,* good-bye forever. Among the images before his eyes may have been some from Judaea: but whether they were of
hills, girls, crosses or temples, nobody knows. All men imagine is that he
was alone, with no one to close his eyes or, in the Roman custom, brush
his lips with theirs to take in his last breath. And then he went abruptly
into the dark.

R AOUL AND HECTOR trudged to the lake, found a flat rock
and collapsed on it. They were not dressed for mountaineering.
The summer of 1868 was hot, and they were wearing the gear
they had bought, more or less as a joke, as they left Paris: silk hats, wide
trousers, high-fashion tunics *à la Garibaldi,* riding coats, silk cravats. As a
precaution each also carried a woollen cape, a metal-tipped umbrella and a
haversack with blister tincture, lip salve, a first-aid manual, several handkerchiefs and two spare pairs of slippers. Now they sweated, and waited.

On another part of the mountain a plump middle-aged woman in
black crepe and a black bonnet labored upward on a small English pony.
Behind her came the Princess Louise, the Prince Arthur, a lady-in-
waiting and several Highland attendants, one of whom carried the royal
box of watercolors. The whole party was traveling incognito. A list of
false names—the Countess of Kent, Lady Louise Kent, Lieutenant the

Hon. Arthur Kent R.E., the Marchioness of Ely—had been inscribed in
the visitors' book at the Bellevue Hotel. Prince Arthur set the pace on
foot, outdoing the guide and no doubt finding the view "inexpressible
grand," as did the panting hack from the *Illustrated London News*. But the
royal party did not stay till the evening, when "the sun . . . colours the
whole of the snowy peaks with molten gold"; they went down again in
the daylight, with Arthur dreaming of dinner.

The trek up Mount Pilatus had become a favorite day trip from
Lucerne, almost too organized and comfortable and often too crowded.
Tourists started on the bridle-path at Hergiswyl and walked for three
and a half hours to the Klimsenhorn Hotel, through meadows and orchards and then up a zigzagging path through pine woods. At the Klimsenhorn the path got steeper, still twisting, until it turned into fifty-two
steps through a chimney of rock, at the top of which unfolded a sweeping panorama of the Bernese Alps. For any of these sections, though less
successfully for the steps, mules could be hired. The paths had been
widened by many boots, and difficult traverses had been fitted with iron
railings. In later years the faint-hearted could take Colonel Locher's cog-
wheel railway from the Pilatus Hotel right up to the Bellevue, which by
then had been superseded by a better establishment with first- and
second-class dining rooms. Twenty-five francs would take you in the
single-coach train, at a maximum speed of eight miles an hour, from watering station to pumping station with occasional views of the gorges;
and at the top it would buy you dinner, a room and breakfast, while the
glowing Alps spread out below the terrace. As Baedeker commented, the
journey presented "no danger even to novices."

Tourists on Mount Pilatus therefore had to make excitements of their
own. Wagner walked there in 1859, the third act of *Tristan* running in
his head, dragging along a friend who was almost sick with vertigo.
Raoul and Hector, the Paris students, made bets about blisters. The hack
from the *News* hoped for a royal stumble, his own exclusive on the plump
ball of black crepe rolling down the hillside. None of these had laid wa-
gers on whether or not they would see Pilate. Yet that, for many
nineteenth-century visitors, was the underlying thrill of the climb. At
any bend of the path, behind any of the steeply serrated crags of the
mountain, and especially near the marshy little lake known as the Pila-
tusee where Raoul and Hector now sat, the governor might suddenly appear. Raoul and Hector's guide told them that he materialized each

Friday, when he paced around the lake with a notebook, taking down the names of visitors to pass them on to the Devil.

The lake itself was nothing much to see. According to the official history of Pilatus, published in 1913, it was just "a gloomy puddle" surrounded by a mighty forest. But any change of weather on this temperamental mountain—a sudden squall, a descent of cloud—was attributed by the superstitious to Pilate's temper; and even the gloomy thoughts of Queen Victoria, her widow's visions of Albert in just such a Gothic setting of rocks and forest light, might have been interrupted by a man in a toga washing his hands.

Some scraps of folklore suggested that Pilate had come here alive. More often, it was supposed to be the place where his spirit had reached the end of its wanderings. It was too easy to send Pilate directly to hell, though one thirteenth-century life of Judas confidently reported that he was being tortured there (together with Judas, Annas, Herod and Caiaphas) every day and night except Sundays, the Christmas season, the Easter season and the feasts of Our Lady. Like all malevolent spirits, he clearly had more walking on the earth to do.

After Pilate's suicide in Rome, according to the *Golden Legend,* the emperor ordered a millstone to be hung around the "evil and sordid" body and the body to be thrown in the Tiber. But it was seized immediately by devils who made the air and water seethe, whipped up storms, lashed the city with hail and made the river flood. An oracle was consulted; it said the storms would continue as long as Pilate's body stayed in the river. But no one dared to fish it out. In the end a condemned man was sent in, fastened to the bank for safety with a long rope. As he went under the surface the rope jerked fantastically, as if hooked to a fighting fish; it took twenty men to hold it. At last the water quietened, the jerks could not be felt, and the men hauled in the body of the diver clamped to the dead Pilate's neck. The struggle had been terrible.

The brave diver was given a state funeral, but the body of Pilate clearly had to be burned. It was taken to Vesuvius and thrown into the crater, in the hope that it would roast slowly while waiting for the Day of Judgment. Instead, the mountain almost exploded. The earth shook, lava poured out, and the cities of Pompeii and Herculaneum were buried under ash. Again the oracle was consulted; again it answered, "It's Pilate." "The bastard!" cried the Romans. "How can we get rid of him?"

In the city's prison lay a Christian, waiting to be eaten by the lions. They ordered him to fetch Pilate out of the volcano. The man agreed, as long as all the other Christians in the prison were spared; the deal done, he set off for Vesuvius. At the edge of the crater, black and red and hissing with fire, he met the Devil.

"You want to go down there?" the Devil asked.

"Yes, I do," the saint replied.

"You won't come up again."

"God is with me."

"If you go down there, you'll belong to me."

"Get lost! You keep my body, God gets my soul."

He climbed down. But Vesuvius was one of the gateways to hell, and the Devil reserved the right to refuse to release anyone who went in. He allowed the Christian to go down in search of Pilate and bring him to the surface, but then he decided not to let the theft go unavenged; instead, grabbing the Christian from behind, he dragged him down into the whirlpool of fire.

Pilate, or rather his body, was found the next day on the flanks of the volcano. The people decided to send him to Gaul, and either threw him into the Rhone at Vienne ("another river that has no bottom, but goes down directly to hell") or buried him near Lausanne. Once again the devils descended with a clatter of leathery wings, shrieking and spitting. They whipped up great whirlpools that sucked ships down, and racked the land with storms. Because there was no oracle at Lausanne, the locals put up with this for a hundred years until, one day, they decided they could do so no longer. One local legend says they sent a boat without oars, but filled with relics of the saints, to still the whirlpool in the river; then, when the water was calm, they sent down a diving machine to search the bottom for Pilate. When he was found they threw him into a flaming pit somewhere in the Alps, "where the devils were delighted to get their man back."

Another local folktale says that the people of Lausanne tolerated Pilate until, after many years, the Wandering Jew came past. He knew Pilate of old. Matthew Paris, in his *Chronica Majora* of about 1260, said that the Jew had been a porter in Pilate's service in the *praetorium* during the trial. As Jesus had stumbled out of the door, he had urged him to go faster. In return for his scorn then, Jesus had condemned him to wander the world until the Second Coming. The Jew, called Cartaphilas, had long since repented; he had been baptized and spent most of his time in Armenia and the east, telling and retelling his stories of the Passion. In a later German version of the fable his name was Ahasverus, and he was spotted in the fifteenth and sixteenth centuries in most of the countries of Europe. He was tall, with an unkempt beard and hair reaching past his shoulders; even in winter he went barefoot, wearing an old belted coat that trailed on the ground. This apparation now offered to rid Lausanne of its plague.

Without a tremor, he stepped into the Rhone and plunged until his long coat, beard and hair had disappeared under the water. When he resurfaced, Pilate was with him. The governor clung to him and let himself be carried, piggyback, all over the world as the Jew wandered. Yet the odd pairing could not last. The Jew grew weary, and wanted to be carried himself. But Pilate was dead, and could not oblige him. One day, as they toiled up a mountain called Fracmont in the Alps, the Wandering Jew took a detour to a marshy little lake among the pine trees and tipped Pilate in.

Most people took this as the end of the journey. Yet all over southern Germany and Alpine Europe villages laid claim to the body of Pilate. If there was any pool, any lake, any well with a disturbing feel to it, this sense of menace was attributed to the governor. Pilate's ghost was seen in the Bavona valley, in the canton of Tessin and in Lake Joch on the Vigilijoch, four hours from Merano, where he fought with a count who lay drowned beside him. It was seen in the bottomless lake at Norcia in the Apennines, to which his body had been taken on an oxcart, and where necromancers still resorted, even in the nineteenth century, to have their books of magic consecrated. On the island of Amrum in the North Sea, the words "Pilate is dead" became a charm to keep bad luck away, and Cornishmen thought his body had been put on a fishing boat and cast adrift for the devils to lay claim to.

Other places saw him, too. Every year, around New Year's Eve, a not-unfriendly-looking man could be found traveling from Aargau to the Rhine. People said it was either the Wandering Jew or Pilate. In Lake Piller he could be heard howling for the whole of Holy Week; in Tiersee, near Kufstein, he took the shape of a roaring bull; on the mountain called Septimer he went on fighting with Herod, and in the Saarland he could be heard at night, crying "I am innocent of the blood of this just man." It was a muffled cry, people said, because he had been buried both deep and facedown; but from time to time it boomed like a foghorn, and from this the old folk of Ehsten said that Pilate had turned into a bittern, the hidden and booming bird of the empty marshlands. The bittern seemed an appropriate guise for history's Great Equivocator, "skulking, solitary and usually crepuscular," as one observer described it; a bird that flew with reluctant, dragging wings and, when it tried to hide itself, blended with the dead reeds and sometimes swayed with them.

It was clear why Pilate could not rest. He was still stained with the blood of Christ, and could not get it off; he would have to go on journeying, struggling and shouting until the hand of mercy was extended to him. In Bulgakov's *The Master and Margarita* it was the Master, the man who had invented Pilate in his novel, who alone had the power to free the governor from the burden of guilt he had placed on his shoulders. On a high mountain ledge he found him, wringing his hands and gazing at the moon, his great dog at his feet. Pilate still had something to say to Jesus; he longed to walk along that path of light with him, as he had done long ago in his dreams. So the Master released him, shouting the words "You are free! Free! He is waiting for you!" It was the moment of redemption. Half-laughing, half-crying, his dog bounding in front of him, Pilate stumbled into the light of the love of Christ.

Yet mercy was not always so certain. In medieval England Pilate was seen as a ghost knight, riding with Herod and Judas through a landscape of unrelenting winter. Walter de la Mare in his poem "The Three Traitors" described them traveling by moonlight, silvered and "shining like hoarfrost," in search of Jesus, who could wash them clean. When day broke, the sun-Christ might indeed shine on them, and they might feel his mercy laid over them like fresh clothes; but their journey had not ended. They were bound to wander on.

> *Babe of the Blessed Trinity*
> *Shall smile their steeds to see:*
> *Herod and Pilate riding by,*
> *And Judas one of three.*

Of all the sites of Pilate's wanderings, none was more haunted than the mountain of Fracmont above Lucerne. From at least the fourteenth century it was called Pilatus, apparently after him. As soon as Pilate's body arrived there, the mountain became a fearsome abode of hail and storms. People in Lucerne began to watch the peak, noting whether the clouds that drifted over it were bunched like Pilate's hat, or long like his sword. A hat meant fair weather, a bare head meant rain; but on a day of sword-clouds, no one would venture up the mountain. Some discounted the ghost, of course. They pointed out that "Pilatus" could well have come from *pileatus,* "capped with clouds." But the shepherds on the higher slopes did not believe that. Their flocks were disturbed and skittish, and if men threw stones into the little lake they stirred up horrors: whirl-pools, black vapors, foul smells, and devils that left the scrape-marks of their hooves in the rocks beside the water.

Every year, at noon on Good Friday, they claimed to see Pilate in his judge's robes of scarlet or purple, sitting on a throne of massive stones or in a purple armchair in the middle of the lake in which the devils had placed him. Man and throne would rise out of the water and, as they rose, Pilate would slowly and solemnly go through the motions of washing his hands. He would look only at his hands, not at any bystanders; and having stayed a little while, he would sink again below the surface of the lake. Anyone who saw him died within the year.

He had to be exorcised, but who would dare? The mountain was so cursed that the burghers of Lucerne forbade people to climb it under pain of fine. If a man had to climb it out of necessity, and needed to approach the lake, he had to be accompanied by a burgher of probity who would see that he did nothing to disturb Pilate's peace. Nothing at all—no stone, or fruit, or plant, or even gold coins—could be thrown into the lake. Some adventurers were executed for disobeying this law; and in 1307 six priests were put in prison for daring to climb the mountain by themselves, without a burgher or a license.

The good citizens of Lucerne continued to look for a man in a state of grace who could rid the mountain of Pilate. At last, around the end of the fifteenth century, they seemed to have found one. By some accounts, he was a Rosicrucian recently returned from Palestine; by others, he was a Spanish scholar who volunteered to put Pilate in a Christian frame of mind. Accordingly he set off up the mountain, completely alone. Torrents and huge chasms blocked his way, but when he made the sign of the cross, magical viaducts appeared across the gorges. He walked over them, and with each step the viaducts dissolved into the mist behind him. Confident of divine protection, he came at last to the edge of Pilate's pool.

Here a terrifying vision reared up before him. Pilate, who had gone on growing after death, was now the height of the tallest tower in Lucerne. He was in full Roman military dress of breastplate, helmet, kilt and nailed boots, and he shook a whole pine tree in his fist. But the Christian, unafraid, engaged him in a tremendous contest that rocked the mountain like a boat on the sea. For thirty-six hours the battle raged, until a great thump ended it. There was silence, followed only by heavy breathing. Down in the valley, the terrified folk of Lucerne laid bets on the winner. It was the Christian, who had teased and harried the giant shadow until he had floored him.

Yet Pilate was dead already, of course. The new defeat winded him, but could not kill him, and so the ghost and the Christian came to terms. The Christian produced from his pocket a fragment of the True Cross, and made Pilate swear that he would stay quietly in his pool all the days of the week except Fridays. On Fridays he could roam through the mountains, and the people of Lucerne would leave him alone. Pilate agreed, and laid his ghostly fingers on the splinter of wood from the cross he had ordered for Christ.

Relieved and exhausted, the Christian went back down the mountain. In the town he found a notary to draw up the official contract between the town and Pilate, and the deed was done. But in one version of the story, the notary was suspicious of the man who came to his office. He imposed such heavy conditions for calming Pilate that the notary felt he could not record them. "Not if you were the Devil himself," he told him.

"Better put your gloves on to deal with people like that," snapped his visitor.

It was Satan.

"All right," he told the notary, "I'll tear that agreement up. Here's another. Pilate keeps one day a week to wander in the mountains."

"Fine. Friday."

"Friday. But on that day, everyone is expressly forbidden to go up there."

"Fine again."

"Sign."

"Sign what?"

"This paper."

"But what about everyone who'll go up there on a Friday? Pilate will get them and give them to you."

"Right! Then you forbid people to go up there!"

The notary scratched his ear.

"I'm sure they'll choose exactly that day to see him."

"A thousand cauldrons!" cried the Devil. "If I hadn't been sure of that I'd never have made this deal."

"Bah! Too bad, I'll sign it," said the notary. "Those who go up on Friday will die the same year without being in a state of grace."

"Done," said the Devil.

After the agreement, Pilate was quiet. Matters unfolded as the notary had predicted. English tourists in particular made a point of climbing the mountain on Fridays to watch His Majesty Pontius Pilate promenading with his notebook. Those who survived crawled back maimed or wounded, and they all died within the year. So the mountain was calmed, but it was not exorcised.

In 1518, a year after Holbein had used the mountain as a background to one of his paintings, four wise men decided to test the truth of the legend. Having obtained the necessary permissions from the notary and the burghers of Lucerne, they began the long climb up Pilatus—on a Friday. Their nicknames showed their seriousness; they were drawn from a study-bound world of encyclopedias, metal-rimmed spectacles and armillary spheres, in which strange phenomena, like botanical specimens, could be pinned down and explained. "Vadianus" of St. Gallen, otherwise known as Joachim von Watt, led the expedition. He had been a professor at Vienna, where he had taken a degree in medicine. Accompanying him were "Xylotectus" of Lucerne, otherwise known as Zimmerman, "a learned and well-bred ecclesiastic"; "Myconius" of Lucerne, otherwise known as Genshaussler, an "erudite and open-hearted" man; and Grebel of Zurich, "a young man of remarkably fine character." They went in a spirit of scientific enquiry, but they could not quite manage to be open-minded; for once on the mountain, strange fears began to assail them. Behind their bravely rational and humanist front, they were still men of the Middle Ages, and their climb became a metaphor for the struggle of Renaissance Europe to get past old ghosts.

They climbed in August. Half the route could be covered on horseback, but the riding was rough and finally impossible. Vadianus reported that they scrambled up a narrow path and over broken ground, guided by a shepherd. At last they came to Pilate's little lake, overgrown and still, with the reeds barely sighing. There seemed to be neither inflow nor outflow, and winds could not reach it; the sky was not reflected in the surface of the water. Vadianus was deeply struck by it, and even more so by the terror of his shepherd-guide, who "practically made us bind ourselves by an oath" not to perform experiments on the lake, nor to throw anything into it. His life was in danger, he kept saying. They must all be careful, they must be reverent and quiet; they should tread as if they were on holy ground. This disturbed Vadianus: it made him "almost pay a certain respect to the reputation of the place, though of course there is not a word of truth in the story which some have imagined concerning Pilate . . . it's utter nonsense."

Yet barely a paragraph on he changed his mind. "I cannot say whether or not things are as the local inhabitants say they are," he wrote,

> because I was not allowed to carry out experiments; and even if I had been allowed, I could not have done so without great danger. Nonetheless, I am moved to accept most of their stories in view of the marvels of nature which are established by the authority of many observers. . . . Not to mention that the character—and more particularly the lie—of the place seemed to me to correspond readily enough with the story that is told about it.

In this mood he went back down the mountain. In order to lay the ghost, the party took two hours over dinner at the hostelry halfway to Lucerne; they did not get back into town until after sunset. Yet in years to come Vadanius changed his mind again. "I have ascertained from persons I can believe," wrote a man who followed him up Pilatus, "that he subsequently got rid of his doubts and recognized that his whole story was a superstitious legend."

The man who followed him was Conrad Gesner, and he wrote with feeling. He considered himself not only a man of reason, but a scholar who loved mountains and refused to believe anything bad of them. "My-

conius" of Lucerne, one of the party that went up Pilatus in 1518, had
been his teacher. But Gesner's approach to mountains was new. They
were no longer a necessary evil, something to be climbed if you could not
avoid it; they were, on the contrary, thrilling and enchanting. He had resolved, he told a friend, "as long as God suffers me to live . . . to climb
one mountain every year, at the season when the vegetation is the best,
partly for the sake of studying botany, and partly for the delight of the
mind and the proper exercise of the body." He added, "The mind is
strangely excited by the amazing altitude. . . ."

But not toward imaginings of ghosts. Gesner's account of his trip up
Pilatus, published in 1555, was as sunny and invigorating as all his others. In passing, he mentioned the irritating necessity of taking a guide
"because of the superstitions of the natives about people approaching the
marsh of Pilate"; but he made something good even of this annoyance,
getting the man to carry the party's wine. They started the trip with a
night in a hayloft, the best bed of all, according to Gesner: soft and fragrant, "compounded of the most wholesome grasses and flowers." After
breakfast of milk and cheese, they climbed beside a cold stream swarming with fat trout and crayfish. Gesner looked for chamois and mountain
goats, spotted white ptarmigan; in a tiny cave he found an icy spring, in
which they dipped bread. He exulted in the warmth of exercise, the
shapes of the crags, the soft grass under his feet. Even in the grass he saw
wonders, "herbs that have a sweeter smell and a greater power of healing
in the mountains than in the plain." At the summit he noted that he
could see "without let or hindrance, the rising and setting of the stars."

He refused to be alarmed by the thought of Pilate. When he approached the lake at last, he had fortified himself with a draft of "rich but
delicate milk," his favorite drink, and had tooted a few deep notes on an
Alpine horn. The party passed a rock on which Pilate was sometimes
supposed to sit, conjuring up storms. Gesner observed with interest "letters carved upon it—the names of climbers who had been there, with
their dates, and their family crests." No other comment. Of the lake, he
remarked that it was more like a marsh, and so small that a dozen people
could barely stand in it. As for the ghost,

> This belief, having no *raison d'être* in the laws of nature, commands no cre-
> dence from me. . . . I am inclined to believe that Pilate has never been

here at all, and that even if he had been here he would not have been accorded the power of either helping or hurting human kind.

If evil spirits accomplish evil deeds, one must not assume that they are privileged to do so, but rather that the Lord God allows it. . . . If there is any sorcery in the lake it is not the work of Nature, but of some evil spirit, whether you call that evil spirit Pilate or by some other name. The whole earth, in fact, is full of evil spirits. . . . But if a man confronts them in a truly pious and believing frame of mind . . . he will assuredly remain tranquil and unharmed.

This report seemed to mark the final exorcism of Pilate, but the work was still not done. Gesner, for all his blitheness, still had his evil spirits, and even after his comforting report the mountain terrified people. In 1585 the pastor of Lucerne, John Muller, felt obliged to make the ascent to prove once again the harmlessness of the story. Before a crowd of witnesses he threw stones and rubbish into the pool, shouting, "Pilate, come out of your den!" "Pilat, wirf aus dein Kath!" There was no answer. After that, witnesses were not needed again; the pastor climbed by himself once a year, threw in his customary pebble, and came down again. It was, as Francis Grebble wrote in *The Early Mountaineers* in 1899, "as though men wished to mark with a solemn and appropriate ceremony the end of the dark ages of superstition and the beginning of the reign of reason and the scientific spirit."

Yet even Pastor Muller's bold defiance of Pilate had not left the mountain calm. In 1649 the prefect of Lucerne, out watching the night sky, saw a bright dragon come out of a cave on Pilatus. It was large, with a long tail and extended neck; its head "terminated in the serrated jaw of a serpent" and it flew about with swift flapping wings, "throwing out sparks like a red-hot horseshoe hammered by a blacksmith." The prefect wanted to be scientific about this. He said he thought at first it was a meteor, "but then after careful observation I recognized it was a dragon, from the nature of its movements and the structure of its various limbs."

I thought it was a meteor, but I recognized it was a dragon. The real Pilate, too, had seemed torn in just this way, between rationalism and superstition. It was ironic that his ghost became a test case of the longevity of legends and the persuasive power of science. In the end, inevitably, the scientists won. The little lake became no more than a curiosity. But there were times even in the nineteenth century when shepherds and climbers out late on Pilatus were startled, like the Rosicrucian, by roaring and sighing, or, like the prefect of Lucerne, by red sparks showering among the crags, and realized too late that it was only the mountain train.

IV.

In mountain Europe, Pilate survived as the wandering spirit of evil; but in Ethiopia he was enshrined in the Canon of the Saints. Once again, water was his medium. He was made a saint—or, strictly speaking, a confessor—because he had washed his hands of the blood of Christ. The Coptic liturgy reflected the fascination with water of any dry-land people subject to inundations. Ritual water made all things new and washed all sins away. On the Feast of the Epiphany in January, the greatest feast of the year, the whole nation of Ethiopia underwent a vast lustration. In the liturgy, toward the end, the priest washed his hands first at the south corner of the church and then toward the west, repeating almost exactly the words of Pilate: "I wash my hands in innocence." He did this as the people recited the last words of the Creed, so that, like Pilate's, his words were barely heard above the chanting of the crowd.

The feast of Pilate and Procula was on the twenty-fifth of June; in Ethiopia the twenty-fifth of *Sane,* the month of the rains. It was commemorated in the Ethiopian calendar with a simple verse:

> *Salutation to Pilate who washed his hands*
> *so that he himself was pure of the blood of Christ*
> *and salutation to Procula, his wife,*
> *who sent him the message: Do not condemn him*
> *because that man is pure and just.*

The story of their "conversion" was read in churches on Good Friday, the same day that children were given license to beg for food and stage mock funerals in the street. Western visitors noticed this strange convention, as they noted, too, that the Ethiopians were summoned to church by kettledrums, ate their meat cut from live cattle, got drunk on mead, and marked the highest pitch of religious excitement by firing off their rifles. Lawrence Durrell met them once in deputation in the 1940s:

Fuzzy-wig, kink-haired, with cocoa-butter shining,
With stoles on poles, sackbuts and silver salvers

Walking the desert ways howling and shining;
A Coptic congregation, red blue and yellow,

With Saints on parchment and stove-pipe hats . . .

In the pantheon of Ethiopian saints, Pilate and Procula were almost dull. They shared the calendar with Naakueto-Laah, an emperor who was celebrated for never having died; with Aaron, who was made a saint for inducing roasted pigeons to fly into his mouth; with Batazun, who fasted so repeatedly that he made himself as light as air; and with John, who extracted a serpent from the womb of a princess. Balaam and his ass each had their feast days, as did Tecla Haimanot, a holy man who was taken up a perpendicular mountain on the back of a boa constrictor. After Pilate in the calendar came the angel Gabriel, who predicted the rising and falling of the Nile by causing the beams of his church at Dabra Naklon, in the desert, to run with drops of sweat.

Pilate was also the subject of a special kind of holy poem, known as "effigies," in which every part of the saint's body was celebrated as a model for the devout. This poem, discovered in 1972 in the Bibliothèque Nationale in Paris, had been written down in the eighteenth century but probably went back as far as the fifteenth. It was attributed to Cyriacus, Archbishop of Oxyrhyncus, and was appended to some of his sermons. Such poems had very little to do with the physical world, although they solemnly saluted each feature of Pilate's body, including his nostrils and his teeth, "disposed with such beauty of whiteness." The body was only a frame for theological and metaphysical speculation, and as the poem progressed Pilate seemed to break up and dissolve into the teeming landscape of the myths that had been built around him.

"Salutation to thy brows," wrote the poet,

frontiers of thine eyes; like an ocean
whose sand in its depths is a mirror of the secret mystery.
Oh Pilate, thou showest to the Lord of Heaven and Earth thy behavior, in its de-
    tails. . . .
Salutation to thy breath, which was exhaling faith
And to thy sweet throat which was open to the taste of the Gospel . . .
Salutation to thy breast, a treasure of deep understanding,

And salutation to thy bosom, which was troubled with the vine of torments . . .
Salutation to the nails of thy hands which were placed
over thy ten fingers in equality.
Salutation to thy heart, full of righteous love,
and to thy kidneys, torrents of water . . .
Salutation to thy internal organs; thy interior kept the knowledge of the Gospel,
    the Law;
and to thy navel, a circle on the breadth of the house . . .
Salutation to the soles of thy feet in their prodigious running, faster than a hur-
    ricane,
and to thy step which was ready for the ascetic struggle . . .
Salutation to the toes of thy feet, branches of cedar,
and to the nails of thy feet too, signs of sweet feeling and acting . . .
Oh Pilate, the thunder of thy hymn in the month of thy feast in the season of the
    rains
was heard from the heavens of the tongues of men, and now let the trumpets sound.

As in the Alps, so in Ethiopia, Pilate became the spirit of the storm. His giant body became ghostly; his misty toga dissolved into clouds, and rainstorms fell from his vanishing hands. In the European mountains his form had diffused into elemental evil: the shadow behind a crag, the darkness at the bottom of a lake. Thunder carried his voice, which rolled around the peaks unable either to rest or to escape. Yet in Ethiopia his body and its functions had become pure goodness, swiftness and wisdom. The mystery he mirrored was divine, not diabolical. It was neither opaque nor terrifying, but bright with blue-green transparency like the depths of the sea. And the thunder was the sound of his awe and understanding.

He was the essence of evil or the essence of goodness: God's rejecter or God's embracer. These opposing legends had taken on lives of their own. Yet they had both sprung, however far back, from a civil servant's moment of uncertainty. There had been potential in Pilate at that moment for darkness or light far beyond the routine experience of a Roman prefect. Even he seemed to sense it. The tiny seed had lodged in his heart or his mind, suggesting infinite possibilities. He could take untraveled roads, open hidden doors, escape the bounds of earth and flesh, exceed himself. Or he could stay as he was: shrug, scratch his ear, write another memorandum.

He stayed as he was. As most of us do.

PILATE ON THE BEACH

How does the song go?

A-B-C-D-1-2-3
Jesus died for you and me

The scene is a beach in the northeast of England on a cardigan afternoon.
The August sun should be hot, but the gray clouds will not leave it
alone. Green corporation wind-breaks have been hammered up to protect
the clutter of family seaside life. Sunday newspapers, plastic picnic boxes,
damp drying swimsuits, flyaway footballs that strain to escape. Fathers,
a little apart, perch on ruined sandcastles to smoke. Grandmothers, surrounded by a ballast of stout bags, sit on the lee side of beached fishing
boats; mothers stretch out their pink veined legs. Thermos cups of tea
shuttle between them. The children cry, throw sand, drip ice cream or
paddle in a pool which bears a yellow slick of scum; but out on the blue
sea the spinnakers dip silently toward Whitby, images of grace.

From below the sand dunes comes the sound of an accordion. The
player is a swarthy young man in a red shirt, backed by two red-shirted
girls with tamborines. They jump in circles on the sand, in front of a
blackboard and a crowd of small children sitting cross-legged. While
their mothers and fathers caress or bicker in caravans suddenly emptied
of noise, the United Beach Mission entertains their offspring on the
patch of beach behind the tea room.

A-B-C-D-1-2-3
Jesus died for you and me

Downwind the song carries to the outside tables, where a waitress in a
white blouse puts down a tray with aluminum jug, pot and spoons, and
a plate of cake. It carries up the bank, to where a couple in their fifties

have put out two canvas chairs at an angle from each other and have settled to the lighter bits of the *Sunday Times*. They glance down in distaste at the gyrations below them. Sunday has its drawbacks, which they always forget.

Yet the wind also blows the sound away, dispersing it among the marram grass. It lies there with sweet papers, empty shells, ashes of old fires, a seagull's feathered bones: things saved from the sea, caressed by the wind, lifting and blowing.

> *A-B-C-D-1-2-3*
> *Jesus died for you and me*
> *He died to make us really free!*

Is that so? Pilate might ask. (He walks in the sand dunes; the wind and the grass snag at him.) Are you free now, jumping, shouting, saved, because I sentenced him? Did I do that for you?

Acknowledgments

T HIS BOOK was written on the sly, in bits and pieces of time
snatched from running a family and doing my job, and there are
many people to thank that it has appeared at all. First, as always,
my husband, Malcolm, and my three sons, for not minding my odd dis-
appearances to the shed at the bottom of the garden, or my scribbling
away in bed after lights out. I tried to put the thing away whenever I was
needed, but I'm sorry for the times when I wasn't as attentive as I should
have been.

Second, I should thank *The Economist* for providing me with a computer on which I could type in the second draft, largely (though not entirely) by dint of coming in an hour earlier in the mornings; and I should
thank all my colleagues who turned a blind eye when they caught sight
of the letters "B.C.," or a slug of Latin, in the story the American editor was working on. A large technical-support team, especially Ginny
O'Riordan, Pauline Cuddihy and Helen Mann, helped me through the
hitches with unfailing patience. Special thanks should go to Graham
Bayfield, who, at a crucial stage in producing the manuscript, came in on
a Saturday to fix the system which had somehow crashed around me.

The Economist should also be thanked for having the foresight to in-
stall itself just around the corner from the London Library, where I spent
any moments I could spare. Thanks to the staff there for putting up with
my queries, extending my borrowing limit, obtaining copies from other
libraries of the rare articles they did not have themselves, and for getting
down on their knees in the dustier parts of the stacks to find obscure volumes translated from the Syriac.

Michael Walsh, the librarian of Heythrop College in the University
of London, allowed me to use the wonderfully ordered library there to
unearth yet more information. And Babette Grolman translated many
bizarre texts from the German, some of them in a gothic script that gave
both of us a headache to read.

Once the book was done, many people encouraged me with their enthusiasm and good advice. Alexandra Pringle, my agent at Toby Eady Associates, gave her usual great moral support. Dan Franklin, my editor at Jonathan Cape, nobly extended the delivery deadline and showed unflagging faith in the enterprise. In America the book was championed tirelessly by Joy de Menil, my editor at Random House, whose suggestions for cuts and tweaks were often inspired—and who happily edited many pages not once but twice when they went astray in mid-Atlantic. My thanks to them, and to Maria Wyke, senior lecturer in Classics at Reading University, who read through the manuscript with an academic's eagle eye. The mistakes that remain can only be mine.

AW

Select Bibliography

The Bible quotations in this book are taken mostly from the Jerusalem Bible, sometimes from the King James. Quotations in Chapter 5 (the trial) are often Raymond L. Brown's literal translations in *The Death of the Messiah* (Doubleday, New York, 1994).

The translations or modernizations of the mystery plays are mine, with the exception of the Gréban play (see under "Medieval Sources, Mystery Plays and Folklore").

The place of publication is London unless otherwise stated.

I: PRIMARY SOURCES (ROMAN AND GREEK)

In the bilingual Loeb editions unless otherwise stated:

Catullus	*Poems*, tr. Peter Whigham (Penguin, 1966)
Cicero	*On Duty*, tr. W. Miller
	The Nature of the Gods, tr. H. Rackham
	Against Verres, tr. L.H.G. Greenwood (2 vols.)
	On Friendship and Old Age, tr. W. A. Falconer
	Letters to Quintus, Brutus and Others, tr. W. Glynn Williams
	Letters to His Friends, tr. W. Glynn Williams
	The Laws and *The Republic*, tr. W. Keyes
	On Consular Provinces, tr. R. Gardner
Dio Cassius	*Roman History*, tr. E. Carry (in 9 volumes; Volumes VI and VII are the relevant ones)
Euripides	*The Bacchae*, tr. W. Arrowsmith (*Complete Greek Tragedies*, ed. Grene and Lattimore: Euripides V; University of Chicago Press, 1959)
Horace	*Odes*, tr. David Ferry (Farrar, Straus & Giroux, New York, 1997)
	Epodes, tr. C. E. Bennett
	Satires and Epistles, tr. H. R. Fairclough
Julius Obsequens	*Prodigies* (appended to Vol. XIV of the Loeb edition of Livy), tr. A. Schlesinger
Juvenal	*Satires*, tr. Peter Green (1967)
Livy	*History of Rome* (see Books IX–XI for the wars against the Samnites), tr. B. Foster

Lucilius	*Fragments* (see E. H. Warmington, *Remains of Old Latin*, III, Heinemann, 1938)
Marcus Aurelius	*Meditations,* tr. J. Collier, rev. A. Zimmern (The Scott Library, undated)
Martial	*Epigrams,* tr. W.C.A. Ker (2 vols.)
Ovid	*The Art of Love,* tr. J. S. Mozley
	Metamorphoses, tr. H. T. Riley
	Tristia and *Letters from Pontus,* tr. A. L. Wheeler
	The Fasti, tr. Sir James Frazer
Petronius Arbiter	*Satyricon* and *Poems,* tr. M. Heseltine
Plato	*The Republic,* tr. Paul Shore (2 vols.)
	Phaedo, tr. Henry Cary (Everyman edition, London 1938)
	Timaeus, tr. Desmond Lee (Penguin, 1965)
	The Trial and Death of Socrates (Euthyphron, Apology, Crito), tr. F. J. Church (London, 1892)
Plautus	*Plays,* tr. Paul Nixon
Pliny the Younger	*Letters,* tr. W. Melmoth, rev. W. Hutchinson (2 vols.)
Pliny the Elder	*Natural History* (in 6 vols., tr. J. Bostock and H. T. Riley, Bohn's Classical Library, 1855–98; in 10 vols., tr. H. Rackham and W.H.S. Jones, Loeb edition)
Propertius	*Elegies,* tr. G. P. Goold (1990)
Seneca	*Moral Letters to Lucilius,* tr. Richard Gummere (Heinemann, 1967)
	Natural Investigations (tr. J. Clarke, as *Physical Science in the Time of Nero,* Macmillan, 1910)
Seneca the Elder	*Suasitorae,* tr. M. Winterbottom
Strabo	*Geography* (Bk. XVI for Judaea), tr. H. Jones
Suetonius	*The Twelve Caesars,* tr. Robert Graves, rev. Michael Grant (Penguin, 1979)
Tacitus	*Histories,* tr. C. H. Moore and J. Jackson
	Annals, tr. Michael Grant (Penguin, 1996)
	Germania, tr. M. Hutton
Tibullus	*Poems,* tr. J. B. Postgate
Valerius Maximus	*Memorable Doings and Sayings* (Latin/French edition, *Oeuvres Complètes de Valère Maxime,* tr. P. Charpentier [2 vols., Paris, undated, c. 1870])
Virgil	*Aeneid,* tr. C. Day Lewis (Hogarth Press, 1952); H. T. Fairclough (Loeb edition)
	Eclogues, tr. H. T. Fairclough

PRIMARY SOURCES (JEWISH)

Josephus	*The Jewish War* and *The Antiquities,* in *The Works of Flavius Josephus,* tr. W. Whiston, rev. A. R. Shilleto, Vols. I–III (1898)
Philo of Alexandria	*Works,* tr. F. H. Colson (Loeb edition, in 10 vols.; see Vol. X for "The Embassy to Gaius," Vol. IX for "Flaccus")
Dead Sea Scrolls	*The Complete Dead Sea Scrolls in English,* ed. Geza Vemes (Penguin, 1997)

II: EARLY CHRISTIAN TEXTS

Augustine	*Sermons* and *Treatises on John's Gospel,* in *Works,* ed. Marcus Dods (Edinburgh, 1873)
	The Harmony of the Evangelists (tr. J. Innes, Vol. II [Edinburgh, 1874])
Bonaventura (attr.)	*Meditations on the Life of Christ* (tr. H. Frowde, 1908)
Eusebius	*The Ecclesiastical History* (tr. K. Lake, 2 vols., 1926)
	Demonstratio Evangelica (tr. K. Lake, 2 vols., 1926)
Gregory of Tours	*Histoire Ecclésiastique des Francs,* in 10 vols., Vol. I (tr. J. Guadet, Paris, 1836)
Gwatkin, H. M., ed.	*Selections from Early Writers Illustrative of Church History in the Time of Constantine* (Macmillan, 1911)
Justin Martyr	*First Apology,* Ante-Nicene Christian Library: *Translations of the Writings of the Fathers Down to A.D. 325*
	Second Apology and *Dialogue with Trypho,* ed. A. Roberts and J. Donaldson (T. & T. Clark, Edinburgh, 1868)
Origen	*Against Celsus, Commentaries on Matthew* and *Commentaries on John,* all tr. H. Chadwick (Cambridge, 1953)
Tertullian	*Against Marcion,* Ante-Nicene Christian Library: *Translations of the Writings of the Fathers Down to A.D. 325,* ed. A. Roberts and J. Donaldson, Vol. VII (Edinburgh, 1868)
	Apologeticus, tr. E. Souter (Cambridge, 1917)
	"The Hymn of the Robe of Glory," tr. G.R.S. Mead (in *Echoes from the Gnosis,* Vol. X [London, 1908])

III: APOCRYPHAL GOSPELS AND HAGIOGRAPHIES

For the *Acta Pilati,* the *Gospel of Stephen,* Pilate's "letters," fragments of the Coptic and Greek *Anaphora* and fragments of Anglo-Saxon apocrypha, see M. R. James, *The Apocryphal New Testament* (Oxford, 1924).

For the *Anaphora of Pilate,* see *Apocrypha Siniatica,* ed. and tr. M. D. Gibson (*Studia Siniatica* 5, 1896).

For the *Gospel of Peter,* see Raymond L. Brown, *The Death of the Messiah,* Appendix I, Vol. II, pp. 1317–1349 (Anchor Bible Reference Library, 2 vols., New York, 1994).

For the Martyrdom of Pilate, see E. Galtier, *Institut français d'archéologie du Caire, Mémoires et fragments inédits, Mémoires tome* 27 (Cairo, 1912).

For Pilate's Sentence, see J. P. Lyell, *The Sentence of Pontius Pilate* (1922).

For the "correspondence" between Pilate and Herod, see W. Wright, *Contributions to the Apocryphal Literature of the New Testament* (1865).

For Pilate's prayer at the tomb, see the *Newbery House Magazine,* Vol. VII, no. 6 (December 1892), pp. 641–46.

For the Hymn of the Soul, see the Acts of Thomas in M. R. James, op. cit., pp. 411–15.

For Pilate's "effigy," see E. Cerulli, "Tiberius and Pontius Pilate in Ethiopian Tradition and Poetry," *Proceedings of the British Academy,* LIX (1973), pp. 141–58.

Sir Wallis E. Budge, *Coptic Apocrypha* (British Museum, 1913) and *Coptic Martyrdoms* (British Museum, 1914).

IV: MEDIEVAL SOURCES, MYSTERY PLAYS AND FOLKLORE

Jacobus de Voragine. *The Golden Legend,* tr. William Granger Ryan (2 vols.; Princeton, 1993)

The York Cycle of Mystery Plays: A Complete Version, ed. J. S. Purvis (1957)

The Chester Plays, revised from the MSS by Dr Matthews, Part II (Early English Text Society 23, 1916)

The Corpus Christi Play of the English Middle Ages (the Coventry Play), ed. R. T. Davies (1972)

The Wakefield Mystery Plays (the Towneley Cycle), ed. Martial Rose (1961)

The Oberammergau Passion Play, official text by J. Daisenberger (1950)

The True History of the Passion, adapted from the French Medieval Mystery Cycle of Arnoul and Simon Gréban, ed. J. Kirkup (1962)

The Redentin Easter Play, tr. A. E. Zucker (Columbia University Press, New York, 1941)

Le Livre de la passion; poème narratif du XIVe siècle, ed. G. Frank (Paris 1930)

Mystères inédits du quinzième siècle, ed. A. Jubinal (Paris 1837)

A Stanzaic Life of Christ, ed. F. Foster (Early English Text Society 166, 1926)

Legends of the Holy Rood (Early English Text Society 46, 1871)

The High History of the Holy Grail, tr. J. Evans (1969)

Baring-Gould, S. *Curious Myths of the Middle Ages* (1868)

Du Meril, E. *Carmina latina: Poésies populaires latines du moyen age* (Paris, 1847)

The Brothers Grimm. *Household Tales,* tr. and ed. F. Hunt (2 vols., 1884)

Hasluck, F. W. *Letters on Religion and Folklore* (1926)

Manitus, M. *Geschichte der Lateinischen Literatur des Mittelalters (3)* (Munich, 1931)

Rappaport, A. S. *Medieval Legends of Christ* (1934)

Records of Early English Drama: Coventry (Manchester University Press, 1981)

V: SECONDARY SOURCES (ROMAN AND JEWISH HISTORY)

Brandon, S.G.F. *Jesus and the Zealots* (Manchester, 1967)

Brent, A. "Luke-Acts and the Imperial Cult in Asia Minor," *Journal of Theological Studies,* Vol. 48, no. 2 (Oct. 1997)

Brunt, P. A. *Roman Imperial Themes* (Oxford, 1990)

Ferguson, J. *The Religions of the Roman Empire* (1970)

Foakes Jackson, F. J. *Josephus and the Jews* (1930)

Grant, M. *The Jews in the Roman World* (London, 1973)

————. *History of Rome* (1978)

Jones, A.H.M. "Procurators and Prefects in the Early Principate," in *Studies in Roman Government and Law* (Oxford, 1960)

Lintoff, A. *Imperium Romanum: Politics and Administration* (1993)

Mommsen, T. "Judaea and the Jews," in *The Provinces of the Roman Empire from Caesar to Diocletian* (1909), Vol. II, ch. XI.

Parker, H.M.D. *The Roman Legions* (1928)

Perowne, S. *The Later Herods: The Political Background of the New Testament* (1958)

Raaflaub, K., and M. Toker. *Between Republic and Empire: Interpretations of Augustus and His Principate* (Berkeley, 1990)

Rajak, T. *Josephus* (1983)

Salmon, G.E.T. *Samnium and the Samnites* (Cambridge, England, 1967)

Sanders, E. P. *The Historical Figure of Jesus* (1993)

Scarborough, J. *Roman Medicine* (1969)

Seager, R. *Tiberius* (1972)

Sherwin-White, A. N. *Roman Society and Roman Law in the New Testament* (Oxford, 1963)

Silberman, N. A. *The Hidden Scrolls* (1995)

Smallwood, E. M. "High Priests and Politics in Roman Palestine," *Journal of Theological Studies,* Vol. XIII (1962)

————. "The Jews under Roman Rule," *Studies in Judaism in Late Antiquity,* Vol. XX (1976)

Smith, G. A. "The Historical Geography of the Holy Land: IV, Judea," *Expositor,* Series 4, Vol. V (1892)

————. "Studies in the History and Topography of Jerusalem: III, The Waters," *Expositor,* Series 4, Vol. VII (1894)

Stevenson, G. H., "The Administration of the Provinces," in *Cambridge Ancient History,* Vol. X: *The Augustan Empire* (Cambridge, England, 1934)

Suolahti, J. "The Junior Officers of the Roman Army in the Republican Period," *Annales Academiae Scientiarum Fennicae,* Vol. 97 (Helsinki, 1955)

Thackeray, H.S.J. *Josephus, the Man and the Historian* (New York, 1929)

Webster, G. *The Roman Army* (Chester, 1956)

Wilson, A. N. *Paul: The Mind of the Apostle* (1997)

SECONDARY SOURCES: PILATE'S CAREER

Cox, E. "A Day in Pilate's Life," *Expositor,* Series 2, Vol. VIII (1884)

Doyle, A. D. "Pilate's Career and the Date of the Crucifixion," *Journal of Theological Studies,* Vol. XLII (1941), pp. 190–93.

Gonzales, Echegaray. *Pilato, Poncio: Enciclopedia de la Biblia,* Vol. V (Barcelona, 1965)

Hedley, P. L. "Pilate's Arrival in Judea," *Journal of Theological Studies,* Vol. XXXV (1934), pp. 56–57 (for details of Pilate's coinage)

Hoffman-Kreyer, E., and H.-B. Staubli. *Handworterbuch des Deutschen Aberglaubens* (Berlin and Leipzig, 1935–36) (for Pilate's supposed German origins)

Lemenon, P. *Pilate et le gouvernement de la Judée: textes et monuments* (Paris, 1980)

Liberty, S. "The Importance of Pontius Pilate in Creed and Gospel," *Journal of Theological Studies,* Vol. XLV (1944), pp. 38–56

Maier, P. L. "Sejanus, Pilate and the Date of the Crucifixion," *Church History,* Vol. XXXVII (1968), pp. 3–13

————. "The Fate of Pontius Pilate," *Hermes,* Vol. XCIX (1971), pp. 362–71.

MacGregor, J. "Christ's Three Judges: Pilate," *Expositor,* Series 6, Vol. II (1900)

Maskell, J. "Pilate a Saint?" *Notes & Queries,* 6th series, Vol. XI (1885)

Ollivier, M. J. *"Ponce Pilate et les Pontii," Révue Biblique,* Vol. V (1896)

Rosadi, G. *The Trial of Jesus,* tr. and ed. E. Reich (1905) (especially for Pilate's supposed Spanish origins)

Smallwood, E. M. "The Date of the Dismissal of Pontius Pilate from Judea," *Journal of Jewish Studies,* Vol. V (1954), pp. 12–21

Spadafora, F. *Pilato* (Rovigo, 1973)

Vardaman, J. "A New Inscription Which Mentions Pilate as 'Prefect,' " *Journal of Biblical Literature,* Vol. LXXXI (Philadelphia, 1962), pp. 70–71

Wansbrough, H. "Suffered under Pontius Pilate," *Scripture,* Vol. XVIII (1966), pp. 84–93

SECONDARY SOURCES: THE TRIAL OF CHRIST

Andrews, S. *Life of Our Lord* (Edinburgh, 1892)

Bammel, E., ed. *The Trial of Jesus* (London, 1970)

Bammel, E., and C.F.D. Moule. *Jesus and the Politics of His Day* (Cambridge University Press, 1984)

Benoit, P. *The Passion and Resurrection of Jesus Christ* (1969)

Blinzler, J. *Der Prozess Jesu* (Stuttgart, 1951)

Bloomfield, S. T. *Recensio Synoptica Annotationis Sacrae* ("Annotations on the New Testament") (1826)

Blunt, H. *Lectures upon the History of Our Lord and Saviour Jesus Christ* (1851)

Brandon, S.G.F. *The Trial of Jesus of Nazareth* (1968)

Brown, R. L. *The Death of the Messiah* (Anchor Bible Reference Library, 2 vols.: Doubleday, New York, 1994)

Catechism of the Catholic Church (Geoffrey Chapman, 1994)

Cook, F. C., ed. *The Holy Bible with Commentary, New Testament,* Vols. I and II (1878)

Craveri, M. *The Life of Jesus* (1967)

Edwards, R. A. *The Gospel According to St. John: Its Criticism and Interpretation* (1954)

Edersheim, A. *Life and Times of Jesus the Messiah* (1863)

Eisler, R. *The Messiah Jesus and John the Baptist* (1931)

Ellicott, C. J. *Historical Lectures on the Life of Our Lord Jesus Christ* (1865)

Fairburn, A. M. *Studies in the Life of Christ* (1881)

Farrar, F. W. *Life of Christ* (1894)

Graves, R., and J. Podro. *The Nazarene Gospel Restored* (1953)

Hastings, J., and T. and T. Clark (eds.) *Dictionary of the Bible* (1900)

Hopkins, G. M. *The Sermons and Devotional Writings,* ed. C. Devlin (1959)

Innes, A. T. *The Trial of Jesus Christ: A Legal Monograph* (Edinburgh, 1899)

Keim, T. *The History of Jesus of Nazara,* Vol. VI (1883)

Lange, J. P. *Life of Our Lord Jesus Christ* (Eng. tr. 1864)

Morison, F. *Who Moved the Stone?* (1930)

Murray, J.O.F. *Jesus According to St. John* (1936)

Papini, G. *The Life of Christ* (tr. D. C. Fisher, 1923)

Powell, Frank J. *The Trial of Jesus Christ* (1948)

Radin, M. *The Trial of Jesus of Nazareth* (Chicago, 1931)

Renan, E. *The Life of Jesus* (Eng. tr., 1863)

Ross Williamson, H. A.D. *33: A Tract for the Times* (1941)

Smith, W., and F. Cheetham. *Dictionary of Christian Antiquities* (1983)

Stalker, J. *The Trial and Death of Jesus Christ* (1894)

Taylor, J. *The Whole Works, in 10 Volumes.* Vol. II, *Life of Christ* (1861)

Wilson, A. N. *Jesus* (1992)

Winter, P. *On the Trial of Jesus* (1961)

SECONDARY SOURCES (MYSTERY PLAYS)

Craig, H. *English Religious Drama* (1955)

Crosse, G. *The Arts of the Church: The Religious Drama* (Mowbray, 1913)

Clarke, S. *The Miracle Play in England: An Account of the Early Religious Drama* (1897)

Tydeman, W. M. *English Medieval Theatre* (1986)

Williams, A. *The Characterization of Pilate in the Towneley Plays* (Michigan, 1950)

PILATUS AND THE ALPINE LEGENDS

Brockendon, W. *Journals of Excursions on the Alps* (1833)

D'Auvergne, E. *Switzerland in Sunshine and Snow* (1917)

Gribble, F. *The Early Mountaineers* (1899)

Hoffman-Krayer, E., and H.-B. Staubli. *Handworterbuch des deutschen Aberglaubens* (Berlin and Leipzig, 1935–36)

Laporte, A. *La Suisse le sac à dos* (Paris, 1869)

Schama, S. *Landscape and Memory* (1995)

Weber, P. X. *Der Pilatus und seine Geschichte* (Lucerne, 1913)

Zurich, Comte P. de. *Les Voyages en Suisse de Madame de la Briche, 1785–1788* (Neuchâtel, 1935)

PILATE FICTION

Bulgakov, M. *The Master and Margarita* (tr. M. Glenny, 1967)

France, A. *Le Procurateur de Judée* (in *L'Etui de Nacre,* 1892)

Kazantzakis, N. *The Last Temptation of Christ* (tr. P. A. Bien, 1960)

Maier, P. *Pontius Pilate* (1968)

Potter, D. *Son of Man* (1970)

Sayers, D. L. *Four Sacred Plays* (1948)

OTHER SOURCES, by chapter

Prologue

"Sinking of the *Captain*": *The Times* (London), September 13–14, 1870

Barnaby, K. C. *Some Ship Disasters and Their Causes* (1968)

1: The Forum and the Forest

Murray's Handbook: Spain, Part 1 (1855)

O'Shea's Guide to Spain and Portugal, ed. J. Lomas (1899)

Steegmuller, F. *Cocteau: A Biography* (1970)

Wilde, O. *De Profundis* (1905)

2: Governing Judaea

Hyde, H. M. *Lord Reading* (1967)

Judd, D. *Lord Reading* (1982)

Segal, R. *The Crisis of India* (1965)

3: God's Secret Agent

Bauckham, R. "Nicodemus and the Gurion Family," *Journal of Theological Studies,* vol. 47, Part I (April 1996)

Frazer, J. G. *Adonis, Attis, Osiris* (1907)

Gavic, A.E. "Studies in the 'Inner Life' of Jesus: Vol. XVI, the Foreshadowings of the Cross," *Expositor,* Series 7, Vol. II (1906)

More, T. *A Treatise upon the Passion* (ed. E. Haupt, Yale, 1980)

Ramsay, W. M., "The Divine Child in Virgil," *Expositor,* Series 7, Vol. III (1907)

Redpath, H. "Christ, the Fulfilment of Prophecy," *Expositor,* Series 7, Vol. III (1907)

Selwyn, E. C. "The Trial-Narratives Based on the Oracles," *Expositor,* Series 8, Vol. IX (1915)

Thoreau, H. *The Journal* (1850), in *Writings,* Walden Edition (New York, 1906)

4: Blood on His Boots

Dostoevsky, F. *The Brothers Karamazov,* tr. D. Magarshack (1958)

Frazer, J. G. *The Golden Bough.* Part 6, "The Scapegoat" (1914)

Gandhi, M. *Non-Violence in Peace and War: 43, Theory and Practice of Non-Violence* (Ahmedabad, 1944)

Gill, E. *Social Justice and the Stations of the Cross* (London, 1939)

———. *The Stations of the Cross: Some Meditations on their Social Aspects* (1944)

———. *Letters,* ed. Walter Shewring (1947)

Keneally, T. *Schindler's Ark* (1982; published in the United States as *Schindler's List*)

Mandeville, J. *Travels,* ed. J. Ashton (1887)

Maude, A. *The Life of Tolstoy: Later Years* (1910)

Nashe, T. *The Unfortunate Traveller* (1594)

Shaw, G. B. *On the Rocks: A Political Comedy* (1933)

Thoreau, H. *On the Duty of Civil Disobedience,* in *Writings,* Walden Edition (New York, 1906)

Tolstoy, N. *Writings on Civil Disobedience and Non-Violence,* ed. P. Owen (1968)

———. *Letters, Vol. II, 1880–1910,* selected, tr. and ed. R. F. Christian (1978)

Wilson, A. N. *Tolstoy* (1988)

5: The Great Equivocator

Bacon, F. *Essays Civil and Moral: Of Truth* (1597), ed. W. A. Wright (1863)

Barratt, A. *Between Two Worlds: The Master and Margarita* (Oxford, 1987)

Brown, C. (ed.) *The New International Dictionary of New Testament Theology.* Vol. 3, "Truth" (1978)

Liddon, H. *Passiontide Sermons: X, "The Silence of Jesus"* (1891)

Luther, M. *Table Talk,* tr. W. Hazlitt, DCCLXV (1848)

Mill, J. S. *On Liberty* (1859)

Niemöller, M. *The Gestapo Defied: The Last 28 Sermons* (1941)

Stephen, J. Fitzjames. *Liberty, Equality, Fraternity* (1873)

Whitaker, G. H. "*Aletheia* in the New Testament and in Polybius," *Expositor,* Series 8, Vol. XX (1920)

6: Witness to Christ

See generally the section on apocrypha and hagiographies.
Nutt, A. *Studies on the Legend of the Holy Grail* (1888)

7: Through Brake, Through Briar

Baedeker, K. *Switzerland and the Adjacent Portions of Italy, Savoy and Tyrol* (1895)
Bonney, T. G. *The Alpine Regions of Switzerland and Neighbouring Countries* (1868)
Baum, J. E. *Savage Abyssinia* (1928)
Bernard, F. *De Lyon à la Méditerranée* (Paris, 1855)
Dufton, H. *A Narrative of a Journey Through Abyssinia in 1862–3* (1867)
Farago, L. *Abyssinia on the Eve* (1935)
LeRoy Ladurie, E. *Le Siècle des Platter 1499–1628,* Vol. I: *Le Mendiant et le professeur*
    (Paris, 1995)
Stanley, A. P. *Lectures on the Eastern Church* (1861)
Wagner, R. *My Life,* tr. A. Gray, ed. M. Whittall (Cambridge, England, 1983)
Budge, Sir Wallis E. *The Book of Saints of the Ethiopian Church: A Translation of the
    Ethiopic Synaxarium* (Cambridge, England, 1928)
For Queen Victoria's trip to Switzerland, see the *Illustrated London News* for August 10
    and 29 and September 12, 1868.

Index

About the Author

ANN WROE is the author of *A Fool and His Money: Life in a Partitioned Town in Fourteenth-Century France* and *Lives, Lies and the Iran-Contra Affair*. She is the editor of the American section of *The Economist* and was formerly its literary editor.

About the Type

This book was set in Garamond, a typeface designed by the French printer Jean Jannon. It is styled after Garamond's original models. The face is dignified, and is light but without fragile lines. The italic is modeled after a font of Granjon, which was probably cut in the middle of the sixteenth century.